Psychology

for the IB Diploma
2nd Edition

CHRISTIAN BRYAN • PETER GIDDENS • CHRISTOS HALKIOPOULOS

Published by Pearson Education Limited, 80 Strand, London, WC2R 0RL.

www.pearsonglobalschools.com

Text © Pearson Education Limited 2018
Edited by Andrea Davison and Jenny Hunt
Indexed by Sanet Le Roux
Designed by © Pearson Education Limited 2018
Typeset by © Evolution Design & Digital Ltd (Kent)
Original illustrations © Pearson Education Limited 2018
Illustrated by © Evolution Design & Digital Ltd (Kent)
Cover design by © Pearson Education Limited 2018
Cover images: Front: © **Getty Images**: ferrantraite
Inside front cover: **Shutterstock.com**: Dmitry Lobanov

The rights of Christian Bryan, Peter Giddens and Christos Halkiopoulos to be
identified as the authors of this work have been asserted by them in accordance
with the Copyright, Designs and Patents Act 1988.

First published 2018

23 22 21 20 19
IMP 10 9 8 7 6 5 4 3 2

British Library Cataloguing in Publication Data
A catalogue record for this book is available from the British Library

ISBN 978 1 292 21099 5

Printed in Slovakia by Neografia

Acknowledgements
The authors and publisher would like to thank the following individuals and
organisations for their kind permission to reproduce copyright material.

Photographs
(Key: b-bottom; c-centre; l-left; r-right; t-top)
Alamy Stock Photo: Calvin Chan 251, Graham Prentice 225, Interfoto/Person-
alities 37b, Jake Lyell 179, Lynn Hilton 299, Migstock 256, Roussel Images 121;
Corbis: Bettmann vitl, vitr, vibl; **Gary Goodwin:** xvii, xviii, xx, xxiv, xxvi, 50, 61,
65, 67, 86, 98, 101, 103, 115, 123, 131, 133, 137, 172, 224, 231, 243, 248, 266, 295,
298, 303, 307, 324, 336, 338, 350, 371; **Getty Images:** Bachrach/Archive Photos
vibr, NurPhoto 51; **Science Photo Library:** Kjell B Sandved vi; **Shutterstock:**
Joel Shawn 271, Kathy Hutchins 205, Rodrique Ngowi/AP/Rex 302, Semnic 4,
Stefan Holm 1, Thoai 87; **123RF:** Okolaa 20t;

All other images © Pearson Education

We are grateful to the following for permission to reproduce copyright material:

Text
page 7–8. Biological psychiatry by SOCIETY OF BIOLOGICAL PSYCHIATRY
Reproduced with permission of ELSEVIER INC. in the format Book via
Copyright Clearance Center; **page 28**. Reprinted with permission from the
Diagnostic and Statistical Manual of Mental Disorders, Fifth Edition (Copyright
© 2013). American Psychiatric Association. All Rights Reserved. **page 55**.
Baddeley, A., and Hitch, G., (1974), Working memory. Psychology of learning
and motivation, 8, 47–89; **pages 242, 249** from Reprinted from Obesity and
overweight. Copyright © 18 October 2017. Used by permission of the World
Health organization; **page 330** By permission. From Merriam-Webster.com
© 2018 by Merriam-Webster, Inc. https://www.merriam-webster.com/dictionary/
scientific+method"

Text extracts relating to the IB syllabus and assessment have been reproduced
from IBO documents. Our thanks go to the International Baccalaureate for
permission to reproduce its copyright.

Dedication
My work within this book is dedicated to my beautiful wife and our two perfect sons.
Christian Bryan

Contents

Introduction

What is psychology?

Psychology is the scientific study of thoughts, feelings and behaviour.

The concept of studying other humans has been around for as long as humans have been aware of each other. However, the academic and scientific approach began in the late 19th century when theorists began to apply scientific ideas and methods to human behaviours. The idea of 'scientific study' can cause problems while studying humans. Science depends on notions such as reliability, validity, measurement and reducing explanations to a level where their component parts can be individually studied. This has benefits for studying humans, but it also means the nuances of human individuality can be lost in the overall approach. Viewing humans as capable of being studied scientifically has meant that more abstract notions of the human condition such as spirituality are often excluded from psychology.

Underpinning psychology is the notion of cause and effect. Psychology researchers usually ask: To what extent does a particular phenomenon (such as a hormone or cultural norm) cause an effect on the thoughts, feelings and behaviours of individuals? Psychology researchers look within (at biological and cognitive factors) and without (at sociocultural norms) to explain behaviour. Moreover, psychology researchers usually want to know to what extent their findings can be applied to larger populations.

Psychology has developed over time to be an accepted academic discipline within the human sciences. It overlaps with a range of other subjects such as biology, philosophy, sociology, anthropology, cultural studies and even literature and the arts, economics and politics. Psychology researchers constantly ask: Why do people do what they do? To what extent is human nature predictable?

History of psychology

Early humans had a keen interest in the behaviour of other humans. They would have the same impulses as modern psychology researchers to understand, explain and apply their knowledge to solving problems. For example, prehistoric skulls have been found with holes seemingly drilled into the top while the individual was still alive – a process known as **trepanning**. It is thought this practice was designed to relieve pressure or allow evil spirits to escape from individuals who we would now consider to be mentally ill.

The desire to understand and explain human behaviour seems to be an instinctive human need, but it has always been a product of the dominant cultural **zeitgeist**. For example, when Communism became the unifying narrative to explain the world in Soviet Russia, people who violated the norms and expectations of the political theory were considered abnormal and persecuted. In other parts of the world and in different eras, behaviour has often been assessed and controlled through the lens of religion.

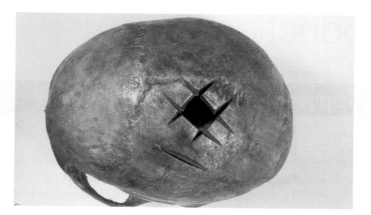

Skull after trepanning

Females have often been the main victims of this approach, with women and girls being targeted by rigidly organized patriarchal cultures that sought to impose control over their sexuality and behaviour. For example, women were often burned as 'witches' or locked away for 'madness' if they were seen to violate codes of conduct for their particular era.

As the explanatory narrative of science took hold in the 19th century (for example, with the increasing acceptance of Darwin's ideas on evolution), academic psychology began to emerge and adopt many of the same basic aims and assumptions of the scientific project. For example, there was a shift toward collecting empirical data and testing using experimental methods.

In 1879, Wilhelm Wundt opened what is thought to be the first psychology laboratory in Leipzig, Germany, to study perception, cognition, and consciousness, and to link them with physical events. Shortly after, Sigmund Freud began to use philosophy to explain unconscious conflict and adopted contemporary themes like the notion of 'repressed sexuality' to explain human conditions such as neuroses and phobias. The reactions against Freud inspired yet further trends, which were in keeping with their cultural zeitgeists. Psychology researchers such as B.F. Skinner and John B. Watson, working after the horrors of the First World War and the increasing political and sociocultural extremism of the 1930s, wanted to see humans as stimulus response organisms that were predictable and controllable.

The 20th century saw many approaches come to the fore to explain human nature. Cognitive psychology focused on internal mental process; humanistic psychology focused on spiritual questions about what it is to be human; and biopsychology began to make use of the development of new technologies to look for physiological explanations.

This range of competing approaches has led some to question whether psychology has too many paradigms within it and if it should seek to reduce them. However, others see the lack of a dominant strand of thinking within the subject as its main strength, as it allows for many varied ideas to co-exist, each of which brings insight into what it means to be human without being subservient to the limitations of one particular approach.

Wilhelm Wundt (1832–1920) was originally a physiologist.

Sigmund Freud (1856–1939), one of the most famous psychologists of all.

John B. Watson (1878–1958)

B.F. Skinner (1904–1990)

IB Diploma Psychology

The IB Diploma Psychology Guide has been developed to reflect current thinking in academic psychology. It is intended to give the student a broad and foundational understanding of the themes within the subject. No single approach is considered to be dominant. Human beings are complex animals, with highly developed frontal lobes, cognitive abilities, involved social structures and cultures. Therefore, the study of behaviour and mental processes requires a multidisciplinary approach and the use of a variety of research techniques while recognizing that behaviour is not a static phenomenon, it is adaptive, and as the world, societies, and challenges facing societies change, so does behaviour.

At the core of the DP psychology course is an introduction to three different approaches to understanding behaviour that are assessed in paper 1:

- biological approach to understanding behaviour

- cognitive approach to understanding behaviour

- sociocultural approach to understanding behaviour.

The contribution and the interaction of the three approaches can be best understood through the options that are assessed in paper 2. There are four options in the course. They focus on areas of applied psychology:

- abnormal psychology

- developmental psychology

- health psychology

- psychology of human relationships.

The options provide an opportunity to take what is learned from the study of the approaches to psychology and put it into the context of specific lines of inquiry, broadening experiences of the discipline and developing critical inquiry skills.

Surrounding the approaches and the options are the overarching themes of research and ethics. A consideration of both is paramount to the nature of the subject.

A representation of how you should approach content in the IB Diploma Psychology course.

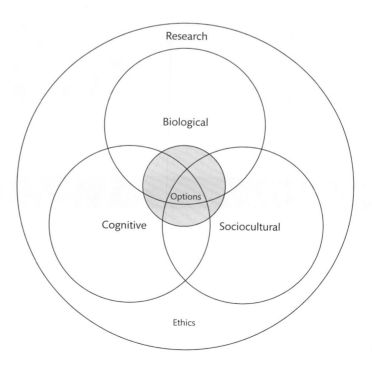

Structure of the course: distinction between standard level and higher level

There are three main distinctions between this course at standard level (SL) and higher level (HL).

The following extensions to the core approaches are studied at HL only:

- the role of animal research in understanding human behaviour

- cognitive processing in the digital world

- the influence of globalization on individual attitudes, identities, and behaviour.

This differentiation is reflected in paper 1, section B of the external assessment.

SL students are required to study one option, while HL students study two options. This differentiation is reflected in paper 2 of the exam.

Both SL and HL students will be expected to show their understanding of approaches to research in the internal assessment and for criterion D (critical thinking) in paper 1, section B and paper 2 responses. Additionally, HL students will be directly assessed on their understanding of approaches to research in paper 3 of the external assessment. This will cover both qualitative and quantitative research methods.

The table below shows the percentage weighting for your grade of each individual component for the SL course.

Assessment component	Weighting
External assessment (3 hours)	**75%**
Paper 1 (2 hours) Section A: Three short-answer questions on the core approaches to psychology (27 marks) Section B: One essay from a choice of three in the biological, cognitive and sociocultural approaches to behaviour (22 marks) (Total 49 marks)	**50%**
Paper 2 (1 hour) One question from a choice of three on one option (22 marks)	**25%**
Internal assessment (20 hours) This component is internally assessed by the teacher and externally moderated by the IB at the end of the course **Experimental study** A report on an experimental study undertaken by the student (22 marks)	**25%**

The table below shows the percentage weighting for your grade of each individual component for the HL course.

Assessment component	Weighting
External assessment (5 hours)	**80%**
Paper 1 (2 hours) Section A: Three short-answer questions on the core approaches to psychology (27 marks) Section B: One essay from a choice of three on the biological, cognitive and sociocultural approaches to behaviour. One, two or all of the essays will reference the additional HL topic (22 marks) (Total 49 marks)	**40%**
Paper 2 (2 hours) Two questions; one from a choice of three on each of two options (44 marks)	**20%**
Paper 3 (1 hour) Three short-answer questions from a list of six static questions on approaches to research (24 marks)	**20%**
Internal assessment (20 hours) This component is internally assessed by the teacher and externally moderated by the IB at the end of the course	**20%**
Experimental study A report on an experimental study undertaken by the student (22 marks)	

Command terms and content focus

You need to be familiar with the following key terms and phrases used in examination questions, which are to be understood as described on the following pages. These come directly from the IB and will form the basis of the exam questions. Although these terms will be used frequently in examination questions, other terms may be used to direct you to present an argument in a specific way. These command terms have been used throughout the book under the heading 'Content focus'. As authors, we needed to interpret the Guide in a way that will best prepare you for the exam. Therefore, we have used the command terms and focused our content around specific focuses.

The command terms used in psychology are arranged into four groups labelled assessment objectives (AO). The first three, AO1, AO2 and AO3, are **hierarchical** with more challenging verbs for assessment as you progress from AO1 to AO3. AO4 is not hierarchical, but represents actions related to subject-specific tasks.

Assessment objective 1 (AO1)

Knowledge and comprehension of specified content

These terms require students to demonstrate knowledge and understanding and learn and comprehend the meaning of information.

Describe	Give a detailed account.
Identify	Provide an answer from a number of possibilities.
Outline	Give a brief account or summary.

Assessment objective 2 (AO2)

Application and analysis of knowledge and understanding

These terms require students to use and analyse knowledge and understanding, explain actual situations, break down ideas into simpler parts and to see how the parts relate.

Explain	Give a detailed account including reasons or causes.
Suggest	Propose a solution, hypothesis or other possible answer.

Assessment objective 3 (AO3)

Synthesis and evaluation

These terms require students to make a judgement based on evidence and, when relevant, construct an argument or rearrange component ideas into a new whole and make judgements based on evidence or a set of criteria.

Contrast	Give an account of the differences between two (or more) items or situations, referring to both (all) of them throughout.
Discuss	Offer a considered and balanced review that includes a range of arguments, factors or hypotheses. Opinions or conclusions should be presented clearly and supported by appropriate evidence.
Evaluate	Make an appraisal by weighing up the strengths and limitations.
To what extent	Consider the merits or otherwise of an argument or concept. Opinions and conclusions should be presented clearly and supported with appropriate evidence and sound argument.

Assessment objective 4 (AO4)

Selection and use of skills appropriate to psychology. The terms require students to take action.

Design	Produce a plan, simulation or model.
Investigate	Observe, study, or make a detailed and systematic examination, in order to establish facts and reach new conclusions.
Predict	Give an expected result.

Question format

Each paper has a specific approach to questions.

Paper 1

Section A consists of three short-answer questions using AO1 and AO2 command terms. All three questions are compulsory. Each question is marked out of 9 marks for a total of 27 marks.

Section B consists of a single essay from a choice of three. One, two or all of the essays will reference the additional HL topic. The essay is marked out of 22 marks. AO3 command terms will be used in the essay questions.

Paper 2

Paper 2 consists of essay questions, one for each option studied. Each option will have a choice of three essays. All essays will use an AO3 command term. The essays are marked out of 22 marks. SL students answer one question from one option; HL students answer two questions from two distinct options they have studied.

Paper 3 (HL only)

Paper 3 assesses the approaches to research in psychology. The paper consists of a research scenario followed by three short-answer questions for a total of 24 marks.

Question 1

Question 1 will consist of all of the following questions, for a total of 9 marks. The questions will be assessed using an analytical markscheme.

Questions	Marks
Identify the research method used and outline two characteristics of the method.	3
Describe the sampling method used in the study.	3
Suggest an alternative or additional research method giving one reason for your choice.	3

Question 2

Question 2 will consist of one of the following questions, for a total of 6 marks. The question will be assessed using an analytical markscheme.

Questions	Marks
Describe the ethical considerations that were applied in the study and explain if further ethical considerations could be applied.	6
Describe the ethical considerations in reporting the results and explain additional ethical considerations that could be taken into account when applying the findings of the study.	6

Question 3

Question 3 will consist of one of the following questions, for a total of 9 marks. The question will be assessed using the rubric below.

Questions	Marks
Discuss the possibility of generalizing/transferring the findings of the study.	9
Discuss how a researcher could ensure that the results of the study are credible.	9
Discuss how the researcher in the study could avoid bias.	9

Rubric for question 3

Markband	Level descriptor
0	The answer does not reach a standard described by the descriptors below.
1–3	The question is misunderstood and the central issue is not identified correctly, resulting in a mostly irrelevant argument. The response contains mostly inaccurate references to the approaches to research or these are irrelevant to the question. The reference to the stimulus material relies heavily on direct quotations from the text.
4–6	The question is understood, but only partially answered resulting in an argument of limited scope. The response contains mostly accurate references to approaches to research which are linked explicitly to the question. The response makes appropriate but limited use of the stimulus material.
7–9	The question is understood and answered in a focused and effective manner with an accurate argument that addresses the requirements of the question. The response contains accurate references to approaches to research with regard to the question, describing their strengths and limitations. The response makes effective use of the stimulus material.

Internal assessment and extended essays

Every IB student must submit one simple experimental study as part of the requirements for the course. This is marked by your teacher and moderated externally by an examiner. The mark for this piece of work makes up 20 per cent (HL) or 25 per cent (SL) of your overall grade for your Diploma Psychology course. It is up to you to plan, carry out and then write up your experiment. The internal assessment is compulsory for both SL and HL students. The requirements for SL and HL students are the same. Full details on how to plan, conduct and write up your internal assessment can be found on page 334.

The extended essay (EE) is an in-depth study of a focused topic chosen from the list of available Diploma Programme subjects. Psychology is a popular choice and an EE in Psychology gives you the chance to broaden your interest in this diverse field. However, there are many pitfalls with an EE in Psychology. Therefore, the following advice should be considered.

- Do not do an EE in Psychology if you are not a Psychology student.

- Do not consider collecting data of any kind.

- Do not see an EE in Psychology as an 'easy' or fall-back subject.

- Do not choose an EE in Psychology because you could not think of a suitable question in your other subjects.

Only consider an EE in Psychology if:

- you are studying Psychology at HL or you want to study Psychology at university

- you have a clear personal interest in the subject outside of school

- you have access to academic psychology journals.

You need to remember, a Psychology EE is not an extension of the internal assessment. Full details on how to plan, conduct and write up your EE can be found on page 372.

IB learner profile

The IB aims to develop inquiring, knowledgeable, and caring young people who help to create a better and more peaceful world through intercultural understanding and respect. To this end the organization works with schools, governments and international organizations to develop challenging programmes of international education and rigorous assessment. These programmes encourage students across the world to become active, compassionate and lifelong learners who understand that other people, with their differences, can also be right.

Therefore, one of the central aims of all IB programmes is to develop internationally minded people who, recognizing their common humanity and shared guardianship of the planet, help to create a better and more peaceful world. It should be noted, the IB learner profile is intended for the teacher, school and student.

IB learners strive to be: Inquirers, Knowledgeable, Thinkers, Communicators, Principled, Open-minded, Caring, Risk-takers, Balanced, Reflective.

In the psychology classroom this means we must:

- be aware of the increasing complexity of an interconnected world when we discuss other cultures and cultural norms

- strive to understand people who are different to us and attempt to explain their behaviour

- be reflexive by acknowledging our biases and how they impact our understanding

- make 'best judgements' based on secure knowledge foundations when the research allows it (e.g. Theory of Evolution; determinants of IQ; origins of gender roles)

- acknowledge, navigate and be prepared to communicate the constraints and impositions on knowledge creation (e.g. gender bias, cultural bias, political correctness)

- listen to others' perspectives while not attempting to impose one perspective on human nature

- be able to communicate ideas using the accepted academic norms of psychology

- be able to work in groups with people who are diverse

- be original and not necessarily agree with a position just because other people do.

The learner profile represents an ideal to strive for. However, it can present a dilemma for students (and teachers). For example, the emphasis on justice, compassion, fairness and risk-taking may compel some students to take a risk and speak out about cultural practices that they see as unfair, unjust, and lacking in compassion. The student could be accused of lacking intercultural understanding or not being open-minded. However, it should be noted, psychology is a subject that depends on debate and constant critical thinking and students who take a position should be applauded.

What this book includes

This book has been written for the syllabus content for IB DP Psychology. It addresses:

- the core (biological, cognitive and sociocultural approaches to understanding behaviour)

- the options (abnormal psychology, developmental psychology, health psychology and the psychology of human relationships)

- research methods (qualitative and quantitative)

- how to write an internal assessment

- how to write an extended essay

- Theory of Knowledge in the context of psychology.

It is intended for use by students who are studying psychology for their IB Diploma and offers complete coverage of the syllabus.

How this book works

In addition to the main text, there are a number of coloured boxes in every chapter, each with a distinctive icon. The boxes provide different information and stimulus.

Key fact boxes

These boxes summarize key information from the text. They are designed to draw your attention to what is considered most important in what you have just read as well as help you articulate the point in an assessment setting.

Structural imaging focuses on what parts of the brain look like in relation to each other.

Investigate the Swayamvara system in ancient India.

When discussing stereotypes, use at least one example to clarify your answer.

How is balance achieved between ethical considerations and the pursuit of knowledge?

To what extent can a specific behaviour be explained by localization?

Activity boxes

These boxes are designed to stimulate action and thought to help you interact with the key themes.

Hints for success

These boxes give you advice on what to do with the key themes in an assessment situation. They focus your attention on what is important and help you structure answers.

TOK boxes

These boxes help you consider TOK issues as they may arise in the text. Sometimes they come in the form of questions to stimulate your thoughts and discussion. In addition there is a TOK chapter to help you understand psychology in the context of TOK.

Extended essay boxes

These boxes are designed to stimulate thought and discussion regarding possible extended essay topics and questions. The topics and questions found within them are quite broad and are designed as starting points for your consideration, not necessarily extended essay questions themselves. You should always consult with your supervisor before embarking on an extended essay topic/question.

Special interest boxes

These boxes provide extra information for your interest.

The Theory of Natural Selection

The Theory of Natural Selection was initially developed by Charles Darwin in the 19th century.

The theory has two main assumptions:

- evolution is caused by **natural selection**
- evolution is caused by **sexual selection**.

Regions of the brain diagram

In the Appendix (page 377), you will find a diagram showing the locations of the different regions of the brain.

Glossary

A list of key terms and their definitions can be found in the eText version of the book.

Reference list

A full list of references can be found in the eText version of the book.

Introduction to research

Knowledge about human behaviour is achieved from research. The research process usually begins with curiosity followed by questions, i.e. someone wondering why a behaviour exists or what causes a behaviour to occur. For example, why are some people shy and some not? Is shyness a problem or not? Does shyness hinder a student's academic achievement or does it help?

Think of five human behaviours about which you are curious in some way. Write your curiosity as questions.

The research process aims to answer questions and so explain human behaviour. The research process could be considered a journey from curiosity toward (although never quite reaching) certainty. Early in the process researchers use observations to gather more information about the behaviour, and the setting in which it is observed, such as in a family home, at work, in school, or perhaps at a crime scene.

The research process aims to answer questions and so explain human behaviour.

Researchers will learn even more about a behaviour by interviewing people either one to one or in small groups. This early stage of the research journey involves gathering information such as **environmental factors** that may affect a behaviour. A **correlational** study will determine whether factors occur coincidentally or whether they occur together because of some factors common to both. For example, observations may reveal that most shy school students study mathematics, eat breakfast every day, and read fiction books. A correlational study may reveal that these are correlational factors or simply coincidental. After determining correlational **variables**, researchers may begin to conduct experiments that may show a **cause-effect relationship**, or not.

In the past, scientists conducted **post-mortem** studies and observed human brains to satisfy their curiosity regarding where in the brain certain behaviours are controlled. More recently, researchers can use functional magnetic resonance imaging (fMRI), which is the creation of a computer-generated image of a brain in action. fMRIs have been used to observe the brains of people who experience **attention deficit hyperactivity disorder** (ADHD) to discover whether brain abnormalities cause the behaviour (Spiers and Maguire, 2006).

Research and methodology is the basis of scientific psychology and references to peer-reviewed studies are the basis of this entire textbook. Each chapter uses published studies as the basis of all claims of fact.

Good researchers understand the theory of knowledge. Seldom is it possible to conclude that any behaviour is caused by a particular variable. For example, the fMRIs of people with ADHD show brain anomalies, but this does not mean these anomalies cause ADHD, or that ADHD causes the anomalies. Most people with ADHD take medication and it may be this that causes the anomalies.

It is seldom possible to say, 'I know with 100 per cent certainty that. . .' Indeed, in science the research process aims to find exceptions to rules so that we can conclude, 'I know that this behaviour is not caused by. . .' or, 'Research shows that this variable does not cause that behaviour'.

An observation is a research method that gathers sensory data such as episodes of behaviour, spoken language, or physical behaviour.

Observations

Observations can be **overt**, i.e. the participants know the researcher is watching them and their behaviour. Observations can also be **covert**, i.e. the participants do not know they are being observed. Covert observations are useful because sometimes participants may change their behaviour when they know they are being observed. However, covert observations may be unethical because participants in research should give their **informed consent**.

Observations may be momentary or one-off, such as a researcher watching students in their lessons and noting their shy or not shy behaviour, or they may be conducted over a period of time. Observations aim to clarify a behaviour, define it, and identify associated phenomena.

Ochs (1982) conducted an overt observational study of children in Western Samoa, observing the way the children learnt to read (see p. 108). The study was the first step in a journey that began with questions about whether a person's culture affects their **cognitive** processes such as 'do children who grow up in a traditional extended family in a village in Western Samoa learn to read differently to children who live in an urban, 'Western' setting?'

Interviews

Researchers may use interviews to delve deeper into the human behaviour that prompted the curiosity. Interviews can be conducted in small groups, or on a one-to-one basis, and it can take a lot of time to gather a large amount of data. Howarth (2002) used focus groups and one-to-one interviews to investigate 44 teenagers' feelings about living in Brixton, South London (see p. 91).

Researchers understand that small numbers of participants in a study can result in weak conclusions. While interviewing individuals can reveal a rich insight into one person's behaviour, making conclusions about all people based on the behaviour of a small number of people would be a misuse of statistics and probability.

Case studies

Case studies are an in-depth study of behaviour. Case studies often focus on one participant or a small group of participants. Henry Molaison may well be psychology's most well-known case, studied by a number of researchers over a number of years (see p. 6).

Longitudinal studies

Longitudinal studies can strengthen a study's conclusions because the behaviour is observed over a sustained period. For example, it is probable that all children exhibit some characteristics of shyness from time to time and in some situations, but not always, and some generally shy children are not shy in some situations. A longitudinal study is conducted over several months or even years in an effort to determine the effect of early life events on later life behaviour. Elinor Ochs (1982) studied children in a traditional Western Samoan village for several months. She returned to the village several years later and conducted even more research.

Correlational studies

After the research process has observed a behaviour and associated phenomena, researchers may conduct a correlational study to determine whether the behaviour and other phenomena are associated in some way. A school teacher is likely to have noticed that some shy students achieve high grades, but it is not clear whether the shyness causes high grades, or high grades cause shyness, or perhaps the two phenomena just occur in the same people as a coincidence, just as ice cream consumption and sunburn often occur at the same time. It may simply be that shy students are a rarity and so they are more noticeable to teachers and so there is an illusory correlation based on flawed thinking. Correlational studies simply show if two events occur at the same time.

Interviews can be conducted in small groups, or on a one-to-one basis, and it can take a lot of time to gather a large amount of data.

TOK Use the internet to read about the Henry Molaison (H.M.) case study. It is often said that H.M. was unique, but all people are unique, so to what extent can the H.M. case study be used to explain the behaviour of all humans?

A longitudinal study is conducted over several months, sometimes years, in an effort to determine the effect of early life events on later life behaviour.

Correlational studies simply show if two events occur at the same time.

Marazziti et al. (1999) noticed obsessive-type behaviour of people in the early stages of love and wondered if it might share the same physiological basis of **obsessive compulsive disorder** (OCD), which earlier research had associated with low **serotonin** levels (see p. 16). This was a correlational study, so caution should be used when assuming low levels of serotonin caused either OCD or 'in love' type behaviour. The low serotonin levels may be the consequence of the in love and OCD behaviour rather than the cause of it. Moreover, only 40 people were included in the study.

Do this activity with a class member. Flip a coin ten times and record the results, i.e. H,T,T,H,H,T,H,H,H,H. Do the same for 40 more coin tosses and continue recording the results. Count the heads and tails, and then predict the result of the 51st coin flip. Explain your prediction, make the coin flip for the 51st time. Was your prediction correct? What is your conclusion?

Psychology is not like physics or chemistry in which the objects of curiosity always behave the same under the same conditions. Humans are unique. One shy student may achieve very good school results while another may not. Unlike in chemistry, it is difficult, perhaps even impossible, to control all variables. A shy student may achieve very good school results, but if he or she were not shy the student may have achieved excellent results. A shy student who achieves poor results may achieve even poorer results if he or she were not shy.

Human behaviour, as we will see in this book, is a consequence of many factors, some biological, some cognitive, some sociocultural, and very often many variables working together. A shy student may also have been encouraged by supportive family members and nurturing teachers so that the shyness is overcome (or supported) by other factors.

Meta-analysis

Rather than conduct a trial with real patients in real clinical settings, researchers often choose to perform a **meta-analysis** of others' work so they can reach broad conclusions. A meta-analysis combines the results of many studies and so allows a large-scale review of work in the same area so conclusions can be drawn. Von Wolff et al. (2013) wanted to assess the efficacy of SSRIs (selective serotonin re-uptake inhibitors or serotonin-specific reuptake inhibitors) and TCA (tricyclic antidepressants) in the treatment of depression (see p. 173). They conducted a systematic search of a number of databases including CENTRAL, MEDLINE, EMBASE, ISI Web of Science, BIOSIS, PsycINFO, etc. They only considered randomized controlled trials. However, while the methodological quality of the primary studies was evaluated as unclear in many cases and they argued that more evidence was needed to assess the efficacy of SSRIs and TCAs in patients suffering from chronic forms of depression other than dysthymia, they were able to claim that both SSRIs and TCAs are effective in the treatment of chronic depression.

Qualitative and quantitative research

Qualitative research tends to be exploratory, aiming to achieve an understanding of underlying causes or motivations. Qualitative research provides insights into a behaviour. Qualitative research methods vary and tend to use unstructured techniques such as focus/discussion groups, interviews, and observations.

Quantitative research tends to focus on phenomena that can be measured in some way, such as the area/volume of a brain area, the time taken to react to a stimulus, the number of items recalled, or the level of a hormone in a person's blood. Instead of observing that a child exhibits some characteristics of shyness, quantitative research will measure the behaviour. For example, a child demonstrated five shy-typical behaviours in a one-hour school lesson. Quantitative data collection methods tend to be more structured than qualitative methods and include surveys, questionnaires, structured interviews, and systematic observations.

Experiments

The research journey, which began with curiosity and questions about a behaviour and then moved through a process of observing and learning about the behaviour, approaches the goal of certainty through the use of experiments.

The experiment is a systematic method of determining knowledge. A simple experiment (sometimes called a 'true experiment') involves isolating one variable (called the **independent variable**, IV), manipulating that variable while ensuring everything else is kept unchanged, and then observing and measuring any change in the phenomenon being studied (called the **dependent variable**, DV). Because everything else has been kept the same, any change in the phenomenon can only have been caused by the change in the one variable that was manipulated.

The process of ensuring everything else remains unchanged is called controlling and is almost impossible to achieve in the human sciences.

In **natural experiments**, the IV is manipulated naturally and not by the researcher, for example, a child's shy behaviour before and after an earthquake. In this situation, extraneous variables cannot be controlled and this means any changes in the DV may not be attributed to the change in the IV. In this example, a researcher may use a natural experiment to observe whether a student's shyness is the result of a natural event (a significant and damaging earthquake). It is likely though that it is not just the physical environment that is different because the child's friends' behaviour may have

A simple experiment (sometimes called a 'true experiment') involves isolating one variable (the IV), manipulating that variable while ensuring everything else is kept unchanged, and then observing and measuring any change in the phenomenon being studied (the DV).

changed, the child's family situation may have changed, and the shyness may simply be because the child is older or has moved into a new class or school.

In **quasi-experiments**, participants are assigned to a condition of the IV on the basis of a characteristic such as gender, ethnicity, nationality, handedness, or IQ.

In quasi-experiments the researcher assigns the criteria for participants being exposed to the different IV conditions, while in natural experiments the assignment occurs 'naturally', i.e. not assigned by the researcher.

The Minnesota Twin Family Study (MTFS) began in 1989 using same-gendered twins age 11 or 17, all born in Minnesota (USA). In 2000, 500 more 11-year-old pairs of twins were included in the study (see p. 33). The MTFS aims to determine whether biological factors can be **causal** factors in behavioural phenomena such as substance abuse, divorce, and leadership.

Twin studies are, fundamentally, quasi-experiments because the **genes** of monozygotic (MZ) twins are 100 per cent the same and dizygotic (DZ) twins are about 50 per cent the same. Twin studies effectively use the participants' genetics as the IV and because the twins were raised in very similar environmental conditions, most variables other than the twins' genetics are controlled.

Twin studies are, fundamentally, quasi-experiments because the genes of monozygotic (MZ) twins are 100 per cent the same and dizygotic (DZ) twins are about 50 per cent the same.

Bouchard et al. (1990) studied identical twins that had been separated at birth and raised in different families and found that identical twins reared apart have about the same likelihood of having similar personalities, interests, and attitudes as twins raised together. This means phenomena such as personality, interest and attitudes are likely to have a genetic rather than an environmental origin. Similarly, any differences between MZ twins reared apart must be due to environmental rather than genetic factors.

Controlled family studies have generally found increased rates of eating disorders in the biological relatives of women with **anorexia** compared to relatives of control groups (e.g. Strober et al., 1990) (see p. 144). However, given that close relatives share both genes and environments, these studies cannot differentiate genetic versus environmental causes for the disorders. Therefore twin studies are used to disentangle the relative **etiological** influence of genes versus environmental causes. They do this by comparing the similarity of MZ and DZ twins. Overall, MZ twin correlations are approximately two times greater than DZ twin correlations for anorexia which suggests genetic factors are involved in the disorder. It can be reasonably assumed that anorexia appears to be moderately **heritable** (Berrettini, 2004).

Experiments are the only method that produce cause-and-effect conclusions with some degree of certainty. However, they lack **ecological validity** because so many other variables need to be controlled and the isolation and control of variables produces an artificial setting that can make participants behave differently in the experimental setting compared to their real-life setting. Experiments in developmental psychology are often not as tightly controlled as they might be, because of the nature of working with children.

Oostermeijer et al. (2014) conducted a study in the Netherlands with 128 sixth-grade students. They found those who spent more free time in construction play performed better on a test of mathematical word problems. However, the study was only correlational, which made it impossible to draw conclusions about any causal relationships among constructive play, spatial ability, and mathematical word problem-solving performance.

Therefore, for causality to be established, tight control over variables needs to occur. For example, Christakis et al. (2007) carried out a study sponsored by the toymaker Mega Bloks (see p. 220 for details). The results of this study showed children in the experimental group scored higher on parent-reported tests of vocabulary, grammar, and verbal comprehension and showed a trend toward watching less TV (although this was not significant). The deliberate manipulation of the variable (presence or absence of playing blocks) made it possible for the researchers to infer a cause-effect relationship that was not present in the equivalent correlational study performed by Oostermejier et al. (2014).

Generalizing research results means taking the conclusion of a study and applying it to a greater population. A study that finds all 20 shy students in a study achieve high grades might conclude that shyness causes good school grades for all people. Generalizing these results to the wider population, i.e. claiming that all shy students will achieve good grades, though, would need to be done cautiously because 20 participants is a small number compared to the greater human population.

Although it is a simplistic statement, at this level of psychology we tend to say that we generalize the results of quantitative research and transfer the results of qualitative research.

Inferential statistical analysis gives an indication of the probability of achieving an experiment's result purely by chance (and not because of manipulating the IV), i.e. what is the probability of selecting 20 shy students and finding that they all do well in school?

Imagine an experiment to determine whether practising improves a person's skill and success at darts. Half of the participants practise throwing darts and half do not. The IV's two conditions are 'practised' and 'not practised', and the DV is whether the participant is successful, i.e. hits the 14 or not. If two participants throw a dart and the one who practised aims for and hits the 14 and one who has not practised aims at the 14 but hits the 5, can we conclude that practising results in success?

The probability that a blind folded person hits the 14 is 1 in 20, i.e. 5 per cent. That the participant who hit the 14 practised is not necessarily reason to conclude that the practising caused the success because there is a 5 per cent chance that that result could have been achieved randomly.

Similarly, it is possible, albeit with a low probability, that all 20 students in the shyness-school-grades study achieved the good grades randomly and not because of their shyness. To improve the study's generalizability, more studies, including more participants, are needed.

Unless research includes all people, researchers cannot be certain that a study's results can apply to all people. This lack of generalizability is the reason that researchers never quite reach certainty.

Although it is a simplistic statement, at this level of psychology we tend to say that we generalize the results of quantitative research and transfer the results of qualitative research.

Inferential statistical analysis gives an indication of the probability of achieving an experiment's result purely by chance.

Critical thinking

To be a critical thinker is one of the IB's learner profile attributes and therefore a goal of all IB students. After research has been peer-reviewed, i.e. checked, verified, and approved by another expert in the same field of study, it may be published and so be available for the general public to learn from. It is important to read research critically.

The first thing to consider when evaluating a study is its context, in particular its date and sociocultural context. Bartlett's (1932) study on the cultural distortions of recall and memory was set in an exclusive British university between the First World War and the Second World War and it is likely that if the study were replicated now, the results would be different (see p. 60).

Reliability and validity

Bias refers to factors that may distort a study's results. Researcher bias occurs when the researcher's behaviour distorts a study. For example, a researcher who experienced a natural disaster such as an earthquake may bring a bias to a qualitative study about people's behaviour during and following an earthquake.

Participant bias (sometimes called demand characteristics) occurs when participants act differently to the way they normally do, perhaps to show themselves in a better light, or to help the researcher achieve better results. People who experienced a devastating earthquake may not want to tell a researcher that they behaved irrationally during the earthquake and that they are now afraid to live in high-rise apartments.

Sampling bias occurs when the participants selected for the study are not representative of the target population. For example, when researching people's post-earthquake behaviour, it is important to include people of all ages, genders, and nationalities, but not people from areas that do not have severe earthquakes.

When evaluating research, it is important to examine the evidence, perhaps by reading transcripts of interviews or looking at data collected in quantitative studies. Researchers may use the data to make a limited set of conclusions and the data may actually reveal more about the phenomenon.

Conclusions tend to be **reductionist**, which means that conclusions tend to state that a behaviour is caused by or affected by one or two variables, while real-life behaviour tends to be **holistic** and so research can sometimes seem limited in explaining behaviour. The reductionist explanation of fear is the increased level of **testosterone** and **adrenaline**, the faster heartbeat and breathing rate. A holistic explanation of fear must also encapsulate the emotional response to a frightening, usually environmental, stimulus such as standing on a high bridge or being attacked.

While research attempts to offer an explanation for a behaviour, there may be alternative explanations and these should also be considered. For example, fMRIs have been used to explain ADHD as the result of brain anomalies, but there are other possible explanations including cultural interpretations of the behaviour.

In psychology, **triangulation** refers to using a range of methods or a range of researchers to study a behaviour and ensure a **reliable** and **credible** conclusion. For example, when researching whether shyness helps or hinders a student's academic achievement, an experiment could be conducted with shy and not-shy student participants as the IV and academic achievement being the DV. To strengthen the conclusion, interviews and naturalistic observations could also be used. Triangulation can help to overcome researcher bias and researchers' different interpretations of shyness.

Replicating a study and achieving similar results strengthens a study's conclusions. It is understood that when studying human behaviour not all variables can be held constant and conditions cannot be exactly replicated. Various studies relating to **flashbulb memory** have created similar results, strengthening the original theory. A study that can be replicated and achieve the same or similar results each time is called reliable. A study that does not have contradictory evidence or alternative theories or explanations is considered credible.

A study that can be replicated and achieve the same or similar results each time is called reliable. A study that does not have contradictory evidence or alternative theories or explanations is considered credible.

A study is described as **valid** if its results accurately reflect what the research was measuring. External validity refers to the extent to which a study's results can be generalized or transferred to another situation or target population. Internal validity refers to the the extent to which the researcher considered alternative explanations. For example, a study investigating whether shyness helps or hinders academic achievement would be externally valid if the results of a study conducted on students in Bahawalpur (a city in Pakistan) can be generalized to students throughout Pakistan. If the same study also considered gender differences, family backgrounds, previous school experiences and all other factors that could affect a student's academic achievement, it would have high internal validity.

Ethics

Ethical concerns regarding a study that has been published are different to those before a study is conducted. It can probably be assumed that research has been approved by a **research ethics committee** (REC) and so while a study may include some deception, for example, a REC has considered it reasonable. The only ethical concern for those reading published research is that the study's conclusions be used correctly. For example, using the results of Bartlett's (1932) study on the cultural distortions of recall and memory, it would be ethical to point out that the study was conducted almost 100 years ago and so generalizing its conclusions may not be appropriate in the current cultural context (see p. 60).

It is acceptable for research to be inconclusive or to present contradictory results. This simply means research has not reached a definitive conclusion and more research is needed. For example, more research is needed to determine whether shyness helps or hinders students' academic achievement.

Strengths and limitations of methodologies

Below is a table listing the strengths and weaknesses of the various methodologies mentioned in this chapter. Further details and explanations of these strengths and weaknesses can be found in the HL paper 3 chapter, page 352.

Method	Strengths	Limitations
Observations	Possible to see behaviour in natural situation. Minimal risk of participant bias/demand characteristics, especially with covert observations. Provides a context for an observed behaviour.	Does not establish any cause-effect relationship or even correlational relationship. Results tend to be subjective. Overt observations can affect the behaviour but covert observations may be unethical.

Method	Strengths	Limitations
Interviews – structured	Data tends to be objective and so is relatively straightforward to accumulate, process, and measure. Can be administered by relatively inexperienced researchers. Interviewer can record non-verbal language cues such as emotions, facial expressions, and body language.	Data tends to have less ecological validity than unstructured interview data.
Interviews – unstructured	Data tends to have greater ecological validity than structured interview data. Interviewer can record non-verbal language cues such as emotions, facial expressions, and body language.	Data tends to be subjective and so is difficult to accumulate, process and measure. The quality of data may rely on the interviewer's ability to draw out valuable information from the participants.
Group interviews / focus groups	More participants can be interviewed in less time. Participants' can enrich each others' responses, i.e. the group can promote individuals' thoughts/ideas.	Requires a high level of expertise to ensure all group members contribute. Participants' responses can be affected by others' responses. Data tends to be subjective and therefore problematic to process.
Case studies	Provide an opportunity to investigate phenomena that could not be studied otherwise. Stimulate new research by highlighting phenomena that need further investigation. Can help develop new theories.	Can be difficult to replicate as a whole research approach. There is a risk of bias. Reliance on memory is subject to distortion.
Correlational studies	Higher degree of ecological validity. Variables can be isolated and researched in a semi-controlled way.	Not possible to establish a cause-effect relationship. Problems with informed consent.
Natural experiments	Higher degree of ecological validity. Allow variables to be isolated and researched in a semi-controlled way.	Not possible to establish a cause-effect relationship. Potential problems with informed consent.

Method	Strengths	Limitations
Field experiments	Higher degree of ecological validity. Participants do not have to know that they are being studied.	Do not allow for complete replication. Potential problems with informed consent.
Quasi-experiments	Higher degree of ecological validity. Allow one characteristic to be isolated and researched in a controlled way.	Care must be taken to create a comparable control group. Causality between variables is difficult to establish.

Biological approach to understanding behaviour

A

The relationship between biology and human behaviour can be seen as a complex interaction of **correlations**. The biological approach can be summarized with a question: To what extent do biological phenomena cause effects in human psychology? Many behaviours are biologically predetermined, but decisions made by individuals as well as **sociocultural** and physical **environmental factors** also influence biology.

Biological explanations of human behaviour show the clear influence of the natural sciences on the human sciences. For example, many biological explanations are **reductive** in nature and resort to experimentation to claim **validity**. Moreover, the technology available to investigate the relationship between biological phenomena and behaviour is becoming ever more sophisticated, allowing for new understanding.

The biological approach to behaviour focuses on:

- the brain and behaviour (SL and HL)

- hormones and behaviour (SL and HL)

- genetics and behaviour (SL and HL)

- the role of animal research in understanding human behaviour (HL only).

1 The brain and behaviour

Topic focus

To what extent can the structure and neurochemistry of the brain be used to explain behaviour?

1.1 Techniques used to study the brain in relation to behaviour

Content focus

Explain how different techniques can be used to study the brain in relation to behaviour.

Modern technology is now extensively used in **neuropsychology** because it provides an opportunity to study the active brain and allows researchers to see where specific brain processes take place. The choice of techniques used to correlate the brain with behaviour is based on a variety of factors, including opportunity, available technology and costs.

One of the key problems with using technology in brain research is that it can lead to reductionist arguments about the causes of behaviour that fail to consider other causes outside of biological factors. Other causes include sociocultural and socioeconomic factors, media norms, and parental and peer influences.

Furthermore, the technologies used do not provide a natural environment for **cognition**, which raises questions of **ecological validity**. The environments the active brain is studied in (with large noisy equipment) are so false and potentially

In Paper 1 (SL and HL), do not spend too long describing each technology. The key focus is whether the technological technique provides functional or structural data. You can use techniques other than the main technologies presented here (such as autopsy and the use of stroke victims) as evidence of critical thinking by showing alternative ways to investigate the brain and behaviour. You might also want to speculate as to what extent:

- reductionist arguments are valid in the human sciences

- cause and effect can be established using these techniques.

off-putting to participants that they do not necessarily give a picture of the brain in a natural environment.

Moreover, the images produced by these technologies, with their use of colours (Figure 1.2, page 4), may exaggerate the different activities of the brain.

There are two main types of imaging technology: **structural imaging** and **functional imaging**.

1.1.1 MRI (structural imaging)

A Magnetic Resonance Imaging (MRI) scan produces a three-dimensional picture of the brain structures. It works by detecting changes in blood flow without using a radioactive tracer. MRIs are non-**invasive** and relatively inexpensive. MRIs can measure the size of certain brain areas, which can then be compared in different groups of people. However, the images can lack clarity and precision and any conclusions are **correlational**, so **causation** cannot be inferred.

Structural imaging focuses on what parts of the brain look like in relation to each other.

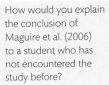
How would you explain the conclusion of Maguire et al. (2006) to a student who has not encountered the study before?

Key study: Maguire et al. (2006)

Aim: To investigate the extent to which the various parts of the hippocampus could be correlated with certain types of **topographical** or **spatial** memory. Topographical or spatial memory refers to the ability to recall the shape of a previously experienced environment.

Procedure: They compared taxi drivers with bus drivers who had similar driving experience and stress levels but differed in the sense that bus drivers follow constrained routes while taxi drivers have to constantly plan varying routes. Thirty-five healthy male volunteers participated in the study. Of these, 18 were licensed London taxi drivers and 17 were London bus drivers. Researchers used a variety of cognitive tests to match the taxi drivers and bus drivers in terms of stress and experience levels, and then gave them a structural MRI scan. Researchers then tested for functional differences between the groups in terms of their ability to acquire new **visuo-spatial** information after a 30-minute delay. They did this by asking participants to draw a reproduction of the Rey–Osterrieth Complex Figure (see Figure 1.1), which is one of the most widely used tests of spatial memory in neuropsychology.

Findings: They found that taxi drivers had greater matter volume in mid-posterior hippocampi and less matter volume in anterior hippocampi than bus drivers did. Furthermore, they found that years of navigation experience correlated with hippocampal matter volume only in taxi drivers, with right posterior matter volume increasing and anterior volume decreasing with more navigation experience. The ability to complete this task was worse in taxi drivers than in bus drivers.

Conclusion: Spatial knowledge, and not stress, driving, or self-motion, is associated with the pattern of hippocampal matter volume in taxi drivers. Maguire et al. speculate that maintaining a spatial representation of a complex object (the London road network) might require a cognitive trade-off, leading to a decreased ability to form spatial memories of new complex objects. The taxi driver's ability to navigate a complex pattern can be associated with greater posterior hippocampal grey matter volume while their lower ability to form new spatial memories can be correlated with decreased matter volume in the anterior hippocampus. Overall, they concluded that learning, representing, and using a spatial representation of a highly complex and large-scale environment are the primary functions of the hippocampus in humans.

In summary: Maguire et al. (2006) were able to show that various parts of the hippocampus could be correlated with certain types of topographical or spatial memory.

Figure 1.1 An image of the Rey–Osterrieth Complex Figure, which is used to test spatial memory. Taxi drivers were less successful than bus drivers in recalling this figure, which was new to them, even though they were more capable of recalling routes around London, which they were familiar with.

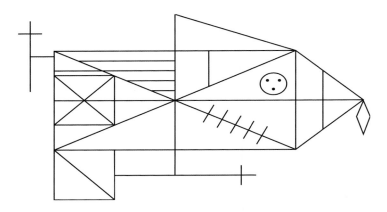

Functional imaging focuses on how the brain works, in terms of its physiology, functional architecture and dynamics.

1.1.2 PET scan (functional imaging)

A Positron Emission Tomography (PET) scan monitors glucose **metabolism** in the brain. The participant is injected with a harmless dose of radioactive glucose, and the radioactive particles emitted by the glucose are detected by the PET scan. The images produced are coloured maps of brain activity, as shown below.

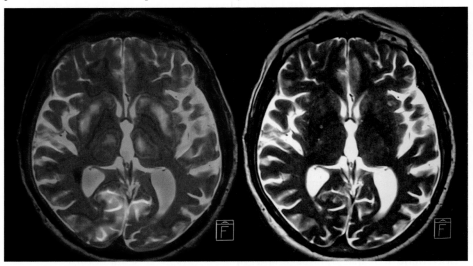

Figure 1.2 Maps of brain activity

The PET scan has been used to compare gender difference and to investigate how the brain responds to particular stimuli. It can measure the function of certain areas of the brain by focusing on metabolic activity, which can then be compared in different groups of people.

PET scans are invasive, because the participant receives a radioactive injection, but very safe, as the radiation dose is small and goes away quickly. The greatest advantage of PET (compared to MRI) is that it can record ongoing activity in the brain rather than produce just one static image. However, there is a high cost associated with the necessary equipment and its maintenance.

Key study: Maguire et al. (1997)

Aim: To investigate the extent to which the right hippocampus could be correlated with spatial memory.

Procedure: London taxi drivers were given a PET scan while they were asked to recall complex routes around London, and then while they were asked to recall famous landmarks that were not on taxi routes.

Findings: When participants were asked to recall complex routes around London, the right hippocampus was shown to be activated. When they were asked to recall famous landmarks of which the participants had no knowledge of the spatial location, the right hippocampus was not activated.

Conclusion: This suggests the right hippocampus is involved in spatial memory.

1.1.3 fMRI (functional imaging)

An fMRI scan studies the structure and physical functions of the brain by monitoring blood-oxygen levels. Blood-oxygen levels in the brain increase as the active parts of the brain require more oxygen.

fMRIs can record brain signals without the risks of radiation and are one of the most common brain-mapping techniques because of the relatively wide availability of the machines. Many researchers are able to access the technology, which promotes **reliability** and comparisons across studies.

The machines have high spatial resolution (up to 1 mm) and are considered more accurate than PET scans. However, they must be used carefully because they can produce false positives. Training is required and the images produced must be interpreted carefully, since brain processes are complex and often non-localized. Furthermore, the signals can be susceptible to non-neural changes in the body, such as diet.

Key study: Eisenberger et al. (2003)

Aim: To investigate the **neural correlates** of **social exclusion** and test the hypothesis that the brain bases of social pain are similar to those of physical pain.

Procedure: Participants were given an fMRI scan while playing a virtual ball-tossing game in which they were ultimately excluded.

Findings: Results showed that the anterior cingulate cortex (ACC) was more active when participants were excluded, which correlated with the results of self-reported distress. They were able to correlate these results that had also showed ACC activation during physical pain.

Conclusion: The social attachment system in humans may have 'piggybacked' onto the physical pain system to promote survival because it would lead to the promotion and maintenance of social bonds.

Alternative techniques to understanding the brain and behaviour

Autopsy

An autopsy is a surgical procedure that examines a corpse through the process of dissection. When used in research, the main aim is to establish if specific areas of the brain can be correlated with specific thoughts, feelings and behaviour by comparing a healthy brain with any abnormalities in the brain of the deceased.

An **autopsy** is a surgical procedure that examines a corpse through the process of **dissection**. It is usually performed to determine the cause of death. When applied to studying the structure and function of the brain it involves removing sections of a deceased person's brain to discover if any abnormalities can be observed.

By comparing a healthy brain to any abnormalities found in the brain of the deceased, assumptions can be made regarding which areas of the brain and which abnormalities may have been responsible for behaviour observed during an individual's lifetime.

Key study: Henry Molaison

An autopsy was performed on Henry Molaison (H.M.), one of the world's most famous **amnesic** patients. His amnesia was caused by an experimental brain operation carried out in 1953 to relieve his symptoms of epilepsy. H.M. died in 2008 and his brain was immediately subjected to a full autopsy. It was found to have partial damage in the medial temporal stem and in particular the parahippocampal cortex, which is an area of the brain that surrounds the hippocampus. The results confirmed these areas play an important role in memory encoding and retrieval (Augustinack et al. 2014) because these were the specific problems H.M. had during his lifetime.

Researchers can also use scanning techniques on portions of brain that are removed. For example, Augustinack et al. (2014) used high-resolution MRI imaging on parts of H.M.'s brain and were able to distinguish between the age-related white matter disease that likely accounted for the dementia he suffered in the final part of his life and the damage caused by the surgery when he was a younger man. By using methodological **triangulation** they were able to add validity to their findings and suggest definitive connections between brain areas and specific behaviours.

Use examples to support any assertions about functional localization. Ask:

• To what extent are reductionist arguments valid in the human sciences?

• To what extent can cause and effect be established using the assumptions of localization?

1.2 Localization

Content focus

Explain localization while addressing the limitations of this model.

1.2.1 Defining localization

Localization refers to the notion that specific areas of the brain are responsible for specific behaviours. It assumes that specific areas can be correlated with specific thoughts, feelings and behaviour.

Studies that show clear localization in the previous pages include:

- Maguire et al. (1997, 2006) investigated to what extent the right hippocampus could be correlated with spatial memory. They used a PET scans and MRI scans over a number of studies and concluded that the right hippocampus is involved in spatial memory as it is more active in spatial tasks and becomes enlarged over time with individuals who are engaged in intense spatial awareness tasks.

- Eisenberger et al. (2003) investigated the neural correlates of social exclusion with fMRIs and tested the hypothesis that the brain bases of social pain are similar to those of physical pain. They concluded that the anterior cingulate cortex (ACC) was involved in feelings of social exclusion.

Key study: Raine et al. (1997)

Aim: To compare specific brain structures in murderers and non-murderers. The researchers measured brain activity to investigate whether there was dysfunction of the same areas in both groups.

Procedure: The 'murderers' were 41 prisoners (39 male, two female) with a mean age of 34.3 years, who had been charged with murder or manslaughter in California, USA.
Participants had been referred for brain imaging scans to obtain evidence or information relating to either a defence of not guilty by reason of **insanity**, incompetence to stand trial, or proof of diminished capacity that could reduce the sentencing after being found guilty.
A **matched-pairs** design was used where each murderer was matched with a 'normal' subject – a control – for age, sex and diagnosis of **schizophrenia** where necessary. Each match was screened to exclude physical and mental illness, history of drug use and a history of murder. Therefore, the variable of 'murder' had been isolated.
No subject took psychoactive medication for two weeks before scanning, to prevent medication affecting the results.
After practice trials, all participants were injected with a tracer substance (fluorodeoxyglucose) that was taken up by the brain to show the location of brain metabolism while conducting a continuous performance task (CPT). A PET scan was then immediately given to show the relative brain activity for **cortical** areas (on the outside of the brain) and **subcortical** areas (inside the brain).

Findings: A summary of results from Raine et al. (1997).

Brain structure	Murderers' metabolic activity level	Interpretation
Prefrontal cortex	Lower activity in murderers than in controls.	Linked to loss of self-control and altered emotion/linked to emotional control.

To what extent does the concept of localization (reducing complex behaviours to specific brain regions) help and hinder understanding of human thoughts, feelings and behaviour?

Localization refers to the notion that specific areas of the brain are responsible for specific behaviours. It assumes specific areas can be correlated with specific thoughts, feelings and behaviour.

Brain structure	Murderers' metabolic activity level	Interpretation
Parietal cortex	Lower activity in murderers than in controls especially in the left angular and bilateral superior gyrus.	Lower left angular gyrus activity linked to lower verbal ability and therefore possibly educational failure/certain levels of frustration at not being able to express themselves – possibly crime.
Amygdala	Lower activity in left than right side of the brain in murderers than in controls.	These structures form part of the limbic system (thought to control emotional expression). Problems with these structures may cause a lack of inhibition for violent behaviour, fearlessness and a failure to learn the negative effects of violence.

Conclusion: Raine et al. demonstrate a clear physiological difference between violent people and non-violent people. The study also shows specific localized brain areas that can be linked with an extreme behaviour such as murder.

The study has many strengths, including gender balance. Although the number of females was low, violent murder is a crime committed more often by men. Ethically this study was very well conducted, as permission was sought and granted from the relevant authorities and no intrusive techniques were used. Methodologically this is a relatively large sample given the cost of PET scans. There was also a clear use of controls to rule out alternative effects on brain activity. Moreover, the effort put into the matched-pairs design is a strength.

The study has some weaknesses, notably the use of PET scans, which can lack precision. Furthermore, the findings apply only to a small subgroup of violent offenders and they were not a **homogenous** group. Some were murderers and some were manslaughterers, and the reasons for their scanning referrals were very diverse, ranging from schizophrenia (six cases) to head injury or organic brain damage (23 cases). Therefore the majority of cases had some kind of brain injury, which limits the generalizability of the results to a wider, non-brain-damaged population.

Extreme caution should be used when correlating specific areas of the brain with specific behaviours, as it may be the damage to the brain that causes those behaviours.

1.2.2 Limitations of localization

Localization can cause errors in analysis.

There is a significant variability in brain anatomy between individuals caused both by **genetic** predisposition and **neuroplasticity** (discussed in section 1.3).

Studies in localization can lead to reductionist arguments for behaviour causation whereby specific behaviours are linked with specific areas of the brain and it is then assumed those areas cause the behaviour. However, because of the processes involved in individual variability and neuroplasticity, a clear causative relationship between location and function can rarely be inferred. Reducing complex behaviours to purely biological factors is tempting for researchers because it ignores factors that are difficult to study, such as the intertwined relationship of sociocultural and cognitive processes, as well as individual responsibility. For example, Raine et al. focus on specific brain areas and assume these are linked to specific behaviours. However, their findings do not mean violence is caused by biology alone as other social, psychological and situational factors are involved in such an extreme and complex behaviour. Moreover, the findings do not demonstrate the murderers are not responsible for their actions and they do not mean PET scans can diagnose murderers. The findings do not reveal whether the brain abnormalities are a cause or effect of behaviour.

The brain is a complex organ; its structure is only just being uncovered. While scanning is an important tool in uncovering localization – as it shows a link between activation and a specific task or behaviour – it is often difficult to identify the area to which the activation corresponds because of poor image quality and the complexity of the area in question. Researchers are only just beginning to standardize parcellations of the brain in terms of function, microanatomy and labelling, although this will increase as technology becomes more accurate.

To some extent, brain locations are human constructions that are not present in actuality because the brain is a highly interconnected organ. There is considerable disagreement as to where certain locations start and end. Different theorists using different technologies often question and redraw boundaries depending on the task and technology used.

Researchers have resorted to two main approaches to solve this problem:

- labelling brain locations through coordinates, usually in relation to the Talairach coordinate system
- labelling through names usually in relation to the accepted anatomic labels of brain locations.

Both systems produce inaccuracies because of the lack of task and equipment standardization. A coordinate is often the most useful label for comparison with other results in neuro-imaging, but it can be difficult to compare coordinates with brain locations obtained from other types of data.

Furthermore, as labels and coordinates become embedded in research conclusions, they become more accepted over time and create a rigidity of understanding for other researchers to base their studies and results on. Such rigidity has advantages, as it produces a basis of understanding, but it could also mean that researchers are more likely to ignore results that do not correlate with established understanding of localizations of function.

1.3 Neuroplasticity

Content focus

Explain how neuroplasticity is influenced by both genes and the environment.

Neuroplasticity refers to how the brain changes over time as a result of environmental influences. It can also be referred to as brain plasticity, cortical plasticity or cortical remapping.

 TOK How can we determine whether the regions of the brain occur in actuality or are just products of the human research process?

 EE To what extent can a specific behaviour be explained by localization?

 Neuroplasticity refers to how the brain changes over time as a result of environmental influences. It can also be referred to as brain plasticity, cortical plasticity or cortical remapping.

Make a clear link between the effect on brain development and environmental stimuli. Clearly label the environmental stimuli throughout your answer. Distinguish between human and animal research.

Although genes provide the basic outline for brain development, environmental influences shape gene expression in the brain through the process of neuroplasticity. Neural networks can change as a result of sociocultural and personal experiences or as a result of brain injury.

Genotype refers to the genetic constitution of an individual organism.

Phenotype refers to the set of observable characteristics of an individual that is a result of the interaction between the genotype and its environment.

A phenotype results from the expression of an organism's genotype and the influence of environmental factors as well as interactions between the two. A single genotype can be expressed in a multiplicity of distinct physiological and behavioural phenotypes.

The field of research that studies the interaction between genetic determinability and environmental interaction has been termed **psychosocial genomics** (Rossi, 2002). Psychosocial genomics is an interdisciplinary study of the processes by which gene expressions are modulated by psychological and sociocultural and personal experiences.

It is an interdisciplinary approach because the union of neuroplasticity and psychosocial genomics research represents a synthesis of the social and biological sciences that is non-reductive: it does not dismiss human experience as the product of a neural machine or predetermined genetic blueprint. Instead, such an approach is integrative, inclusive, and holistic (Garland and Howard, 2009).

The brain structure is highly **heritable**, but the extent of heritability remains open to debate.

Key study: Watanabe et al. (2016)

Aim: To investigate how genetics and environmental factors influence the brain.

Procedure: They used PET scans to measure glucose metabolism in 40 pairs of monozygotic (identical) twins and 18 pairs of dizygotic (fraternal) twins. They assumed any differences in glucose metabolism between monozygotic twins could be attributed to environmental factors, since they are genetically identical. Therefore, when a genetic influence is dominant, the monozygotic twins would have more trait similarity than the dizygotic twins. When an environmental influence is dominant, the trait similarity would be the same for identical and fraternal twins.

Findings: Both genetic and environmental factors influenced glucose metabolism in the brain, but different parts of the brain were influenced by genetic or environmental factors to differing degrees. For example, genetic influences were found to play a significant role in the left and right parietal lobes where sensory information such as taste, temperature and touch are processed. Genetic influences were also found to play a significant role in the left temporal lobe where sounds and speech comprehension are processed.

To what extent do interdisciplinary approaches help or hinder knowledge creation?

Conclusion: More research is needed to ascertain why certain areas of the brain are more open to influence from genetic or environmental factors, but it seems reasonable to conclude that the regions of the brain that are shaped more by environmental forces will be more susceptible to neuroplasticity.

The causes of neuroplasticity are difficult to research conclusively in humans because of the highly varied nature of the environment and the early stages of genetic research into the phenomena.

However, neuroplasticity has been well documented in animal studies. For example, Rosenzweig and Bennett (1972) demonstrated the effect of a physically enriched environment on the thickness of the **frontal lobe** in rats. The enriched, stimulating environment was characterized by interesting toys to play with while the deprived environment was operationalized by no toys. The rats spent 30 or 60 days in their respective environments and then they were euthanized. The post-mortem studies of their brains showed those that had been in the stimulating environment had an increased thickness in the frontal lobe, which is associated with thinking, planning, and decision making. Similar research studies demonstrated how cortical thickness increases even further if rats are placed with other rats.

The experimental nature of the study, with a clear independent variable (IV) and dependent vaariable (DV), allows causation to be inferred. However, this is an animal study and caution should be used when generalizing the results to humans. The manipulation of an environmental IV to measure the impact on a physiological DV would be not possible on humans for ethical reasons.

Isolating key variables and then documenting the effect on brain growth is challenging from a research standpoint because of these **ethical considerations** and the unpredictability of environmental factors. However, it is possible through careful isolation and measurement.

Key study: Luby et al. (2012)

Aim: To investigate the effect of **nurturing** mothers on the hippocampal development of their children by isolating the variables of nurturing and hippocampal development.

Procedure: The researchers used 92 children aged between 3 and 6 years old in a longitudinal study. Because of ethical considerations, researchers cannot deliberately create a non-nurturing environment and then measure the effect on brain development, so Luby et al. used a **natural experimental** method and pre-determined which parents were nurturing and which were non-nurturing. The children were put into a frustrating situation whereby they and their mothers were left in a room with a brightly wrapped package. The children were not allowed to open the gift and they were told to wait while the mother filled out a series of forms. The researchers observed how the children and mothers handled this situation, which was meant to replicate the typical stressors of daily parenting. Mothers who offered reassurance and support that helped their child control their impulses were rated as being nurturing. Mothers who either ignored the child or harshly scolded the child were rated as non-nurturing. When the children were between 7 and 10 years old, Luby et al. performed MRI brain scans on them.

Findings: The children with the nurturing mothers had a hippocampus that was 10 per cent larger than the hippocampi of children with non-nurturing mothers.

Conclusion: A nurturing environment impacts children's brain development.

In summary: Luby et al. (2012) used a natural experimental method to measure the effect of non-nurturing environments on hippocampal growth in children. They found that children from non-nurturing environments had a smaller hippocampus than children from nurturing environments.

The study highlights the positive relationship between early experiences of maternal nurturing and hippocampal volume. However, the key failing of any study that cannot account for extraneous variables is that it is difficult to pinpoint which aspects of parental nurturing cause the effect in the hippocampal volume. Non-nurturing is a very broad concept and encompasses many behaviours. For example, non-nurturing mothers may also neglect to feed their children healthily, or read to them regularly, both of which may also impact their children's brain development.

Maguire et al. (2006) were able to isolate the variables of complex navigational experience and hippocampal development by comparing taxi drivers with bus drivers. The isolation of these variables occurred by splitting them into two distinct groups: taxi drivers and bus drivers. Bus drivers follow constrained routes while taxi drivers had to constantly plan varying routes. They then used a variety of cognitive tests to match the drivers in terms of stress levels and driving experience and then gave them a structural MRI scan.

They found that taxi drivers had greater matter volume in mid-posterior hippocampi and less volume in anterior hippocampi. The years of navigation experience correlated with hippocampal matter volume in the taxi drivers, with right posterior matter volume increasing and anterior volume decreasing with more navigation experience. Maguire et al. (2006) were able to cautiously suggest this was an example of neuroplasticity in action, as the taxi drivers' constant need to use complex spatial memory had meant a development of the mid-posterior hippocampi.

Gilles et al. (1996) aimed to create an animal model to show the effects of continuous **chronic** stress on **corticosterone** secretion in response to an **acute environmental stressor**.

Previous studies had used an absence of the mother to induce stress but the researchers wanted a model that could be comparable with human experiences. Therefore, stress was moderated by placing newborn rats into an environment with their mothers that featured either good or limited bedding before they were euthanized and their bodies subjected to an autopsy.

The group with limited bedding manifested increased corticosterone. Gilles et al. were able to suggest the experiences they had created in the laboratory were approximate to the human situation of chronically stressed, neglected infants.

The research is important because corticosterone secretion has a profound effect on the structure, development and function of the hippocampus particularly via **dendritic retraction** – a form of neuroplasticity. Dendritic retraction involves reductions in dendritic length and reduced branch numbers, and has traditionally corresponded to hippocampus-dependent spatial memory deficits (Conrad, 2006), further suggesting the hippocampus is involved in spatial memory.

Other studies have shown the effects of environmental stress on the development of the hippocampus can be reversed when maternal care is reintroduced, which again shows that environmental change can cause neuroplasticity (Edwards and Burnham, 2001).

1.4 Neurotransmitters and their effect on behaviour

Content focus

Explain how neurotransmitters cause behaviour through agonistic and antagonistic mechanisms and comment on to what extent cause and effect can be inferred.

The nervous system is comprised of **neurons** (nerve cells) and they are one of the building blocks of behaviour. Neurons send electrochemical messages to the brain so that people can respond to stimuli – either from the environment or from internal changes in the body.

The method by which these messages are sent is called **neurotransmission**. When an electrical impulse travels down the axon (the body) of the neuron, it releases neurotransmitters, which then cross the gap between two neurons. This gap is called a synapse.

The neurotransmitters are stored in the neurons' terminal buttons. After crossing the synapse, the neurotransmitters fit into receptor sites on the post-synaptic membrane. Once the message is passed on, the neurotransmitters are either broken down or reabsorbed.

Neurotransmitters are affected by **agonists**, which amplify their effect, and **antagonists**, which reduce their effect. Neurons working together can produce a large variety of effects resulting in a complex repertoire of thoughts, feelings and behaviours. Neurotransmitters also have different effects in different systems in the human body. For example, **acetylcholine (ACh)** is involved in muscle contraction when it acts on motor neurons, but is involved in memory in the hippocampus. Therefore, the complexity of these chemical interactions, together with the range of effects, makes cause–effect difficult to establish.

Neurotransmitters are involved in a range of thoughts, feelings and behaviours.

Neurotransmitter	Some effects
ACh	Muscle contraction and memory
Dopamine	Voluntary movement, learning, and feelings of pleasure
Norepinephrine (noradrenaline)	Arousal, alertness, and stimulation
Serotonin	Sleep, arousal levels, and emotion

Speculate as to what extent a cause-effect relationship can be inferred regarding neurotransmitters and their effects.

- Critique the studies, but remember all methodologies have flaws and always consider to what extent these flaws undermine the entire validity of the conclusion.

- Avoid coming to definitive conclusions about specific hormones. Instead, come to cautious conclusions based on the findings of varied research.

- Use animal studies to show how the manipulations of certain variables can be carried out on animals, but not humans, and thereby demonstrate cause and effect. Caution should be used if generalizing the findings of animal studies to humans.

Neurotransmitters are the body's natural chemical messengers, they transmit information from one neuron to another across the synapse.

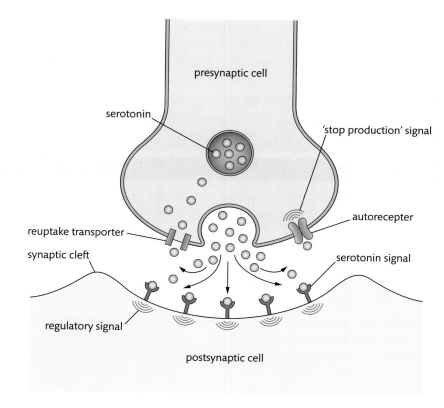

Figure 1.3 Synaptic transmission

An agonist is a chemical that binds to a receptor and activates it to provoke a biological response.

An antagonist is a chemical that binds to a receptor and blocks it to dampen a biological response (they are sometimes called blockers).

The complexity of these chemical interactions makes cause–effect difficult to establish, but researchers can use agonists and antagonists to manipulate the levels and effects of neurotransmitters.

1.4.1 Acetylcholine

The main role of ACh is to change the state of neuronal networks throughout the brain and modify their response to internal and external stimuli. The diverse effects of ACh depend on the site of release and the receptor subtypes. However, a common theme is that it has a role in behaviours that are **adaptive** to environmental stimuli as well as decreasing responses to stimuli that do not require immediate action (Picciotto et al. 2012). ACh is also thought to play a role in memory formation.

Key study: Martinez and Kesner (1991)

Aim: To investigate the role of ACh in learning and memory.

Procedure: Rats were trained to go through a maze at the end of which they received food. Once the rats were able to do this, they injected one group of rats with an antagonist substance (scopolamine) that blocks ACh receptor sites, thus decreasing available ACh. They then injected a second group of rats with an agonist (physostigmine) that led to the increase of ACh and stopped the synapse returning to its 'resting state'. A third group, the control group, were not given any injections. Therefore, the researchers either boosted or blocked levels of ACh in two groups of rats. The dependent variable (DV) was memory, measured by how fast the rats could run a maze.

Findings: The rats that had their ACh levels boosted were better at running the maze and they found the food more quickly.

Conclusion: The researchers concluded that ACh played an important role in creating a memory of the maze.

Criticism: This study has a clear IV (levels of ACh) and a clear DV (ability and time taken to run the maze), so the use of an experimental method with a control group makes it possible to establish a **cause-and-effect relationship** between levels of ACh and memory. However, the limitation of the research is that it is questionable to what extent these findings can be generalized to humans, but human research has shown that ACh-producing cells in the basal forebrain are damaged in the early stages of Alzheimer's disease, which suggests that ACh does have a role to play in memory formation in humans.

The nervous system involves complex interactions, making clear cause-effect with isolated variables difficult to establish. Experimental evidence suggests that memory processing is mediated by parallel, and to some extent independent, neural systems. Because different memory systems appear to acquire different classes of information, the processing of different attributes of memory may at times come into conflict with one another (White and McDonald, 2002). Therefore, while experimentation through manipulation of clear **independent variables** to measure the effect on clear **dependent variables** makes researchers confident they can claim cause-effect, it is essential that caution is used when coming to conclusions. While Martinez and Kesner appear to show a clear link between spatial memory formation and ACh in this study, researchers cannot simply conclude ACh increases memory.

The complexity of brain functionality means that researchers must be very cautious when claiming simple cause-effect relationships between neurotransmitters and specific responses.

McIntyre et al. (2002) suggest ACh release may reflect activation and participation of the hippocampus in learning and memory, but in a manner that can be detrimental to performance on another brain area such as the **amygdala**, which is also involved in memory. They were able to measure ACh levels in rat hippocampi. When the levels were high in the hippocampus the rats were more able to perform spontaneous spatial awareness tasks but less able to perform tasks needing conditioned responses, which are associated with the amygdala.

They concluded that ACh can be linked with certain brain areas, such as the hippocampus, which are themselves responsible for certain types of memory, but high levels may impair other functions that require a different type of memory.

1.4.2 Serotonin

Like ACh, **serotonin** has a number of roles and performs differently in different parts of the body where it exists in varying amounts. In most humans, serotonin is found in the digestive tract where it regulates food digestion. A small amount is found in the central nervous system (CNS) where it is involved in mood regulation, appetite, and sleep, as well as cognitive functions such as learning and memory. Again, this means researchers need to be cautious in claiming any single cause-effect relationship.

'Falling in love' is deeply intertwined with feelings and emotions, and humans expend energy and devote resources to the person they fall in love with. Therefore, researchers assume the **evolutionary** consequences of love are so important that there must be some long-established biological mechanism that regulates and promotes it. For example, it has been noted that in the early stages of love, the object of love becomes an overvalued idea, similar to the thought processes of someone suffering from **obsessive compulsive disorder (OCD)**. Research has pointed to the possibility that the two conditions, love and OCD, might share some physiological similarities.

Key study: Marazziti et al. (1999)

Aim: To test whether the obsessional nature of early phase love might share the same physiological basis as obsessive compulsive disorder (OCD), which has a similar psychological framework of obsessiveness.

Procedure: Twenty subjects who had fallen in love within the previous six months were compared with 20 non-medicated OCD patients and 20 controls. The density of the platelet 5-HT transporter was measured – a low measurement would indicate a low level of serotonin.

Findings: The main finding of the study was that subjects who were in the early romantic phase of a love relationship were no different from OCD patients in terms of the low density level of the platelet 5-HT and both groups had significantly lower levels than in the normal controls.

Conclusion: Love and OCD were physiologically similar and serotonin could act as a biological mechanism to explain 'falling in love' and pair-bonding behaviour.

Criticism: This was a correlational study, so caution should be used when assuming low levels of serotonin caused either OCD or 'in-love'-type behaviour because the low serotonin levels may be the consequence of the in love and OCD behaviour rather than the cause of it. Moreover, the sample group was small and should be seen more as a pilot study rather than a definitive account of the effects of serotonin.

TOK

To what extent does the process of reducing complex behaviour to biological mechanisms help or hinder knowledge creation?

How does the language in the phrase 'falling in love' impart meaning about this process? Do other languages use similar metaphors?

There has been a philosophical criticism of reducing the explanation of a complex behaviour such as falling in love to the workings of neurotransmitters alone. Given the complexity of the thoughts, feelings and behaviour of falling in love, it is likely that more than one chemical interaction is involved. It should also be considered that neurotransmitters have different effects in different regions. For example, it is possible that serotonin, rather than activating a region associated with pair bonding, actually deactivates a region associated with negative emotions, social judgement, and 'mentalizing' that is, the cognitive assessment of other people's intentions and emotions (Zeki, 2007), thereby allowing falling in love to take place.

The lack of cause-effect inference from certain studies can be addressed by experimental manipulation of variables. This is challenging with humans and must be carefully considered.

Key study: Passamonti et al. (2012)

Aim: To manipulate serotonin levels through diet with an aim to measure the effects via an fMRI scan of the participants' brains. As well as 'falling in love', reduced serotonin levels have also been implicated in aggression and therefore, Passamonti et al. wanted to test if such overt manipulation produced an effect.

Procedure: They used **tryptophan**, which can be used as a serotonin agonist; its presence increases the effects of serotonin. Thirty healthy volunteers' serotonin levels were manipulated by giving them a mixture of amino acids that lacked tryptophan, which is a building block for serotonin, on the experimental day, and the same mixture but with a normal amount of tryptophan on the placebo day. On the experimental day, they were artificially having their serotonin levels lowered. Passamonti et al. then used a personality questionnaire to generate **quantitative** data associated with personality characteristics. They were able to determine which individuals had a natural tendency to behave aggressively.

All participants were then scanned using an fMRI as they viewed faces with angry, sad, and neutral expressions. Using the fMRI, researchers were able to measure how different brain regions reacted and communicated with one another when the volunteers viewed the different faces.

Findings: The research showed that low brain serotonin levels inhibited communication between the amygdala and the frontal lobes compared to communication present under normal levels of serotonin.

Conclusion: The amygdala is thought to be associated with generating emotional reactions and the frontal lobe is thought to be associated with regulating them. Therefore, the findings suggest that when serotonin levels are low, it may be more difficult for the forces of the prefrontal cortex to control the emotional responses to anger that are generated within the amygdala.

In individuals determined to have a natural tendency toward agression, the communications between the amygdala and the prefrontal cortex was even weaker following serotonin depletion. This finding suggests those individuals who might be predisposed to aggression were the most sensitive to low levels of serotonin. These results also support the localization data from Raine et al. (1997) who found lower activity of the frontal lobe in murderers when compared to controls.

EE

To what extent can a specific neurotransmitter be used to explain a specific behaviour?

Speculate as to what extent a cause-effect relationship can be inferred regarding hormones and their effects.

- Critique the studies. All methodologies have flaws so consider to what extent these flaws undermine the conclusion's validity.

- Avoid definitive conclusions about specific hormones. Instead, make cautious conclusions based on the findings of varied research.

- Use animal studies to show how the manipulations of certain variables can be carried out on animals, but not humans, and thereby demonstrate cause-effect. Caution should be used in generalizing the findings of animal studies to humans.

2 Hormones and pheromones and behaviour

Topic focus

To what extent can hormones be used to explain behaviour?

2.1 Hormones and behaviour

Content focus

Explain how hormones cause changes in thoughts (attention), feelings (mood), and behaviour.

Hormones are chemicals released by specific **glands** in the body to regulate medium- and long-term behaviour changes. However, some hormones (e.g. adrenaline) also act as **neurotransmitters** and can produce more instantaneous effects on mood and attention.

Hormones are chemicals released by specific glands in the body to regulate medium- and long-term behaviour changes. However, some hormones (e.g. adrenaline) also act as neurotransmitters and can produce more instantaneous effects on mood and attention.

Hormones are involved in a range of thoughts, feelings and behaviours.

Hormone	Gland(s)	Function
Adrenaline	Adrenals	Flight or fight response, arousal
Cortisol	Adrenals	Arousal, stress, memory
Oxytocin	Pituitary and hypothalamus	Social recognition via facial expression, mother–child attachment, and attachment
Testosterone	Gonads	Development, social status via aggression

Hormones enter the bloodstream and they take longer to produce changes in behaviour than neurotransmitters.

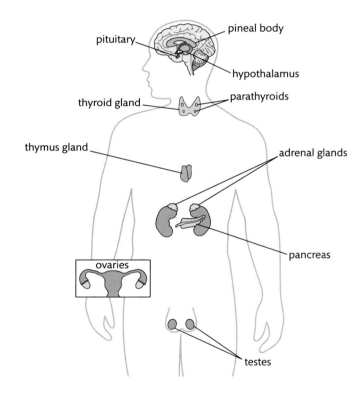

Figure 2.1 The glands that produce hormones make up the endocrine system.

2.1.1 Oxytocin

Oxytocin is a hormone that is produced by the hypothalamus after being stimulated by the pituitary gland. Oxytocin release is often triggered by touches and hugs and it is associated with bonding between lovers, and mothers and offspring, as well as wider social emotions.

Oxytocin appears to change the brain signals related to social recognition via facial expression, perhaps by changing the firing of the neurons of the amygdala. This is the part of the brain that plays an important role in processing emotional stimuli.

Does ethical and non-ethical behaviour depend on free will? Can the concept of free will in human behaviour be measured?

If oxytocin is given to healthy individuals it seems there is an increase in feelings of trust and generosity. The inability to secrete oxytocin and feel empathy has been linked to psychopathic behaviour, which is a disorder characterized by shallow feelings, a lack of guilt, and showing superficial charm and criminality as well an increase in feelings and behaviour associated with **narcissism**.

Key study: Guastella et al. (2008)

Aim: To measure the effects of **oxytocin** on male humans and how it enhances the **encoding** of positive social information.

Procedure: Oxytocin or a placebo was given in the form of a nasal spray to 69 healthy male volunteers. They were then presented with 36 happy, angry, or neutral human faces. Participants returned the following day to make 'remember' and 'know' judgements for a mixture of 72 new and previously seen faces.

Findings: Oxytocin-administered participants were more likely to make 'remember' and 'know' judgments for previously seen happy faces compared with angry and neutral human faces. In contrast, oxytocin did not influence judgements for faces that had not been presented previously.

Conclusion: The administration of oxytocin to male humans enhances the encoding of positive social information to make it more memorable. The results suggest that oxytocin could enhance intimacy and bonding in humans by strengthening encoding to make the recall of positive social information more likely. The study used only male participants, therefore caution should be used when generalizing the results to females.

It would be inaccurate to describe oxytocin as a 'pro-social' hormone, because human interaction is complex. For example, a study showing the 'negative' social effects of oxytocin was conducted by Shamay-Tsoory et al. (2009), who aimed to measure the effect of oxytocin on envy and schadenfreude (enjoyment over others' misfortune).

The researchers argued that humans have a strong social tendency to compare themselves with others and they tend to feel envious when they receive less valuable rewards. They also tend to rejoice when their own payoffs are more advantageous. Envy and schadenfreude are social feelings widely agreed to be a symptom of the human social tendency to compare one's payoffs with those of others.

Shamay-Tsoory et al. speculated that oxytocin may have a moderating effect on the intensity of these emotions. Fifty-six participants were either given nasal doses of oxytocin or a placebo. They then played a game of chance with another (fake) participant who either won more money (envy manipulation), lost more money (schadenfreude manipulation), or won/lost equal amounts of money. In comparison with the placebo, oxytocin increased the envy ratings during unequal monetary gain conditions. Oxytocin also increased the ratings of schadenfreude during gain conditions. However, oxytocin appeared to have no effect on the emotional ratings following equal monetary gains and did not affect general mood ratings. Therefore, this study shows oxytocin is involved in moderating envy and schadenfreude and not just 'positive' pro-social behaviours.

Key study: Guastella et al. (2010)

Aim: To measure the effects of oxytocin on the Reading the Mind in the Eyes Task, which is a widely used and reliable test of emotion recognition. It involves participants being shown a picture of eyes and asked to discern what emotion they are showing.

Oxytocin should not be simply described as a 'pro-social' hormone as human interaction is too complex. It is thought to be involved in envy and schadenfreude.

19

Procedure: In a **double-blind**, **randomized**, **placebo**-controlled design, oxytocin nasal spray or a placebo was administered to 16 males aged 12 to 19 who had been diagnosed with **autistic** or **Asperger's** disorders. Participants then completed the Reading the Mind in the Eyes Task.

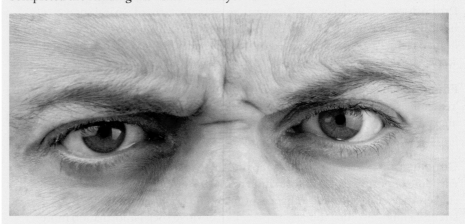

An example of the Reading the Mind in the Eyes Task.

Findings: In comparison with placebo, the results showed that oxytocin administration improved performance on the Reading the Mind in the Eyes Task. This effect was also shown when analysis was restricted to the younger participants, aged 12 to 15, who received a lower dose.

Conclusion: Oxytocin is linked to perception of emotions and the study provides the first evidence that oxytocin nasal spray improves emotion recognition in young people diagnosed with autism spectrum disorders (ASD). Findings suggest the potential of earlier intervention and further evaluation of oxytocin nasal spray as a treatment to improve social communication and interaction in young people with these disorders.

In summary: Although oxytocin has been called 'the love hormone' because it seems to be involved in pro-social behaviour such as bonding and remembering positive faces, it is more accurate to call it the 'pleasure hormone' as it is also involved with more negative social emotions such as envy and schadenfreude. The term 'love hormone' is too simplistic when the pleasure induced comes from the misfortune of others.

Furthermore, oxytocin appears to be closely linked with improved emotional recognition and provides insight into male-dominated disorders such as ASD. A strong male bias in ASD prevalence has been observed with striking consistency, with a male to female ratio of 4 : 1 (Werling and Geschwind, 2013). No mechanism has been identified to account for this gender difference, and oxytocin may provide an avenue of future investigation.

2.1.2 Testosterone

Testosterone is a **steroid** hormone from the androgen group. In mammals, testosterone is primarily secreted in the testes of males and the ovaries of females, although small amounts are also secreted by the **adrenal glands**. It is the principal male sex hormone. In men, testosterone plays a key role in health and well-being. A typical adult human male produces about 40–60 times more testosterone than an adult human female, but females are, from a behavioural perspective (rather than from an anatomical or biological perspective), more sensitive to the hormone.

Wagner et al. (1979) measured the effects of reduced levels of testosterone on aggression in male mice. They used a clear experimental method with the manipulation of the independent variable (IV) to measure an effect on a dependent variable (DV). The IV was the level of testosterone, **operationalized** by the mice being first castrated and then injected with testosterone. The DV was levels of aggression, operationalized by the number of bites exhibited. They found castration reduces aggression and then testosterone restores aggression in castrated mice who were previously judged to be aggressive. When the injections ceased, it led to reduced levels of aggression again.

Therefore, while there is a **causal** link between aggression and testosterone, caution should be used when inferring a unitary **causal relationship**. Methodologically this is a very tightly controlled study with a clear IV (testosterone) and a clear, quantifiable DV (number of bites exhibited). However, caution should always be used when **generalizing** the results of animal studies to humans.

Key study: Dreher et al. (2016)

Aim: To test whether testosterone can increase status-relevant aggressive behaviours, such as responses to provocation, while also being linked to status-relevant non-aggressive behaviours, such as feelings of generosity toward others.

Procedure: Forty healthy young human males were injected with testosterone or a placebo in a double-blind randomized design. Therefore, neither the participants nor the experimenter knew which participants were the experimental group or the placebo group.
Participants played a version of the Ultimatum Game (UG), a game in which two players must decide how to split a sum of money between them. In each round, the first player (the proposer) presents a proposal to the second player (the responder), which describes how this money should be divided. The responder accepts this proposal and the split is implemented, or rejects it and both players win nothing. The game was modified so that the participants who played the role of the responder, having accepted or rejected a proposed split, had the option to reward or punish the proposer by increasing or decreasing their monetary payoff at a proportional cost to themselves. Therefore, it was a game of risk that allowed participants to reward and punish the proposer.

Findings: The results showed participants treated with testosterone were more likely to punish the proposer and that higher testosterone levels were associated with increased punishment of proposers who were deemed to make unfair offers. This supports the long-held assumption that testosterone can be linked with aggressive responses to provocation. When participants who had been administered with testosterone received large offers, they were more likely to reward the proposer and also chose rewards of greater magnitude.

Conclusion: This increased generosity in the absence of provocation indicates that testosterone can also be linked with pro-social behaviours that are appropriate for increasing status.

Research undermines the simple causal link between testosterone and male aggression. Instead, testosterone's effect on male behaviour depends on the social context in which it occurs and is more likely linked to social status rather than simply aggression.

Dreher et al. suggest that testosterone, by playing on both positive and negative incentives, could have played a key evolutionary role by not only promoting aggressive behaviour but also increasing feelings of generosity, which leads to more generous behaviour and in turn a higher social status. They note how observations in non-human primates also indicate that the social hierarchy may be maintained by alpha males who have higher testosterone levels by not only aggressive behaviour but also sharing resources, such as access to food and females (Czoty et al., 2009). The findings undermine the notion of a simple causal link between testosterone and male aggression. Instead, testosterone's effect on male behaviour depends on the social context in which it occurs.

Key study: Gettler et al. (2011)

Aim: To determine whether fatherhood suppresses testosterone. Previous studies had shown childcare can lower testosterone levels.

Procedure: Six hundred and twenty-four Filipino men were followed in a **longitudinal study** for four and half years and had their testosterone levels measured at regular intervals.

Findings: Men with high waking testosterone were more likely to become partnered fathers by the time of the follow-up, four and a half years later.
Men who became partnered fathers then experienced significant declines in waking and evening testosterone, which were significantly greater than declines in single non-fathers.
Fathers reporting three hours or more of daily childcare had lower testosterone at follow-up compared with fathers not involved in childcare.

Conclusion: The findings suggest testosterone is involved with mating success because the men with high waking testosterone were more likely to become partnered fathers. The findings also suggest testosterone then declines rapidly after the men become fathers as a result of childcare because men involved in daily childcare had lower testosterone compared with fathers not involved in care. It appears testosterone levels involve a trade-off between mating and parenting in human males, which is also seen in other species in which fathers care for young. It may be that testosterone helps men become socially dominant, which increases their chances of mating by competing with other males and then declines once children are born as more nurturing behaviours are needed.

EE

To what extent can a specific hormone be used to explain a specific behaviour?

In paper 1 (SL and HL), speculate to what extent a cause-effect relationship can be inferred regarding pheromones and their effects. You also need to question whether or not pheromones can be said to exist as a researchable phenomenon in humans.

2.2 Pheromones and behaviour

Content focus

Comment on the validity of evidence that pheromones may cause behaviour.

Pheromones are chemicals that are **secreted** outside of the body and may play a role in human behaviour by acting on other individuals who sense them and then respond in certain ways. Species use different pheromones for different roles, including marking territory or signalling a threat to other members of the same group.

Research regarding human pheromonal interactions is still in its infancy so firm conclusions cannot be drawn. However, discussions about the effect of pheromones on behaviour can be seen as a useful exercise in critical thinking.

2.2.1 Establishing validity

The validity of a study refers to its 'correctness' or 'accuracy' and can usually be established by asking: To what extent are researchers confident an identifiable cause has had an identifiable effect? Therefore, to satisfy notions of validity, researchers need to be able to show the actions of an identified pheromone and how it causes an odour-mediated behavioural or **physiological** response.

Given the biological assumptions of the subject matter, validity would have to be established through cause-effect experimental methods that are open to **peer review**. There would also have to be a clear identification of the active molecule involved in both the secretion and the response.

The following considerations can be discussed when attempting to establish the validity of a cause-effect relationship between pheromones and human behaviour: definitions, **theoretical evidence** and **empirical evidence**.

Definitions

While there has been peer-reviewed research on other species regarding definitions and pheromonal effects, there has yet to be an established, coherent, peer-accepted definition of what a human pheromone constitutes, let alone what the effects on other individuals may be.

Researchers have agreed on certain aspects of pheromones. For example, for a pheromone to be considered a researchable phenomenon it has to be established as a coherent and singular entity that can be isolated and agreed upon in peer-reviewed research. It also has to be characteristic of an entire group rather than an individual. For example, all males of a species, rather than one individual, would have to secrete the chemical compound for it to be considered a pheromone. Moreover, it needs to be present in naturally-occurring sufficient quantities to cause an effect.

Researchers also know that, while some males may have more of a particular chemical compound and females may prefer those males, all individuals in the group have to be capable of producing that particular chemical compound for it to be considered a pheromone (Wyatt, 2014). According to Wyatt, pheromones have been identified in every part of the animal kingdom, including mammals, and are involved in a wide range of functions, including attraction, trail following, and interactions between parents and offspring. Although the effect of pheromones is dependent on the species, there is clear evidence that pheremones are a physiological mechanism that causes an effect in other non-human animals.

However, even with this understanding of pheromones, it has been difficult to establish whether or not they can be seen as a coherent and singular entity that can result in an agreed-upon definition. Most pheromones are not single compounds, but tend to be multi-component combinations of various other molecules (Logan, 2015).

TOK To what extent should peer-reviewed reliability be a consideration when establishing validity? If researchers continuously demonstrate the same result are they more correct than researchers who cannot achieve reliability?

 A key problem has been establishing whether or not pheromones can be seen as a coherent and singular entity that can result in an agreed-upon definition. Most pheromones are not single compounds, but tend to be multi-component combinations of various other molecules (Logan, 2015).

Moreover, the behaviour and actions of pheromone molecules create further problems for definition. For example, they can be volatile or involatile, soluble or insoluble, large or small, depending on whether they are carried to the receiver in air or water or deposited on the nasal sensors of the receiver (Wyatt, 2014). Humans produce many different chemicals for excretion, but research is still in its infancy regarding which of these could be considered pheromones and/or have an effect on another individual.

Theoretical evidence

Humans are mammals and have been subject to the processes of evolution. Evolution involves **natural selection** as well as **sexual selection** (see p. 35). Darwin (1871) noted that adult males of mammal species such as goats and elephants have characteristic strong odours during their breeding season. He reasoned the evolution of specialized odour glands in male mammals is 'intelligible through sexual selection, if the most odiferous males are the most successful in winning the females, and in leaving offspring to inherit their gradually perfected glands and odours' (1871, vol. 2, p. 281, cited in Wyatt, 2015).

While different pheromones can be found across different species, it does not follow that because one species uses a molecule for the pheromonal effects, other unrelated species are necessarily likely to use the same molecules for the pheromonal effects.

In common with other mammals, humans show changes in gland development as they move toward sexual maturity via the processes associated with puberty. Other mammals have been found to have chemicals they use as pheromones in common with humans. For example, molecules with pheromonal effects in pigs were also detectable in human armpits. This was enough to lead some researchers (e.g. Kirk-Smith and Booth, 1980) to consider the same chemicals as being used by humans as pheromones. Therefore, it is reasonable to theorize that humans have developed communication strategies through the use of pheromones. However, while different pheromones can be found across different species, it does not follow that because one species uses a molecule for the pheromonal effects, other unrelated species are necessarily likely to use the same molecules for the pheromonal effects.

Empirical evidence

For it to be asserted that pheromones play a role in human psychology it would need to be shown that humans have advanced **olfactory** abilities. Bushdid et al. (2014) sought to measure how effective humans were in distinguishing different odours. They designed a double-blind experiment where subjects were presented with three vials, two of which contained the same mixture, and the third contained a different mixture. The subjects were instructed to identify the odd odour vial based on odour quality.

Twenty different stimuli pairs were tested for a total of 260 mixture discrimination tests. Through computer programs the researchers calculated that humans can discriminate at least 1 trillion olfactory stimuli, suggesting humans have evolved to be highly effective smellers.

Given the physical abilities of humans to distinguish odours, it seems reasonable to assume that pheromones play a role in behavioural outcomes. Moreover, given the use of pheromones in other species in pair-bonding behaviour, it might be reasonable to assume they also play a role in human mating systems.

However, non-human mammals and non-mammal animal species like reptiles have a specific tissue in the nasal cavity, known as the **vomeronasal organ** (VNO), that detects most pheromones. While human fetuses are known to have a VNO, most current evidence holds that it is functionally inactive after birth (Verhaeghe et al. 2013).

Attraction is an important motivation in human pair-bonding behaviour and a key part of the sexual selection process outlined by Darwin. A biological approach to attraction assumes that it occurs between two people because the combination of their genes will result in healthy offspring.

Evidence for this assumption can be found in the attraction to individual odours in sweat, which carry information about a person's **immune system**. It is assumed genetically different immune systems complement each other and the mixture of the two immune systems should produce a child with a good immune system.

MHC genes, for example, control the immunological self/non-self discrimination and subsequently, tissue rejection and immune recognition of infectious diseases. Therefore, MHC genes help to ensure that people stay healthy. It is assumed MHC genes are the product of sexual selection to improve the immune system of offspring and avoid inbreeding. Studies in house mice indicate that both males and females prefer MHC-dissimilar mates, which they apparently recognize by odour cues. Studies in humans have also found MHC-associated odour and mating preferences (Wedekind and Penn, 2000).

Key study: Wedekind et al. (1995)

Aim: To test whether a female will rate a sweaty t-shirt as more attractive if it is from a man with different immune system genes to her own.

Procedure: Forty-nine female and 44 male students were tested to see what type of immune system genes they had. The males were asked to wear a plain white t-shirt for two days. The t-shirts were put into closed boxes until the females were asked to smell them. The females were asked to rate the shirts for pleasantness and sexiness. The women rated the t-shirts as more pleasant and sexy if they came from a man with a different set of MHC genes.

Conclusion: Wedekind et al. concluded that people are motivated to find a mate with different immune system genes so their offspring will have stronger immune systems. This information is encoded in the body odour of the potential mate. It can be concluded as a result of this small-scale study that body odour, but not necessarily pheromones, is an important element of human **sociosexual** behaviour.

Studies in house mice indicate that both males and females prefer MHC-dissimilar mates. However, in humans, it seems body odour but not necessarily pheromones is an important element of human sociosexual behaviour.

Research with humans does not show that pheromones cause the effect of attraction simply because some individuals prefer the smell of certain other individuals.

At the current level of understanding, for a pheromone to be considered a researchable phenomenon it has to be established as a coherent and singular entity that can be isolated and agreed upon in peer-reviewed research. Moreover, it has to be characteristic of an entire group rather than an individual.

Wedekind et al.'s research focuses on individual body odour and, while it is likely molecules characteristic of all males of the species may well appear among the other molecules in an individual male's chemical profile (and can therefore be individually identified as pheromones), the research does not show that pheromones cause the effect of attraction in humans simply because some individuals prefer the smell of certain other individuals.

Pheromones may be present in all bodily secretions, but most attention has been focused on 'sweat', which is thought to contain the steroid **androstadienone** (AND). It is present at much higher concentrations in male sweat and can be detected by women, albeit with wide variation in sensitivity (Verhaeghe et al. 2013).

AND has been described as having pheromone-like activities in humans. For example, Wyart et al. (2007) measured salivary levels of the hormone cortisol in 21 **heterosexual** women after a brief exposure (20 sniffs) to AND and compared it to a control substance with similar olfactory qualities. They found smelling AND maintained a better mood, increased sexual arousal, and increased physiological arousal via significantly higher levels of cortisol.

These results are supported by Jacob et al. (2002), who compared the effects of AND with two controls by measuring the psychological states of a mixed-gender group of 37 participants who all identified as heterosexual. They used a double-blind repeated-measures experiment and found female participants showed increased positive-stimulated mood and reduced negative mood after exposure to AND when compared to male participants.

Verhaeghe et al. (2013) reviewed a number of studies regarding the effects of AND on women and found further empirical evidence for a mood uplift for women who were exposed to AND, although this was dependent both on its dose (Bensafi et al. 2004b) and on the pre-exposure mood prompted by a 'sad' or 'happy' video (Bensafi et al. 2004a). Other studies have shown AND can increase cooperation between heterosexual men (e.g. Huoviala and Rantala, 2013).

The studies presented here can be used to present a cautious conclusion that AND does have an effect on mood if presented in sufficiently large concentrations. However, the questions remain: Can AND can be defined as a pheromone at all? Can the naturally occurring concentrations produce an effect?

- Wyart et al. (2007) state in their research that 'whether [androstadienone] AND satisfies the key criterion for pheromonal action, influencing endocrine balance, remains unknown' (p. 1261). Therefore, they do not claim AND is a pheromone.

- Jacob et al. (2002) state that AND is a pheromone by claiming (without citation) how 'other researchers' have found AND has had unique effects on the surface of the vomeronasal tissue. They state: 'This apparent stimulus specificity was used to justify calling AND a pheromone' (p. 275) with no further justification. This claim is made despite other researchers suggesting the functionality of the vomeronasal tissue is inactive after birth in humans (Verhaeghe et al. 2013).

Ecological validity is lacking in the designs of many studies measuring the effects of pheromones. The methodology of various studies actually undermines the validity of any claim that suggests a 'pheromone' causes certain responses.

For example, chemicals are placed near or inside the nasal membranes in large amounts. This may be because the naturally occurring physiological levels appear to be too low to induce a response under experimental conditions and so researchers have to augment the amount and present it in unnatural ways.

TOK How can researchers in the human sciences measure human experience and claim validity?

Empirical evidence is a very significant phrase in psychology. Make a wall chart that explains to passers-by the meaning of empirical evidence. Use examples of theories for which there is empirical evidence and examples for which there is no empirical evidence.

Researchers need to show the actions of an identified pheromone and how it causes an odour-mediated behavioural and/or physiological response in a reliable, naturally occurring way in a peer-reviewed journal for scientific notions of validity to be satisfied.

Another key problem with studies relating to pheromones is finding a homogenous group of participants. For example, if asked to identify their sex and sexuality in order to account for it in the study, participants are prompted to the true purpose of the study, affecting its validity.

Furthermore, when participants are asked to smell a pheromone and then asked to report their mood, they can immediately guess the nature of the study and may also cognitively associate the smell with a boyfriend or husband rather than have a genuine physiological response to the chemical compound.

In summary, empirical evidence is open to question about the supposed effects of pheromones. Researchers make mistakes in their approach, for example:

- They use small sample sizes.

- They use unnaturally large amounts of the chemical and forcibly present it in an unnatural way, questioning the ecological validity of their findings.

- They assume that if humans share chemical molecules with other mammals who use them for their pheromonal effects, humans must do too.

- Participants are often able to guess the nature of the study and associate certain smells with memories. Therefore, true validity via an odour-mediated behavioural or physiological response is difficult to establish.

- The effects of individual body odour are combined with pheromonal effects, which does not satisfy the definition of a pheromone.

TOK

To what extent does the practice of reducing complex behaviours to singular or less complex entities help or hinder knowledge creation in Psychology?

3 Genetics and behaviour

Topic focus

To what extent can genetics be used to explain behaviour?

3.1 Genes and behaviour

Content focus

Discuss the links between genes and behaviour in the light of environmental factors.

Genes are made up of **DNA**, which provides the blueprint for the structure and function of the human body and may include thoughts, feelings, and behaviour. Animals, including humans, are born with **innate** behaviours to allow them to react instinctively to some environmental stimuli in a way that enhances their prospects for survival (O'Brien, 2000). Therefore, genes are increasingly considered as candidates to explain complex behavioural traits (Stockinger et al. 2005).

Assume substantial links can be made between genes and behaviour. Use the deeply personal nature of human experience as well as the influence of the environment to add moderation to your argument. Do not assume definitive conclusions can be drawn about the relationship between genes and behaviour.

Genotype refers to the genetic constitution of an individual organism.

Phenotype refers to the set of observable characteristics of an individual that is a result of the interaction between the genotype and its own environment.

What ethical principles are relevant to the design of one's own offspring through technology?

However, not all genes that an individual might possess are expressed at all times, as genes can be switched on and off via various mechanisms. This gene regulation will result in differential gene expression, which means having a gene for a particular behaviour does not necessarily mean that an individual will exhibit that behaviour.

In sum, there is a difference between the **genome**, which refers to all the genes that an individual possesses, and the behavioural phenotypes, which refers to the patterns or sets of behaviours that are expressed and are dependent on genotype (DeCamp and Sugarman, 2004).

3.1.1 Major depressive disorder

According to the *Diagnostic and Statistical Manual of Mental Disorders*, Fifth Edition (DSM-5), a person is suffering from major depressive disorder (MDD) if five or more of the following symptoms have been present during a two-week period and represent a change from previous functioning; and at least one of the symptoms is either (1) depressed mood or (2) loss of interest or pleasure.

- Depressed mood most of the day, nearly every day, as indicated by either subjective report (e.g. feels sad, empty, hopeless) or observation made by others (e.g. appears tearful). (Note: in children and adolescents, can be irritable mood.)

- Markedly diminished interest or pleasure in all, or almost all, activities most of the day, nearly every day (as indicated by either subjective account or observation.)

- Significant weight loss when not dieting or weight gain (e.g. a change of more than 5 per cent of body weight in a month), or decrease or increase in appetite nearly every day. (Note: in children, consider failure to make expected weight gain.)

- **Insomnia** or hypersomnia nearly every day.

- **Psychomotor** agitation or retardation nearly every day (observable by others, not merely subjective feelings of restlessness or being slowed down).

- Fatigue or loss of energy nearly every day.

- Feelings of worthlessness or excessive or inappropriate guilt (which may be delusional) nearly every day (not merely self-reproach or guilt about being sick).

- Diminished ability to think or concentrate, or indecisiveness, nearly every day (either by subjective account or as observed by others).

- Recurrent thoughts of death (not just fear of dying), recurrent suicidal ideation without a specific plan, or a suicide attempt or a specific plan for committing suicide.

Reprinted with permission from the *Diagnostic and Statistical Manual of Mental Disorders*, Fifth Edition (Copyright © 2013). American Psychiatric Association. All Rights Reserved.

There is a significant body of evidence that demonstrates MDD has its causes rooted in biology, which suggests a clear link between the disorder and genes. However, it can also be noted that no single genetic variation has been identified to increase the risk of depression. It seems likely that multiple genetic factors, in conjunction with environmental factors, lead to the development of MDD (Lohoff, 2010).

The study of twins – namely comparisons between identical twins and fraternal twins – can be used to disentangle the relative **etiological** influence of genes versus environmental causes. Identical (MZ) twins share all of their genes, whereas fraternal (DZ) twins only share about half. Therefore, any significant differences between MZ twins can be attributed to the environment. The study of twins is also useful in showing the importance of a unique environment, one that is specific to one twin. Unique environments can occur in multiple ways, for example when the twins have been separated or one has suffered a head injury or maintained a different diet.

A traditional twin design compares the similarity of MZ twins with DZ twins. If MZ twins have significantly more similarities than DZ twins this suggests that genes play an important role in these traits.

For example, Kendler et al. (2006) compared the incidence of the symptoms of depression among MZ and DZ twins. The researchers used telephone interviews to ask 42,000 twins if they and their family members had symptoms of depression. The findings showed a significantly higher rate of correlation among MZ twins than DZ twins, suggesting a clear genetic component.

The basic principle of **genetic association** studies is that a genetic variant is investigated in a group of cases and controls. By determining the allele or genotype frequencies and comparing them statistically, the probability that a gene is more frequent in one group than the other can be investigated (Lohoff, 2010). For example, the serotonin-transporter (5-HTT) gene has come under particular scrutiny because it is connected to the reuptake of serotonin in the synapses. It is assumed adaptations in this gene may influence the incidence of MDD in an individual.

Twin studies can be used to disentangle the relative etiological influence of genes versus environmental causes. They do this by comparing the similarity of identical twins and fraternal twins.

TOK Can universal assumptions be applied to all humans? Does the methodology of psychology downplay individual differences as well as culturally specific details?

Key study: Caspi et al. (2003)

Aim: To investigate whether a functional change in the 5-HTT gene is linked to a higher or lower risk of depression in an individual.

Procedure: A natural experiment was conducted where the naturally occurring IV was the length of the alleles on the 5-HTT gene. An opportunity sample was used, consisting of 847 participants all aged 26 who were taking part in another study. Their age was controlled to isolate the variable of 'number of stressful life events' between the ages of 21 and 26. The participants were split into three groups, depending on the length of the alleles on their 5-HTT transporter gene.

Group 1 – two short alleles
Group 2 – one short and one long allele
Group 3 – two long alleles

Stressful life events that occurred after the 21st birthday and before the 26th birthday were assessed using a life-history calendar so the participants could show when the events occurred as well as their intensity. They were standardized around the following themes: employment, financial, housing, health and relationships. Instances of depression were assessed using the Diagnostic Interview Schedule that occurred during the year preceding the study. A correlation assessed: between stressful life events and depression; between the length of the alleles and depression; and for any interaction between perception of stress and the length of the alleles.

Findings: Group 1 participants with two short alleles in the 5-HTT gene reported more depression symptoms in response to stressful life events than the other two groups.

Experiences of childhood maltreatment were predictive of depression in adulthood, but only in adults with either one or two short alleles.

Participants with two long alleles reported fewer depression symptoms.

Conclusion: The serotonin transporter (5-HTT) gene was found to moderate the influence of stressful life events on depression. The study provides evidence of a gene-by-environment interaction, in which an individual's response to environmental stimuli is moderated by his or her genetic make-up. In particular, the presence of short alleles on the 5-HTT gene may increase the risk of developing MDD.

However, since a large proportion of the population carries the mutation of the 5-HTT gene, which may make them susceptible to depression after traumatic events, it can be difficult to conclude that the gene is a major contributor to depression because most people do not have significant MDD symptoms.

The findings suggest the long alleles may protect against suffering depression as a result of stress.

Criticism: It should be noted that the effects of the gene adaptation are dependent on the type of environmental exposure to stress. People who did not carry the mutation can also become depressed. Another limitation of this study is the symptoms of depression were **self-reported**. One person's perception of being depressed will not be the same as another's. This problem is compounded by the perception of what constitutes a 'stressful life event'.

A key problem with gene–environment research is deciding what should be measured and how. MDD is a complex and deeply personal illness and can manifest in different ways for different individuals. Moreover, there are **gender** and sociocultural influences on how MDD manifests.

One approach is for researchers to use **clinically diagnosed** patients and then use quantifiable data. For example, Peyrot et al. (2013) compared MDD patients (defined by a lifetime DSM-IV based diagnosis) to healthy controls who had not been diagnosed, as well as suicidal MDD patients to healthy controls.

Data from 1727 unrelated MDD patients and 1792 healthy controls from the Netherlands Study of Depression and Anxiety (NESDA) and the Netherlands Twin Registry (NTR) were analysed. The MDD patients were compared to healthy controls with respect to age, gender, and the environmental factors of 'lifetime and recent stressful life-events', 'sexual abuse', 'low educational attainment', and 'childhood trauma'. They examined whether the gene that codes for the serotonin transporter (5-HTTLPR) could have a direct effect on the outcomes of MDD patients.

They used t-test and chi-square statistics and found no significant effect for 5-HTTLPR on outcomes for MDD patients. However, there was a possible small influence of the gene on how the illness will develop over time. They found environmental factors had large and consistent direct effects on both prevalence and course of MDD (how an illness develops over time) and they state the environmental impact is stronger for the more severe outcomes, such as suicide.

Sullivan et al. (2000), conducted a **meta-analysis** of relevant data from primary studies of the genetic links to major depression. They concluded that MDD is a familial disorder that mostly or entirely results from genetic influences. However, environmental influences specific to an individual are also etiologically significant, but this is not the case for the broader environmental influences shared by other members of the family.

Therefore, MDD is a complex disorder that does not result from either genetic or environmental influences alone, but rather from both, but with a particular emphasis on individual interactions with their environment.

The studies suggest that MDD is a deeply personal disorder with a complex mode of **inheritance**. Therefore, it is likely that multiple genes with small effects are involved. Moreover, identifying genetic factors is complicated by the significant environmental components that affect each individual differently (Lohoff, 2010). Trying to identify singular causes is further complicated by different perceptions of what constitutes MDD symptoms as well as what a stressful environmental factor may well vary from one individual to the next.

3.1.2 Factors that affect gene expression

Epigenetics is the study of changes in organisms caused by **genetic expression** rather than changes in the underlying genetic code. The protective package of proteins around which genetic material is wrapped can be influenced by environmental factors, which in turn influence how the genes express themselves. Therefore, the **epigenome** plays a crucial role in determining which genes actually express themselves in a creature's traits: in effect, it switches certain genes on or off, or turns them up or down in intensity. Not only can these changes influence genetic expression, they can also be passed on to the individual's offspring.

Epigenetics is the study of changes in organisms caused by genetic expression rather than changes in the underlying genetic code.

Epigenetic modifications are thought to be one mechanism to explain how environmental stressors influence gene expression and can therefore help explain risk to abnormal behaviours (Klengel et al. 2014; Menke and Binder, 2014).

In particular, childhood adversities have been associated with onset of MDD via epigenetic changes (Kang et al. 2013). One way epigenetic influence may occur is via the process of methylation, which is used by cells to control gene expression. Methylation is the process where methyl groups are added to the DNA molecule, which can change the activity of a DNA segment without changing the underlying sequence.

Kang et al. (2013) measured the methylation status in the promoter of gene encoding serotonin transporter (SLC6A4) in 108 patients with MDD and correlated it with childhood adversity. They found that higher SLC6A4 promoter methylation status was significantly associated with childhood adversities, suggesting a link between environmental experiences and gene activity.

Key study: Natt et al. (2009)

Aim: To test whether unpredictable food access would act as an environmental stressor to chickens and cause them to adopt a more dominant feeding strategy.

Procedure: Chickens were placed in a controlled environment. The IV was either predictable or unpredictable feeding environment and was operationalized by manipulating light and darkness. The DV was the level of dominance in feeding and was operationalized by counting the amount of pecks for food. The chickens were allowed to breed and then all offspring were separated from their parents.

Findings: Chickens adapted their feeding behaviours in response to changes in their environment. The offspring of such chickens can retain these adaptive behaviours despite never being directly exposed to the same environment. Furthermore, levels of **estradiol** (a hormone chiefly secreted by the ovaries) were significantly higher in egg yolk from birds exposed to unpredictable feeding environments, suggesting one possible mechanism for these effects.

Conclusion: Chickens that became dominant passed their dominant behaviour on to their offspring despite not interacting with them. Hormonal changes in the chickens influenced their genetic expression and made their offspring better adapted to a problematic environment.

To what extent can specific genes be used to explain a specific behaviour?

Show an awareness of the degree of relatedness between MZ and DZ twins, siblings, parents and children, and parents and adopted children. This will provide a critical perspective in evaluating twin or kinship studies.

Genetic similarity is referred to as relatedness and it is assumed the greater the genetic similarities between two individuals or a group of individuals the higher the degree of relatedness.

3.2 Genetic similarities

Content focus

Explain the concept that the greater the genetic similarities between two individuals or a group of individuals, the higher the degree of relatedness.

Genetic similarity is referred to as **relatedness** and it is assumed the greater the genetic similarities between two or more individuals, the higher the degree of relatedness.

Relatedness is measurable and is known as the coefficient of the relationship between two individuals. It is usually expressed on a scale of 0–1 with 1 representing the highest level of genetic similarity and 0 representing individuals who have arbitrarily remote common ancestors. It is a useful construct for societal and legal purposes to measure levels of inbreeding and to help courts decide who should be allowed to form relationships.

Twin studies are used to disentangle the relative etiological influence of genes versus environmental causes. They do this by comparing the similarity of identical twins (MZ) and fraternal twins (DZ). MZ twins share all of their genes whereas DZ twins only share about half. Therefore any significant differences between MZ twins can be attributed to the environment. Twins are also useful in showing the importance of a unique environment that is specific to one twin. Unique environments can occur when the twins have been separated or one has had a head injury or a different diet, etc. A traditional twin design compares the similarity of MZ twins with DZ twins. If MZ

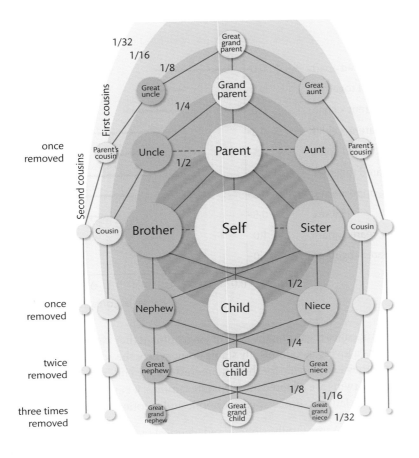

Figure 3.1 Common family relationships, where the area of each coloured circle is scaled relative to the degree of relatedness. All relatives of the same relatedness are included together in the green ellipses.

twins have significantly more similarities than DZ twins, this suggests that genes play an important role in these traits.

The Minnesota Twin Family Study (MTFS) is a longitudinal study of twins conducted by various researchers associated with the University of Minnesota. The aim of the study is to identify and measure the level of genetic and environmental influences on the development of psychological traits such as IQ, academic ability, personality, interests, family and social relationships, mental and physical health. It involves several independent but related projects that use different measurements, researchers, and participants to meet the aim of the overall study.

For the intelligence area of the study, they measured statistical correlations between performance on IQ tests with degree of genetic relatedness. This was modified by the degree of **familiarity**, which refers to whether or not they were raised in the same family. There are three degrees of genetic relationships, R=0.0 for unrelated persons, R=0.5 for either Parent x Child or Sibling x Sibling (including DZ twins), and R=1.0 for MZ identical twins. The data shows that related persons have more similar IQ test scores than unrelated persons. The results also show that the similarity of scores increases with degree of relatedness.

The results show that identical twins raised together are more similar than those raised apart. This clearly shows an environmental influence on IQ test scores. However, a note of caution is needed when considering the influence of the environment on identical twins raised apart. Western countries, when placing children up for adoption,

TOK

Some cultures allow individuals with a high degree of genetic relatedness – such as first cousins – to form relationships and have children. This cultural norm can produce birth defects such as the blood disorder thalassemia, which leads to anemia. Can cultural norms be measured and ranked within a system of ethics?

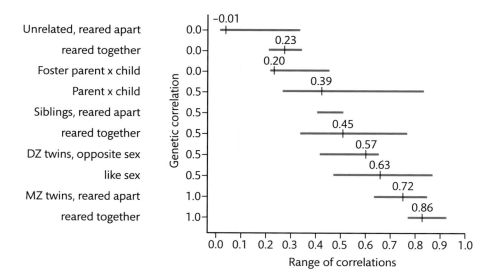

Figure 3.2 The similarity of IQ scores when compared to the degree of genetic relatedness.

have strict guidelines regarding the type of environment they can be placed into. This usually means a loving, economically stable home where the adopting parents can clearly show they can provide for the best interests of the children. Therefore, even when identical twins are adopted into separate families, it can be assumed they are being raised in relatively similar socioeconomic and emotional environments.

When raised in the same family, siblings and identical twins are on average more similar than those raised apart. This result even applies to pairs of unrelated persons. Therefore, this indicates that familiarity (similarity of family background) has a significant influence on IQ test scores.

The results indicate that performance on IQ tests is highly heritable, but they also show a significant influence of environmental factors on IQ test scores.

Plomin and Deary (2015) propose three 'laws' of genetics for complex behavioural traits that can be used to summarize the debate over genetic versus environmental influence:

- all traits show significant genetic influence
- no traits are 100 per cent heritable
- heritability is caused by many genes of small effect.

They also argue that intelligence is one of the most heritable behavioural traits.

3.3 Evolutionary explanations for behaviour

Content focus

To what extent can evolutionary pressures be used to explain behaviour?

Evolutionary psychology is a theoretical approach that assumes human thoughts, feelings, and behaviours have been subjected to **evolutionary pressures**.

Clearly label a very specific behaviour and use research to show why it can be considered an adaptation. To show critical thinking, use sociocultural explanations to argue that while human behaviour can be explained by evolutionary pressures, humans are also subject to other influences, which means there are very few behaviours with an absolute delineable relationship between biology and behaviour.

The approach seeks to identify which human psychological traits have evolved as adaptations.

The term adaptation refers to functional products of natural selection or sexual selection in human evolution. In the following section human attachment, human sexual behaviour, and Major Depressive Disorder (MDD) will be discussed.

 Evolutionary psychology is a theoretical approach that assumes human thoughts, feelings and behaviours have been subjected to evolutionary pressures.

The Theory of Natural Selection

The Theory of Natural Selection was initially developed by Charles Darwin in the 19th century.

The theory has two main assumptions:

- evolution is caused by natural selection
- evolution is caused by sexual selection.

Basic assumptions of natural selection

- The resources needed for survival are limited.
- There is a struggle to survive in the environment.
- Environments present challenges to individuals and species.
- Individuals in the population have variations in their traits due to genetic mutations (although Darwin did not fully understand this). Such variations in traits make the individual organism more or less suited to its environment.
- Individuals with better adapted traits have more chance of surviving and passing their better adapted genes on to the next generation.
- Individuals with less well adapted traits have less chance of surviving and passing their less well adapted genes on to the next generation.
- Over time, genes that render the individual better adapted will exist in greater numbers and the trait that was successful will be seen more in the population.
- Genes that render the individual less well adapted will exist in fewer numbers and the trait that was less successful will be seen less in the population – possibly eventually dying out.

A note on language

The phrase 'survival of the fittest' is often applied to summarize Darwin's theory. In the 19th century when the term was coined it was interpreted as 'survival of the best fitted' but over time 'fittest' became less synonymous with 'fitted' and became more synonymous with 'healthy' or 'physically fit'. The underlying assumptions of Darwin's theory became misinterpreted by poor language choice on the part of subsequent authors and theorists who still continue to use the term 'fittest' when the meaning has changed in mainstream society. To be clear, the underlying notion of 'survival of the fittest' should interpreted as 'survival of the best adapted' whereby organisms with the most appropriate traits in the context of their environment are the most likely to survive, thrive and reproduce.

TOK

To what extent does language impact knowledge creation? To what extent should language be standardized across the social sciences? What can other languages offer in terms of bringing new meaning and understandings to knowledge?

TOK

To what extent do theories help and hinder knowledge creation in the human sciences?

Basic assumptions of sexual selection

- There is a struggle to breed in the environment. (Note: Darwin referred to it as the 'sexual struggle'.)

- Sexual selection takes place between individuals of the same sex (generally the males) in order to drive away or kill their rivals; to attract those of the opposite sex (generally the females) who then select the more agreeable partners.

- Better adapted organisms have characteristics that render the individual more sexually attractive – and therefore more likely to mate.

- Individuals with better adapted sexual traits have more chance of breeding and passing their better adapted genes on to the next generation.

- Individuals with less well adapted sexual traits have less chance of breeding and passing their less well adapted genes on to the next generation.

- Over time, genes that render the individual better sexually adapted will exist in greater numbers and the trait that was successful will be seen more in the population.

- Genes that render the individual less sexually adapted will exist in fewer numbers and the trait that was less successful will be seen less in the population – possibly eventually dying out.

A note on genes

When Darwin presented his theory in the book *On the Origin of Species*, he was not aware of the biological processes through which traits are inherited (now known as genes). Therefore, it is not accurate to talk of genes or genetic adaptability in terms of Darwin's own writings, but it is accurate to talk of genes or genetic adaptability in terms of the Theory of Natural Selection.

3.3.1 Attachment

Attachment behaviours show the basic mechanisms of natural selection. Attachment is a deep and enduring emotional bond that connects one person to another across time and space (Ainsworth, 1973; Bowlby 1969). Bowlby defined attachment as a 'lasting psychological connectedness between human beings' (1969, p. 194).

Infants have a universal need to seek close proximity with their caregiver when under stress or threatened (Prior and Glaser, 2006) and therefore, attachment in children is characterized by specific behaviours, such as seeking proximity with the **attachment figure** when upset or threatened (Bowlby, 1969). Attachment behaviour in adults toward a child includes responding sensitively and appropriately to the child's needs. Such behaviour appears universal across cultures.

Attachment theory provides an explanation of how parent–child relationships emerge and then influence further development. Bowlby and Robertson (1952) observed that children experienced intense distress when separated from their mothers. Even when such children were fed by other caregivers, this did not diminish the child's anxiety.

The behavioural theory of attachment assumed children became attached to the mother because she simply fed the infant and attachment was a learned response through association. However, Bowlby (1958) proposed that attachment can be understood within an evolutionary context in that the caregiver provides safety and security for the infant and attachment should therefore be seen as an adaptive trait as it enhances the infant's chance of surviving and thriving.

Attachment and the evolutionary benefits are illustrated by the work of Lorenz (1935) on imprinting. Lorenz took a large clutch of goose eggs and kept them until they were about to hatch. Half of the eggs were then placed under a goose mother, while Lorenz kept the other half beside himself for several hours.

When the geese hatched, Lorenz imitated a mother duck's quacking sound so the young birds regarded him as their mother and followed him accordingly. The other group followed the mother goose.

Lorenz found that geese follow the first moving object they saw, during a 12- to 17-hour critical period after hatching. This process became known as **imprinting**, and suggests that attachment is innate and programmed genetically. To ensure imprinting had occurred Lorenz put all the goslings together under an upturned box and allowed them to mix. When the box was removed the two groups separated to go to their respective 'mothers' – half to the goose and half to Lorenz.

Hess (1958) showed that although the imprinting process could occur as early as one hour after hatching, the strongest responses occurred between 12 and 17 hours after hatching, and that after 32 hours the response was unlikely to occur at all. Imprinting occurs without any feeding taking place, undermining any stimulus-response explanation via external stimuli.

Using animals in this way allowed a variable to be isolated (proximity of an attachment figure) and then measured (mixing the geese with other non-attached youngsters), which would not be possible with humans.

Bowlby (1958) proposed that attachment can be understood within an evolutionary context in that the caregiver provides safety and security for the infant and attachment should therefore be seen as an adaptive trait as it enhances the infant's chance of surviving and thriving.

Attachment and the evolutionary benefits are illustrated by the work of Lorenz (1935) on imprinting.

Lorenz worked with geese to demonstrate how the mechanism of imprinting is important for attachment.

37

3.3.2 Major Depressive Disorder

There is a significant body of evidence that demonstrates MDD has its causes rooted in biology and, therefore, evolutionary psychologists ask if there could be evolutionary benefits to the disorder – can it be seen as a **Darwinian adaptation**?

Given the deeply personal, as well as cultural, elements to MDD, it can be challenging to disentangle the relative sociocultural versus biological elements of the disorder. Therefore, twin studies are often used.

Kendler et al. (2006) compared the incidence of the symptoms of depression among identical and non-identical twins. The researchers used telephone interviews to ask 42,000 twins if they and their family members had symptoms of depression. They found a significantly higher rate of correlation among MZ twins than DZ twins, suggesting a clear genetic component.

Genes manifest in complex ways. It is enough to assume they influence neurological frameworks as well as hormonal and neurotransmitter levels and sensitivity. The monoamine hypothesis assumes there is a lack of certain neurotransmitters that are responsible for varied outcomes, which then leads to depression. For example, a lack of serotonin may be related to anxiety, obsessions, and compulsions. A lack of dopamine may be related to reduced attention, motivation, pleasure, and reward, as well as interest in life (Nutt, 2008). Evidence of this comes from certain drugs that raise the levels of serotonin and dopamine and improve the mood of sufferers.

The presence of genetic determinants for MDD suggest there could be evolutionary benefits to the disorder. For example, the conservation of resource theories assume depression is a mechanism that leads to the inhibition of certain desires. This could be beneficial because they would enable the individual to give up unattainable goals, to conserve resources, and to redirect them to more productive tasks (Nesse, 2000).

Social competition theories assume depressed mood is an answer to a perceived descent in social hierarchy. Any descent in social hierarchy may lead to further attacks, as higher ranking individuals may seek to assert their dominance over perceived lower ranking individuals. Therefore, specific behaviours accompanying depression would correspond to the loss in social rank and project messages that might serve to protect an individual from possible attacks (Price, 1998).

In keeping with the notion of depression serving to regulate group dynamics, the **attachment theory of depression** assumes depressive responses serve as a distress call (Frijda, 1994) to other members of the group as a way of signaling for help and reassurance and improving group bonds.

Given the underlying assumption that depression fulfills a **social projection** role within group dynamics it could be assumed that rates between males and females would be approximate. However, this is not proven by the research. Kessler et al. (1994) reported that women in the US are about two-thirds more likely than men to be depressed, with a similar trend in the UK. However, seen through an evolutionary lens, women and men have different social functions within groups as well as distinct gender roles and identities.

It could be assumed that if depression is a social projection, it might affect men and women differently. Therefore, gender differences in depression rates may be the result of the two genders responding to sociocultural pressures, which would mean their underlying depression symptoms manifest themselves in gender-specific ways (Nazroo, 2001).

For example, men may have been **socialized** to express depression symptoms in the form of anger, seeking solitude, or turning to drugs, or other forms of acting out; whereas women are more likely to talk about their feelings in social settings and peer groups, prompting them to be labelled as 'depressed' and seek help.

Women may also feel more comfortable seeking help with personal problems from healthcare professionals as a result of sociocultural expectations regarding women's behaviour. Studies have shown that expected gender differences in depressive disorders were balanced out by higher male rates of alcohol abuse and drug dependency (e.g. Metzler et al., 1995), suggesting there is no underlying biological difference between men and women in experiencing these feelings, but the social projections are dependent on sociocultural norms.

 To what extent can a specific behaviour be explained as an evolutionary adaptation?

4 Research methods: biological approach

Learning focus

Discuss the contribution of research methods used in the biological approach to understanding human behaviour.

Research within the biological approach aims to uncover how biological phenomena influence psychology. Therefore, it is very scientific in nature, which assumes a reductionist position on many behaviors with attempts made to make causal links between biology and psychology. These underlying scientific assumptions are reflected in the type of methods discussed below.

 Show an awareness of the specific research methods used in the biological approach. They should be clearly labelled, defined and supported with examples that illustrate their strengths and limitations. It is important to show a practical awareness of how psychology research is carried out.

4.1 Experiments

Experiments are usually designed with one clear independent variable (IV) that is manipulated, and a dependent variable (DV) that is measured. All other factors that may affect the dependent variable are controlled as far as possible. The precise nature of experiments allows other researchers to attempt to replicate the methodology to test the findings for reliability.

Experiments are used to test the validity of claims by asking to what extent there is a causal relationship between two variables. However, because of their tightly controlled nature they lack ecological validity and caution should be used when generalizing the data to more realistic scenarios.

For example, Wagner et al. (1979) measured the effects of reduced levels of testosterone on aggression in male mice. The IV was the level of testosterone operationalized by the mice being first castrated and then injected with testosterone. The DV was levels of aggression operationalized by the number of bites.

 Experiments are usually designed with one clear independent variable that is manipulated and a dependent variable that is measured. All other factors that may affect the dependent variable are controlled as far as possible.

They found that castration reduces aggression and then testosterone restores aggression in castrated mice who were previously judged to be aggressive. When the injections ceased, it led to reduced levels of aggression again. Therefore, they were able to show that testosterone does have a causal relationship with aggression in mice.

This study lacks ecological validity because the isolation of singular or a small number of variables in experiments investigating biological phenomena is reductionist in nature and has the benefit of isolating biological mechanisms and testing to what extent they cause effects. The drawback is they fail to take wider factors that influence behaviour, such as sociocultural influences, into account.

4.2 Natural experiments

In a natural experiment researchers find naturally occurring variables and study them. They have the benefit of studying behaviour as it naturally occurs, which increases the ecological validity.

In a natural experiment researchers find naturally occurring variables and study them. They have the benefit of studying behaviour as it naturally occurs, which increases the ecological validity. Moreover, it allows researchers to conduct research that would otherwise be unethical. For example, Gettler et al. (2011) conducted a longitudinal study where they measured testosterone levels in men over time.

As researchers they would not be allowed to deliberately or artificially manipulate these levels because they wanted to determine if fatherhood suppresses testosterone (previous studies had shown childcare can lower testosterone levels), or if men with lower testosterone were more likely to become fathers – thereby establishing clear cause and effect. Six hundred and twenty-four Filipino men were followed for four and half years. They found:

- Men with high waking testosterone were more likely to become partnered fathers by the time of the follow-up four and a half years later.

- Men who became partnered fathers then experienced significant declines in waking and evening testosterone, which were significantly greater than declines in single non-fathers.

- Fathers reporting three hours or more of daily childcare had lower testosterone at follow-up compared with fathers not involved in childcare.

While this may appear to establish causality, the use of natural experiments meant they did not have full control over confounding variables, which undermines any claims to causality.

4.3 Correlations research

By now you have read about behaviours or behaviour-related issues, such as memory, aggression, and depression. Make a list of any three behaviours or behaviour-related issues that you would like to investigate or know more about. Why do you want to know more? Make a poster that asks a psychology-related question and the reason why you think it is an important question.

Correlations research has a focus on two variables and researchers attempt to uncover the strength of the relationship between the two. Correlations research provides an initial platform allowing later studies to narrow the findings down and, if possible, determine causation via more focused means. Correlational research also allows researchers to collect much more data of a greater variety than simple experiments can.

For example, Kendler et al. (2006) compared the incidence of the symptoms of depression among identical (MZ) and non-identical (DZ) twins. The researchers used telephone interviews to ask 42,000 twins if they and their family members had symptoms of depression. The findings showed a significantly higher rate of symptoms of depression among MZ twins than DZ twins, suggesting a correlation between a genetic component and incidences of depression. However, it did not allow the researchers to claim a cause-effect relationship as so many other variables were involved.

4.4 Quasi-experiments

Quasi-experiments allow participants to be grouped based on a characteristic of interest to the researcher. For example, Raine et al. (1997) was interested in the brain activity of murderers versus non-murderers. The characteristic of 'murderer' was defined by the researchers and then they set about locating individuals who met their definition and were prepared to take part in research.

They used a PET scan to investigate whether there was dysfunction in the same brain areas of all participants. With quasi-experiments there is a lack of random assignment into test groups because the groups are chosen on the grounds of their inherent characteristics. This makes conclusions about causality less definitive and makes it more difficult to compare test groups, which can limit the generalizability of the results to a larger population.

Therefore, many quasi-experiments use a matched-pairs design so that the variables can be isolated and compared as much as possible. Raine et al. matched each murderer with a 'normal' subject for age, sex and diagnosis of schizophrenia, where necessary. Other variables were excluded because each participant was screened to exclude physical and mental illness, drug taking and a history of murder. Therefore, the variable of 'murder' had been isolated.

In this way, the groups become comparable, although it should be remembered that quasi-experiments are almost always performed retrospectively (in this case after the murders had taken place), which means the researcher has less control over past or hidden variables. For example, Raine et al. could not exclude participants who lied about taking drugs or had a hidden mental illness, and the participants' past criminal background was a naturally occurring variable outside of the study's control.

Quasi-experiments allow participants to be grouped based on a characteristic of interest to the researcher.

5 Ethical considerations: biological approach

Learning focus

Discuss ethical considerations used in the investigation of the biological approach to understanding human behaviour.

Ethics refers to a moral framework that differentiates 'right' from 'wrong'. All social science research carries ethical responsibilities because researchers interact with their participants and have to respect the **autonomy** and dignity of persons they research. In the research context this means that there is a clear duty to participants' knowledge, insight, experience, and expertise.

Show an awareness of the specific ethical considerations related to the biological approach. They should be clearly labelled and supported with examples of good and bad practice. It is important to show a practical awareness of how psychology research is carried out.

41

Ethics refers to a moral framework that differentiates 'right' from 'wrong'. All social science research carries with it ethical responsibilities because researchers interact with their participants.

Ethical considerations are more relaxed when working with animals, which allows researchers to focus on the variables and their effects rather than worry about the emotional welfare of participants.

Biopsychology is engaged in trying to uncover biological causations of behaviour. The search for biological mechanisms will inevitably mean a thorough investigation into human bodies and the effects on their thoughts, feelings, and behaviour.

5.1 The use of non-invasive techniques

With non-invasive techniques, human participants can be used to investigate biological causes of behaviour. For example, Maguire et al. (2006) made good use of MRI scans in conjunction with cognitive tests to investigate to what extent the various parts of the hippocampus could be correlated with certain types of topographical or spatial memory.

Non-invasive techniques do not cause harm to subjects and still give valuable insights into links between biological factors and behaviour. However, they can lack the accuracy of **post-mortem** techniques, such as autopsy, which are more normally used on animals (or after the natural death of the humans with explicit **consent** from them or their families). For example, post-mortems on Henry Molaison (see 1.1.3 fMRI) revealed damage to his brain tissue that previous non-invasive scans had not revealed.

How is balance achieved between ethical considerations and the pursuit of knowledge?

5.2 Informed consent

The Ethics Code of the American Psychological Association (2017) describes **informed consent** as follows.

Researchers should inform participants about:

- the purpose of the research, expected duration, and procedures

- their right to decline to participate and to withdraw from the research once participation has begun

- the foreseeable consequences of declining or withdrawing

- reasonably foreseeable factors that may be expected to influence their willingness to participate such as potential risks, discomfort, or adverse effects

- any prospective research benefits

- limits of confidentiality

- incentives for participation

- who to contact for questions about the research and research participants' rights.

Researchers should also provide opportunities for the prospective participants to ask questions and receive answers.

The case study of Henry Molaison (see 1.1.3, page 6) offers a good example of research into rare disorders caused by biological problems. Molaison is reported to have given consent in 1992 for his brain to be used for research after death. However, serious questions can be asked as to how he could give informed consent as he could not retain the information presented to him, so did not have the ability to understand the research process. Lead researcher Suzanne Corkin eventually received informed consent from a living relative of Molaison's (a third cousin), but this raises questions about the 'closeness' of relatives and whether it refers to biological relatedness or an emotional closeness.

These matters are usually settled by a legal court. However, in the case of Molaison, a journalist, Luke Dittrich, was able to find relatives who could be considered closer to the participant (first cousins) but who were apparently not contacted by the researchers. Dittrich also documented that Corkin told him that Molaison was the only person signing his informed consent forms from at least 1981 to 1992 (Dittrich, 2016).

5.3 Minor deceptions

There are instances where informed consent is not necessary for researchers. Psychology researchers may dispense with informed consent:

- where research would not reasonably be assumed to create distress or harm and involves, for example, the study of normal educational practices, curricula, or classroom management methods conducted in educational settings; only anonymous questionnaires, **naturalistic** observations, or archival research for which disclosure of responses would not place participants at risk of criminal or civil liability or damage their financial standing, employability, or reputation, and confidentiality is protected; where there is no risk to participants' employability, and confidentiality is protected

- where otherwise permitted by law or federal or institutional regulations

- where mild deception is a reasonable approach to research, such as when the prospective scientific, educational, applied value, or non-deceptive alternative procedures are not feasible (Ethics Code of the American Psychological Association, 2017).

However, psychology researchers are not allowed to deceive prospective participants about research that is reasonably expected to cause physical pain or severe emotional distress. Researchers must also explain any deception that is an integral feature of the design and conduct of a study to participants as early as is feasible, which is usually at the conclusion of their participation, and allow participants to withdraw their data from the research if they wish.

5.4 Genetic research

Research with genetics requires a special set of ethical considerations because of the amount of data stored in genes. For example, predispositions for illness or certain behaviours, such as addictions, could be uncovered. A discussion always needs to happen within the research team and with the participants about what to do with this information and if and how it should be communicated back to the participants.

Research surrounding genetics:

- can reveal unexpected information that may harm or cause undue stress to research participants. For example, evidence of true parentage or unrevealed adoptions within a family or when a person discovers that he or she carries the gene for a particular genetic disorder.

- can often be complex and misunderstood. Participants and their families should be kept informed about the nature of genetic research.

Participants should know how their confidentiality will be protected, and what will happen to any genetic information obtained as part of the study. The aims and procedure of the study must be explained in plain language and participants must sign an informed consent form to show they have a clear understanding of the study they are participating in and its implications, including any potential harm.

TOK

To what extent can ethical frameworks be placed on a hierarchy? On what basis should ethical decisions be established and on what basis should ethical dilemmas be resolved?

Some groups may object to genetic studies as a cultural principle and, given the existence of other forms of discrimination against groups and the history of the **eugenics** movement, it is important to consult with relevant community leaders and organizations before genetic research is carried out. In such circumstances, consent must be seen as a community matter, not just an individual concern.

One way for researchers to protect the privacy of their participants is to use **coding**. Codes are assigned to the research material and only a small number of researchers have access to the codes. In this way researchers cannot link samples or information to particular people. This protects the confidentiality of individuals from insurance companies, employers, police, and others, but it also can limit the scientific value of the study by preventing follow-up and further investigation.

!

Present a balanced argument about the use of animal research. Do not dismiss the role of animal models in psychology research as they are used widely and have a clear role to play in helping to uncover biological mechanisms that may cause human behaviour. However, your argument needs to show that researchers must be cautious when generalizing the findings of animal studies to human behaviour.

6 The role of animal research in understanding human behaviour (HL)

General focus

Discuss the role of animal research in understanding human behaviour.

6.1 The value of animal models

Learning focus

Discuss the value of animal models in psychology research.

Animal models are used in psychology research with the assumption that discoveries made will provide insight into the workings of human beings.

The value of animal models in understanding human behaviour can be seen in the following areas.

6.1.1 The manipulation and isolation of variables

Variables in areas of behaviour can be manipulated and isolated to a higher degree with animals than would be possible with human participants. Reductionist arguments can then be discussed in the context of causation.

For example, Wagner et al. (1979) measured the effects of reduced testosterone levels on aggression in male mice. The IV was the level of testosterone, operationalized by the mice being first castrated and then injected with testosterone. The DV was level of aggression, evident by the number of bites exhibited. They found castration reduces aggression and then testosterone restores aggression in castrated mice who were previously judged to be aggressive. When the injections ceased, it led to reduced levels of aggression again.

Methodologically this is a very tightly controlled study with a clear IV (testosterone) and a clear, quantifiable DV (number of bites exhibited), which would not have been possible if they had used human participants.

6.1.2 The benefit of a relatively quick breeding cycle

The breeding cycle of animals used in research is quicker than that of humans, which allows researchers to study the effects of **heredity** and environmental factors on behaviour.

For example, Natt et al. (2009) wanted to test the extent to which an unpredictable feeding environment would cause chickens to show a more dominant feeding strategy and whether that could be passed on to future generations purely by genetic means. They manipulated the feeding environment of chickens by manipulating the levels of light and darkness.

The DV was the level of dominance in feeding, found by counting the amount of pecks for food while separating the offspring from their parents. They found chickens adapted their feeding behaviours in response to changes in their environment, and the offspring of such chickens retained these adaptive behaviours despite never being directly exposed to the same environment.

They also found estradiol levels (a hormone chiefly secreted by the ovaries) were significantly higher in egg yolk from birds exposed to unpredictable feeding environments, suggesting one possible mechanism for these effects. Therefore, they were able to show how chickens who became dominant passed their dominant behaviour on, despite not interacting with their offspring. The hormonal changes in the chickens had influenced their genetic expression and made their offspring better adapted to a problematic environment.

6.1.3 The benefit of animal post-mortem study

The nature of animal research means brains can be accessed, manipulated and then measured post-mortem within a time frame convenient to researchers. The only way human brains can be accessed for post-mortem study is after the participant's natural death, having received permission.

For example, Gilles et al. (1996) aimed to create an animal model to show the effects of continuous chronic stress on corticosterone secretion in response to an acute

Without giving your opinion, ask five of your friends or family members if they think using animals in research is ethical. Ask them to explain why they think the way they do. Write a summary of all five of the discussions, synthesizing (combining) all of the arguments for and against, and then write a conclusion.

Animals are useful for researchers because variables can be manipulated and isolated to a high degree; the breeding cycle of animals allows researchers to study the effects of heredity and environmental factors on behaviour.

environmental stressor. Previous studies had used an absence of the mother to induce stress but the researchers wanted a model that could be comparable with human experiences. Stress was induced by placing newborn rats into an environment with their mothers that featured good or limited bedding before the rats were euthanized for the post-mortem. The group with limited bedding manifested increased corticosterone.

Gilles et al. were able to suggest the **paradigm** may more closely approximate the human situation of chronically stressed, neglected infants. The research is important because corticosterone secretion has a profound effect on the structure, development and function of the hippocampus, particularly via dendritic retraction – a form of neuroplasticity.

6.1.4 Caution in using animals to understand human behaviour

Assumptions of similarity

The fact that humans are mammals and have been subjected to the processes of evolution can lead researchers to assume that traits with adaptive functions in other species have similar adaptive functions when found in humans. This can be problematic, as illustrated by the example of pheromones.

Darwin (1871) noted that male adult mammals of some species, such as goats and elephants, have strong odours during their breeding season. According to Wyatt (2014), these pheromones have been identified in every part of the animal kingdom, including mammals, and are involved in a wide range of functions including attraction, trail following, and interactions between parents and offspring.

Although the effect of pheromones is dependent on the species, there is clear evidence that pheromones are a physiological mechanism that cause an effect in other non-human animals. However, it has been difficult to establish whether or not pheromones can be seen as a coherent and singular entity that can result in an agreed-upon definition for humans.

Humans produce many different chemicals for excretion but research is still in its infancy regarding which of these could be considered pheromones and/or have an effect on another individual.

So, while there has been peer-reviewed research in other species regarding definitions and pheromonal effects, and these animal models have stimulated debate about the role of pheromones in humans, there has yet to be an established, coherent, peer-accepted definition of what a human pheromone constitutes, let alone what its effects on other individuals may be.

Moreover, while mammals share similar biological traits and structures with humans, they do not always respond to stimuli in the same way. For example, there are significant differences in the way that mice respond to diet and exercise when compared to human participants.

Assumptions of objectivity

Researchers may assume that an animal is merely a research platform to test a hypothesis in living tissue. However, animals are also thinking and feeling organisms that respond in subtle and complex ways to their environment.

For example, Sorge (2014) measured the response of mice and rats to an injection in the ankle administered by a man or a woman. They measured the animal response using two methods: A **mouse grimace scale** (MGS) that examines facial expressions of pain in non-human animals, and the level of the stress hormone corticosterone in the animals' blood. In the results, the animals seemed to show a decrease in pain response of about 40 per cent when a man rather than a woman performed the injection.

They concluded that male researchers caused stress to the animals, which produced greater quantities of the stress hormone corticosterone in the blood and dampened the pain that the animals could potentially feel. The presence of a t-shirt placed with the animals also confirmed the findings, as the animals showed elevated levels of stress if it had been worn by a man rather than a woman.

These results show how the gender of the person handling the animals can have a significant effect on the biology of the animal in the study. Such findings should at least prompt researchers to report the gender of experimenters in their publications and to include their gender as a variable in any subsequent analysis.

6.2 Measuring the value of animal research

Learning focus

Discuss whether animal research can provide insight into human behaviour.

One way to measure whether animal research can provide insight into human behaviour is to ask to what extent the knowledge is genuinely new.

For example, the extent to which the insight gained from Lorenz's geese experiments can be generalized to human emotional interactions is extremely limited. The need for vulnerable mammals to cling to older protective members of the group was a well established, observable trait before Lorenz sought to measure and replicate it. Therefore, questions remain about what level of 'new knowledge' was created in his studies.

It could be argued that using animals in this way allowed a variable to be isolated (proximity of an attachment figure) and then measured (mixing the geese with other non-attached youngsters), which would not be possible with humans. However, if the knowledge was already known before the experiments were conducted, questions can be asked about the purpose of the scientific study and the use of animals in the pursuit of insight regarding human behaviour.

Researchers have to be cautious in assuming humans and non-human animals are similar, and must be aware of how their own interaction with the animals will impact their results.

EE To what extent can animal research help in understanding a specific human behaviour?

! Clearly define the notion of insight. Animal research has clear uses in psychology but there are also limitations to using it. Present a balanced argument with a clear thesis statement using examples from research to support them. Use the information from other higher level sections to build an argument.

TOK To what extent will humans learn more about human life and personality from novels than from scientific psychology?

What is the purpose of the scientific approach in psychology?

47

A common theme in bio-psychology is the influence of reductionism and to what extent it helps generate insight into human behaviour. If the use of animals can help identify specific biological mechanisms that are connected to specific behaviours then this might qualify as insight. For example:

- Martinez and Kesner (1991) concluded that ACh played an important role in creating a memory of a maze in rats

- Rosenzweig and Bennett (1972) demonstrated the effect of a physically enriched environment on the thickness of the frontal lobe in rats.

In both examples, the manipulation of an environmental IV to measure the impact on a physiological DV would be ethically unacceptable on humans. Establishing a clear causal mechanism between the environment and a physiological response would only be possible with animal subjects. However, the main limitation of the research is that it is questionable to what extent these findings can be generalized to humans.

Another way to measure the extent to which animal research can provide insight into human behaviour is the level of predictability it can provide. Shanks et al. (2009) argue that the validity of any model can be assessed by its ability to predict what will happen. This is rooted in the testing of scientific hypotheses, which compare what is expected to occur with what actually occurs.

Animal models must be assessed on their ability to predict human responses. At the end of the series of animal experiments the researcher has a hypothesis that predicts a likely human response to the same stimulus.

Thus, those claiming animal models are predictive of human responses must show that what they claim is true. Shanks et al. (2009) argue there is an overarching hypothesis in the animal model community that assumes results from experiments on animals can be directly applied to humans and that animal models should be considered predictive. This assumption has led to an unquestioned methodological approach that means animals are used as surrogate humans.

However, animals and humans have markedly different biological reactions to the same stimuli despite having similar biological systems. For example, the Japanese Pharmaceutical Manufacturers Association found that 43 per cent of **clinical** toxicities for humans were not forecast from animal studies (Igarashi, 1994). Sankar (2005) argues that the majority of the drugs shown to be safe in animals end up failing in clinical trials and animal models have only a 10 per cent predictive power, since 90 per cent of drugs fail in the human trials.

In summary, caution should be used when assuming biological causation. This is especially true when the complex social systems of various species are taken into account. For example, Wagner et al. (1979) were able to connect testosterone to aggression in male mice. However, Dreher et al. (2016) suggest that testosterone could have played a key evolutionary role for humans by not only promoting aggressive behaviour but also increasing feelings of generosity, leading to more generous behaviour, which leads to a higher social status.

Human studies undermine the impression of a simple causal link between testosterone and male aggression that animal models can create. Instead, it seems likely that testosterone's effect on human male behaviour depends on the social context in

TOK

To what extent should animal models be reliably predictive? How should levels of prediction be measured? To what extent should psychology be held to the same standards as the natural sciences, or should some leniency be used when discussing prediction in complex social systems?

which it occurs. In other words, while testosterone is linked to aggression, it is simply a hormone that leads to higher ranking of human males. Aggression is one route to achieve that, but not the only route. Rats have no option but to be aggressive because they are less complex creatures.

6.3 Ethical considerations

Learning focus

Discuss ethical considerations in animal research.

The treatment of animals is rooted in cultural norms. Western psychology researchers work within a culture influenced by Judeo-Christian teachings, which have an assumption that humans hold dominion over animals, allowing them to use them for their needs. However, Judeo-Christian teachings also encourage the kind treatment of animals while suggesting that deliberate cruelty represents a flawed moral character on the part of the human.

The underlying moral assumptions that have evolved for the ethical treatment of animals are as follows.

* It is acceptable to use animals for human ends. However, the purpose of the use must be of some benefit.

* The use of animals should be minimized.

* Pain and distress should be minimized.

Most work with animals takes place within an academic or research setting. To receive funding and recognition for their work, institutions have to adhere to a code of ethics regarding their animal use. For example, the British Society of Animal Science's ethical guidelines for the use of animals in research experimentation refers to the 3 Rs.

* Refinement: any animal science research undertaken should be as focused as possible and have realistic and achievable aims of increasing knowledge of the species of interest in relation to our understanding of its functioning, performance, health or welfare. Researchers should avoid the causation of pain wherever possible but where there is deliberate infection of the animals, deliberate withholding of nutrition or genetic manipulation, then special justification must be made by the researcher.

* Replacement: researchers must consider all available options to replace animals with other techniques that will fulfill the research objectives. Researchers should always actively look for non-animal methods of investigation (e.g. computer models using statistical programs based on previous data).

* Reduction: there is a scientific, moral and legal requirement to expose as few animals to pain, suffering and distress as possible. Researchers should calculate how few animals are required to ensure they are able to obtain meaningful results. Furthermore, power calculations should be made to ensure that sample sizes in experiments are appropriate so as to not lead to wastage of animals and potential unnecessary suffering. Therefore, a statistician with expertise in experimental design should always be consulted before carrying out any experimental work.

Show an awareness of the specific ethical considerations related to animal research. They should be clearly labelled and supported with examples of good and bad practice. Show a practical awareness of how psychology research is carried out using animals.

The 3 Rs refers to Refinement, Reduction and Replacement and relate to a set of ethical guidelines written by the British Society of Animal Science.

Can animals be placed on an ethical hierarchy? Should animals with more human-like characteristics be more protected from harm? What ideologies can be used to create ethical frameworks?

To what extent does one's culture affect one's opinion toward using animals in research?

However, it could be argued that any animal with psychological and social abilities has the capacity to feel and understand pain. This raises philosophical questions about what rights animals should have in their interactions with humans.

Activity

Find all of the new words or expressions from this chapter and write them into a document with their definitions and explanations next to them. Be creative and use diagrams or boxes to help make your personal glossary unique and effective.

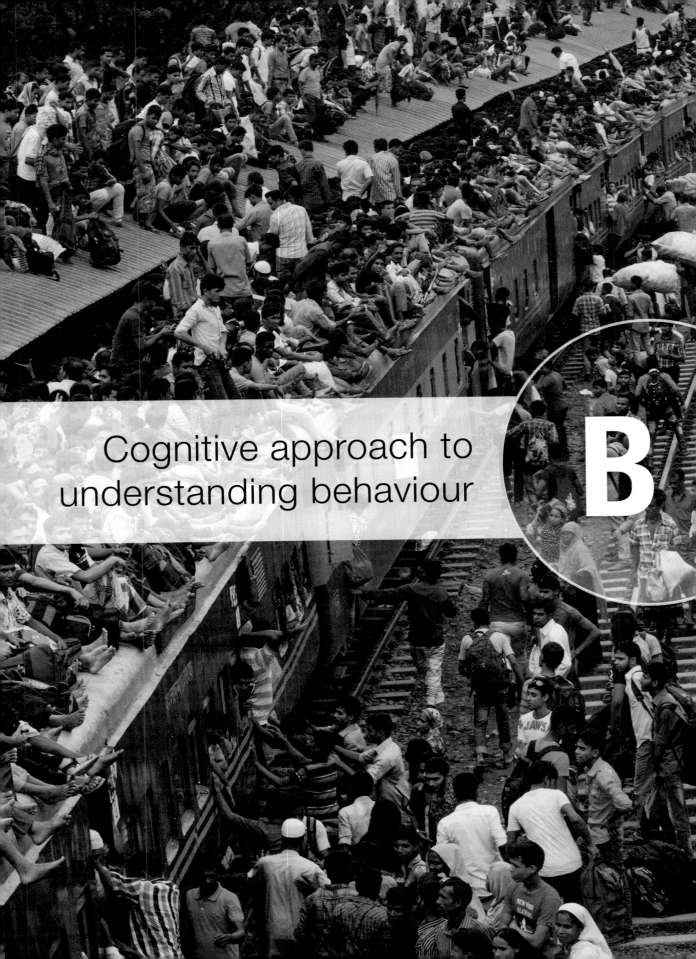

Cognitive approach to understanding behaviour

B

Cognitive approach to understanding behaviour

The cognitive approach to behaviour views human beings as processors of information in much the same way as a computer processes information. The cognitive approach to behaviour focuses on areas of research such as schema processing, memory processing, and thinking, and how cognition may influence behaviour. Researchers are also interested in the extent to which cognitive processes are reliable, for example, in relation to thinking and memory. How cognitive processes may be affected in the modern digitalized world is an emerging field within the cognitive approach to behaviour.

Cognitive processes are often influenced in complex ways by emotions. The influence of emotions on cognitive processes is studied not only by cognitive psychologists but is developing as an area of interest for cognitive neuroscientists as well as social psychologists.

Research methods in the cognitive approach to understanding of behaviour rely on experiments and brain imaging technologies as well as qualitative approaches to understanding everyday memory and thinking, making the cognitive approach an example of the holistic approach to understanding human behaviour.

The cognitive approach to understanding behaviour looks at:

- cognitive processing (SL and HL)

- reliability of cognitive processes (SL and HL)

- emotion and cognition (SL and HL)

- cognitive processing in the digital world (HL only).

7 Cognitive processing

Topic focus

To what extent can cognitive processes be used to explain behaviour?

7.1 Models of memory

Content focus

To what extent do the working memory model and the multi-store model represent human memory processes?

7.1.1 The multi-store model of memory

Atkinson and Shiffrin (1968) proposed a simple representation of human memory called the **multi-store model**. Their initial model comprised a group of sensory registers, each linked to the short-term store (STS), which is linked to the long-term store (LTS).

The multi-store model proposed that when an environmental stimulus is detected, it is 'stored' very briefly in the appropriate sensory register (or buffer). If the information

The multi-store model proposed a separate register for each of the senses.

in the sensory registers is given attention, it is passed to the STS where it may be rehearsed and then passed into the LTS. Once information has been transferred to the short-term memory, it can remain there for up to 30 seconds.

Information in the sensory registers that is not given attention, and information in the STS that is not rehearsed, quickly decays and is lost.

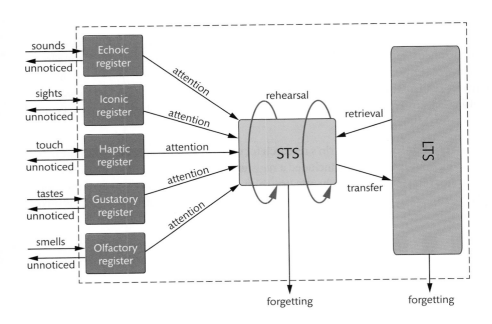

Figure 7.1 The multi-store model (Atkinson and Shiffrin, 1968)

According to the model, people detect many environmental stimuli (such as faces or sounds) during a day, and these stimuli are all captured in the sensory register. The model proposes a separate register for each of the senses: echoic register (sounds), iconic register (visual stimulus), haptic register (touch), gustatory register (taste), olfactory register (smell).

Atkinson and Shiffrin (1968) claimed that most information held in the sensory registers quickly decays and is lost, but information that receives attention is transferred to the STS. Attention, in the model's description, refers to 'noticing' in everyday language.

Only some of the environmental stimuli detected every day gets noticed; perhaps a face that looks unusual or familiar, the sound of the school principal's voice, or a catchy tune. If a stimulus is attended to (given attention) it is transferred from the appropriate sensory register to the STS. The rest, anything that does not get noticed, is not stored.

The model also proposed that information can be stored in a different mode to that in which it was first detected. For example, a sound (a spoken sentence) could be stored as a visual stimulus.

Information that is rehearsed sufficiently can be stored in the long-term or (relatively) permanent memory. The model proposes that the more the information is rehearsed, the stronger its position is in long-term memory. The model assumes that the long-term memory's capacity is limitless in both capacity and duration.

Redraw the multi-store model as a flow diagram highlighting the flow of information that gets stored in long-term memory and information that is lost or forgotten.

As you walk through the school corridor, try to pay attention to all of the material on the walls. When you get to the next classroom, immediately write down all of the things you saw on the walls. Do the walk again later and see what material you noticed and what you did not notice.

53

How reliable is memory as a way of knowing?

The hippocampus plays a significant role in the formation of long-term memories, i.e. the transfer of information from the short-term store to the long-term store.

Evidence in support of the multi-store model

The Atkinson and Shiffrin (1968) model relied on hippocampal **lesion studies**, which showed that people with damaged hippocampal regions could create short-term memories, but not long-term memories. This showed that short- and long-term memory are distinctly different cognitive processes.

Bekhterev (in Milner, 2005) showed that the medial temporal lobes have a role in memory formation. Bekhterev demonstrated that the brain of a patient who had shown severe memory impairment displayed significant 'softening in the regions of the uncus, hippocampus, and adjoining medial temporal cortex'. The strongest evidence supporting the hypothesis that the hippocampal region plays a role in memory formation came from studying patients who had developed **amnesia** after **ablation** surgery on the medial temporal lobe as a way of controlling certain types of epilepsy (Milner, 2005).

Most of Atkinson and Shiffrin's research focused on visual (seen) and aural (heard) stimuli, but the model also included a register for each of the senses including a gustatory (taste) store and a haptic (touch) store. Supporting this aspect of the model, D'Esposito et al. (2000) used fMRI images to show that the prefrontal cortex is involved in haptic memory.

Strengths of the multi-store model

Many memory-related studies, such as Glanzer and Cunitz's (1966) study relating to the **primacy and recency effect** and Scoville and Milner's (1957) studies relating to memory formation, are consistent with the multi-store model.

Limitations of the multi-store model

What are the implications of the multi-store model's process for remembering information presented during a lesson?

- The multi-store model describes rather than explains. It does not tell us why information is stored.

- The model suggests memory formation processes are grouped and distinct, but lesion studies have shown that memories are spread out through the brain.

- Memory formation processes are more complex than the model implies. The model does not account for how memories are stored based on their importance, nor does it account for the effect of emotion on memory.

- The model does not account for the type of information taken into memory. Some information seems to pass into LTS more readily than other information. For example, information that is emotional or distinctive in some way is also stored and retrieved more readily.

- Rehearsal alone is too simple to account for the transfer of information from STS to LTS; the model ignores factors such as effort and the strategies that people may use when learning; elaborate rehearsal methods lead to better recall than simple rehearsal.

- The model does not account for the process of forgetting; forgetting is seen as a by-product, rather than an active process.

- The model does not account for the retrieval process. Information storage is only one part of the memory process; in order to be remembered, information must also be retrieved, and this retrieval process must be more complex than represented in the model.

7.1.2 The working memory model

Baddeley and Hitch (1974) expanded this short-term aspect of the Atkinson and Shiffrin model, proposing a three-part working memory model that separates primary memory into three components: the phonological loop; the visuo-spatial sketchpad; and the central executive. In 2000, the model was expanded again to include an episodic register.

The phonological loop

The phonological loop stores sound-based content. According to the model, the phonological loop is made up of a short-term phonological (sound) store from which information can decay very quickly, and an articulatory rehearsal component that can revive or recall sound-based memories. The phonological store is thought to detect and receive sounds and the articulatory loop process repeats or rehearses the sounds, preventing decay. This phonological loop, or repetition/rehearsal process, likely plays a significant role in language acquisition.

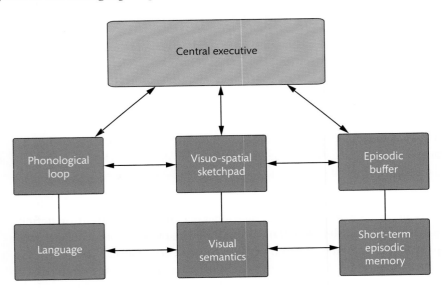

Figure 7.2 The three-part working memory model (Baddeley and Hitch, 1974)

The visuo-spatial sketchpad

The visuo-spatial sketchpad stores visual and spatial information. Mental images can be created, recalled, and manipulated as spatial tasks. The visuo-spatial sketchpad is made up of the spatial short-term memory, which remembers locations (i.e. where images are relative to each other); and the object memory, which stores objects' characteristics such as size, shape, surface texture, and colour (Logie, 1995).

The visuo-spatial sketchpad component of the model has been expanded to include a visual buffer (or cache) that stores information about objects' characteristics, and an inner scribe that rehearses information in the visuo-spatial sketchpad and passes it to the central executive for task processing.

The episodic buffer

The episodic buffer stores events or episodes made up of related information such as the sights, sounds, and chronologies associated with a particular event. This buffer is also assumed to link to the long-term memory. Baddeley (2000) found that patients who did not have the ability to form new long-term memories were able to recall stories, i.e. combinations of sights and sounds that would be too great to store together in the phonological loop.

The central executive

The central executive (CE) controls cognitive processes, including the flow of information. It combines information from different sources into episodes by coordinating the phonological loop, the visuo-spatial sketchpad and the episodic buffer. The CE also co-manages retrieval, attention, and inhibition.

Norman and Shallice (1986) proposed a model of the CE that split control of behaviour based on memories between two processes:

- the control of behaviour by habit patterns or schemas

- the control of behaviour by a supervisory activating system (SAS).

The split could be considered a way of applying minimal effort to controlling routine behaviours, leaving maximum energy for controlling non-routine behaviours.

Schemas are mental representations. They are practised or rehearsed, and so become memory by which future similar behaviour is controlled. Evidence for some behaviour being controlled through the use of schemas and habits came from 'slips of action' such as getting out of bed on a Saturday morning and dressing for school rather than dressing for Saturday morning sports.

By contrast, the SAS monitors for unique or new stimuli and modifies general strategies to resolve new or unique situations. The SAS is relatively slow and deliberate and employs a range of strategies to solve unique or new problems.

Evidence supporting the existence of an SAS came from frontal lobe studies. Bayliss and Roodenrys (2000) studied the frontal lobes of children with **attention deficit hyperactivity disorder (ADHD)** who displayed many behaviours consistent with impaired CE functioning. The study applied Norman and Shallice's (1986) SAS as a model of the executive functioning that is impaired in ADHD. Fifteen children with ADHD were compared to a sample of non-ADHD learning disabled (LD) children and a group of children with neither ADHD nor LD. The groups were matched for age, gender, and IQ. The study used tasks that assessed inhibition or impulsive responding and found that the ADHD group was significantly impaired in comparison to the LD, non-LD, and non-ADHD groups. This study's findings supported the existence of the supervisory activating system and its role in controlling behaviour.

Location within the brain

fMRIs of brain-damaged patients indicate that the phonological loop is associated with the brain's left temporal lobe while the visuo-spatial sketchpad is associated with the occipital lobe and the parietal lobe. Research indicates the central executive is located

Schemas are mental representations. They are practised or rehearsed, and so become memory by which future similar behaviour is controlled.

fMRIs of brain-damaged patients indicate that the phonological loop is associated with the brain's left temporal lobe while the visuo-spatial sketchpad is associated with the occipital lobe and the parietal lobe.

in the frontal lobes (Alvarez and Emroy, 2006). The episodic buffer is less isolated and associated with both of the brain's hemispheres, the frontal and temporal lobes, and the hippocampus.

7.1.3 Long-term memory

The multi-store model's long-term memory component has also been expanded upon by researchers proposing a split between explicit and implicit memories, each of which have subsequently been expanded.

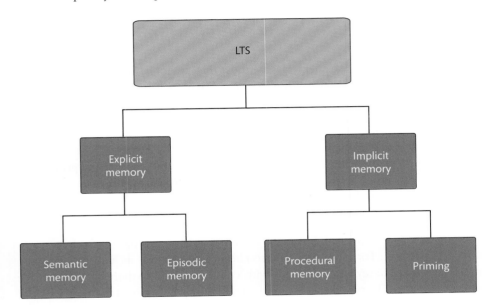

Figure 7.3 The expanded multi-store model of memory

Explicit memory

Explicit, or declarative, memories are memories that can be verbalized, such as a description of what happened while playing a game of cards or an account of driving through a city. Explicit memories tend to exist in a specific context. Tulving (1972) proposed two categories of explicit memory: **episodic memories**, which are events that happen to someone; and **semantic memories**, which are facts or details.

Episodic memories are actual and personal experiences from the past, such as a detailed description of what happened during a person's first day at school. They can also be called autobiographical memories. Tulving and others identified three key characteristics of episodic memory:

- a sense of time or mental time travel

- a connection to the self and the ability to create a personal narrative

- **autonoetic consciousness**, which means the ability to imagine ourselves in mentally-generated situations.

Semantic memories are non-specific information such as facts, ideas, meaning, and concepts, which are blended through personal experiences. For example, a semantic memory might be information about what a smartphone is, i.e. a screen, the physical design, weight, feel, and an operating system. Semantic memory is what allows people

 To what extent do models over-simplify reality and therefore become inaccurate?

to see a previously unseen smartphone and identify it as a smartphone. By contrast, episodic memory would be a memory of holding and using an actual smartphone.

Prince et al. (2007) used fMRIs and found: (1) the temporal lobes and the left hippocampus were associated with episodic memories, but not with semantic memories; (2) the lateral temporal cortex was associated with semantic memories, but not with episodic memories; (3) a more posterior region within the lateral intraparietal cortex was associated with semantic memories; (4) a mid-region was involved with both semantic and episodic memories; and (5) a more anterior region was associated with episodic memories, but only when semantic memories were also involved.

Implicit memory

Implicit, or non-declarative, memories are those that cannot be described. They tend to involve procedures such as how to eat a meal politely or how to write a job application letter. Similarly, an emotional response to a situation, such as reading a poem or listening to a song, cannot be accurately or objectively described and so is stored as an implicit memory.

Two categories of implicit memory are proposed: procedural memory and priming (Tulving, 1972). Procedural memories inform or guide processes. They are automatically retrieved and used to execute cognitive and motor skills, such as reading and swimming. These memories are executed without conscious effort.

Priming is likely to happen after repeating or rehearsing perceptual, semantic, or conceptual stimuli. For example, if a person hears a list of words including 'computer' and is later asked to say a word starting with 'comp', they will be more likely to give the word 'computer'. Hearing the word 'computer' in the list has primed the brain for that response.

7.1.4 Cross-cultural studies

Ismatullina et al. (2014) sought to determine whether there are cross-cultural differences in working memory. A spatial working memory task was given to 289 adolescents (aged 10–17 years old) from Russia and Kyrgyzstan. The study found no significant differences in working memory between the Russian and Kyrgyz participants, although working memory performance was greater in the older adolescent participants in each country.

Conway et al. (2005) conducted a content-analysis study on participants from Japan, China, Bangladesh, England, and the USA and found no cross-cultural differences in creating episodic (autobiographical) memories, although they did find that the content of memories was sensitive to the participants' different cultural influences. The Chinese participants' memories were of events that had a group or social basis, while the US participants' memories were of events oriented to the individual.

Create diagrams to show the approximate locations within the brain that seem to be associated with the different memory functions.

Explicit, or declarative, memories are memories that can be verbalized or described. Implicit, or non-declarative, memories are those that cannot be described.

Initiate a discussion with friends or family about their significant memories and simply listen to their language – do they retell the event from their personal perspective, using 'I', 'my', and 'me' or do they retell the event from a social perspective using language such as 'we' and 'our'? Be careful not to make any cross-cultural conclusions about these responses because the people you interact with are most likely to be of your local culture and you will only consider a very small number of people.

Studies have not shown significant cross-cultural differences in working memory or in creating episodic (autobiographical) memories.

7.2 Schema theory

Content focus

To what extent do schemas support our understanding of long-term memory?

Refer to studies to support your answers. Be cautious with **assertions** because, although schemas are well supported, they are not proven to exist, nor are they **universally defined**.

There are many theories of knowledge organization and schema theory is one of them. The way we process information or the way we act in specific settings is determined to a significant extent by relevant previous knowledge stored in our memories and organised as schemas. A schema is a cognitive structure that provides a framework for organizing information about the world, events, people and actions.

Schema theory assumes that people give meaning to new experiences by fitting them to mental representations (schemas) previously stored in long-term memory. Morton et al. (2017) proposed that schemas encapsulate the common features of events and so allow for predictions relating to new, similar situations.

There is little common agreement on a definition of schemas, (Sadoski et al., 1991). For this text though, schemas are defined as tools that allow information to be processed relatively quickly and with minimal cognitive effort. Alba and Hasher (1983) identified the following five processes incorporated into all schema theories.

- Selection – the process that selects information for storing and representing.

- Abstraction – the process that stores an event's meaning.

- Interpretation – the process through which background knowledge is used to help comprehension.

- Integration – the process by which a mental representation is formed.

- Reconstruction – the process that uses details from the event and general knowledge to refabricate the event.

A schema is a simplified mental representation of an event or situation. For example, many people have a mental image, or schema, of a typical office that includes typical office furniture and fittings. To demonstrate this, Brewer and Treyens (1981) asked participants to wait in a room that resembled a graduate student's office and later tested them for memory of the room's contents. Many participants said they had seen objects that would be expected in an academic's office, but were not there.

7.2.1 Effort after meaning

Bartlett (1932) referred to the 'effort after meaning' that people make to try to convert information that they cannot comprehend into a form that they can: '. . . it is fitting to speak of every human cognitive reaction—perceiving, imaging, remembering, thinking, and reasoning—as an effort after meaning' (Bartlett, 1932, cited in Roediger, 2003). The tendency to use metaphors and similes in language, such as describing someone as 'quiet as a mouse', is an example of 'effort after meaning'.

As people experience the world through their perceptions they store new events in long-term memory, but then apply past knowledge to try to make better sense of these new events. This can mean that experiences are changed after they have been memorized so that they are more sensible to us.

For example, if a van arrives at a neighbour's house and a person wearing blue overalls walks from the van to the house, then ten minutes later returns to the van and leaves, this episode is likely to be stored by the neighbour who saw it. Soon afterwards though, 'effort after meaning' is likely to distort the event when it's retold. Perhaps the van becomes a service vehicle and the person who went into the house becomes a pest exterminator.

Schema theory proposes that details that do not fit into the general mental representation may be deleted (forgotten) or adapted (changed) to match the schema. Bartlett (1932) found that when asked to retell the War of the Ghosts, a Native-American legend, some Cambridge University (UK) participants seemed to adapt it to fit the more culturally familiar fairy-tale schema, beginning their retelling with 'once upon a time' and ending it with a moral of the story.

A schema is a mental representation of an event. Details that do not fit into the general mental representation may be deleted (forgotten) or adapted (changed) to match the schema.

> ### Key study: Bartlett (1932)
>
> **Aim:** To determine if recall from memory is affected by schema.
>
> **Procedure:** An unstated number of Cambridge University students, male and female, were instructed to read a Native American story twice. The story included a number of cultural references. Fifteen minutes later, the participants were asked to recall and retell the story. The participants were asked to retell the story again some time later (for some participants this second delay was weeks, for others it was months or years).
>
> **Findings:** The participants remembered the global idea of the story but changed unfamiliar elements, such as using the word kayak instead of canoe. The remembered story was shorter than the original and tended to have the supernatural elements removed.
>
> **Conclusion:** Recollections or memories are not accurate copies, but reconstructions of the original stimuli. These reconstructions can be influenced by people's schemas.
>
> **Evaluation:** The procedure was conducted in relatively uncontrolled conditions and so lacks ecological validity. The rehearsal phase was not overseen by the researchers so there is no way to be sure that rehearsal happened as per the instructions. The participants did not receive standardized instructions. The study was conducted with Cambridge University (UK) students in about 1915 (the study was published in 1932 in a book rather than a peer-reviewed journal), so its conclusion may not generalize/transfer to the general population today.

Identify the research method employed in Bartlett's (1932) War of the Ghosts study. Explain your answer.

To what extent has research such as Bartlett (1932) been influential, despite being based on weak methodology? Is Bartlett (1932) a case of 'Argument from False Authority'?

7.2.2 Pattern recognition

Pattern recognition is an example of schema theory in action. A pattern can be any recognizable set of external stimuli, such as a short piece of music associated with a television advertisement, a person's facial features, components of language, or the grimacing mouse character in this book's cartoons. Any newly detected external stimuli are recognised against previously stored information.

Gestalt psychology is largely based on the concept of forming global wholes from collections of separate elements, such as interpreting a simple stick figure as a person. **Apophenia** is the irrational tendency to recognise patterns that do not exist, such as faces in burnt toast, the man in the moon, and the ancient Greeks' constellations.

7.2.3 Stereotyping

Stereotyping is an example of a schema based on a mental representation of a group of people. Stereotypes are simplified generalizations about identifiable groups. Examples of gender, nationality, race, and sexuality stereotypes abound. Stereotyping of groups of people is the basis of racism, homophobia, xenophobia, age and gender discrimination, and profiling.

Tao et al. (2016) used a self-report questionnaire and found that 'middle-class' Chinese had formed stereotypes about the rich and poor that focused on competence, sociability, and morality. Rich people were seen as highly competent, having low sociability and bad morals, while poor people were seen as being incompetent, with 'average' sociability and good morals.

Key study: Tao et al. (2016)

Aim: To investigate stereotypes about rich and poor Chinese people.

Procedure: One hundred and fifty-two participants (69 males, 83 females, aged 20–47) were selected from 28 professions and from 24 cities and provinces including Beijing, Shanghai, Tianjin, Guangxi, Heilongjiang, Jiangxi and Hunan, with annual household income 80 000–350 000 RMB. The researchers considered this sample to comprise 'ordinary people in China, not belonging to the rich or the poor'. The participants were instructed to write ten adjectives to describe poor and rich people. The sequence was balanced: half the participants were asked to write about rich people first and the other half wrote about poor people first.

Ask people to draw a simple but actual object, for example the cup they are using or the book they are looking at. Observe whether they draw 'the' object or a mental representation of the object, i.e. 'a' cup or 'a' book. To what extent is this an application of schemas?

Stereotyping is an example of a schema based on a mental representation of a group of people. Stereotypes are simplified generalizations about identifiable groups of people.

Findings: The researchers filtered out non-adjectives to yield 1317 adjectives for rich people and 1399 for poor people. Rich people were commonly described as 'intelligent, self-confident, motivated, hard-working, active, knowledgeable, flexible, and innovative'. Adjectives associated with poor people were 'uneducated, conservative, pessimistic, lazy, low-capacity, hard-working, and strong'. The researchers separated the adjectives for sociability and in this respect the rich were described as arrogant, supercilious, hypocritical, indifferent, and showing off. They were said to have good communication skills, but they developed relationships calculatingly, for material gain. On the sociability dimension, the poor were described as 'warm, kind, tolerant and displaying affinity, willing to help others, but vain and impulsive'.

Conclusion: The study concluded that stereotypes about rich and poor people can be viewed on three dimensions: competence, sociability, and morality. Rich people were considered highly competent, having low sociability and bad morality. Poor people were seen as incompetent, with average sociability and good morality.

Evaluation: The participants were selected and balanced for gender and socioeconomic status. The method was a free-report questionnaire and so the researchers did not affect the participants' choice of adjectives by giving a list of their own. The study is very recent and so has not lost validity over time. The study focused on Chinese people only, so the findings may not transfer to wider populations. The inherent weakness of questionnaires is participant unreliability, e.g. **demand characteristics**.

7.2.4 Evaluation of schema theory

Strengths

Schema theory helps to understand stereotyping, prejudice, discrimination, and inaccurate or unreliable memory.

Limitations

Schemas have not been universally defined and so schema theory is based on a fundamental concept, the meaning of which has not been universally agreed upon by researchers.

Schema theory describes but does not explain how and why schemas are formed. The theory does not explain why information that does not match a person's schemas can be forgotten or distorted to match schemas.

7.3 Thinking and decision making

Content focus

Evaluate one model of thinking and decision making.

7.3.1 Systems of thinking

Thinking and decision making research frequently refers to two distinct types of thinking and decision making: rational (logical, careful, controlled) and intuitive

If you watch television or movies, identify stereotypes associated with nationality, sexuality, gender, or age.

Do not mistake several weaknesses but only one strength as meaning a theory is weak. One strength may outweigh several weaknesses. Cautious and conditional conclusions that use language such as, 'it seems that...' are more appropriate than definitive statements.

(automatic, impulsive, emotion-driven). It is widely believed that rational thinkers give the time and effort needed to make correct decisions, while intuitive thinkers tend to make impulsive and emotion-driven decisions and are therefore less likely to make correct decisions.

Phillips et al. (2016) conducted a **meta-analysis** to determine whether intuitive or rational thinking is more likely to result in accurate decision making. With a combined sample of 17 704 participants from 89 studies, their meta-analysis found no significant difference in the accuracy of decisions made using either intuitive or rational thinking, suggesting that people apply the most appropriate thinking style to decision making situations.

Thinking, fast and slow

Kahneman (2011) proposed a model of thinking made up of two types of thinking: System 1 thinking and System 2 thinking.

System 1 thinking	System 2 thinking
relatively fast	relatively slow
intuitive	rational/logical and therefore calculated
emotional	purposeful
seemingly automatic	requiring more cognitive effort and therefore time
requiring minimal cognitive effort	
influenced by bias and perhaps schemas	less influenced by prejudice, bias, and schemas
uses associations and metaphors to quickly reach a simple representation of reality	uses reasoned beliefs and choices to slowly reach a less simple representation of reality

System 1 thinking can manage these relatively simple cognitive tasks:

- compare and contrast objects
- identify the source of a sound
- complete a common phrase such as 'as quiet as a . . .'
- display an emotion in response to a stimulus, such as smile at a funny cartoon
- solve simple maths problems such as 'the square root of 16'
- read text on signs.

System 2 thinking can manage these more demanding cognitive tasks:

- prepare to dive into a swimming pool
- direct attention to one actor on a stage of many actors
- look for a person who has been described in an airport arrivals area
- recognize a familiar voice
- determine appropriate behaviour in a social setting
- evaluate several similar products, such as smartphones
- interpret a logical conundrum.

Initiate a discussion with friends and list ten decisions that were taken by prominent world figures such as heads of very large companies, religious leaders, or government leaders. Suggest whether the decisions were made spontaneously by the person or by a consultative process, i.e. with other people.

Key study: Tversky and Kahneman (1983)

Aim: To test whether people mistake representativeness for similarity.

Procedure: Eighty-eight US statistically naive (undergraduates), informed (graduates) and sophisticated (PhD candidates) participants completed a questionnaire. They were asked the following question: Linda is 31 years old, single, outspoken, and very bright. She majored in philosophy. As a student, she was deeply concerned with issues of discrimination and social justice, and also participated in anti-nuclear demonstrations.

Which is more probable?

- Linda is a bank teller.
- Linda is a bank teller and is active in the feminist movement.

Findings: A significant percentage (almost 90 per cent) of the participants answered the questionnaire incorrectly by stating that Linda was more likely to be a bank teller and active in the feminist movement.

Conclusion: Naive, informed, and even sophisticated users of statistics were inclined to make incorrect decisions, indicating System 1 thinking overrode System 2 thinking. Quick, intuitive, perhaps emotion-driven thinking made the respondents answer that it is more likely that Linda is both a bank teller and a feminist than just a bank teller. This is an example of the conjunction fallacy: that specific conditions have a higher probability than a single general condition.

Evaluation: The study has a number of weaknesses. The participants were not a representative sample of the general population. The study was conducted on students from the US in two US universities. If the study was carried out in cultures where statistics and probability are more prominent in the school curriculum the results could be different. For example, one of the participants, when shown the statistical error responded with, 'I thought you just asked for my opinion' (Kahneman, 2011). The study's main strength is that it has been replicated many times with similar results.

7.3.2 Irrational thinking and decision making

The large body of work by Kahneman and Tversky on flawed, illogical decision making is supported by other researchers. For example, Kivetz and Simonson (2002) asked 85 Americans aged 18 to 80 whether they would prefer a lottery prize of $55 in cash or a $50 bottle of wine. They found that 24 participants (i.e. 28 per cent) chose the wine rather than the cash. The study concluded that people made the seemingly irrational decision of choosing the wine, even though if they had chosen the cash they could buy the wine and have $5 extra, because if they won the $50, they would spend it on a necessity rather than a luxury.

Framing

Tversky and Kahneman (1981) explored how the phrasing of a choice affected decision making outcomes. Framing refers to the way a statement is presented, for example whether the focus is on loss or gain.

Use the internet to investigate Nobel Laurete Richard Thaler and his work relating to apparently irrational decision making. To what extent are these seemingly irrational decisions likely to be culture-bound or culture-affected? Would the findings of these studies apply in all cultures?

In their study, participants were asked to choose between two health programmes for 600 people with a potentially fatal disease. Treatment A was expected to result in 400 deaths; Treatment B had a 33 per cent probability of no deaths and a 66 per cent probability of 100 per cent deaths. This choice was presented to participants framed either positively (focusing on how many patients would live) or negatively (how many would die).

Seventy-two per cent of participants chose Treatment A when it was framed positively (it saves 200 lives) but only 22 per cent chose the same treatment when it was negatively framed (400 people will die).

Loss aversion

Kahneman and Tversky (1984) demonstrated people's tendency to choose to avoid losses rather than make equivalent gains. For example, most people seemed to prefer not to lose $10 over finding $10, even though logically they amount to the same thing and so there should be no significant preference shown either way. Critics of this study have suggested it is the way the problem is stated, i.e. simply framing with a money focus.

SYSTEM 1 MICE

SYSTEM 2 MICE

FOOLS RUSH IN WHERE ANGELS FEAR TO TREAD...

Peters et al. (2006) showed that highly numerate people make more accurate decisions than those with poor numeracy skills. This suggests that the poor (i.e. inaccurate) decision making demonstrated in some studies and attributed to decision making biases may simply be the result of a poor understanding of statistics and probability.

7.3.3 Cultural considerations

Strohschneider (2002) considered the effect of cultural factors on decision making by using the results of two empirical studies that investigated complex decision making by participants in India and Germany. According to Strohschneider (2002), thinking

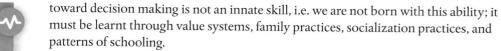

Initiate an informal discussion, perhaps at lunchtime, asking whether people think different cultures have different decision making styles or strategies. You may have to explain that 'culture' is not the same as race or nationality.

toward decision making is not an innate skill, i.e. we are not born with this ability; it must be learnt through value systems, family practices, socialization practices, and patterns of schooling.

Strohschneider (2002) found that there are culture-specific decision making processes, developed according to the environment's functional requirements. Differences in predictability and certainty lead to differences in the 'strength' of decisions, or decisiveness. The cost of incorrect decisions, attitude toward risk and assertiveness are all likely to differ across cultures and lead to different decision making styles.

7.3.4 The influence of emotions on thinking and decision making

There is a tendency for people to associate their current mood or the emotions they are feeling when a decision is being made with the decision's outcome (Clore and Huntsinger, 2007). Johnson and Tversky (1983) found that happy people tend to overestimate the probability of positive results, and the opposite tendency for sad people. Happy people tend to adopt a top-down, or heuristic, processing strategy with a heavy dependency on pre-existing knowledge and schema, and little reliance on the current situation's details – consistent with Kahneman's System 1 thinking style. Lerner and Keltner (2000) found that fear resulted in pessimistic decisions and anger resulted in optimistic decisions.

The relationship between emotions and decision making is bi-directional: emotions affect decision making and decision making affects emotions.

Fenton-O'Creevy et al. (2012) used heart rate variability data to investigate the influence of emotions on the decision making of investment bank traders in London and Copenhagen. The study focused on thinking and decision making in a real-world situation. With the large sums of money and high risk involved, financial trading is a job that most would expect relies on rational thinking, but many of the participants' (traders') decisions had to be made relatively quickly. Fenton-O'Creevy et al. (2012) used interviews with the traders and their managers, and concluded that antecedent-focused, emotional strategies (Kahneman's System 1 thinking) achieved better decision making outcomes than strategies that were response-focused (Kahneman's System 2 thinking).

The relationship between emotions and decision making is bi-directional: emotions affect decision making and decision making affects emotions.

Does fear help or hinder decision making effectiveness?

If the hormones associated with being in love are similar to those associated with OCD, does love help or hinder thinking and decision making?

To what extent are thinking and decision making theories culture-bound?

8 Reliability of cognitive processes

Topic focus

To what extent are cognitive processes reliable?

8.1 Reconstructive memory

Content focus

Discuss the reconstruction of memories.

The process of encoding, storage and retrieval is still not well understood. Be cautious in how you use terms such as short-term and long-term memory. Be similarly cautious when referring to schemas because there is not a universally agreed definition of schemas.

8.1.1 Constructing and deconstructing memories

The construction of memories is a complex process. Memories are not simply bundles of recordings that can be replayed like a file on a smartphone. They are not constructed of just images and sounds, but also traces of semantics and emotions. The memory construction process works by encoding sense perceptions such as sound, touch, and sight, with emotion and semantics.

The concept of **engrams**, or memory traces, was first proposed by Richard Semon (1859–1918) and subsequent research showed there is not one single brain location where complete engrams are stored. Instead, memories are deconstructed into several engrams, each possibly stored in different locations in the brain, which together make up a memory. These traces are rebundled or reconstructed when the memory is recalled.

Stark et al. (2010) used fMRIs to show that memories are reconstructed from fragments of information previously encoded into memory (Semon's engrams) and that these are reactivated at retrieval. The study showed that the auditory cortex was active during the retrieval of auditory information and the visual cortex was activated when visual information was retrieved.

It is during the reconstruction process that errors such as false memories, **confabulation** and schemas can occur. In general, true information and false memories showed similar brain activation in the fMRI studies of Stark et al. (2010).

8.1.2 False memories

A false memory occurs when a person 'remembers' something that simply did not happen, although they believe it did. False memories must not be confused with repressed memories, which were proposed by Freud and thought to be associated with childhood trauma and are described as memories that an individual refuses to recall. There is no evidence to support the existence of repressed memories.

False memories are believed by the person to be true accounts.

Ramirez et al. (2013) showed that it is possible to create an inaccurate memory of a fearful event in mice. The researchers created a false memory in mice by **optogenetically** manipulating memory cells in the hippocampus. Optogenetics is a technique that uses light to control living cells, in this case neurons. In the study, neurons were activated and later optically reactivated. Mice were deceived into recalling and therefore reacting to an electric shock that did not occur. The results showed that recall of a false memory was context-specific and could also initiate a fear response. The study showed that it is possible to generate an internally represented and behaviourally expressed fear memory artificially.

Loftus (1996) used the 'lost in the mall' technique to determine if false memories can be created in participants. Over the course of several days, one participant was told a convincing story by several family members of being lost in a shopping mall and found by an elderly man. Not only did the participant 'remember' the event when later questioned about it, he added new details to it. Loftus (1996) found that about 25 per cent of participants can be made to create a false memory of an event during their childhood.

Pezdek and Hodge (1999) used the same 'lost in the mall' technique with 19 5–7-year-old children and 20 9–12-year-old children to determine whether children can have false memories planted or created. The children were read descriptions of two events: (1) a plausible event (being lost in a shopping mall); and (2) an implausible event (receiving a rectal enema), each said to have occurred when the children were 4 years old. Neither event actually happened. Fifty-four per cent of the 39 children did not remember either event. Twenty-four per cent of the children remembered the plausible event, but not the implausible event. One of the 39 children remembered the implausible event, but not the plausible event. Three of the children, all in the 5–7-year-old group, remembered both being lost in a shopping mall and receiving a rectal enema.

Key study: Loftus (1975)

Aim: To test whether a false presupposition can affect a witness's answer to a later question about that presupposition.

Procedure: Forty undergraduate University of Washington students were shown a short video recording, showing a group of eight students disrupting a lesson. After watching the video recording, the participants were given one of two questionnaires, each containing 19 filler questions and one key question. Half of the participants were asked, 'Was the leader of the four demonstrators who entered the classroom a male?' The other 20 participants were asked, 'Was the leader of the 12 demonstrators who entered the classroom a male?' One week later the participants answered another questionnaire. The key question was, 'How many demonstrators did you see entering the classroom?' They were asked to answer from memory rather than inference.

Findings: Ten per cent of those participants who were prompted with 12, answered '12' and 10 per cent who were prompted with four answered 'four'. The mean response for the group prompted with four was 6.4 while the mean response from the group prompted with 12 was 8.85.

Conclusion: A question that contains false numerical data can affect an eyewitness's answer to a question about that data.

8.1.3 Confabulation

Confabulation is an error of memory reconstruction because it involves fabricated or distorted narratives, especially about the individual. People who confabulate are not deliberately or consciously dishonest. Inaccurate memories can be subtle or grandiose and the individuals are usually very confident about their memories.

Benson and Ardila (1996) reported a patient who recounted detailed accounts of conversations with physicians who she had never met, and accounts of trips she had made that had not happened. Confabulation seems to be associated with under-development or degeneration, or with brain damage, and is symptomatic of Alzheimer's disease, brain damage, dementia, and Korsakoff's syndrome (Johnson and Raye, 1998).

8.1.4 Schema processing and errors in memory

Schema processing, described earlier in this chapter, can also be a source of errors in memory, both in the construction of memories and their retrieval. Schemas are simplified mental representations. Jean Piaget proposed that information is **assimilated** or moulded with previously learned information to make sense of it. Piaget also proposed the concept of accommodation, a cognitive process in which pre-existing information is altered to accommodate new information. Piaget and Cook (1952) proposed that accommodation and assimilation work simultaneously, altering new and existing memories to assist memory construction.

For example, if a person has childhood memories of an enjoyable family holiday in Fiji, he or she is likely to assimilate new information, perhaps a television documentary about Fiji, to fit this generally positive schema or mental representation of Fiji. It is likely that subsequent memories of that television documentary will be generally positive. The existing schema is also likely to accommodate new information from the documentary, perhaps details of dangerous hurricanes or military coups, so that the schema is slightly altered, slightly less 'cheerful' perhaps. Schemas and schema processing, accommodation and assimilation result in errors of both memory construction and retrieval.

8.1.5 Implications of the unreliability of memory

There is little doubt that human memory is unreliable, and this can have significant implications.

People being interviewed for jobs are often asked to recall details about their previous work or their studies. It is clear from research that memory is unreliable, and interviewers should be aware that inaccuracy in memory recollection is not the same as deception or dishonesty.

Eyewitness accounts of historical events, such as the Yugoslav War, the Fukushima earthquake, or the 2004 tsunami around the Indian Ocean, are often vivid, emotional, and compelling, but research shows that they may not be very accurate and other evidence should also be used to verify people's accounts of events.

Eyewitness testimony is often thought to be accurate, but numerous studies and an increasing number of legal cases that use CCTV evidence or DNA testing have shown the opposite. In 1984, in Maryland USA, Kirk Bloodsworth was convicted of rape and murder and was sentenced to death. Five eyewitnesses testified that they had seen Mr Bloodsworth with the victim, at or near the crime scene at the time of the murder. After almost nine years in prison, DNA testing established Mr Bloodsworth's innocence, showing that the five eyewitnesses' testimonies were inaccurate.

TOK

If false memories can be created, can memory be a reliable way of knowing?

While not being able to remember what we ate for dinner three days ago may seem trivial, inaccurate eyewitness accounts can have significant consequences for many people.

8.2 Biases in thinking and decision making

Content focus

To what extent do biases in thinking affect the accuracy of decision making?

Kahneman and Tversky are clearly experts in thinking and decision making research but be aware that their work is mono-cultural and so it may not be possible to transfer their conclusions to wider populations. Be cautious when describing all studies' results and generalizing their conclusions.

Biases are normal human tendencies to think in certain ways, often contrary to, or without considering, evidence. Humans are irrational thinkers, relying on intuition or inaccurate cognitive processes that result in biases. Factors involved in biased thinking and decision making include the use of inappropriate thinking styles such as was discussed with Kahneman's System 1 and System 2 thinking, heuristics, algorithms, framing and representativeness, as well as cognitive biases.

8.2.1 Heuristics

Heuristics are simple decision making rules that people use to make decisions efficiently, i.e. with minimal cognitive effort. They usually focus on one of many aspects of a decision making situation, ignoring the rest. For example, given the complexity of technical specifications, pricing structures, and the opinions of friends, some people choose to just buy the latest model of a popular brand of smartphone rather than conducting their own research into the best option. Normally this works well enough, which is why people tend to use heuristics in complex decision making situations.

Heuristics are simple decision making rules that people use to make decisions efficiently.

Tversky and Kahneman (1974) demonstrated three heuristics that hinder effective thinking and decision making: anchoring and adjustment, representativeness, and availability.

Anchoring and adjustment

Anchoring and adjustment is a heuristic that begins with a statement or suggestion to influence a person's subsequent decision. For example, if a person is asked whether Te Rauparaha (a Māori chief) was more than 100 years old when he died, they are more likely to estimate his age at death as higher than if the same question were asked with the age 35 instead of 100. The anchoring and adjustment heuristic has been used in promotional activities such as signs stating, 'limit 12 per customer', which tends to result in people buying more than if the signs state, 'limit six per customer'.

Caverni and Péris (1990) conducted an experiment in which 48 teachers (participants) were given sets of students' essays to be graded along with a list of the students' fictional grades. The higher the mean of the fictional grades, the higher the grade given by the teachers for the essays they graded. The fictional grades were the teachers' 'anchors'. They affected the teachers' judgement and the distorted grade given was the 'adjustment' or the changed behaviour.

Representativeness

Tversky and Kahneman (1974) identified the 'representativeness heuristic': when people mistake representativeness with likelihood or probability. For example, John lives in a medium-sized city with a university and is described as logical, unemotional, and interested in patterns. If research participants are asked whether John is more likely to be a doctor, a police officer, or a mathematics professor, most predict that he is a mathematics professor even though the percentage of mathematics professors in the population is less than 1 per cent while the percentage who are police officers is closer to 5 per cent.

Like all heuristics, the representativeness heuristic is used because it is simple and so demands less cognitive effort than logically thinking through calculations.

Availability

The availability heuristic is the error of mistaking readily available examples as the typical sample. Tversky and Kahneman (1974) explained the heuristic as the ease with which examples come to one's mind. For example, if several close friends and family members suffer from heart disease in their mid-fifties, the availability heuristic would lead to the conclusion that many or most people in their mid-fifties suffer heart disease.

This has been tested by researchers asking participants if there are more words starting with an 'm' than words with 'm' as their third letter. It is easier, i.e. it requires less cognitive effort to think of words beginning with an 'm' than thinking of words with 'm' as the third letter (Gilovich and Griffin, 2002). As a result, people tend to say there are more words that start with an 'm' than have 'm' as their third letter.

8.2.2 Confirmation bias

Confirmation bias is a broad term to describe what occurs when people select or interpret information to confirm their existing knowledge, including the tendency to interpret ambiguous information so that it supports their existing ideas or beliefs. Confirmation biases contribute to the formation and strengthening of schemas and stereotypes.

Confirmation bias tends to result in overconfidence in personal beliefs, even when contrary evidence is presented. People tend not to search for, and even avoid or deny, information that would contradict a belief and therefore show decisions based on these beliefs to be incorrect (Koriat et al., 1980). Confirmation biases are often present in poor decision making.

Snyder and Swann (1978) provided participants with information about another person that strongly suggested the other person was either an **extrovert** or an **introvert**. Participants were instructed to select questions to ask the person to test the hypothesis that the person was extroverted or introverted. Participants tended to seek information that supported the hypothesis. The study also found that when interviewees were asked questions that confirmed the hypothesis, they tended to behave in ways that also confirmed the hypothesis.

8.2.3 The illusory correlation

The illusory correlation describes the conclusion people reach when they decide that events occurring at the same time are related, sometimes going as far as stating that one event causes the other. For example, a student who did well in a test when writing with a pencil may conclude that writing with a pencil caused the success.

The illusory correlation likely plays a role in stereotype formation (Peeters, 1983). Often, when behaviour is negative (such as crime) and the group is of a clearly identifiable minority (such as immigrants), negative stereotypes are formed and strengthened. This is because the two factors (the crime and the minority) both seem significant and the casual observer assumes they are related.

8.2.4 Implicit personality theories

Implicit personality theories relate to people's understandings about which personality characteristics they think co-occur in others. For example, if a person observes someone else acting in a quiet, reserved way and considers reserved behaviour to be related to intelligence, then the observer will probably conclude that the shy person is intelligent.

The halo effect is the false correlation of positive characteristics, i.e. the assumption that someone who has a few positive characteristics has many. A halo effect is sometimes associated with physical attractiveness: people tend to assume that physically attractive people have other positive characteristics. Verhulst et al. (2010) found attractiveness and familiarity to be strong predictors for selecting people for leadership roles. Palmer and Peterson (2012) found that even after factual knowledge is considered, candidates that voters rated as more attractive were still considered more knowledgeable. The halo effect, then, is thought to have an effect on how political candidates are elected.

Key study: Zebrowitz and McDonald (1991)

Aim: To investigate the effect of plaintiffs' and defendants' facial appearance on decisions made in a small claims court.

Procedure: Twenty-five decisions relating to 506 cases were observed in a Massachusetts small claims court. Fifty-one per cent of the cases were presided over

---

Think of a recent decision you made. With the advantage of hindsight, would you describe the decision as accurate? How did you make the decision? Slowly and carefully, using a lot of cognitive effort? Or quickly?

To what extent is confirmation bias a cross-cultural or a culture-bound behaviour?

Implicit personality theories relate to people's understandings about which personality characteristics they think co-occur in others.

by three judges and the rest by 22 judges. Two observers independently rated the plaintiffs' and defendants' appearance. Seventy-two per cent of the plaintiffs and 78 per cent of the defendants were male. Ninety-six per cent were white and 81 per cent were between 21 and 50 years old.

Results of cases were obtained from court records by a different researcher. The appearance ratings were compared with the case outcomes.

Findings: The greater a plaintiff's physical attractiveness, the more likely defendants were to lose the case.

As a defendant's rating of baby-facedness increased, the more likely they were to win cases involving intentional behaviour, and more likely to lose cases involving negligence.

As the rating of a defendant's facial maturity increased, the greater the monetary awards were to baby-faced plaintiffs.

Conclusion: The study concluded that the outcome of a small claims court case is correlated with the plaintiff's and defendant's facial attractiveness and a halo effect is evident.

The study also measured for a possible correlation between nine other variables such as height, weight, clothes, and whether the defendant/plaintiff wore glasses, and no correlation was found.

Evaluation: The study's conclusion is reasonably robust: a halo effect, i.e. a positive correlation between attractiveness and innocence is apparent.

No information about the judges, i.e. gender, age, or experience, is included in the study. The study's participants are the judges because it is the relationship between the litigants' appearance and the judges' decision making that the study investigated, so the omission of the participants' characteristics is a serious limitation of the study.

The study was limited to Massachusetts and the subjects within the study were a fairly homogeneous group – predominantly white, male, and middle-aged – and so the conclusion cannot be widely generalized. The study did not conclude a cause-effect relationship, simply a correlation.

Zebrowitz and McDonald (2012) investigated whether the halo effect is a cross-cultural phenomenon by comparing judgements made by US judges and decision making by Tsimané people living in the Bolivian rainforest. The study found that a within-culture halo effect was present in decision making by Tsimané people, i.e. the attractiveness rating was culture-bound, but the correlation of attractiveness and favourable decision making is cross-cultural.

8.2.5 Algorithms

An algorithm is a step-by-step approach to reaching a conclusion. Algorithms are often associated with mathematics and computer coding. The same methodical approach can be applied to problem solving or decision making. Algorithms are often described graphically with squares representing each step in the path to an accurate decision. Sometimes there is a simple one-path set of steps, and in other situations there are alternatives to be considered when coming to a decision.

Draw a flow diagram that represents the algorithm used to calculate the mean of a set of people's heights rounded to the nearest centimetre.

Draw a flow diagram that represents the algorithm used by a doctor to determine an unwell patient's diagnosis.

Algorithmic thinking has been applied to medical diagnostic decision making and to procedures for aircraft pilots, so that the most accurate and efficient decision making process can be applied in critical situations to reach the best outcome every time. Algorithms are often contrasted with heuristics, which involve cognitive shortcuts and do not always achieve accurate outcomes.

9 Emotion and cognition

Topic focus

To what extent are emotion and cognition related?

9.1 The influence of emotion on cognitive processes

Content focus

Discuss the role of emotion in one cognitive process.

Be cautious when you write about causes and effects, because emotion and cognition are intertwined: emotions affect cognitive processes and cognitive processes affect emotions.

There was a time when science considered emotion and cognition to be separate, but there is now evidence showing brain areas and psychological processes that are commonly associated with cognition. For example, the dorsolateral prefrontal cortex and working memory are strongly associated with emotion. This research shows that emotion and cognition are interwoven.

Emotions such as stress and anxiety influence cognitive activities such as selective attention, working memory, and cognitive control (Pessoa, 2013). Other research, for example Ochsner and Gross (2007), has shown that the neural activity associated with cognitive activities is involved in the regulation of emotions.

9.1.1 Valence theory

Valence refers to the inherent positiveness or negativeness of an event, object, situation, or emotion. Emotions with a negative valence include disgust and fear, while emotions with a positive valence include happiness and love. Emotions that are positively valenced are produced by events or situations that are similarly valenced. The valence approach proposes that emotions with the same valence have a similar effect on decision making.

Emotional reactions help people manage and respond to difficult situations, often when that person is experiencing stress. Emotions perform an adaptive function by motivating people to act quickly and take action that maximises the likelihood of survival.

Darwin (1872) proposed that emotional states are adaptive, and only those who can express certain emotions can pass on their characteristics to their offspring. When the human body creates a state of fear, anger, disgust, or happiness, it produces withdrawal or approach behaviours that have been perpetuated through evolution because they have been advantageous to survival (Damasio et al., 2000). Positive emotions such as joy, interest, and love are also thought to be adaptive. They broaden the range of people's thoughts and actions, 'to play and create when experiencing joy, to explore when experiencing interest, to savour and integrate when experiencing contentment, and to combine play, exploration and savouring when experiencing love,' (Fredrickson, 1998).

Tugade and Frederickson (2002) showed that the adaptive benefits of positive emotions are more significant when people are experiencing stress. Resilient people use positive emotions to recover from stressful situations.

To what extent are emotions an adaptive behaviour?

Are positive emotions as valuable to humans as negative emotions?

Do emotions hinder or help cognitive processes?

9.1.2 Arousal theory

The arousal theory of emotion and memory proposes that emotionally arousing information is encoded to a higher standard, resulting in better retention and more accurate retrieval of the information.

Significant autobiographical memories tend to be accompanied by strong emotions. Our memories of happy family gatherings, deaths of close friends, traumatic incidents such as car accidents, or bullying incidents in school, all involve intense emotions. These memories are likely to be recalled more often and more vividly than neutral memories such as brushing your teeth, researching your extended essay, or eating lunch.

Arousal theory is likely explained by, or at least associated with, greater attention during the initial stage of memory formation. Arousal theory proposes that retention is strengthened when the information is associated with arousing events or information, and the information is also remembered more vividly and more accurately (Sharot and Phelps, 2004). Schachter and Singer (1962) found that participants remembered arousing words better one week after learning them, compared to just two minutes after learning the words. This is probably because during the later time the memories were recalled and rehearsed.

Memories that are supported or strengthened by intense emotions are likely to be adaptive, i.e. evolutionary. Survival often relies on behaviour that has been repeated, rehearsed, and reinforced. The 'fight or flight' instinct is an example of such an adaptive behaviour. A physically or emotionally traumatic event creates a physiological response which excites neurochemical activity affecting brain areas associated with encoding and recalling memories. Intense emotion, however, does not always enhance memory.

9.1.3 The two-factor theory of emotion

Schachter and Singer (1962) proposed the two-factor theory of emotion: that emotion is based on a physiological arousal and a cognitive label. When a person experiences an emotion, a physiological arousal follows. The person then searches the immediate environment to identify the physiological arousal. For example, a person on a high suspension bridge would experience stress or anxiety and, based on the immediate environment, label the emotion as a fear of height or a fear of falling.

Lesion studies and **neuroimaging** studies have shown that the amygdala is a critical structure for the development of memory by emotion (Adolphs et al., 1997). The right

Lesion studies and neuroimaging studies have shown that the amygdala is a critical structure for the development of memory by emotion.

amygdala is more significantly associated with the formation of emotional memories and the left amygdala with the retrieval of those memories (Sergerie et al., 2007). The amygdala is also associated with classifying information as new rather than old (Sergerie et al., 2007).

9.1.4 Flashbulb memory

First proposed by Brown and Kulik (1977), the flashbulb memory model proposes that unexpected, personally significant episodes may be stored unchanged in people's memories for years. While some research has found people reporting remarkably accurate and stable memories (Neisser et al., 1996), others have shown that memories that would qualify as flashbulb are just as inaccurate as other kinds of memories (Neisser, 1982).

Most studies into the existence of flashbulb memory have focused on negative public events such as ferry sinkings, assassinations, or large-scale disasters in which the studies' participants have been personally involved, rather than private or personal events such as car accidents or home invasions, or positive personal events such as weddings or the birth of a child.

Key study: Er (2003)

Aim: To test flashbulb memory models by sampling subjects who experienced the Marmara earthquake on 17 August 1999 directly, or who learned about it in the news.

Procedure: Six hundred and fifty-five Turkish volunteers, of whom 335 (140 female, 195 male) experienced the Marmara earthquake directly (age range 18–48, mean age 34.4) and 320 (150 female, 170 male) were not directly affected, but lived nearby (age range 18–53, mean age 30.22), completed self-report questionnaires. Questionnaires were distributed by the experimenter to small groups of participants asking about their experiences of the earthquake. Data collection occurred six to nine months after the earthquake. A subsample from both the victim and the comparison groups was tested again after another six months.

Findings: The findings indicated participants from both groups had been significantly affected by the earthquake, that the earthquake was consequential (important), and that it generated high levels of surprise and emotional reaction. Two important similarities were found for both groups: firstly, importance or consequentiality determined the intensity of the participants' emotional states; and secondly, rehearsal (retelling and reliving the event) had a direct effect on flashbulb memory.

Conclusion: This study concludes that the Marmara earthquake is a flashbulb event, especially for the victim group, and had consequences for all participants. The study also concludes that the greater the event's importance and the more intense the emotional reactions to it, the more vivid and detailed the memory.

Evaluation: The study is recent and was conducted with a large number of volunteer participants with a reasonable age and gender balance. The participants were all either personally involved in, or well informed about, the earthquake and so the study has strong ecological validity. Most flashbulb memory studies involve memory of public events in which the studies' participants were not directly involved and this may explain why the memories 'fade'.

The study could not isolate the cause of the flashbulb memory effect – the personal significance, the consequentiality, and the rehearsal may each be responsible for the flashbulb memory effect. Although the study's method was largely **quantitative**, the findings and conclusion are qualitative, so the study ought to have included a reflexivity statement from the researcher to expose any possible researcher biases.

Ask your parents and teachers where they were and what they were doing when they first learnt about the Indian Ocean tsunami on 26 December 2004. To what extent are their responses flashbulb memories?

10 Research methods: cognitive approach

Learning focus

Discuss the contribution of research methods used in the cognitive approach to understanding human behaviour.

Most research methods have weaknesses as well as strengths. Adopt a critical but balanced attitude when evaluating the contribution of different methods.

10.1 Field experiments

Field experiments are experiments conducted in real-life settings rather than in laboratory settings. Hippocampal lesion studies, i.e. research that studies the effects of damage to the hippocampus, are an example of a field experiment because they occur outside a laboratory in real-life settings.

The Atkinson and Shiffrin (1968) model of memory (the multi-store model) relied on hippocampal lesion studies that showed people with damaged hippocampal regions could create short-term memories, but not long-term memories. The independent variable (IV) in this study is the state of the hippocampus and this takes two conditions. IV1 is the undamaged hippocampus and IV2 is the damaged hippocampus. The dependent variable (DV) in the experiment is the function of the hippocampus, i.e. the formation of long-term memories.

Milner (2005) also conducted a field experiment that used hippocampal lesion studies to support the hypothesis that the hippocampal region plays a role in memory formation. Milner (2005) studied the development of amnesia after ablation surgery on the medial temporal lobe as a way of controlling certain types of epilepsy.

In a laboratory experiment all the variables other than the IV are controlled so that any change in the DV can only be attributed to the change in the IV. In a field experiment, all other variables may not necessarily be controlled because the study is conducted in a real-life setting. This means that there is less certainty that any change in the DV can be attributed to the change in the IV.

In a laboratory experiment all the variables other than the IV are controlled so that any change in the DV can only be attributed to the change in the IV. In a field experiment, other variables are not able to be controlled because the study is conducted in a real-life setting.

Moreover, participants in laboratory experiments are usually representative of a wider population, while in a field experiment the participants are usually purposively selected and are unlikely to be representative of wider populations. This reduces the extent to which the field experiment's conclusions can be generalized.

10.2 Interviews and questionnaires

Interviews are a qualitative research method and may be used in conjunction with a questionnaire, which is a quantitative method, to collect data from a representative sample so that the findings can be transferred to a larger population.

Tao et al. (2016) used a questionnaire to investigate stereotypes about rich and poor Chinese people (see page 61). The researchers considered their sample to be 'ordinary people in China, not belonging to the rich or the poor'.

The study concluded that stereotypes about rich and poor people existed. Rich people were considered highly competent, having low sociability and bad morality. Poor people were seen as incompetent, with average sociability, and good morality. The research method was a free-report questionnaire and so the researchers did not affect the participants' choice of adjectives by giving a list of their own.

The inherent weakness of questionnaires is participant unreliability, e.g. demand characteristics. This occurs when the participant responses are distorted, perhaps because the participants want to please the researcher or perhaps because the participants simply do not want to give a truthful response.

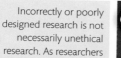

Conduct a simple questionnaire with your friends using three or four questions to determine how much time they spend using their smartphones. Knowing your friends, do you think they gave accurate responses to your questions? Why might their responses be inaccurate?

11 Ethical considerations: cognitive approach

Learning focus

To what extent are ethical considerations significant in the cognitive approach to understanding human behaviour?

Ethics are the rules imposed on researchers by their professions, their cultures, and themselves. The simplest two ethics are 'do the right thing' and 'do no harm'.

Loftus (1996) used the 'lost in the mall' technique to determine if false memories can be created. Over time, a participant was told a convincing story by several family members of being lost in a shopping mall and found by an elderly man. Not only did the participant just 'remember' the event, but when later questioned about it for the study, new details were added.

This study involved deception and so if the participant consented to the study, their consent was not given from a position of full information. The study, therefore, would be considered by most to be unethical.

Pezdek and Hodge (1999) used the same 'lost in the mall' technique with 19 5–7-year-old children and 20 9–12-year-old children to determine whether children can have false memories planted or created. The children were read descriptions of two events – a plausible event (being lost in a shopping mall) and an implausible event (receiving a rectal enema). Both events were said to have occurred when the children were 4 years old. The study concluded that some children can have memories planted or created.

Incorrectly or poorly designed research is not necessarily unethical research. As researchers have become more aware of their actions, studies that were once considered ethical would not be now.

Children cannot give 'fully informed consent' because they cannot understand the implications of their involvement in such research. A child cannot understand how having a false memory planted would affect him or her. Creating false memories, whether these are memories of positive or negative events, is unethical because the participant believes the event occurred, when it did not. Pezdek and Hodge (1999) would, in most cultural situations, be considered unethical because it harms the participant and because children cannot give fully informed consent.

One might reasonably ask, 'Is a little harm to some participants an acceptable cost to pay for the benefit accrued to many as a result of this research?' This is the type of question an ethics committee might discuss before giving a researcher its approval to proceed.

12 Cognitive processing in the digital world (HL)

General focus

To what extent is cognitive processing affected by the digital world?

Research has shown that technology affects cognitive processes such as attention, memory formation, and thinking. Just as printed pages, numbers, clocks, abacuses, and typewriters levered human intellectual performance, the internet and other digital technologies are shaping, possibly even reshaping, how people think. Some neuroscientists are concerned that digital technology not only has positive neurological impacts, but also significant negative effects. China's psychological body has made internet addiction a clinical disorder and the Chinese government has established more than 400 rehabilitation camps for the condition.

Digital technology includes many aspects that simultaneously compete for people's attention, some of which may be useful but some of which may be better described as a distraction. Some argue that we cannot process vast quantities of information from numerous sources and therefore the internet may be degrading the way that we think, learn, and make decisions. Others argue that the information overload through technology is no different to the information overload of everyday life.

Hebb (1947) looked at information overload by comparing the problem-solving capabilities of rats kept in a confined space with rats that had been reared in a stimulating environment. The 'free-range' rats outperformed the rats kept in captivity in problem-solving activities later in the rats' lives. The study concluded that exposure to more information may lead to increased brain weight, greater neuron cell size, and greater cortex thickness.

Children cannot give 'fully informed consent' because they cannot understand the implications of their involvement in such research.

TOK
Is it ethical to use the results of unethical research?

Take care when using the broad and ill-defined term 'technology', which has been used in research to mean television, computers, video games, and mobile phones. It is more likely that the technology that actually affects behaviour is the software or content, rather than the hardware.

Use the internet to determine statistics of daily internet use.

TOK
To what extent did the invention of the clock affect the way humans behave?

To what extent does a lack of clarity regarding the term 'digital technology' hinder research into the effects of using technology?

12.1 The influence of digital technology on cognitive processes

Learning focus

To what extent does digital technology affect one cognitive process?

There is a worldwide shortage of research determining cause-effect relationships between modern technology and effects on cognitive processes, so claims should be considered cautiously, using critical-thinking skills.

The technology in question includes television, calculators, the internet, and smartphones. Perhaps because the peer-reviewed research process is relatively slow compared to the rate of technology development, there is a shortage of research examining a possible cause-effect relationship between technology and cognitive processes.

While current research focuses on smartphones and the internet, older technology has also affected cognitive processes. Murzyn (2008) found that people who had lived in a home with a black and white television were more likely to dream in black and white than those who had lived with colour televisions, who almost always dream in colour. Before the introduction of black and white television, dreams were in colour. King and Robinson (2012) indicated that some students' use of calculators means they do not understand what the calculator is doing in mathematics, although the evidence for this seems more **anecdotal** than the result of empirical research.

12.1.1 Attention

Stothart et al. (2015) showed that exposure to notifications from smartphones decreased participants' performance on a concurrent attention-based task. Simply hearing or feeling the alert distracted the participants and affected their attention to the primary task. This result is not very surprising as the purpose of a smartphone's alerts is to draw the user's attention to the incoming message or call. However, when Drouin et al. (2012) surveyed 290 undergraduates, 89 per cent reported that they had felt their phone was vibrating when it was not. They reported that this distraction occurred at least once every two weeks. Rothberg et al. (2010) found 68 per cent of 176 medical workers reported feeling similar phantom vibrations and therefore distractions from their primary task. Thornton et al. (2014) found that just being in possession of a smartphone is sufficiently distracting to affect cognitive functioning, although only during demanding tasks.

Numerous studies (for example, Caird et al., 2014) have found that texting while driving consistently decreased attention to the road and traffic conditions and correlated with slower response times to hazards and, not surprisingly, more crashes. In 2011, 31 per cent of adults in the US, and in 2015, 42 per cent of teen drivers in the US, said they had read or sent text messages while driving within the past 30 days.

Design and conduct a simple survey of 20 classmates to determine whether a correlation exists between hours of smartphone use and one cognitive process such as attention or memory.

Loh and Kanai (2015) found less than expected grey matter in the anterior cingulate cortex of heavy users of multimedia, suggesting that multi-tasking with technology may affect the structure of a region in the brain known to be associated with attentional control. It is therefore clear that smartphones have an effect on attention, but of course this is a deliberate feature of smartphones.

12.1.2 Memory

Studies show that the effects of technology on memory and knowledge acquisition are limited. For example, Sparrow et al. (2011) had participants type a series of newly learned, but trivial pieces of information into a computer. Half were told the computer would save their information and the others were told the information would not be saved. All were told to remember the information.

Those who thought their information would be saved did less well on a recall task. This suggests that knowing we will be able to read the information later leads to poor encoding and storing of information in long-term memory.

Sparrow et al. (2011) also proposed that technology users remember less information, but they are better at remembering where and how information can be found. To investigate this, Sparrow et al. (2011) conducted an experiment similar to the one described above, but with three conditions: for one third of the questions, participants were simply told that the information they entered was saved; for another third of the questions the participants were told that the information was saved into one of six named folders (Facts, Data, Info, Names, Items, and Points) and the remaining third of the questions were followed by a prompt that informed the participants that the information they typed was immediately deleted. The results showed that participants recalled the name of the folder in which the information was located more readily than the information itself and the researchers concluded that, 'the processes of human memory are adapting to the advent of new computing and communication technology' (Sparrow et al., 2011).

Henkel (2013) investigated the impact of cameras on autobiographical memory formation. Participants took their smartphones on a tour of an art museum and were told to (1) photograph specific objects, and (2) observe other objects, but not photograph them. The next day the participants were tested on their recall of the objects. The results showed that the photographed objects were recalled less than those not photographed. The effect was less pronounced if the participants were instructed to zoom the camera in on the object, supporting Atkinson and Shiffrin's (1968) conclusion that memory formation is more effective when stimuli are given more attention.

Memory formation is more effective when stimuli are given more attention.

12.1.3 Thinking

Barr et al. (2015) assessed participants with a set of cognitively demanding questions, including numeracy and verbal intelligence tests, and then asked participants to estimate how much time they spent using their smartphones and how much of that time they spent using internet search engines. The results showed that participants who reported using their smartphones the most had weaker analytical thinking skills and lower knowledge measures. Tempting as it is to conclude that smartphones cause diminished cognition, it may simply be that those with poor cognitive ability are more likely to make use of their smartphone's internet search capabilities.

12.2 The positive and negative effects of modern technology on cognitive processes

Learning focus

Discuss the effects of modern technology on one cognitive process.

Modern technology appears to have both negative and positive effects on cognitive processes. In most cases, it is reductionist to state that modern technology has a negative or a positive effect on any cognitive process. For example, smartphones appear to have both positive and negative effects on attention and on different aspects of memory, such as encoding and recall. Further, in some instances, what some consider to be a negative effect, others may consider a positive effect. For example, as people switch from encoding and storing memories to using technology-based information storage mechanisms such as digital contact lists and reminder apps, they conserve cognitive energy that they can then use for more sophisticated mental tasks.

12.2.1 Positive effects of technology on memory, attention, and emotion

Memory

Kahneman (2011) described humans as 'cognitive misers'. This means that humans tend to use cognitive shortcuts that require little effort, such as schemas and heuristics. It is likely that this cognitive 'miserliness' is what motivates people to use memory-assistive technology. This suggests that any effects of technology on memory that are perceived to be negative are in fact positive, and given the well-documented unreliability of memory, people are probably better served using technology to store and retrieve information than to rely on human memory.

Attention

Some people, some of the time, experience greater attention to a primary task if they complete it while also listening to music. This is one of the few exceptions to the idea of true multi-tasking. Most of the time, when people believe they are multi-tasking they are actually switching between two tasks. Switching attention between tasks requires significant and fast cognitive effort, which is challenging, but it appears that we can learn to do it with rehearsal or practice. Lui and Wong (2012) had participants perform a task that required integrating information of multiple sensory **modalities** (i.e. sights and sounds) and found that those who reported greater multi-tasking significantly outperformed those who were light multi-taskers. This suggests a positive effect on people's attention of exposure to multimedia.

Emotion

While technology has been shown to have a negative effect on emotions such as exacerbating depression and anxiety, it has also been shown to have a positive effect. Computer software, often in the form of smartphone apps, has been developed to improve the mood of people suffering from depression by showing them photos, video, and audio of, for example, their friends and families. Similarly, apps have been

---

Be careful not to be too simplistic – it is reductionist to state that modern technology has either a negative or a positive effect on any cognitive process because the technology is varied, and the cognitive processes are complex.

Humans are cognitive misers: they tend to use cognitive shortcuts that require little effort, such as schemas and heuristics.

Most of the time, when people believe they are multi-tasking they are actually switching between two tasks.

Design and conduct a survey of students in your school to investigate whether smartphone use helps or hinders students' attention. Do any students use apps that help focus attention?

developed to treat phobias, and computer games have been developed to provide therapy for people who are, for some reason, reluctant to interact with a human therapist. For example, a fantasy role-playing game called SPARX was found to be at least as effective as human face-to-face therapy (Horne-Moyer et al., 2014).

12.2.2 Negative effects of technology on memory, attention, and emotion

Memory

Sparrow et al. (2011) showed what they called the 'Google effect' or 'digital amnesia' – that knowing or expecting to have later access to information tends to make people less inclined to encode and store information in long-term memory. Other studies have shown some technology has a negative effect on spatial memory. Heavy users of GPS technology drew significantly simpler and more disjointed (and therefore inaccurate) maps of commonly used routes than non-GPS users, who could recall maps with significantly greater accuracy.

Other research has shown that technology such as digital cameras may have a negative effect on the formation of autobiographical memories.

Attention

There is evidence suggesting that when it comes to distractions, the richer the information in the distraction, the more significant a negative effect it will have on the successful completion of a primary task (Levy, 2016). Information that includes text, graphics, sound, and perhaps even movement, is more distracting than information that has fewer elements. This of course should not come as a surprise, because distraction is usually the designed purpose of technology's disruptive features.

The extent of the effect of disruption may be less about technology and more about the person's susceptibility to distractions, i.e. the person's pre-existing lack of cognitive ability to self-regulate attention and control over behaviour.

Emotion

Both depression and anxiety are known to have negative effects on cognitive functioning. Mark et al. (2016) found that restricting email access reduced people's anxiety and improved their focus on work-related tasks. However, research indicates that separation from smart devices also causes anxiety. Cheever et al. (2014) found that people who did not have their phones with them experienced increasing levels of anxiety as time without their phone passed.

Some research, for example Chiu (2014), suggests general stress (life-stress) is a strong predictor of smartphone use, i.e. generally more stressed people tend to use smartphones for social support and other stress-mitigating uses.

Discuss with others in your class how researchers might design research to determine a cause-effect relationship between high smartphone–internet use and diminished cognitive skills. The challenge, to establish effective cause-effect results, is in controlling all variables except the independent variable. How could researchers do this?

To what extent is research into the effects of modern technology on cognitive processes likely to be distorted by socioeconomic and cross-cultural factors? How could researchers strengthen their research to account for cross-cultural factors?

12.3 Methods to study interactions between digital technology and cognitive processes

Learning focus

Discuss methods used to study the interaction between digital technology and cognitive processes.

A range of data-collection techniques, such as fMRI scans and self-report questionnaires, have been used as elements of research methods that include observations, correlational studies, and experiments to study the interaction between digital technology and cognitive processes. There appears to be a need for longitudinal studies, although there are inherent problems with this type of research for studying the effects of technology on cognition because new technology is being developed faster than longitudinal research can be conducted, peer-reviewed, and published.

It should be noted that many studies use the term 'technology' to describe television, video games, the internet, smartphones, and social media, when in fact these are all very different. Many studies also fail to control socioeconomic or environmental factors that correlate with technology use. For example, while students who use smartphones in lessons may achieve better results, they may also be the students who can afford to employ private tutors. Despite this, it seems reasonable to assume that the internet, smartphone use, and video games will change brain structure and cognitive processes, but then so has playing sports, reading books, and driving taxis in inner London.

12.3.1 Animal research and fMRI scans

Animal research could be used to observe the effects of technology on cognition. Dombeck et al. (2010) used a virtual reality system with mice to study decision making and learning in fast-paced 'mice-enticing' environments. The mice interacted with a spherical treadmill to navigate a virtual maze while researchers used fMRI scanning to study the effect on the CA1 region of the hippocampus.

Animal research incorporating fMRIs is useful because the ethical limitations of animal research are less restrictive than those for human research. fMRIs are non-invasive and do not require the mice to be killed. Conclusions from animal behaviour research, however, usually cannot be generalized to human behaviour.

12.3.2 Meta-analysis

A meta-analysis is a research method in which researchers consider the results of many previous studies, effectively combining the number of participants and factoring in cross-cultural and inter-temporal effects by including studies done in different countries and in different time periods. A meta-analysis is useful because it involves very large numbers of participants. Meta-studies are relatively low cost as they do not involve the cost of new studies being conducted.

Caird et al. (2014) performed a meta-analysis to examine 28 experimental studies involving 977 participants and reached a conclusion regarding the effect on attention of sending and receiving text messages while driving. The meta-analysis found that texting while driving produces cognitive distraction.

Be clear not to confuse data-collection methods with research methods. For example, brain scans and questionnaires usually are data-collection techniques that contribute toward research methods such as correlational studies or experiments.

12.3.3 Self-report questionnaires

Self-report questionnaires are often used as a data-collection technique in many studies to identify variables such as how many hours per week participants use their smartphone or access the internet. Self-report questionnaires are useful because they are relatively low cost and they are direct, i.e. the respondents provide the information, so the responses are not prone to errors of interpretation.

However, self-report estimates are of limited reliability, and because technology is being developed rapidly and usage rates are increasing even more rapidly, many of the studies based on self-report questionnaires are obsolete before they can be applied to studies.

12.3.4 Longitudinal studies

A longitudinal study involves repeated observations, or repeated experiments, over long periods of time (often years or even decades) to determine long-term effects. There is almost no long-term data relating to the effect of modern technology on cognitive processes, partly because the technology itself changes fundamentally across short periods of time. For example, the technology that children were using in schools just ten years ago is significantly different to that used now.

Longitudinal studies that investigate the effects of technology should take this into account at the design stage, or the conclusions should be clearly stated to show that the study relates to technology in general rather than a particular technology such as a tablet or a smartphone.

12.3.5 Experiments

Experiments are designed and conducted to determine (or rule out) a cause-effect relationship.

They are useful because by showing whether a cause-effect relationship exists, they can usually give a definitive answer to a research question such as, 'Do students who make class notes with a tablet achieve better exam results than students who do not use tablets?'

To confidently show that modern technology has a negative effect on memory, an experiment would have to show that all variables other than 'modern technology' have been controlled so that the only factor that could have produced a change in a dependent variable (in this case memory) is the modern technology.

One issue faced by researchers is finding participants who match in age and socioeconomic status who make little or no use of modern technology to contrast with those with high exposure to technology.

Finally, the few experimental studies conducted on technology's effect on cognition have almost all investigated momentary, or very short-term, effects rather than long-term effects.

Self-report estimates of behaviour are of limited reliability.

There is almost no long-term data relating to the effect of modern technology on cognitive processes.

Design and conduct an interview or self-report questionnaire to use with people of different ages in your school community, aiming to find out the approximate usage level of technology during their school-age years. Use the results to create a wall chart that shows a longitudinal trend. Describe the flaws in this data-collection method.

Experiments are designed and conducted to determine (or rule out) a cause-effect relationship.

Key study: Sparrow et al. (2011)

Aim: To determine whether people recall where to find information more than they recall the actual information.

Procedure: Thirty-two undergraduate students at Columbia University (USA) read standardized instructions from a computer screen. Participants had to write trivial facts into the computer and then read that the information was saved into a folder called Facts (or Data, Info, Names, Items, Points). Participants were led to believe that they could access what had been saved. The order of the statements was randomised. Participants were allowed ten minutes to write down the statements they had written. Participants were then asked a general question about each piece of information they had written (e.g. In which folder is the statement about ostriches saved?) Participants were not reminded of the folder names.

Findings: Participants recalled the names of the folders where the information was stored more accurately than the information itself.

Conclusion: These results suggest that processes of human memory are adapting to the advent of new computing and communication technology.

Evaluation: Strengths include being conducted in laboratory conditions with most variables controlled. This leads to low ecological validity. The participant group was relatively small in number and relatively homogeneous (although the group was approximately gender-balanced), so the conclusions cannot be generalized to the wider population.

A weakness in this study's procedure is that remembering a full statement is likely to require more cognitive effort than recalling one relatively odd (because it is unrelated) word associated with the informational statement.

Activity

Find all of the new words or expressions from this chapter and write them into a document with their definitions and explanations next to them. Be creative and use diagrams or boxes to help make your personal glossary unique and effective.

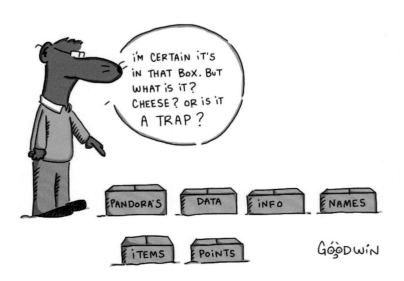

Sociocultural approach to understanding behaviour

C

The sociocultural approach to behaviour investigates the role of social and cultural influences in shaping thinking and human behaviour. An increasing body of culturally informed research has made **cross-cultural** psychology, as well as cultural psychology, a contemporary topic of debate among psychologists working in the field. Theories, concepts, and research studies provide the background for a more nuanced understanding of the variety and complexity of human behaviour. This is important in the modern globalized world where issues related to migration and integration are on the rise.

Key figures in the field of modern social psychology have often favoured experimental methods to understand how social context influences behaviours, identities, attitudes, and **cognitions**. However, by studying **acculturation** in terms of intergroup relations, we can start to understand that the same processes may be seen in the interaction between cultural groups. Social and cultural psychologists now also use **qualitative** research methods to get a better understanding of intergroup relations as well as the process of acculturation.

The sociocultural approach to behaviour looks at:

- the individual and the group (SL and HL)

- cultural origins of behaviour (SL and HL)

- cultural influences on individual attitudes, identities, and behaviours (SL and HL)

- the influence of globalization on individual attitudes, identities, and behaviours (HL only).

13 The individual and the group

Topic focus

To what extent is a person's behaviour affected by membership of a group?

13.1 Social identity theory

Content focus

Evaluate social identity theory (SIT) as an explanation of human behaviour.

The strength and relevance of social identity theory may depend on individuals' cultures.

Tajfel and Turner (1979) proposed **social identity theory** (SIT) to explain that people's concept of **self-identity** is derived, at least in part, from the groups they belong to. People belong to many groups, such as their family, school community, workplace and sports teams. SIT proposes that people derive much of their identity from the behaviour of other people within these groups.

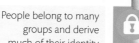

People belong to many groups and derive much of their identity from the behaviour of other people within these groups.

When people consider themselves a member of one group and not a member of another similar group, their group becomes an ingroup for them. The other, similar groups become their outgroups. Ingroups and outgroups are defined in terms of comparisons and contrasts (Yuki, 2003). This ingroup/outgroup, or 'us' versus 'them' situation, is derived from SIT's three basic assumptions: social categorization, social identification, and social comparison.

Social categorization

People categorize others in order to easily identify them and to begin to understand them. By understanding the categories others belong to, they can better understand themselves and begin to develop a sense of identity. People tend to define behaviour as 'right' according to their group's behaviour. Individuals usually belong to many groups at the same time and depending on the group they are with, their behaviour is likely to change to match the group's behaviour.

Social identification

People tend to assimilate into their group by behaving in ways that the group members behave and therefore taking on the group's identity. The group becomes the person's ingroup.

Social comparison

Once people have categorized themselves within a group and identified themselves as members of that group, they tend to compare their ingroup with respect to their outgroups. To improve their **self-esteem**, group members see their ingroup in a positive light and their outgroups in a negative light. This is not just true for the groups as a whole – people also tend to perceive the individuals within their outgroups negatively.

13.1.1 Ingroup bias

According to the theory, people's **biased** evaluations of their outgroups are a result of their need to feel good about themselves. People seem to improve their perception of themselves after discriminating against their outgroups (Lemyre and Smith, 1985).

Struch and Schwartz (1989) found that conflict between religiously defined groups in Israel was due to outgroup aggression and that this perception was strongest for those who identified most strongly with their ingroup. Brown et al. (2001) observed the same effect between passengers on a UK–France ferry (ingroup) and French fishermen (outgroup). The passengers had been prevented from travelling because of a blockade by French fishermen. The ingroup had significantly less favourable attitudes toward French people in general than those who were not affected by the French fishermen's behaviour. This negative attitude among the ingroup was stronger for those who identified most strongly with their English nationality. Identification of a person's nationality was the most consistent predictor of negative attitudes toward those of other nationalities. The strength of ingroup identification is a powerful predictor of intergroup attitudes.

13.1.2 Responses to intergroup inequality

SIT has shown how collective protest can sometimes be predicted by people's level of identification with their ingroups. Participation in trade union, gay, and elderly people's protests was generally predicted by the strength of people's identification with their ingroups (Kelly and Breinlinger, 1995). Wright et al. (1990) unjustly deprived a

Interview three people from your class by just asking them who they are. To what extent did they define themselves by identifying groups they belong to?

SIT is based on three assumptions: social categorization, social identification, and social comparison.

According to SIT, people's biased evaluations of their outgroups are a result of their need to feel good about themselves.

To what extent does social identity theory predict intergroup behaviour such as disputes between different political groups, different nationalities, and supporters of different sports teams?

group of people and then offered individuals the possibility of leaving the group. The study found that collective protest only occurred when people felt they could not leave their group and concluded that even when just a few from the deprived group could join a more privileged group, collective protest was unlikely to occur.

13.1.3 Stereotyping

SIT affects the way psychologists think about **stereotyping** and the perception of ingroups and outgroups. Stereotypes may not be reliable mental tools for decision making. The categorization process that underlies stereotyping implies members of an outgroup share common attributes, i.e they are seen as more similar to each other than they are to members of other groups. SIT shows that perceptions of group **homogeneity**, of both ingroups and outgroups, are linked to social identity processes. Stereotypes, then, cannot be understood by considering them solely as cognitive devices to simplify thinking.

Stereotypes may not be reliable mental tools for decision making.

> **Key study: Yuki (2003)**
>
> **Aim:** To investigate the extent to which social identity theory is applicable within US and Japanese contexts.
>
> **Procedure:** One hundred and twenty-two Japanese (72 men and 50 women, mean age 19.7 years old) and 126 Americans (62 men and 64 women, mean age 19.3 years old) completed a questionnaire (presented in each group's own language).
>
> **Findings:** (1) Loyalty to and identification with their ingroup was greater with American participants than with Japanese participants; (2) evidence suggests that discrimination against outgroups is more pronounced in individualistic cultures; and (3) there is no evidence to support the theory that there is ingroup favouritism.
>
> **Conclusion:** SIT 'may not accurately represent group behaviours among East Asians' and therefore is not a cross-cultural phenomenon.

13.1.4 Limitations of SIT

Research supporting SIT theory is limited.

- SIT assumes that a positive social identity is based on favourable intergroup comparisons. There should, therefore, be a positive correlation between strength of group identification and the amount of positive ingroup bias, but research shows only modest support for this (Yuki, 2003).

- SIT assumes that ingroup bias is driven by the desire to perceive one's ingroup, and oneself, positively. There should, therefore, be a causal relationship between intergroup **differentiation** and self-esteem, i.e. positive intergroup differentiation should cause people to feel better about themselves when they judge or treat their ingroup better than their outgroup. Yuki (2003) has not supported this claim.

- SIT is a theory of how people make their ingroups different from and better than outgroups. Therefore, groups that find they are similar should be motivated to demonstrate intergroup differences. Yuki (2003) does not support this.

To what extent do schema theory and social identity theory lead to stereotyping?

SIT was largely developed within 'Western' contexts. Yuki (2003) suggests SIT is less reliable in explaining behaviour in 'non-Western' communities. Yuki (2003) investigated the extent to which SIT is applicable within US and Japanese contexts and found:

- loyalty to and identification with their ingroup was greater with American participants than with Japanese participants

- evidence suggests that discrimination against outgroups is more pronounced in individualistic cultures

- there is no evidence to support the theory that there is ingroup favouritism.

Yuki (2003) concluded that SIT 'may not accurately represent group behaviours among East Asians'.

Stewart et al. (1998) found that Chinese students living in Hong Kong perceived intergroup differentiation to be less important than British students living in Hong Kong did. The British students felt that their group membership was more important and that it generated more positive images of their group than the Chinese students did. Although the results did not contradict SIT, they did suggest that differentiation among the Chinese students is weaker than among the British students. This study focused only on students and so its findings cannot be **generalized** to the wider Western and Eastern populations.

EE To what extent does the lack of supporting empirical evidence weaken SIT as an explanation of human behaviour?

Key study: Howarth (2002)

Aim: To examine 'how the struggle for recognition and esteem **permeates** everyday experiences in the contexts of young people living in Brixton (South London, UK)'.

Procedure: Eight focus groups with a total of 44 teenagers (12–16 years old) separated into friendship groups, and interviews with the three head teachers of Brixton's secondary schools. Questions and discussion prompts included, 'Tell me about Brixton. What it is like for you to live here and how do people outside Brixton think about Brixton?' (Howarth, 2002, p.4).
Follow-up interviews were conducted a short while later to clarify and expand on several themes.

Findings: The study found that many, but not all, of the young participants held positive perceptions of living in Brixton but believed people who did not live in Brixton did not think highly of it.

Conclusion: At least some adolescents develop social and psychological ways to protect themselves from others' perceptions and judgements about them. The study showed how teenagers' relationships and the cultures of the institutions to which they belong are able to empower them in respect to their identity. The young participants created a positive identity because of the sense of belonging they felt to their group, i.e. to Brixton residents.

Evaluation:

Strengths: Interviews can gather rich and varied qualitative information and focus groups have particular strengths, as participants can be prompted to discuss issues that other group members think of. Interviews can be flexible, allowing the interviewer to delve into themes by developing questions into discussions. The focus group interviews were followed with one-to-one interviews with the heads of the three schools in the area as a means of triangulation, or at least to gather information from a different perspective. The study was gender-balanced and focused on a specific age range that was consistent with its aim and conclusion.

Limitations: Qualitative research such as focus group interviews is usually difficult to replicate with the same results. As the essence of the study was about the teenagers' perceptions of their ingroup, interviewing the participants in small friendship-based focus groups rather than conducting individual interviews raises the possibility of peer pressure compromising the authenticity of the teenagers' responses.

13.2 Social cognitive theory

Content focus

Evaluate social cognitive theory (SCT) as an explanation of human behaviour.

Social cognitive theory (SCT) is a learning theory: it attempts to explain how people learn new behaviours. SCT suggests behaviour is acquired through observation or imitation of others. The theory proposes that when a learner observes another person's behaviour and sees the consequences of that behaviour (rewards or punishments), they remember and use this information with respect to their own behaviour.

The model whose behaviour is mimicked or learned can be real (e.g. a family member, school teacher, or sports player) or fictional (e.g. a movie or television character).

Bandura et al. (1961) argued that people's behaviour is caused by personal, behavioural, and environmental influences. Whether a learner reproduces a behaviour that has been modelled or demonstrated is influenced by:

* personal factors: the extent to which the learner has low or high **self-efficacy** (their belief that they will succeed)

* behavioural factors: the extent to which the learner is rewarded after performing the behaviour correctly

* environmental factors: external barriers or supports that affect the learner's ability to reproduce the behaviour.

13.2.1 Social cognitive theory and self-efficacy

Self-efficacy refers to a person's perception of the likelihood that they will succeed. It relates to SCT in that if learners do not think they can succeed, they are less likely to try to replicate a model's behaviour.

White et al. (2012) tested whether SCT could affect physical activity participation in middle-aged and older adults. Participants' self-efficacy level, ability limitations, goals,

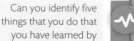

Theories and models are simplified explanations of human behaviour. These theories are often adapted over time as research attempts more detailed explanations. Being simplifications, they come with limitations as well as strengths. Always offer balanced discussions of theories and models.

Can you identify five things that you do that you have learned by observing others, perhaps family members or school friends? It may be a way of thinking, talking, or walking. It may be the way you tie your shoelaces or eat your breakfast.

SCT's basic hypothesis is that people learn some behaviours by observing others' behaviours and the consequences of those behaviours.

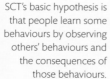

outcome expectations, and physical activity were measured at the beginning and end of an 18-month period. Self-efficacy was thought to influence the participants' level of physical activity directly, but also indirectly by affecting the participants' goals and expectations. The researchers found that participants with higher levels of self-efficacy participated in greater levels of physical activity and had fewer disability limitations impeding their participation.

SCT has been applied to health psychology to help people stop cigarette smoking by increasing smoker's self-efficacy (their belief that they will be able to quit). Smokers were shown ways of experiencing success through role-playing and imagination. Smokers were also shown models who had successfully quit smoking, i.e. behaviour they could mimic. This method was effective in helping smokers to stop smoking.

Stajkovic and Luthans (1979) clarified self-efficacy in the workplace by stating that unless employees believe they can bring together required behavioural, cognitive, and motivational resources needed to execute a task, they will most likely focus on the most difficult aspects of a task and apply insufficient effort (Stajkovic et al., 1979).

Ahmed and Sands (2009) aimed to determine if more mothers of pre-term infants breastfed their babies after a SCT-influenced breastfeeding education programme. Sixty Egyptian mothers were randomly assigned to groups: (1) participating in the programme, or (2) routine care. The education programme was made up of SCT strategies: (1) showing role models who breastfed correctly to improve the participants' self-efficacy; (2) weekly check-ups over the course of three months to reinforce the participants' breastfeeding skills; and (3) a self-report checklist for the participants to encourage the breastfeeding. The study found that mothers in the education programme showed significant improvement in breastfeeding and were more likely to only breastfeed their babies, i.e. no bottle feeding. These mothers also had significantly fewer breastfeeding issues than the mothers who were not in the education programme.

13.2.2 Social cognitive theory and aggression

Bandura et al. (1961) aimed to find out when and why children display aggressive behaviours. They conducted a study where adults demonstrated verbal and physical aggression toward an inflatable doll (called a Bobo doll) in the presence of preschool-aged children, many of whom subsequently reproduced the aggressive behaviour.

Key study: Bandura et al. (1961)

Aim: To find out why and when children display aggressive behaviours.

Procedure: An experiment was conducted with 72 children (36 boys and 36 girls) aged 3–6, all of whom were enrolled in Stanford University's day-care programme. While the participants (children) played with books and stickers, an aggressive adult model (sometimes a male model, sometimes a female model) played briefly but shortly afterwards spent the rest of the time behaving aggressively (both physically and verbally) toward the Bobo doll, in a standardized way that would be used with each of the children. At the same time another (adult) model played in a subdued, non-aggressive way.

The children were then taken to another room where they played with some toys for about two minutes. A researcher then took these toys away, but the children were left with other toys they could play with.

The children were then taken (individually) into another room that contained toys that were considered aggressive or non-aggressive. The aggressive toys were a Bobo doll, a mallet, and dart-guns. The non-aggressive toys were a tea set, cars, and dolls. Several researchers observed the children and recorded details of their behaviour.

Findings: Of the children who were exposed to the aggressive adult model, the boys showed an average of 38.2 physically aggressive acts and the girls showed 12.7 physically aggressive acts.

Boys and girls imitated the male models more than the female models with respect to physical aggression but imitated the model of their gender more with respect to verbal aggression.

Conclusion: The study concluded that children can learn behaviour by observing an adult's behaviour. The study also concluded that boys are more likely to mimic the behaviour of men, and girls are more likely to mimic the behaviour of women, and females tend to be less aggressive than males.

Evaluation: The study was conducted under laboratory conditions and so the procedure was controlled, as were environmental **variables**. Although the group of participants was gender balanced they were of a relatively homogeneous **socioeconomic** background. The study's dependent variable (acts of aggression) was subjectively measured, with all acts of aggression treated as equal in value, i.e. each act was simply counted and not measured for intensity. More research is needed before the study's conclusions can be generalized to wider populations. The study was conducted on very young children and so further research is needed to determine whether the study's conclusions can be generalized to people of older ages.

EE

To what extent can social cognitive theory help to explain unhealthy behaviours such as cigarette smoking, misuse of alcohol, and eating disorders?

To what extent has the use of social cognitive theory in fictional television programmes been effective in modifying individuals' behaviour?

13.2.3 Social cognitive theory and mass influence

SCT has been used by governments to influence social behaviour. For example, in 1975 a soap opera, *Ven Conmigo* (*Come with Me*), was created in Mexico to entertain, but primarily to promote adult literacy. The soap opera centred on the lives of adults in a literacy class and captured large viewing audiences. The soap opera generated a 900 per cent increase in enrollments in adult literacy classes compared to the previous year. After an episode that mentioned how to access free literacy booklets, 25 000 people approached the organization to get copies of the same booklet.

13.2.4 Evaluation of social cognitive theory

SCT is derived from studies that have been replicated. While the original studies lacked ecological validity and were conducted with a group of participants who limited the study's ability to be generalized, SCT has been studied with broader ranges of participants and the conclusions support SCT's basic hypothesis that people learn some behaviours by observing others' behaviours.

SCT is a broad and ill-defined theory of learning or **behaviour-acquisition** that is still evolving. It neglects the role of emotions and cognitive learning in explaining behaviour. SCT does not explain why some people replicate or mimic behaviour that has been modelled and some do not.

13.3 Stereotypes

Content focus

Discuss the formation of stereotypes.

When discussing stereotypes, use at least one example to clarify your answer.

13.3.1 Development of stereotypes

One theory of stereotype development is that stereotypes are the cognitive component of people's attitudes toward other people or groups (Harding et al., 1969). Others suggest that stereotypes are functional, allowing rationalization of people's **prejudice** with respect to a group (Allport, 1954). Others still suggest that prejudice is an inevitable consequence of the simple categorization processes inherent in stereotype formation (Tajfel, 1981).

Stereotypes appear to be heuristically applied to members of a stereotyped group, meaning people use them as a simple decision making technique that may not lead to an accurate or correct conclusion.

Key study: Katz and Braly (1933)

Aim: To determine whether stereotypes were 'not based upon **animosity** toward a member of a proscribed group' because of individual characteristics, but rather because of attitudes against 'race names'.

Procedure: One hundred Princeton undergraduates (age and gender unknown) completed a self-report questionnaire in which they were asked to identify the attributes of ten social groups that were prominent in the US at the time of the study, including Germans, Italians, Jews, Americans, Chinese, and Japanese, and then check the five traits from a list of 84 (such as happy, lazy, superstitious, and hard-working) they considered most typical of each group.

Findings: The students showed a range of agreement about the attributes given to different ethnic groups, from 84 per cent of participants who said African Americans were superstitious to 11 per cent who said Germans were practical.

Conclusion: The study concluded that actual contact with individual members of groups was not a requirement for people to form racial/ethnic stereotypes.

To what extent does television perpetuate, or even create, stereotypes? Think about television programmes that are watched in countries different to the country they were created in.

Evaluation: The study was based on verbal reports from the participants, so the responses required little effort. The study only aimed to investigate stereotypes held by US students, so the study's conclusion is of limited value with regards to stereotypes held by wider populations. The study does not explain why the stereotypes exists, just that they do. The study was conducted in 1933, at a time when prejudices were strongly held and widespread, so the study's findings simply gave confirmation to widely known information. The study was conducted on participants at a prestigious university, so it is likely that the participants were mostly young, Caucasian males from a relatively upper socioeconomic sector of US society, meaning the conclusion cannot be generalized to wider populations. There is no evidence of attempting to correct the participants' stereotypes.

In a follow-up study, Gilbert (1951) found the same stereotypes still existed but the extent of consensus was lower. Devine and Elliott (1995) modified Katz and Braley's (1933) attribute list with new attributes, such as ostentatious and pleasure-seeking. There was low consensus for Katz and Braley's attributes, and high consensus for the new ones, suggesting Katz and Braley's attribute list may be outdated and current beliefs are less negative. An inherent weakness of self-report questionnaires is that participants may not report accurately.

Once stereotypes have been formed they tend to persist because of correspondence bias, the illusory correlation, upbringing, and ingroup and outgroup relations.

13.3.2 Correspondence bias and stereotype formation

Correspondence bias can play an important role in stereotype formation. Correspondence bias is the tendency to over-attribute a person's behaviour to their personality (**dispositional**) factors, and to under-attribute the extent to which external (**situational**) factors caused the behaviour. Nier and Gaertner (2012) found that people who display correspondence bias tend to stereotype high-status groups as competent and low-status groups as incompetent. Participants who scored highly on correspondence bias assessment stereotyped the poor, women, and a fictitious group of low-status Pacific Islanders as incompetent. The same participants stereotyped the rich, men, and the fictitious group of high-status Pacific Islanders as competent. After controlling for other variables, correspondence bias was the most significant predictor of stereotyping by the participants.

To what extent did your responses in the previous activity include stereotypes of people living in Pakistan, Germany, and Russia?

Research successful entrepreneurs or sportspeople and look for examples of correspondence bias.

13.3.3 Illusory correlation and stereotype formation

An illusory correlation is a simple error of association: the incorrect conclusion that two events that occur at the same time are related. For example, if someone breaks a mirror and the same day breaks their arm, they may correlate the two events and conclude that the broken mirror caused the broken arm, when in fact the two events are unrelated.

Unusual events are distinctive and so people notice them more than mundane, normal events. The increased attention leads to stronger or more effective encoding, which strengthens the perception that the events are associated. In an intergroup context, illusory correlations cause people to wrongly attribute uncommon behaviours to minority groups or outgroups.

An illusory correlation is a simple error of association. It is the incorrect conclusion that two events that occur at the same time are related.

Hamilton and Gifford (1976) tested the extent to which illusory correlation leads to stereotype formation. The study found illusory correlation is stronger when the infrequent and distinctive information is negative.

Key Study: Hamilton and Gifford (1976)

Aim: To investigate the illusory correlation of group size and negative behaviour.

Procedure: Researchers asked 114 university students from the US to read descriptions and then make conclusions about two made-up groups, Group A and Group B. The descriptions were based on a number of positive and negative behaviours. Group A, the larger group with 26 members, performed 18 positive and 8 negative behaviours. Group B, the smaller group with 13 members, performed 9 positive and 4 negative behaviours.

	Group A	Group B
Number of members in the group	26	13
Number of positive behaviours	18	9
Number of negative behaviours	8	4

Findings: Although there was no correlation between group membership and the types of behaviours exhibited by the groups (the proportion of negative and positive behaviours was the same for both groups) the participants did seem to make an illusory correlation because more of the undesirable/negative behaviours were attributed to the minority Group B, than the majority Group A.

Conclusion: The findings support the theory that distinctive information draws attention. The number of Group B members and negative behaviours are both numerically fewer than those of Group A and therefore more distinctive than Group A's. The participants' responses were not logically correct and so showed an illusory correlation.

Evaluation: The study concludes that the illusory correlation exists because people's attention is drawn to distinctive or unusual phenomena, such as the small number of people in Group B. This is the explanation given for some people making an illusory correlation relating to minority groups and their behaviour, such as Aboriginal Australians and alcohol abuse. This illusory correlation could also be called a failure of understanding simple statistics. The study was conducted under partially controlled conditions, but the most significant variable, the participants' level of understanding of mathematics and statistics, is not considered.

EE To what extent are superstitions formed because of illusory correlations?

McConnell et al. (1994) found that people formed stereotypes based on information that was considered distinctive at the time of judgement rather than when the information was first encountered. Consistent with Bartlett's (1932) cognitive concept of 'effort after meaning', when a person decides that previously non-distinctive information already encoded into memory is distinctive, that information is re-encoded as if it were distinctive when it was first noticed.

13.3.4 Upbringing and stereotype formation

Stereotypes may also be the consequence of a person's upbringing. Some stereotypes may develop in early childhood because they are presented to children by parents, teachers, friends, and the media.

Bar-Tal (1996) investigated the role of upbringing in the formation of a stereotype of Arabs in Jewish children in Israel. Two hundred and fourteen children (102 boys and 112 girls, aged 2–6 years) from two socioeconomically different Tel-Aviv neighbourhoods were individually shown a photograph of an Arab man wearing the traditional kaffia. Each child was then asked to rate him against four traits (good/bad, dirty/clean, handsome/ugly, and weak/strong). The results showed that almost all the children had already developed a negative stereotype of Arabs.

The study concluded that children acquire or develop some stereotypes from their environmental experiences, i.e. from parents, media, peers, and teachers, as well as direct contact with the outgroup members.

13.3.5 Ingroup and outgroup relations and stereotype formation

The ingroup-outgroup explanation of stereotypes suggests that stereotypes are formed and shared because group members are motivated to strengthen their perceived similarities with their ingroup and strengthen their perceived differences with their outgroups. This means the stereotypes are a consequence, not a cause, of intergroup relationships.

In the same way that research shows that intergroup problems based on perceived ingroup-outgroup differences can be overcome by merging the groups and initiating contact and communication between group members, stereotypes can also be overcome.

> People acquire or develop some stereotypes from their environmental experiences, i.e. from parents, the media, peers, and teachers, as well as direct contact with the outgroup members.

> **TOK** If stereotype formation is a normal human behaviour, are discriminatory practices such as ageism, sexism, and racism also normal human behaviour?

> **EE** To what extent do the cultural aspects of a study's participant sample hinder the ability to generalize that study's results?
>
> Can studies of human behaviour conducted more than ten years ago apply to behaviour now?
>
> To what extent can a study of young children in one country or culture conclude that all people form stereotypes from their environment?

HMM... IN GROUPS AND OUTGROUPS, VERY INTERESTING. NOAM CHOMSKY SAID WE'LL LEARN MORE ABOUT MOUSE BEHAVIOUR FROM NOVELS THAN SCIENTIFIC PSYCHOLOGY. I THINK HE'S RIGHT.

GOODWIN

RESEARCHING AN EXTENDED ESSAY ON IN GROUPS AND OUTGROUPS ... OR MAYBE IT WILL BE ON STEREOTYPES.

13.3.6 Stereotype threat

Stereotype threat occurs when people know about a negative stereotype associated with them or their ingroup and develop anxiety that they might confirm the stereotype. Stereotype threat is not a universally accepted concept, and some consider it to be the subject of publication bias.

Publication bias is the idea that some research is more likely to be published simply because its findings are interesting. Although there have been many studies relating to stereotype threat, this may be because researchers know that studies into the phenomenon will be published, so pursue this research over other, less publisher-friendly, topics.

Steele (1988) conducted experiments to show that stereotype threat can have a negative effect on performance in standardized tests. The study found that African American college students performed worse than white students when a task was presented as an intelligence test, but when it was not presented as an intelligence test the African American students performed better.

An essential aspect of reliable research is **replicability**.

For a theory to be widely accepted it is usually supported by empirical evidence that has been achieved in replications of original research. While stereotype threat is a widely cited psychological phenomenon with apparently real-world consequences, after allowing for publication bias there is little evidence that it has any significant effect on, for example, women's performance in mathematics (Flore and Wicherts, 2014). Zigerell's (2017) meta-analysis concluded that the evidence for stereotype threat was inconclusive.

EE To what extent does stereotype threat affect the behaviour of some elderly people?

---

14 Cultural origins of behaviour and cognition

Topic focus

Discuss the cultural origins of behaviour.

14.1 Culture and its influence on behaviour

Content focus

To what extent does culture affect one cognitive process?

A group's culture is its generally agreed beliefs, norms, and conventions and is made up of its shared attitudes, behaviours, and symbols. Culture is learnt by instruction and observation, and is passed down through generations.

Until relatively recently, the psychology community considered human behaviour to be the product of human biology, i.e. physiology, genes, and hormones. The role of culture in explaining behaviour in general and cognition in particular has become more prominent in recent decades.

 Take care not to confuse culture with ethnicity and nationality. A person with Australian nationality but who has lived in Pakistan for most of her life is more likely to be of the Pakistani culture than the Australian culture. A person of Tongan ethnicity who was born and raised in France is more likely to behave according to French cultural norms.

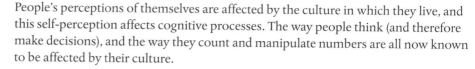

People's perceptions of themselves are affected by the culture in which they live, and this self-perception affects cognitive processes. The way people think (and therefore make decisions), and the way they count and manipulate numbers are all now known to be affected by their culture.

Derry (1996) argued that there is a degree of 'cultural-boundness' to cognitive processes such as memory, language, and thinking. For example, Bartlett (1932) showed that the participants' British-English language (compared to American-English) affected the way they remembered the Native American story, 'The War of the Ghosts'.

A cultural group's language serves to interpret, classify, and structure perception of external reality. There are many instances of a person's beliefs or values affecting what they observe empirically, for example explanations of illness/disease, weather events, and earthquakes, and the meaning of people's facial expressions, body language, and hand gestures.

14.1.1 Role of culture in behaviour

Wong and Hong (2005) investigated the role of culture in behaviour by priming Chinese-American participants with cultural icons (either a Chinese dragon or an image of Mickey Mouse) before asking them to participate in the Prisoner's Dilemma game with friends and strangers. The bicultural participants showed higher levels of cooperation with friends after they had been shown icons from their Chinese culture than when primed with icons from their American culture. Similarly, they showed lower levels of cooperation with strangers when primed with Chinese-culture symbols than American-culture symbols. The study concluded that a person's culture affects interpersonal decision making.

Culture affects judgements and decision making, including the extent to which the fundamental attribution error (FAE) applies (Kashima, 2001, cited in Wong and Hong, 2005). The FAE is the theory that people overstate dispositional factors (factors about themselves) in their successes and understate the role of situational factors (factors that are external to them), such as the weather or other people's behaviour. There is evidence to suggest the FAE is less powerful in some cultures, such as Russian and Indian.

14.1.2 Social class and behaviour

Grossmann and Varnum (2010) investigated the extent to which social class affects cognition by examining the role of American (independent) culture and Russian (interdependent) social class, on people's dispositional and situational bias. The study found a positive correlation between lower social class, **holistic** cognition, and interdependent self-views (i.e. **self-inflation**) in both the USA and Russia. Participants from lower social class American backgrounds and Russians (who were considered to be less class-distinct) demonstrated less dispositional bias. These people attributed fewer outcomes to themselves or their own behaviour. People from lower social class backgrounds and Russians demonstrated more contextual attention, more non-linear reasoning about change, and more interdependent self-views (less self-inflation).

Sidebar (left column):

Ask your friends what they understand by the expression, 'lost in translation'. Have they or you experienced situations where language or a culture-specific behaviour has caused some confusion?

Discuss with your friends the different ways they speak to each other, their parents, their grandparents, and perhaps people in positions of authority. Do they use the same language (vocabulary) and paralanguage (such as tone of voice, slang, and body language) with all people? To what extent does their culture determine this behaviour? Remember that culture is not the same as ethnicity or nationality.

EE Can any generalizations be made about people based on their cultures that are not stereotypes?

To what extent are some emotions culture-bound?

TOK Investigate different cultural interpretations of weather events. Can we say that some cultures' explanations of weather events are incorrect?

The FAE is altered in the Indian context to the extent that dispositional factors tend to be more interpersonal rather than purely personal (Markus and Kitayama, 1991). For example, Indian people tend to understate the role of situational factors such as the weather in their successes and overstate the role of factors such as the effect of their friends and family members as well as their own dispositional factors (Markus and Kitayama, 1991).

These studies showed that FAE is less of a universal human behaviour than previously thought, and that it is instead affected by a person's culture.

GRIMACING MOUSE DISCOVERS FAE.

14.1.3 Counting and arithmetic

Saxe (2015) demonstrated that the cognitive processes of counting and arithmetic are affected by culture. For example, the body-part counting system used by the Oksapmin people in Papua New Guinea is the 27-number equivalent of the 'Western' ten-number counting system based on counting with fingers and thumbs (Saxe, 2015).

Reed and Lave (1979) conducted a natural experiment, which was supplemented with observations and interviews, involving tailors from the Vai and Gola tribes in Monrovia (Liberia) to investigate the effect of culture on arithmetic thinking. The study found that the tailors who used the Vai/Gola numerical system had a very different cognitive process for counting and conducting arithmetic problem solving.

Beller and Bender (2008) used examples from Melanesian and Polynesian culture to show the cultural origins of their unique arithmetic problem-solving skill: adding and subtracting the large numbers required by large-scale and long-distance trading systems. In the High Fijian language, a different word is used to count 100 (bolu) canoes and 100 (koro) coconuts. In Managreva (French Polynesia) different number sequences are used for counting tools, breadfruit, and octopus. (Beller and Bender, 2008).

Oksapmin 27-body-part counting system

The Oksapmin 27-body-part counting system uses body parts' names, starting with the thumb of one hand as 1, moving around the fingers to 5, up the arm and to the shoulder, 10, up the neck and across the ears, eyes, nose and down to the neck, 17, and then down the other arm, hand, and to the other thumb, 27. When shown a group of five piles of ten sticks, teachers will teach children that this is a little finger (representing 5) followed by a shoulder (representing 10) (Saxe, 2015).

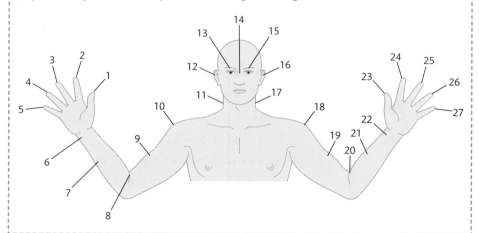

Figure 14.1 The Oksapmin 27-body-part counting system

If you know people from other countries, or perhaps from earlier generations, ask them to explain the way they add, subtract, multiply, or divide.

Key study: Reed and Lave (1979)

Aim: To investigate the role of culture on counting and arithmetic problem solving.

Procedure: The research was based on participant observation and informal interviews with 140 males of the Vai and Gola tribes working as tailors in shops of Tailors' Alley in Monrovia, Liberia. The interviews covered apprentices' personal history, family background, and beliefs about teaching and learning. Some tasks were aimed at understanding arithmetic skills.

Tailors used either the apprenticed Vai/Gola arithmetic system or the school-taught Western arithmetic system to solve a series of arithmetic problems. The Vai/Gola arithmetic is a spoken numeration system (i.e. it's not written) and seldom uses numbers larger than 20. Vai/Gola arithmetic operations are done either 'in the head' or by manipulating sets of markers.

Findings: The study demonstrated consistent differences in the methods employed by tailors who had learned arithmetic in the tailor shop as apprentices and in school. Problem-solving procedures were closely related to the tailors' culture-dependent learning experiences.

The traditionally taught (apprenticed) Vai/Gola tailors used counters, such as pebbles, or marks on paper, to count and conduct arithmetic problem solving, as well as mental arithmetic problem solving. The tailors trained in the Western school system used algorithmic manipulations learnt in school and strategies using number names. Using data based on arithmetic problem solving, observations and recordings of **verbal protocols**, and interviews about the apprenticeship and schooling experiences, the study showed that the 'folk arithmetic system' was as systematic as the Western, school-taught system.

There was strong evidence to show that all except the least experienced apprentices had a clear understanding of the general idea of arithmetic problem solving consistent with their arithmetic system.

Conclusion: The study found that there is an arithmetic problem-solving system unique to the Vai and Gola tribes and that this is used by tailors trained through traditional apprenticeship methods, i.e. not in school, and that there is another, different system used by those with five or more years of schooling.
The tailors who used the Vai/Gola numerical system had a very different cognitive process for counting and conducting arithmetic problem solving. Instead of re-coding quantities as words or numerals, apprentices using the Vai/Gola counting system simply used pebbles or counters, one for each unit counted.

Evaluation: The study has high ecological validity as it was conducted in context. The tailors were observed while they were using their arithmetic systems, not in a laboratory setting. This meant that other variables were not controlled. Interviews and experiments supported the researchers' numerous observations.

Investigate counting systems such as the Oksapmin 27-body-part counting system and the Vai/Gola system. To what extent does culture affect people's system of counting and arithmetic?

14.1.4 Surface and deep culture

Surface culture refers to the obvious or readily discernible differences between a person's **indigenous** and host countries, for example language, gestures, diet, clothing, and interpersonal behaviour. Deep culture refers to more profound cultural norms; those that are considerably less obvious and therefore less accessible to newcomers, such as social hierarchies, interpretations of dignity and respect, religion, and humour.

Individuals who have a low level of acculturation with respect to a dominant culture are more likely to retain the cultural values of their indigenous community and therefore behave less in response to their new culture's norms (Betancourt and Lopez, 1993).

14.2 Cultural dimensions

Content focus

To what extent do cultural values affect human behaviour?

Discuss with your friends or family members their attitude toward honesty. Are there any situations where it is acceptable to be dishonest?

Discuss the attitude toward punctuality – why do you think some people think and behave as if absolute punctuality is essential for respectful living while others have a more casual attitude toward arriving at events on time. To what extent does the discussion reveal cultural attitudes toward some values?

A value is a subjective belief relating to a desirable outcome or behaviour, and one that transcends specific situations.

A value is a subjective belief relating to a desirable outcome or a behaviour that transcends specific situations. A value guides a person's choice of behaviour (Schwartz, 1992). **Cultural dimensions** are the commonly held values of a group that affect behaviour, for example reliability and trustworthiness, the attitude toward truthfulness, the extent to which punctuality is considered important, and the attitude toward planning. They can be thought of as **continuums**. For example, the 'truth dimension' continuum would have a total expectation of truthfulness at one extreme and no sense of honesty at the other.

Key study: Schwartz (1992)

Aim: To determine the existence of a universal set of cultural dimensions or values.

Procedure: 25 863 participants in 44 countries (school teachers, university teachers, and adolescents) participated in a survey and identified the following cultural dimensions or values:

- power (social status, prestige, control/dominance)
- achievement (personal success)
- hedonism (pleasure and gratification)
- stimulation (excitement, novelty, challenge)
- self-direction (independent thinking, self-determinism, free will)
- universalism (appreciating, tolerating, and protecting all people and nature)
- benevolence (protecting and enhancing the welfare of people with whom one is in frequent contact)
- tradition (respect, commitment, and acceptance of one's traditions and culture)
- conformity (restraining oneself to not harm or offend others)
- security (safety and stability of self, society, and relationships).

Fifty-six values were included in a core survey. The values were presented as nouns (e.g. security) or adjectives (e.g. helpful), each with a short explanation. The researchers' colleagues in the countries that were surveyed were encouraged to add any values from their cultures that they felt were missing from the survey. The participants were asked to rate each value with the statement, 'As a guiding principle in my life.' The rating was made on a 9-point scale from 7 'supreme importance', 6 'very important', to 3 'important', 0 'not important', to −1 'opposed to my values'. Prior to rating the values, respondents chose and rated their most and least important values. This anchored their use of the scale.

Findings: The study found that cultural dimensions of countries in Eastern Europe, Western Europe, the Far East, USA/Canada, and countries influenced by Islam each show uniquely different patterns. These cultural dimensions support the continuums such as Triandis' (1990) individualism/collectivism, and Markus and Kitayama's

(1991) independent/interdependent selves. Profiles from Japan and the US suggest distinctive cultures, but neither occupies an extreme position on any dimension.

Conclusion: The study concluded that there is not a universal set of cultural dimensions. However, there is wide acceptance of the following ten cultural dimensions or values: universalism, self-direction, stimulation, hedonism, achievement, power, security, tradition, conformity, and benevolence.

Evaluation: The study included a very large sample of participants from 44 countries from a wide age range. However, participants were only drawn from modern and well-educated countries (e.g. UK, Singapore, and New Zealand), which is relatively inconsistent with the study's aim of determining whether there are universal cultural dimensions. The study used a self-report questionnaire, which can be unreliable because of demand characteristics or simply because respondents do not respond accurately.

14.2.1 Chinese cultural values

Yau (1988) investigated the dimensions of Chinese culture that have formed a consistent values system for many generations. Reflecting Confucianism as the basic pillar of Chinese life, Chinese cultural values are largely formed and created from interpersonal relationships and social orientations. Kluckhohn and Strodtbeck (1961) described Chinese culture with a model using five dimensions or orientations:

- man-to-nature orientation (harmony with nature)

- man-to-himself orientation (modesty)

- relational orientation (interdependence; group orientation, face, and respect for authority)

- time orientation (continuity and past/historical orientation)

- personal-activity orientation (harmony with others).

While the classical value system was disrupted during the Cultural Revolution, the values are still evident (Yau, 1988). The man-to-nature orientation is founded on the belief that Chinese people regard humans as a part of nature and that humans should not try to control or overrule nature, but should instead adapt to it and so be in harmony with nature.

The man-to-himself orientation assumes abasement or self-degradation. By studying Chinese families' child-rearing practices, it is clear that from an early stage, a Chinese child is brought up to understand his or her role with respect to others. Modesty and self-effacement are expected of children (and subordinates). When praised, Westerners say, 'Thank you', but Chinese people often say, 'No, I am not worthy'. Chinese people try to avoid saying, 'no' because they do not want to embarrass or offend (Yau, 1988).

Kluckhohn and Strodtbeck (1961) proposed that Chinese people value family traditions and their cultural history and so proposed a past-time orientation.

The personal-activity orientation implies that the strongest value is to live properly, i.e. being polite and obeying the rules makes social transactions supremely important. In Chinese culture, being considerate to others is a salient aspect of living properly.

Create an interactive wall chart or classroom display that shows Schwartz's cultural dimensions and encourages those looking at the chart to place themselves on each dimension's continuum.

TOK To what extent is the IB Learner Profile a set of cultural dimensions?

EE To what extent does the concept of cultural dimensions of values reinforce stereotypes?

Use the five dimensions to Chinese culture as described and place yourself on the continuum. To what extent does each dimension influence your behaviour?

Can you think of any practical applications of cultural dimensions?

These five orientations combine to create a set of cultural dimensions, each of which can be considered a continuum on which a person can be placed in answer to the question, 'To what extent do you value this orientation in your daily life decisions?'

14.2.2 Cultural dimensions

Hofstede (1984) proposed four cultural dimensions:

- power distance
- individualism
- masculinity
- uncertainty avoidance.

Power distance refers to the extent to which less powerful individuals accept inequality as the norm. Inequality exists in all cultures, but individuals' acceptance of it varies across cultures.

Individualist societies are those in which people place the greatest focus on themselves and their immediate family and friends while collectivist societies are made up of people who place greater value on wider, extended family groups from which they have great difficulty separating themselves. These extended families can be considered an individual's 'ingroup'.

The masculinity dimension refers to individuals' expectation that men will be assertive, ambitious, and competitive and to respect things that are big, strong, and fast. Masculine cultures expect women to care for children and others who cannot care for themselves, while feminine cultures expect men and women to be equally ambitious and caring.

Uncertainty avoidance, according to Hofstede (1984), refers to the extent to which individuals are tolerant of uncertainty. Cultures with a strong tolerance of uncertainty are active, emotional and tolerant while those with a low tolerance of uncertainty are less aggressive, more accepting of personal risk, and relatively intolerant.

15 Cultural influences on individual attitudes, identity, and behaviours

Topic focus

Discuss cultural influences on individual attitudes, identity, and behaviour.

15.1 Enculturation

Content focus

Using one or more examples, discuss the role enculturation plays in one behaviour.

Enculturation is the process of acquiring a culture's norms. At its simplest level, it is the way people learn the 'rules' of their culture or what is expected by a group of its

---

TOK

To what extent might the concept of cultural dimensions contribute to stereotypes of nationalities or cultures?

Do you think cultural dimensions might change over time, perhaps due to globalization or technology use?

A person's values are described as cultural dimensions and are measured or quantified on a continuum, i.e. to what extent is a particular value a strong force in a person's decisions about behaviour.

Culture is not the same as ethnicity or nationality. Use specific language to be clear about this, for example, 'the way children of the Samoan culture learn the nuances of their language is affected by the way they are "encultured", i.e by the way they acquire the norms and expectations of their Samoan culture'.

members. For example, learning the unwritten rules when starting at a new school, or how to behave appropriately when joining a new workplace, sports team, or group of friends is done through enculturation.

People teach their group's norms and expected behaviour, i.e. their group's culture, to new members of the group. People can learn from each other because of social cognition. People take others' perspectives to an extent that allows them to experience the group's behaviour (Tomasello et al., 1993).

At the simplest level, enculturation occurs through direct instruction. Parents teach their children the appropriate way to behave by telling them what is right and wrong, for example they tell them to speak quietly in restaurants. New workers to an organization are instructed by supervisors during orientation about how and when to carry out their assigned duties, how to dress, and which communication protocols to follow. Teaching culture this way occurs because it is direct, deliberate, and effective.

Enculturation can also occur through social learning, i.e. learning by an individual who is influenced by the social environment (Bandura et al., 1961). This influence may be minimal or superficial, for example parents or teachers may simply give young children objects such as a ball, which they explore or play with to discover new behaviour. In such cases the social environment only exposes the culture's new member to the object; the actual learning process is individual.

New students often learn the social rules of their new school (expected norms such as popular hairstyles), in-class behaviours (such as hand raising), and the accepted way to greet classmates and teachers by observing other students' behaviour. This is possible because of social cognition.

People can also learn cultural expectations through cultural learning. New group members do not just observe and then mimic others' behaviour (as with social cognition), they try to see a situation the way other group members see it. This learning is social; the new group member tries to learn the group's norms by empathizing with or imagining another person's perspective or point of view.

15.1.1 Enculturation's effect on language

Enculturation affects the way one learns language. Pinker (1994) proposes children begin life being aware, to some extent, that the sounds their mother produces are elements of a language and that those sounds have meaning, as compared to sounds such as a door closing, which does not have meaning. Others, however, believe that language is a cognitive consequence of enculturation.

Tomasello and Rakoczy (2003) propose that while children's understanding of language occurs **ontogenetically** in all cultural settings at about 1 year old, the understanding of beliefs occurs some years later, and at different ages in different cultural settings. There is strong evidence that participating in language-based communication with other people is a necessary condition for a child's development (Tomasello and Rakoczy, 2003).

Ochs (1982) showed that Samoan culture places great emphasis on learning by observation and so the cognitive process of language acquisition by Samoan children is affected significantly by their families' cultures. For example, as Samoan children

Enculturation is the process of acquiring or learning what is expected by a group of its members.

Discuss with three or four others in your class the process of enculturation when a new student starts in your school. Write down ten 'rules' or expectations imposed by the school, some of which are formal and overt (known to all) and some which are covert (known only to the students). How do students learn these rules or expectations of behaving in the school?

How did you learn the rules of your school? What were the five most important rules that you were not told about?

learn to become members of their society or culture, they also learn to become competent users of their language, meaning enculturation and language acquisition occur simultaneously. A significant part of their enculturation is the way they use their language.

Key study: Ochs (1982)

Aim: To investigate language development and language socialization in traditional Samoan households.

Procedure: A **longitudinal** case study observed 23 children (under 6 years old) from different households every five weeks over a period of ten months. Recordings were transcribed by the children's households and checked by the researchers.

Findings: The study found that language instruction is conducted by a child's caregiver, who is most often an older sibling, and that language instruction is characterized by three culture-laden features: (1) decentring, (2) a lack of expansion by caregivers, and (3) elicited imitation. Higher status people, such as parents, do not lower their perspective to communicate with lower status people, such as children.

Conclusion: Traditional Samoan culture places great emphasis on learning by observation and so the cognitive process of language acquisition by Samoan children is significantly affected by their families' and community's cultures and by the process of learning that culture, i.e. enculturation. The way the children's caregivers use language while being observed by the children affects the way the children learn about their culture's norms. This means that child–parent communication is often 'child-to-parent-to-caregiver-to-child' so that children observe the cultural status of their parent but observe the language of their caregiver, most likely a slightly older sibling.

Within Samoan culture, people believe they have little control over their own actions. For example, they tend to say 'legs walk', 'hands write', 'mouths eat', and 'the head is dizzy', and they have no vocabulary for 'individual' or 'personality' (Ochs, 1982). This means that Samoans are less inclined to communicate with their children. Children are not treated as socially responsive beings, i.e. not cooperative, and they are not considered to be in control of themselves and their actions. The vocal utterances of Samoan children are treated as sounds rather than the beginnings of language.

The social stratification of Samoan society, as well as the emphasis Samoan society places on observational learning, determines the ways children learn and use their language (Ochs 1982). Higher status Samoans, including those caring for children, are not expected to adjust their perspective to that of lower status people. Higher status Samoans are allowed to express their opinions while lower status Samoans are expected to speak about the collective rather than themselves. The children learn their language because they are cared for by a broad range of relatives; initially their mother and then by male and female grandparents and older siblings. Often several older siblings are responsible for caring for and teaching younger children. Samoan society is status-oriented and those of high status are not involved in child-rearing.

Three consequences of Samoan culture are seen in the cognitive process of language acquisition by Samoan children: (1) decentring, (2) a lack of expansion by caregivers, and (3) elicited imitation. Decentring means the child's language learning is predominantly about other people, for example, 'Who is that?' and 'Where are they going?' Expansion occurs when a caregiver expands and so corrects a child's attempts at language, for example may say, 'That my grandfather' and the caregiver expands with, 'He is my grandfather'. Elicited imitation occurs when a caregiver urges a child to repeat or imitate the caregiver's language.

The enculturation, i.e. the process of children learning Samoan norms and expectations such as hierarchy and social status, has a direct effect on the children's cognitive process of language acquisition because the cultural expectations are fundamental to the way children are taught language.

Evaluation: The study has strong ecological validity because it was conducted in the children's home setting and over a significant time period. Both genders were included in the study and the age range of the children was appropriate for the study of language acquisition. There were, however, just a small number of participants and they were all of the same culture, so caution is required in generalizing the study's findings.

15.2 Acculturation

Content focus

Explain how people may change as a result of contact with other cultures in order to assimilate with a new culture.

Acculturation is the process people go through as they adapt to a new culture. It is the socialization process by which outsiders adopt the values of their new culture, affecting a person's attitudes, identity, and behaviour.

Acculturation occurs at many levels, including when:

- people move to a new country to work or to seek refuge from intolerable circumstances in their home country

- people move from one workplace to another

- children start a new school

- children move into a new family situation, perhaps due to foster care or adoption

- a person marries and becomes a member of another extended family.

In each of these situations, the people enduring the acculturation process learn the accepted norms and behaviour of the group in which they have become a new member.

Sam and Berry (2010) state that Tajfel and Turner's (1979, 1986) social identity theory (SIT) explains how people define their identity within their original culture and within the culture to which they are acculturating, and therefore their national identity. SIT

Acculturation occurs at many levels and in many situations.

Do all people think about colour in the same way? Do you think all people 'like' or think positively about colours such as green, yellow, and blue? Discuss with your friends whether a person's culture affects the way they think about, or like or dislike, colours. Do you think people from cultures around the Mediterranean coast think about colours in the same way as people from Patagonia or Scandinavia or the Yukon? To what extent does this discussion reveal a person's assumptions about culture's effect on behaviour, i.e. whether people adopt a universalist or relativist perspective to studying behaviour?

explains that while people tend to identify with their ingroup, they may attempt to move out of their ingroup if the outgroup is perceived to be more successful.

Sam and Berry (2010) take a universalist approach, by assuming there are shared psychological processes in all human behaviour.

Berry et al. (2006) showed strong relationships between how young people acculturate and how well they adapt: those who applied integration strategies such as learning the host country's language and maintaining friendships or peer contacts with those in the host culture achieved the best psychological and sociocultural adaptations. The study also showed that those who had poor host country language skills and few host country relationships also had the worst adaptation outcomes (Berry et al., 2006). Those who used ethnic-group strategies developed good psychological adaptation, but relatively poor sociocultural adaptation, and those who used national-group strategies achieved relatively poor psychological adaptation and slightly negative sociocultural adaptation (Berry et al., 2006).

Key study: Berry et al. (2006)

Aim: To determine how **immigrant** youth acculturate compared to how well they adapt to their new cultures.

Procedure: A questionnaire was given to 7997 adolescents, aged 13–18 years, of whom 5366 were immigrants and 2631 were nationals living in 13 host countries. The sample included both first generation (34.7 per cent) and second generation (65.3 per cent) immigrants. The female-to-male ratio was 52:48. The questionnaire assessed the participants' acculturation attitudes, cultural identity, language proficiency, degree of contact with ethnic and national peers, family relationship values, perceived discrimination, and psychological and sociocultural adaptation.

Findings: The study revealed four acculturation profiles: (1) integration, (2) ethnic, (3) national, and (4) diffuse. 36.4% of the immigrant youth sought to acculturate by being involved with both their original culture and that of their host country; 22.5 per cent tried to acculturate, orienting toward their own culture and with limited involvement in the host country's culture; 18.7 per cent of the participants tried to acculturate by being primarily with the host country's culture; 22.4 per cent of the participants lacked a clear orientation and appeared to be marginalized and confused regarding which culture they identified with most.

The Integration group (1576 participants)	Indicated relatively high involvement and identity with both their own and host countries' cultures.
	Strongly supported integration.
	Had strong proficiency in their host country's language, with proficiency in their own language; typically used both languages.
	Maintained friendships/peer contacts with people from their own and their host groups.
	Maintained 'average' family values and felt comfortable in both their own and the host country contexts, with respect to identity, language ability and language use, peer contacts, and family values.

TOK

Consider the consequences of large groups of people simultaneously moving to another culture in another location and the effect of the two cultures merging. Recent history provides examples of large numbers of refugees moving from one country to another.

Consider the situation an immigrant family from a specific country faces when arriving into your neighbourhood. Give three reasons why they might move to your area. List ten things that the family would find familiar and ten that would be unfamiliar. How can people in the host country help newcomers adapt and assimilate?

The Ethnic group (975 participants)	Showed a strong identity with their own culture and a strong proficiency and usage in their own language as well as maintaining strong relationships with those from their own culture. Supported the separation attitude. Support for family values was high. Remained embedded in their own culture and demonstrated little involvement in their host country's culture.
The National group (810 participants)	Demonstrated a relatively strong orientation toward their new culture. Identified with their host country and demonstrated low identity with respect to their original culture. Proficient in the host country's language and used it most often. Friendships/peer contacts were mostly with people from their host country. Demonstrated relatively low support for family obligations. In general, retained little of their own culture and their original identity.
The Diffuse group (973 participants)	Reported high ability and usage of their own language, but low identity with regards to their original culture. Reported low proficiency in the language of their host country and low identity with respect to their host country. Had few peer contacts outside their own cultural group. Appeared to want to be part of the larger society but lacked the language and social skills or opportunities to make contacts.

Conclusion: Involvement and engagement in both their host country's and their ethnic cultures are associated with better adaptation for immigrant youth than a preference for either their original or their new culture alone. Integration had a positive effect on the immigrants' adaptation. Adolescents' attitude and engagement with respect to their own cultural group is more important for their psychological well-being than their sociocultural adaptation.

Evaluation: The study was conducted with a very large number of participants in 13 host countries. The study was based on self-report questionnaires that are subject to demand characteristics and a possible lack of honesty.
The host countries in the study (Australia, Canada, Finland, France, Germany, Israel, Netherlands, New Zealand, Norway, Portugal, Sweden, UK and USA) are all loosely described as Judeo-Christian. Berry et al. (2006) found that participants in the study who also identified with Judeo-Christian belief systems or with Eastern religions integrated better than those who did not. Participants from a Muslim background integrated least well although this may have been distorted by the large number of Turkish immigrants to Europe who were expected to return to Turkey and therefore were less inclined to integrate with their host country's culture.

To what extent do the circumstances prompting emigration from a country affect the extent to which an immigrant adapts and assimilates into a new culture?

To what extent does acculturation promote or overcome nationality-based stereotypes?

Try to meet someone who came into your cultural group some time ago and discuss with them the process they went through to adapt/assimilate. (This may not necessarily be an immigrant to your country.) What did they find most difficult about their acculturation process? What was not difficult? Did they have to learn a new language? How do they feel they have changed as a result of their acculturation?

The text refers to geographical mobility as a motivation for acculturation. To what extent can acculturation theory be applied to other situations, such as moving to a new sports club?

16 Research methods: sociocultural approach

Learning focus

Explain the contribution of one research method to the sociocultural approach to understanding human behaviour.

Social and cultural psychologists use both qualitative and quantitative research methods to gain an understanding of intergroup relations as well as the process of acculturation.

16.1 Quasi-experiments

A **quasi-experiment** studies variables that are inherent to the participants, for example the participants' height, handedness, nationality or ethnicity. This means the participants are not allocated by the experimenter to the **Independent variable's** (IV) different conditions. Typically, cross-cultural studies are quasi-experiments, using participants' cultures as the IV and a behaviour as the **dependent variable** (DV). Quasi-experiments tend to be conducted outside 'laboratory conditions' and so other variables are less likely to be controlled. This means the studies are difficult to replicate.

Cross-cultural studies can be used to determine whether a behaviour is unique to some cultures, i.e. culture-bound, or whether it is cross-cultural, i.e. observed in all cultures.

Yuki (2003) conducted a cross-cultural study using quasi-experiments to investigate the extent to which SIT is applicable within US and Japanese contexts, i.e. to determine whether it is a culture-bound or cross-cultural phenomenon. In this study the IV is the participants' culture (Japanese or American). The DV is the extent to which SIT applies to each context. Questionnaires were used to gather data relating to the participants' attitudes toward groups and their behaviour within groups. The study found (1) loyalty to and identification with their ingroup was greater with American participants than with Japanese participants; (2) evidence suggests that discrimination against outgroups is more pronounced in individualistic cultures; and (3) there is no evidence to support the theory that there is ingroup favouritism. Yuki (2003) concluded that SIT 'may not accurately represent group behaviours among East Asians' and therefore is not a cross-cultural phenomenon.

16.2 Correlation study using a self-report questionnaire

A correlation study focuses on variables to determine if they are co-variables, i.e. if they co-occur. Correlation means two variables occur together or are related. Berry et al. (2006) focused on the variables of acculturation strategies and the success of adaptation and assimilation to determine a correlation. The study found that acculturation strategies that included involvement and engagement with the host culture (such as high language proficiency and peer contact with those from the host culture) was a co-variable with successful adaptation and assimilation. The study

---

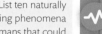

Be clear to distinguish between research methods, such as natural experiments, and data-collection techniques, such as self-report questionnaires.

List ten naturally occurring phenomena in humans that could be used as the IV in a quasi-experiment.

A correlation study focuses on variables to determine if they are co-variables, i.e. if they co-occur. The experimental method tests for a cause-effect link between co-variables.

did not show a **cause-effect** link between the variables. Further study, using the experimental method, is needed to test for a cause-effect link between variables.

Self-report questionnaires are a simple, relatively quick, and inexpensive way to collect data and are easy to replicate. Questionnaires, however, rely on participants' honesty. Participants may unwittingly give inaccurate responses out of a desire to please the researchers, or to appear to be better than they really are. The reliability of questionnaires is dependent on participants' ability to understand the questions. Berry et al. (2006) used responses to self-report questionnaires to gather data relating to acculturation despite a significant number of participants not having strong language proficiency.

16.3 Emic and etic approaches to research

Cultures can be studied by an insider or by an outsider. When research is conducted by an insider, it is considered **emic**. In emic studies, the researcher has first-hand experience, often acquired over a sustained period. The disadvantage is that the researcher lacks a professional distance, the necessary separation to be objective about the research.

When research is conducted by an outsider, it is considered **etic**. Ochs (1982) studied the enculturation process of Samoan children's language acquisition using an etic approach. The behaviour was observed by outsiders, i.e. non-Samoan researchers lived within the culture, but were of another culture. Howarth's (2002) study of teenagers living in Brixton was also etic, because the researcher was an outsider.

Malhotra et al. (1996) stated that the emic approach examines phenomena from within, investigates just one culture, and the criteria adopted are relative; while the etic approach examines phenomena from outside the system, investigates many cultures, and the criteria adopted are universal. The **universalist** approach assumes there are psychological processes shared in all human cultures, for example the language acquisition process. By contrast, the **relativist** approach assumes cultural groups' psychological processes, for example the perception of beauty and intelligence, are different, and so they cannot be compared. Yuki (2003) examined the extent to which social identity theory is cross-cultural, adopting an emic approach when studying Japanese participants and an etic approach when studying American participants.

17 Ethical considerations: sociocultural approach

Learning focus

To what extent are ethical considerations necessary in the investigation of the sociocultural approach to understanding human behaviour?

17.1 Studies involving children

A fundamental rule of most ethical systems is to do no harm. Bandura et al. (1961) was unethical because it exposed young children to aggressive behaviour and taught

When conducted by an insider, the research is emic and when studied by an outsider it is etic.

List some strengths and weaknesses of both etic and emic research into people's attitudes toward time.

The universalist approach assumes there are shared psychological processes in all human behaviour (including the acculturation process). The relativist approach assumes cultural groups' psychological processes are different and so the groups cannot be compared.

Show that ethical considerations are the right thing to do for everyone involved in research, supporting your claims with examples of good or bad practice.

A fundamental rule of most ethical systems is to do no harm.

Describe Bandura et al. (1961) to several of your friends and ask, 'Would you allow your 3 or 4-year-old son or daughter (or brother or sister) to be exposed to aggressive behaviour as was done in the study?' Ask them to give reasons for their responses.

There is an ethical obligation to use research with integrity.

If it is unethical to use children as participants is it also unethical to make use of research that uses children as participants?

Can there be fundamental, universally held ethics?

them to be physically and verbally aggressive. The study's aim was to find out why and when children display aggressive behaviour, so there was reasonable expectation that exposing children to aggressive behaviour would mean the children would mimic aggression. Of the children who were exposed to the aggressive adult model, the boys showed an average of 38.2 physically aggressive acts and the girls showed 12.7 physically aggressive acts. The study concluded that children can learn behaviour by observing an adult's behaviour. The study also concluded that boys are more likely to mimic the behaviour of men, and girls are more likely to mimic women's behaviour, and females tend to be less aggressive than males.

Children, especially very young children, cannot give informed consent because they cannot comprehend the implications of being involved in research. There is no indication that the researchers attempted to address any aggressive behaviour that the study had created in the participants by debriefing the children and by 'undoing' in some way the harm that had been done by teaching them aggressive behaviour.

There is an ethical obligation to use research with integrity. Bandura et al. (1961) made use of a relatively homogeneous and monocultural group of participants, all of a very young age, and yet the study's conclusion (that people learn by observation) has often been applied to adults from other socioeconomic groups and cultures. This is a misuse of research and therefore is unethical.

Some ethical systems may adopt an alternative to 'do no harm'. One alternative is to consider the costs and benefits of research to society. Some may feel that the harm done to a small number of children is outweighed by the benefit to many others as a result of the research, the findings of which may be used, for example, as evidence to support laws prohibiting aggressive behaviour in children's television programmes and video games.

17.2 Cross-cultural studies and stereotypes

There is a risk that conclusions relating to cultural dimensions are misinterpreted as descriptors of all people from a particular culture or nationality. This becomes a generalization about people from a particular country or ethnic group and then this becomes a stereotype. Once a person has formed stereotypes, they tend to persist because people are cognitive misers, meaning less effort is involved in allowing stereotypes to persist than to challenge and change them.

Researchers have an ethical obligation to present their results in such a way as to minimize the risk of misunderstanding and misuse. This often means simply writing the report in language that is unambiguous.

The traditional Western Samoan culture described in Ochs (1982) is likely to be different to the culture of families living in the capital city Apia and the relatively large Western Samoan communities living in New Zealand. The expression 'American culture' occurs frequently in the literature, yet even the casual observer will understand profound differences in the accepted norms and behaviour of people living in New York, New Orleans, and New Hampshire.

17.3 Cross-cultural studies and researcher effect

Researchers have an ethical obligation not to 'disturb' the culture and participants being studied. Ochs (1982) was a longitudinal observation study of children and their families in traditional Western Samoan households. The researchers were of the American-European culture, which tends to be relatively **egalitarian** and responsive to the needs of others. Western Samoan culture, in contrast, is hierarchical with higher status people remaining aloof and unresponsive to the needs of lower status people. 'If a young child begins to fret, the high status party will act in such a way as not to acknowledge these situations' (Ochs, 1982). One can imagine that researchers would find it difficult not to intervene in such a situation, to help a child in distress, but to do so would be to impose their culture onto that which they are studying, and therefore 'disturb' the subject of the research.

17.4 Unethical use of research

The Fundamental Attribution Error that people tend to overstate dispositional (internal/personal) factors and understate situational (external/environmental) factors in their successes, which had previously been assumed to apply to all people, was found by Grossmann and Varnum (2010) to apply less to Russian people than to American people. To assume that the FAE applies to people of all cultures is an unethical use of research. Students should take care when generalising the results of culture-bound studies to people from other cultures.

A CROSS - CULTURAL
OBSERVATIONAL STUDY

Dr Edmond Locard (who became known as the real-life Sherlock Holmes of France) proposed that a criminal always brings something into a crime scene and leaves with something from it. To what extent does Locard's principle add to your understanding of the effect of cross-cultural research methods? To what extent do studies like Ochs (1982) have a similar effect: taking something from the study's culture as well as leaving something from the researcher's culture behind?

To what extent are ethical considerations, such as 'do no harm', hindering our understanding of human behaviour?

18 The influence of globalization on individual behaviour (HL)

General focus

Discuss the influence of globalization on individual behaviour.

18.1 Globalization may influence culture

Learning focus

Discuss how globalization may influence behaviour.

Arnett (2002) states that the most salient psychological consequence of globalization is the effect on people's identity, i.e. how people perceive themselves with respect to the social environment in which they live. Two aspects of identity are affected by globalization: (1) because of globalization many people in the world develop a **bicultural** identity – part of their identity comes from their local or indigenous culture and another part comes from their relationship with the global culture; and (2) there are people who purposefully form themselves into self-selected cultures that are 'pure of infection' from the global culture (Arnett, 2002).

18.1.1 Bicultural identities

Young people develop a global identity that gives them a sense of belonging to a worldwide culture as well as their local identity. Books, theatre, cinema, and television have all played a significant role in developing people's global identities because they have exposed people to the rest of the world, although mostly to the dominant Western world. The internet is likely to play an even more important role in people's global identity, because it allows direct, instant, and two-way communication with other people anywhere in the world.

While most people develop a global identity that allows them to interact with people from all over the world, people still develop their local identities based on their local culture; and this is their 'default' identity (Arnett, 2002).

A bicultural identity is found among many young 'middle-class' Indians; young, Western-educated Indians. While they are active participants in the globalized world, they still generally prefer an arranged marriage and expect to care for their elderly parents, as is the Indian tradition (Verma and Saraswathi, 2002). These young, globalized people retain their traditional Indian identity while also developing a global identity.

Immigration promotes globalization (Hermans and Kempen, 1998). The identities of immigrants and, to a lesser extent, those from the host country's culture incorporate aspects of each other's culture. Berry (1997) found that people who acculturate with bicultural identity show the best psychological adaptation.

Discuss globalization with your classmates. The word is used frequently in many school subjects, but what does it mean? What causes it? Is it a good thing? Or a bad thing? How does it manifest in you and your classmates' lives?

Books, theatre, cinema, and television have all played a significant role in developing people's global identities because they have exposed people to the rest of the world, although mostly to the dominant Western world.

Create an interactive wall chart that invites passers-by to write comments on it about what they value, and why. You should begin with some examples such as, 'I value honesty because it means I can trust and rely on others', or 'I value my family and friends because . . .' After one week, replace the wall chart with a summary of the values and value statements.

People who acculturate with bicultural identity show the best psychological adaptation.

18.1.2 Self-selected cultures

Core values of the global culture are: individual/personal rights; the freedom of choice for individuals; open-mindedness to change, and tolerance of differences. These values are prevalent and dominant in the global culture because they are the generally held values of people within the cultures that power globalization, i.e. the wealthy and 'the West'.

For most people these values are appealing, but some people choose to reject them and join a culture that provides a more personalized identity, as they refuse to be one of the global crowd.

The global culture is, in general, **secular** and often the self-selected cultures of people who shun the global culture have a religious basis. For example, when some women who grew up in secular Jewish homes in the US reached adulthood they decided that the secular values their families raised them with provided an inadequate foundation for their lives and they embraced Orthodox Judaism (Arnett, 2002). Despite the strict gender roles and limitations on women, Orthodox Judaism gave the women the structure and meaning of Orthodox Jewish theology, and a sense of belonging to an enduring tradition (Arnett, 2002). Similarly, Samoans have recently revived their practice of tattooing adolescent males' bodies; traditionally, this was considered essential for achieving adult status, but now seems to be a part of an attempt to resist the loss of their indigenous culture (Arnett, 2002). The revival of interest in indigenous languages is also likely to be a consequence of people rejecting, at least in part, the global culture and the strengthening of one's local culture and therefore local culture-based identity.

18.2 The effect of the interaction of local and global influences on behaviour

Learning focus

Discuss the interaction of local and global influences on behaviour.

Arnett (2002) highlights another psychological consequence of globalization: the effect of the interaction of local and global influences on behaviour. This shows in two ways: (1) the pervasiveness of identity confusion among young people who find themselves identifying with neither their local culture nor the global culture; and (2) people's pre-adulthood discovery process regarding their identity in work and in relationships increases in duration, going beyond the adolescent period (10–18 years old) into the emerging adulthood period (18–25 years old).

Berry (1997) proposed the term 'acculturative stress' to describe the conflict between one's original culture and a new culture, and the effect they have on a person's identity. The stress is greatest when the values of the indigenous culture are incompatible with those of the global culture. This acculturative stress contributes to identity confusion, so the greater the acculturative stress the greater the identity confusion (Berry, 1997).

 To what extent do students in Aotearoa/New Zealand feel their indigenous identity is being protected from the global culture through the teaching and learning of te reo Maori (the Maori language)?

 Find and interview someone who remembers life before the internet. Interview them to determine what behaviours may have changed for this person since the internet's creation.

 The terms global and local are relative. Local, for example, can refer to family, region, country, as well as social groups.

 Can you describe two cultures with values that are compatible? And then two cultures with values that are incompatible?

18.2.1 Identity hybridisation

Having a bicultural identity means that a person adopts a local identity as well as a distinct and separate global identity. In some cases, globalization alters a person's indigenous beliefs and values to the extent that the local and global cultures are blended, generating a hybrid identity (Arnett, 2002). As globalization causes local cultures to develop, most people's identities also adapt to either become a bicultural or a hybrid identity, which allows them to live in their indigenous culture as well as engage with their global culture (Arnett, 2002).

A hybrid identity is an identity that forms on the basis of the local and global culture.

18.2.2 Identity confusion

Some people, however, experience identity confusion because they lose contact with their indigenous culture but are also unable or unwilling to engage with the global culture. Berry (1997) identified marginalization: an acculturation pattern in which people have little interest or an inability to maintain their indigenous culture, but also reject the global culture.

Globalization seems to have the greatest effect on young people's identity. Where a child lives is now less important than it was in the past, with respect to what he or she understands of the world, because of the extent to which young people learn the global culture through television, cinema, and the internet (Arnett, 2002).

Globalization leads to culture shedding, as the global culture affects indigenous cultures. For example, traditionally paternal or patriarchal cultures that are exposed to 'Western' family structures are becoming more egalitarian as a consequence of exposure to the global culture through television, cinema, and the internet (Nsamenang, 2002).

The people most likely to suffer identity confusion because of globalization are those living in cultures that have the greatest cultural distance between them and the global culture. Some cultures have experienced an increase in social problems, especially in young people, likely to be due to identity confusion arising from globalization. Using interviews with young people, supported by data from police and social workers, Delafosse et al. (1993) studied changes in problems among young people aged 16–20 years in Côte d'Ivoire from 1980 to 1991 and found 'an increase over this period in suicide, drug abuse, armed aggression, and male and female prostitution'. Researchers attributed these behaviours to globalization.

18.2.3 Postponed adulthood

Another worldwide psychological consequence of globalization is the timing of the transition into adulthood, with more young people choosing to postpone work, marriage, and parenthood. This is occurring in every part of the world because of a global trend of people spending more time in education, meaning the transition into adulthood roles is delayed (Arnett, 2000). As traditional family structures change through exposure to the global culture on television, cinema, books, magazines, and the internet, all of which are dominated by 'Western values', young people tend to take more control over their lives and, although not universal, the median ages for the transition to adulthood is rising rapidly in all countries (Arnett, 2000).

This postponed adulthood is often associated with self-focused exploration and investigation and is possible only if the person's socioeconomic circumstances are such that their labour is not needed, i.e. relatively well-off young people are able to delay their entry to adulthood because they or their families can afford it.

Economic growth and development gives young people the luxury to choose a career and an adulthood they believe fits their identity, as above. In some regions however, young people's expectations, based on the global culture, are unrealistic for their local situation and the number of university graduates, and the specialisms of their education are often such that they are unable to find work in their chosen field and so many find themselves unemployed, resulting in identity stress (Nsamenang, 2002).

In most developing countries, this postponed adulthood only exists for the relatively rich; the poor, typically those with little or no ability to engage with the world culture, still begin adulthood roles (work, marriage and parenthood) at a relatively young age, as above.

18.3 Methods used to study the influence of globalization on behaviour

Learning focus

To what extent can research methods explain the influence of globalization on behaviour?

As globalization is a process over time, a longitudinal study is a useful research method to study the influence of globalization on behaviour. A longitudinal study involves repeated observations of the same people and a specific behaviour over long periods of time and so they can show trends. Examples of longitudinal studies include looking at methods of language acquisition or identity formation.

Longitudinal studies are observational, so they may show correlations, but they cannot reach cause-effect conclusions. Longitudinal studies are usually done in the participants' environment, so they usually have high ecological validity, but can be expensive and take a long time to complete. Ochs (1982) was a longitudinal observation study of children and their families in traditional Western Samoan households.

A cross-cultural study is typically a quasi-experiment in which the independent variable (IV) is the participants' culture and the dependent variable (DV) is the behaviour being studied, for example identity formation. Chen et al. (2008) used two cultural groups (Mainland Chinese and domestic workers from the Philippines) as their study's IV to examine the impact of different bicultural identities and bilingualism on the psychological adjustment of the two groups living Hong Kong. A common fault with cross-cultural studies is that people of the same nationality are assumed to be of the same culture.

Economic growth and development gives young people the luxury to choose a career and an adulthood they believe fits their identity.

There are weaknesses to all research methods, but these do not necessarily make a study's conclusions wrong or unusable.

A longitudinal study involves repeated observations of the same people and a specific behaviour.

A cross-cultural study is typically a quasi-experiment in which the IV is the participants' culture and the DV is the behaviour being studied.

Key study: Chen et al. (2008)

Aim: To examine the impact of different bicultural identities and bilingualism on the psychological adjustment of two groups living in Hong Kong.

Procedure: The participants completed questionnaires presented in their own language.

Findings: (1) Psychological acculturation factors are significant to the adaptation of migrants; (2) objective environmental factors, e.g. income, housing, work conditions, and language proficiency are also significant, and (3) the strength of first- and second-culture identification, and proficiency in the host language are associated with psychological well-being.

Conclusion: (1) Stress associated with globalization with respect to language proficiency, employment, and intercultural relations have a negative effect on psychological adjustment. For example, poor second-language skills are likely to have a negative effect on work performance; and (2) acculturative stress, e.g. discrimination, language and interpersonal difficulties, and feelings of isolation, are negatively associated with well-being.

Evaluation: The study involved a significant number of participants from clearly different groups and used self-report questionnaires in the participants' own languages with support to complete the questionnaires. This means that the data has a high degree of reliability. The main limitation of the study is that it showed only correlational results and so no conclusions about cause-and-effect directionality between bicultural identity, bilingualism, and well-being can be made.

To what extent do cross-cultural studies perpetuate nationality or cultural stereotypes?

EE

Activity

Find all of the new words or expressions from this chapter and write them into a document with their definitions and explanations next to them. Be creative and use diagrams or boxes to help make your personal glossary unique and effective.

Abnormal psychology

Abnormal psychology focuses on the diagnosis, explanation, and treatment of abnormal behaviour within a **clinical** context. A clinical context refers to a professionally recognized process involving healthcare professionals (clinicians) who are qualified to diagnose and treat abnormal behaviour. Clinical psychology is the applied field of psychology that seeks to assess, understand, and treat abnormal psychological conditions.

The term 'abnormal' is controversial and is rarely used by clinical psychologists who treat people with **disorders**. Terms such as 'dysfunctional', '**maladaptive**', 'psychopathy', and 'mental illness' are often used interchangeably in academia and by mental healthcare professionals. However, for reasons of consistency, the term 'abnormal' will be used as much as possible in the following chapter.

The three topics for this option are:

- factors influencing diagnosis
- etiology of abnormal psychology
- treatment of disorders.

Each of these topics should draw on what has been learned in the biological, cognitive and sociocultural approaches to behaviour where appropriate. In addition, you should have the opportunity to explore the different approaches taken in research and should be made aware of the ethical considerations and the sensitivity required in a discussion of this subject. There is no clear definition of what constitutes normal behaviour and, by the same token, what constitutes abnormal behaviour. Concepts of normal and abnormal change over time and are influenced by such factors as clinical **biases**, social **norms**, gender, culture and **socioeconomic** status. This is an important consideration in diagnosis and in decisions on the treatment of disorders as well as when considering the factors that cause abnormal behaviour.

19 Factors influencing diagnosis

Topic focus

Discuss factors influencing the diagnosis of abnormality.

19.1 Defining abnormality

Content focus

Discuss definitions of abnormality.

How and by whom should notions of abnormality and normality be defined and implemented? To what extent should relativist notions regarding abnormality and normality be incorporated into academic discourses in multicultural societies? To what extent are definitive notions of abnormality useful or realistic?

The concept of normality assumes that there is a most appropriate behaviour that is healthy. The concept of abnormality assumes that deviation from what is normal is a sign of problems. Therefore, normality/abnormality is a sliding scale of nuanced gradation. The question is always: At what degree of gradation does normal become abnormal and vice versa?

The word 'normal' usually refers to conformity to standard or regular patterns of behaviour. The concept of abnormality is essentially a label applied to behaviour that does not conform. Unfortunately, this explanation is not very precise, and it remains difficult for mental health professionals to agree on who is abnormal enough to require or deserve treatment.

In order to diagnose someone as being 'abnormal', a healthcare professional (such as a psychiatrist) would usually have undertaken:

- a clinical interview with the patient to gain a picture of their lifestyle, habits, personal history, and to see if the patient can shed any light on their predicament

- careful observation of the patient's behaviour, mood states, etc. over a period of time

- a thorough review of the patient's medical records and any other formal literature such as criminal records, housing applications etc.

- a series of **psychometric** tests to assess the patient's general level of psychological functioning.

There are two main approaches to defining abnormality: a biological approach and a psychological approach.

19.1.1 Biological approach

A biological approach broadly assumes abnormal behaviour can be attributed to medical or physical causes. Such an approach can be seen as an attempt to be **objective** about human thoughts, feelings and behaviour while standardizing diagnosis and treatment.

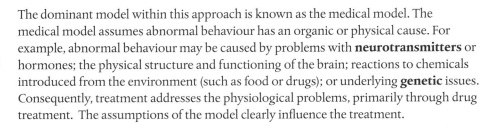

A biological approach to abnormality broadly assumes abnormal behaviour can be attributed to medical or physical causes. Such an approach can be seen as an attempt to be objective about human thoughts, feelings, and behaviour while standardizing diagnosis and treatment.

The dominant model within this approach is known as the medical model. The medical model assumes abnormal behaviour has an organic or physical cause. For example, abnormal behaviour may be caused by problems with **neurotransmitters** or hormones; the physical structure and functioning of the brain; reactions to chemicals introduced from the environment (such as food or drugs); or underlying **genetic** issues. Consequently, treatment addresses the physiological problems, primarily through drug treatment. The assumptions of the model clearly influence the treatment.

Furthermore, the medical model assumes different illnesses can be grouped together and then identified as **syndromes**. These groupings allow clinicians to apply a standardized **diagnostic** criteria to make a 'diagnosis' that has some degree of **reliability** and **validity**. In practice, this means there is a good chance that other clinicians will agree with their diagnosis (reliability) and they are 'correct' in assuming a specific cause has led to a specific behaviour (validity).

There are several ethical concerns about the use of the medical model to define abnormal behaviour. This model argues that it is better to regard someone suffering from a mental disorder as sick rather than morally defective because responsibility is removed from the patient. Today, psychiatrists diagnose using a classification system that is supposed to be objective. The traditional medical model in psychiatry is now assumed to be **reductionist**, and most psychiatrists use a **biopsychosocial** approach to diagnosis and treatment. However, this does not prevent a clinical diagnosis resulting in the patient being labelled as different, or 'not normal'.

19.1.2 Psychological approach

A psychological approach broadly assumes abnormal behaviour can be attributed to faulty psychological processes or a failure to adapt to sociocultural processes.

A psychological approach broadly assumes abnormal behaviour can be attributed to faulty psychological processes or a failure to adapt to **sociocultural** processes. Such an approach can be seen as an attempt to acknowledge the impact of **cognition** and sociocultural factors in causing people to think, feel, and behave 'abnormally'. However, it also makes diagnosis and treatment less standardized.

A psychological approach seeks to understand abnormality as a process between the individual and society rather than as an 'illness' that needs to be 'treated'. One of the most radical critics of the concept of mental illness was the US psychiatrist Thomas Szasz. In *The Myth of Mental Illness* (1962), he argued that while some **neurophysiological** disorders were diseases of the brain, most of the so-called 'mental disorders' should be considered as problems in living. By saying this, Szasz went against the idea of organic **pathology** in psychological disorders and placed the focus on sociocultural processes and the problem some people have in adapting to them.

In Szasz's view, even though people behave strangely and this is classified as mental illness by psychiatrists, such behaviours are not a symptom of an underlying brain disease. Consequently, the concept of mental illness is not used correctly by psychiatrists. According to Frude (1998) there are relatively few psychological disorders that can be associated with identifiable organic pathology.

It should be noted that Szasz's argument fails to address the misery and suffering of real people with real disorders. A failure to find an organic cause for behaviour does not automatically mean the illness is socially constructed; it may simply mean the technology is not advanced enough to pinpoint an organic cause. Szasz's position can be seen as a useful academic debating point, but caution should be used when applying it to real-world situations and people.

Rosenhan and Seligman (1984) suggested that there are seven criteria that could be used to decide whether a person or a behaviour is normal or not.

- Suffering – does the person experience distress and discomfort?

- Maladaptiveness – does the person engage in behaviours that make life difficult for him or her rather than being helpful?

- Irrationality – is the person incomprehensible or unable to communicate in a reasonable manner?

- Unpredictability – does the person act in ways that are unexpected by himself or herself or by other people?

- Vividness and unconventionality – does the person experience things that are different from most people?

- Observer discomfort – is the person acting in a way that is difficult to watch or that makes other people embarrassed? There is a clear violation of social norms.

- Violation of moral or ideal standards – does the person habitually break the accepted ethical and moral standards of their culture?

These criteria demonstrate the fine line between defining abnormality in ways that focus on distress to the individual, and defining it in terms of what is or is not acceptable to society. The first four deal with how the person is living life; the fifth represents a social judgement because it deals with what is seen as conventional or not; and the remaining criteria clearly represent social norms. The danger of social judgements is that they often fail to consider diversity in how people live their lives. For example, there is an increasing awareness of how psychiatric diagnosis of ethnic minorities has been misapplied because doctors do not understand the cultural norms of the groups people come from.

19.2 Strengths and limitations of definitions

Content focus

Discuss definitions of abnormality.

Within the two broad paradigms of a biological approach or a psychological approach it is worth considering the following factors when discussing definitions of abnormality and normality.

19.2.1 Statistical abnormality

Abnormality can be measured using a statistical approach. If a behaviour is statistically rare then it can be considered abnormal. This is based on the assumption that human characteristics that are open to being measured tend to be **normally distributed**,

Abnormality can be measured using a statistical approach. If a behaviour is statistically rare then it can be considered abnormal.

which means the distribution from a sample of people tends to fall within a bell-shaped curve.

By convention, we tend to agree that any observations that occur outside the range of three **standard deviations** from the mean (above or below) are abnormal. As can be seen in Figure 19.1, just 0.5 per cent of people exhibit an abnormally high level of shyness and 0.5 per cent exhibit an abnormally low level of shyness.

This is frequently referred to as a bell curve in statistical descriptions of behaviour, although its more formal name is a normal distribution curve. Most, although not all, naturally occurring phenomena are distributed in this pattern.

In a bell curve, the data occurring nearest the mean can be described as normal or typical. Sixty-eight per cent of the data occurs in the range of one standard deviation above and below the mean. Ninety-five per cent of the data occurs within two standard deviations above and below the mean. The abnormal data is the very small percentage that falls outside the range of three standard deviations above and below the mean.

The normal distribution curve is a useful tool for showing the distribution of **quantitative** data such as height, weight, and reaction times. However, it is less useful for describing behaviours such as shyness or depression. There are many behaviours, like shyness, that occur in a low percentage of a population but do not warrant professional intervention. There are also behaviours that are statistically common that do warrant professional intervention (such as depression). The statistical concept of abnormal, therefore, should not be confused with the clinical concept of abnormal.

Figure 19.1 The normal distribution curve for shyness

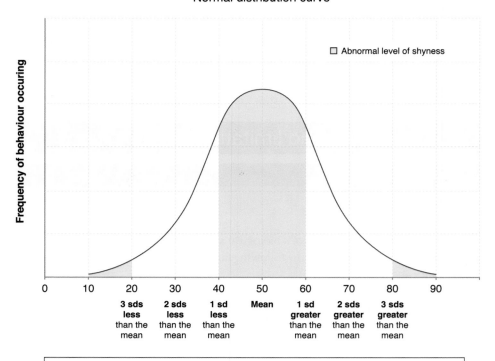

SHYNESS RATING 0–100
Normal distribution curve

☐ Abnormal level of shyness

Frequency of behaviour occuring

| 0 | 10 | 20 | 30 | 40 | 50 | 60 | 70 | 80 | 90 |

| | | 3 sds less than the mean | 2 sds less than the mean | 1 sd less than the mean | Mean | 1 sd greater than the mean | 2 sds greater than the mean | 3 sds greater than the mean | |

99% of behaviour falls within the range of the 3 standard deviations greater than the mean and 3 standard deviations below the mean. Abnormal behaviour is the 0.5% of behaviour above the (mean +3 sds) and below the (mean -3sds) boundaries.

19.2.2 Individual considerations

An individual-centric view of abnormality may consider the levels of distress an individual endures as part of the assessment. Such a **subjective** view would focus on feelings of anxiety, unhappiness, or distress. This is often enough to seek help.

However, the subjective experience of distress is not always a reliable indicator of serious psychiatric problems, since patients with **schizophrenia** or people who wish harm on others as a result of their abnormal feelings may be indifferent or unaware of their condition.

In addition, feelings and subjective experiences are deeply personal and can be difficult to report to healthcare professionals if they are strangers. However, personal insight can skew perception of what is normal.

Taylor and Brown (1988), wanted to see if 'normal' people have more of an accurate perception of themselves than people with a psychological disorder. They conducted a literature review from studies about the attitudes and beliefs of people with a psychological disorder. 'Normal' people were found to have an unrealistically positive view of themselves. For example, it is typical in happiness research that 60 per cent of people report that they are happier than average. 'Normal' people describe themselves using more positive words than other people use when they describe them. Taylor and Brown concluded that 'normal' people often use positive words to protect self-esteem, and therefore to be normal means to overemphasize positive traits. Consequently, people with low **self-esteem** and moderate depression are more likely to be aware of their negative traits.

19.2.3 Political and cultural considerations

Politics and culture are often intertwined and can influence what is considered normal and what is considered abnormal. For example, in the former Soviet Union political dissidents were diagnosed as schizophrenic, implying that they were not responsible for their deviant political beliefs. In the UK during the last century, women who were pregnant but not married could be admitted to an asylum because sex outside marriage was considered 'deviant'. Within 100 years, homosexuality has gone from being seen as a religious sin, a criminal act, and a treatable disease, to being accepted as a normal part of the human condition supported by empirical and **evolutionary** theories. In Germany, **paedophilia** is explicitly viewed as a treatable condition whereby the patient or 'sufferer' can access state-funded help through healthcare professionals. In the UK and USA, people who are sexually attracted to children receive zero or very little state-funded help unless they have committed a crime. They are often branded as 'wicked' and punished severely after acting on their desires. A German who has sexual feelings around children can seek help through their doctor.

Consequently, the help someone may receive for any given condition is contingent on the political or cultural view of what is abnormal and how it should be treated. In the UK and USA, many would not seek help through healthcare professionals for fear of being branded a criminal and receiving a legal rather than a medical reaction.

19.2.4 Concluding comments

The two broad approaches of biology and psychology should not be seen in isolation. There are some elements of abnormality that can be seen as socially constructed and

An individual-centric view of abnormality may consider the levels of distress an individual endures as part of the assessment. Such a subjective view would focus on feelings of anxiety, unhappiness, or distress.

Politics and culture often influence what is considered abnormal. They project constructions of what is considered normal and what is considered abnormal.

127

clinicians need to be cautious about applying standardized expectations to people from varied cultural backgrounds.

However, the medical model has noble aims, as it is an attempt to apply rigorous, reliable, and definitive criteria to a multifaceted subject which, although it may have some degrees of cultural and personal relativity, also has many constants and universals that can be grouped together for diagnosis and treatment purposes to help people who are genuinely suffering.

A clinician who is closely wedded to the basic assumptions of the medical model would also consider the sociocultural environment and the thought processes of the patient, while a clinician who is closely wedded to a psychological approach would also consider biological causes and possible medical treatments.

For example, the *Diagnostic and Statistical Manual of Mental Disorders* (DSM), a handbook used by psychiatrists in the US to identify and classify symptoms of psychiatric disorders, clearly states any diagnosis should be based on the person's clinical and medical conditions, a consideration of psychosocial **stressors** (unemployment, number of children, relationship status) and the extent to which a person's mental state interferes with his or her daily life. Whether they function on a daily basis is a key question in diagnosis and for eventual treatment.

19.3 Classification systems

Content focus

Contrast two diagnostic systems for the classification of mental illness.

Psychiatric disease constructs can be seen as representative of sociocultural constructs that represent sociocultural realities in their culture of origin. Different countries have different systems and these can be used to analyse sociocultural realities in these areas. For example, in the US, the DSM, published by the American Psychiatric Association, could be seen as an entire **schema** that lists every possible mental condition as a disease to allow for remuneration to practitioners from private medical insurance and government programmes. This particular social use may be irrelevant to other societies where healthcare is financed differently (Lee, 2001).

It could be argued that classification systems themselves are a direct consequence of the medical model. The medical model assumes different illnesses can be grouped together by characteristics they have in common. These are then identified as syndromes. Such groupings allow clinicians to apply standardized diagnostic criteria to make a 'diagnosis' that has some degree of reliability and validity. To achieve this, classification systems are compiled and shared. They not only act as a classification system but also as a diagnostic tool that is a universal authority for clinical diagnoses that professionals can use.

A key aim of any classification system is for a disorder to be described in terms that would lead clinicians referring to the system to agree with the diagnosis it suggests. Furthermore, classification systems are open to review and allow for change over time. For example, modern diagnosis is often able to take advantage of medical

EE

Choose a disorder (for example, gender dysphoria) and ask: To what extent can it be objectively measured as an abnormal behaviour within current diagnostic approaches?

TOK

To what extent does the classification of human behaviour help or hinder knowledge production in abnormal psychology?

Psychiatric disease constructs can be seen as representative of sociocultural constructs that represent notions of abnormality in their culture of origin.

breakthroughs such as advances in brain-imaging technology, which adds to our understanding of changes in brain structure or functioning.

The classification systems discussed below are the US-centric DSM, the more global International Classification of Diseases (ICD) and the Chinese-originated Chinese Classification of Mental Disorders (CCMD).

19.3.1 *The Diagnostic and Statistical Manual of Mental Disorders* (DSM)

This publication by the American Psychiatric Association was first published in 1952 and has been revised several times; it is now in its revised fifth edition. The DSM-5 was published on 18 May 2013, superseding the DSM-IV-TR, which was published in 2000. Each revision is intended to make the diagnosis of mental disorders a more reliable process and a more valid reflection of general wisdom at the time of each edition. Disorders are added and removed as time goes on. Revisions are part of the process to ensure the classification system reflects changing sociocultural and political norms and values. For example, homosexuality was removed from the DSM as a disorder in 1980, and alterations have been made to the class of eating disorders several times since then.

The DSM groups disorders into categories and then offers specific guidance to psychiatrists by listing the symptoms required for a diagnosis to be given. A key advantage of the DSM system is its requirement that a diagnosing clinician should consider the individual under investigation not only in terms of whether they qualify for diagnosis, but also whether they have medical conditions, psychosocial and environmental problems, and how well they function generally. This approach has encouraged psychiatrists using the system to take a more **holistic** approach to understanding the person who has presented with problems. This reflects a widely held belief among mental health practitioners today that the origin of each person's problems should be analysed according to a biopsychosocial framework.

A key advantage of the DSM system is the requirement that the diagnosing clinician should consider the individual under investigation not only in terms of whether they qualify for diagnosis, but also whether they have medical conditions, psychosocial and environmental problems, and how well they function generally.

There were a number of changes made between DSM-IV and DSM-5. For example, binge-eating disorder has been moved from an appendix into a proper diagnosis of its own. A **gender dysphoria** category for children, separate to adults and adolescents, has been created, while the original label of 'gender identity disorder' was changed. The name change was partly made because of stigmatization associated with the word 'disorder'. Furthermore, a specific diagnosis for gender issues in children has been created, which reflects the assumption that children are less able to have insight into what they are experiencing and a lesser ability to express their experiences.

There are some key criticisms of DSM-5. For example, DSM-5 task-force members were asked to sign a non-disclosure agreement that meant the process of revision was conducted in relative secrecy. This has led to suspicion that the DSM-5 task force was being unduly influenced by the pharmaceutical industry. It was noted that 69 per cent of the members of the task force reported having ties to the pharmaceutical industry. However, 57 per cent of members of the DSM-IV task force also reported having ties to the pharmaceutical industry (Cosgrove and Drimsky, 2012).

It should also be noted that public input was solicited and members of the public could sign up at the DSM-5 website to comment on proposals as the DSM-5 team worked through the process, allowing a new level of apparent transparency that was made possible by the internet.

The DSM-5 has made much-needed reforms, including adding a structured programme for assessing cultural influence on mental illness and dropping the category of culture-bound syndrome, although the underlying logic of DSM-5 is still prone to see Western psychology as the human norm (Murphy, 2015). For example, Murphy (2015) suggests that the DSM-5 does not allow for the possibility that Westerners may be the ones who suffer from culture-bound syndromes and cites that depression in the West is unlike other forms of depression from different cultures.

19.3.2 *The International Classification of Diseases*

The ICD is now in its tenth edition (ICD-10) and is more commonly used internationally than the DSM (Mezzich, 2002). It was originally intended by the World Health Organization (WHO) to be a means of standardizing the recording of cause of death. WHO seeks a scientific basis for mental health criteria to ensure comparability and consistency across scenarios, although ICD-10 focuses more on covering a wide range of diseases and conditions for the sake of classification rather than diagnosis.

There is a great deal of overlap between the ICD classifications and DSM, and with each revision, differences between the ICD and the DSM are becoming fewer. It can be noted ICD-10 is now relatively old compared to the DSM-5. Work began on ICD-10 in 1983 but was completed in 1992.

ICD-10 is widely used around the world by both developed and developing countries. A key strength of the ICD system is an assumption that it will be used in different settings. As such, it provides different sets of diagnostic criteria for each disorder. One list is used by the diagnostician and allows for some latitude and for the practitioner's exercise of judgement; another is more precise and intended to be used by scholars and researchers in an academic environment; a third is a simplified classification and is applicable to primary-care settings as it contains only broad categories (e.g. dementia, eating disorder, psychotic disorder, and so on) to help clinicians who are on the front line of medicine.

There are some key criticisms of ICD-10. For example, the overly long and often tediously formulated text has caused problems in interpretation but more importantly, has caused problems in translation. For a document intended for international use, the lack of simplistic language has meant different meanings have resulted from the different interpretations (Mombour et al., 1990).

The coding has also been seen as too complex and difficult to use. The argument is that the sheer amount of codes for each illness (which run into the tens of thousands) make the system unwieldly and unworkable. This criticism has been countered by the suggestion that individual clinicians are not expected to know, or work with, the entire classification system and would only be expected to know and understand codes within their specialty (Averill and Butler, 2013). Furthermore, Averill and Butler point out there are electronic aids that allow for quick and easy searching (including an ICD-10 iPhone® app) that should not pose a problem for experienced clinicians.

ICD-10 is widely used around the world, both by developed and developing countries. A key strength of the ICD system is an assumption it will be used in different settings. It provides different sets of diagnostic criteria for each disorder.

19.3.3 *The Chinese Classification of Mental Disorders*

This system has not yet **generalized** far outside Chinese territory. It is currently in its third edition (CCMD-3, published in 2001). It was not intended to capture the full range of human diagnoses but was instead intended to maintain a focus on issues that are of interest in Chinese culture. Therefore, it is characterized by its simplicity, stability, the inclusion of culture-distinctive categories, and the exclusion of certain Western diagnostic categories. For this reason, some disorders identified in the ICD-10 and DSM-5 that are not common in China are left out, and others that are included appear to be culture-bound disorders found only within Chinese culture. Examples include koro – a kind of anxiety or depression – and mental disorder due to Qigong – a form of meditative exercise – which is also now included in the DSM. **Ego-dystonic** homosexuality is also included in the CCMD; this disorder is characterized by homosexual urges that are unwanted.

The CCMD was also written partly in response to the complexity of the language inherent within the ICD-10 system, which caused problems when translated into Chinese. A key criticism of the CCMD is that it is used as a tool to politicize psychiatry. Such a tactic was borrowed from the Soviet Union and is used to detain, imprison, and forcibly medicate dissidents and activists who show signs of political criticism (Lubman, 2016). For example, the creation of psychiatric hospitals (called Ankangs or 'peace and health' institutions) that are actually administered by the police. These institutions are overseen by China's Ministry of Public Security rather than a health ministry. Therefore, while the classification system itself may provide cultural insight into China, the politicization of psychiatry within China makes comparison and academic evaluation of the CCMD difficult, if not impossible.

 The CCMD was not intended to capture the full range of human diagnoses but was instead intended to maintain a focus on issues that are of interest in Chinese culture.

19.4 The role of clinical bias in diagnosis

Content focus

Discuss the role of clinical bias in diagnosis.

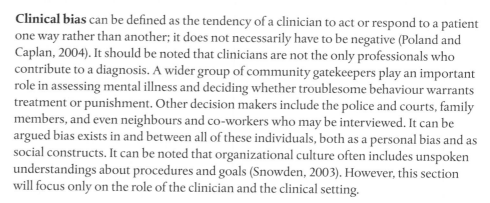

Clinical bias can be defined as the tendency of a clinician to act or respond to a patient one way rather than another; it does not necessarily have to be negative.

Clinical bias can be defined as the tendency of a clinician to act or respond to a patient one way rather than another; it does not necessarily have to be negative (Poland and Caplan, 2004). It should be noted that clinicians are not the only professionals who contribute to a diagnosis. A wider group of community gatekeepers play an important role in assessing mental illness and deciding whether troublesome behaviour warrants treatment or punishment. Other decision makers include the police and courts, family members, and even neighbours and co-workers who may be interviewed. It can be argued bias exists in and between all of these individuals, both as a personal bias and as social constructs. It can be noted that organizational culture often includes unspoken understandings about procedures and goals (Snowden, 2003). However, this section will focus only on the role of the clinician and the clinical setting.

According to Poland and Caplan (2004), clinicians can manifest the following biases:

- focusing on certain kinds of information rather than others

- uncritically interpreting information acquired in the artificial context of a clinic

- making a decision about the normality or pathology of a patient on the basis of little information and little time spent with the patient

- making a decision about the appropriateness of prescribing medication on the basis of very limited information

- more readily taking at face value what male patients say rather than what female patients say

- more readily judging a patient mentally ill if the patient is a woman and/or member of a racialized group and/or poor

- more readily judging women than men to be overly emotional

- more readily assuming that women need protection from men

- more readily prescribing mood-altering medication for women than for men

- more readily offering men the option to take medication than women

- more readily assuming that women need more ongoing monitoring and treatment than men

- tending to assign a higher status role to men, such as making male patients part of the decision making process.

19.4.1 Potential reasons for clinical bias

Poland and Caplan (2004) outline potential reasons why clinical biases occur in diagnosis.

The clinician's individual psychology

The process of trying to understand the nature of people's anguish, fears, and depression is complex, while also being potentially personal for the clinician. There are usually many unknowns, and the prospect of settling on a tidy diagnosis will be more attractive for some clinicians than others. In addition, professional abilities vary widely among clinicians and these can be sources of bias, including perspective-taking; critical self-reflection; tolerance for informational complexity, ambiguity, and uncertainty; tolerance for stress and fear; and tolerance for difference.

Professional identity and clinical practice

Bias can come from professional terminology, such as the labels used for diagnostic categories; accepted beliefs, theories, and models of human functioning and pathology; and questions believed to be of primary importance (e.g. What mental disorder does a person have? Were they abused?), which can lead to assumptions that might not be present if different questions were asked.

In addition, clinicians may engage in defensive clinical practices, designed to avoid lawsuits or other legal and professional consequences, that are ultimately harmful to the patient. For example, to reduce the potential of damage to their reputations or loss of their jobs some therapists will avoid any deviations from usual practices in diagnosis and stick to rudimentary and professionally accepted approaches. There is also pressure from insurance companies in the USA, who will only pay for treatment if the client/patient has an accepted label of mental illness.

Context and labelling

Caetano (1973) was able to demonstrate the power of labelling and context on diagnosis. In an ambiguous situation of a diagnostic interview, any suggestion that the subject is or has been mentally ill has a powerful influence on any decision and makes it more likely that they will be labelled as mentally ill. This not only has a self-fulling prophecy on the part of the patient (I have been labelled mentally ill so I should act mentally ill), but it also has an element of **confirmation bias** on the part of the clinician (this person is in a clinician's room therefore there must be something wrong with them).

Key study: Caetano (1973)

Aim: To investigate the influence of 'labelling' on diagnosis.

Procedure: A male psychiatrist was filmed carrying out separate, standardized interviews with either a paid university student or with a hospitalized mental patient. Two groups of people were shown these interviews: a group of 77 psychology students and a group of 36 psychiatrists attending a meeting. They were asked to diagnose the interviewees and rate their degree of mental illness. Within each sample of viewers, there was random assignment to two different groups, each of which received different information about the interviewees: either that both were volunteers who were paid to participate, or that both were patients in a state mental hospital.

Findings: The psychiatrists with clinical experience were more likely to be persuaded by the information given. For example, they were more likely to label the participants mentally ill if they were described as patients or not mentally ill if they were described as volunteers.

Conclusion: This study demonstrates **labelling theory**: the theory that the behaviour of the person being diagnosed is not the most important component of diagnosis and, in the ambiguous situation of a diagnostic interview, any suggestion that the subject is or has been mentally ill will be a powerful influence on any decision.

Evaluation: The manipulation of the **independent variable** (the description of the interviewees) means a **cause-effect relationship** can be established. However, the age of the study means the findings need to be treated with caution for contemporary situations.

19.4.2 Perceived group identity

The following section focuses on the role of perceived group membership as an example of clinical bias in diagnosis. Clinicians can make unwarranted judgements about people on the basis of perceived group identity (such as gender or ethnicity). The clinician bases their views of a patient on a perception of them as a member of a single human category, ignoring other category memberships and other personal attributes

(Fiske, 2002). In addition, biased views about this category can be held knowingly or unknowingly and can result in action or a failure to act (Snowden, 2003). The second section will discuss potential causes of these biases.

Gender bias

Clinical biases in diagnosis can arise when clinicians make unwarranted judgements about people on the basis of their gender identity. The clinician bases their views of a patient on the fact that they perceive them to be a member of the single human category of male or female. They ignore other category memberships and other personal attributes. It should be noted, taking gender into account does not in itself constitute bias as this may be highly relevant to the patient and their illness. It can be argued that to ignore gender-related issues with diagnosis represents a form of bias in itself. Furthermore, it should not be assumed the higher rate of a disorder within one gender represents a clinical bias toward or against the gender in question.

The gender imbalance may reflect social roles and expectations, specific biological and reproductive differences, higher rates of victimization and poverty, and the under-diagnosis of the disorder in the other gender. In addition, given the biological differences and sociocultural expectations associated with being male or female, it would be odd to expect a normal and symmetrical distribution of diagnoses across the genders.

For example, women are more likely to be diagnosed with depression and the stability of this trend across cultures suggests a biological **causative** factor. Therefore, other biological factors should also be taken into account, such as diet, exercise, and medication, all of which are influenced by sociocultural factors. In addition, given that women are more likely to suffer from depression, this can lead to a feminization of the illness (Norman, 2004) within sociocultural constructs, thereby prompting fewer men to identify as being depressed and seek professional help. Therefore, complex constructs interact before the patient has reached the point of clinical diagnosis.

Clinicians base their diagnosis on their professional experiences. These experiences can take the form of a **sampling bias**, whereby the over-representation of one gender influences the informal findings of the clinician. For example, if more women seek help with symptoms of depression, then over time, a clinician may begin to see the illness through a female paradigm, rendering it potentially more likely they will over-diagnose women in the future and under-diagnose men.

Caution should be used when assuming **gender bias** in diagnosis. Clinicians are aware of the debates and potential for biases around these issues and professionalism, open-mindedness, and compassion should always be assumed. It might also be assumed that gender bias can be overestimated as a factor influencing diagnosis as researchers become more aware of these issues. For example, Woodward et al. (2009) used a sample of volunteers from a group of 119 randomly selected psychologists in New York State in a mail survey. They provided a primary diagnosis and ruled out diagnoses for a potential patient in the form of a vignette that had either a male or female patient. The primary diagnosis suggested **borderline personality disorder** (BPD) and **post-traumatic stress disorder** (PTSD). Despite a large sample and a standardized presentation of the patient there was no evidence that any of the 119 psychologists showed a gender bias in their diagnoses.

Clinical biases in diagnosis can arise when clinicians make unwarranted judgements about people on the basis of their gender identity. The clinician bases their views of a patient on a perception of them as a member of the single human category.

What is the role of objectivity in measuring notions of abnormality if diagnosis is possibly the product of a personal dynamic between clinician and patient?

Ethnicity bias

Clinical biases in diagnosis can arise when clinicians make unwarranted judgements about people on the basis of their ethnic identity. The clinician bases their views of a patient on the perception that they are a member of the single human ethnic category and they ignore other category memberships and other personal attributes. As noted with gender bias, taking account of ethnic differences does not in itself constitute bias as these may be highly relevant to the patient and their illness. It can be argued that to ignore ethnicity-related issues with diagnosis represents a form of bias in itself. In fact, it is probably essential that a clinician does take ethnicity into account when diagnosing a patient (Cross et al., 1989).

However, it can also be noted that behaviours defining mental illness usually violate societal expectations of acceptable behaviour and this applies to ethnic groups who may be perceived as natural 'outgroups' from the majority. If mental illness can be seen as a kind of deviance then it can elicit forces of social control from within groups who see themselves as keepers of social order (Snowden, 2003).

Examples of the outcomes of ethnicity bias.

- African Americans, Latinos, Asian Americans, and Native Americans have been shown to be more likely than white people to leave treatment prematurely (Sue et al., 1994) and perceive treatment as less beneficial (Snowden, 2003).

- Members of ethnic minorities are more likely to be prescribed higher doses of psychiatric medications (Segal et al., 1996).

- In the USA, African Americans are more likely to be brought to a mental health facility by a police officer than white people and more likely to be committed against their will (Snowden, 2003).

Two potential causes of ethnicity bias.

- Visibility: The **visibility hypothesis** assumes that people who are perceived to be members of an ethnic minority stand out more in society and are therefore more likely to receive attention. They are deemed 'attention worthy' by wider community gatekeepers as well as officials and by being visible, any deviant behaviour is recognized more readily (Garland et al., 1998). In the sociocultural approach to behaviour, Hamilton and Gifford (1976) demonstrated the same effect under laboratory conditions, labelling the behaviour 'the illusory correlation' (see page 97).

- Economic: An economic explanation assumes that economic contraction produces greater insecurity, greater frustration, and less tolerance of deviant behaviour toward ethnic minorities. Therefore, during economic downturns, forces of social control appear to be aimed more at minority individuals. This is especially true for African American males who exhibit symptoms of mental illness (Catalano et al., 2002).

19.5 Validity and reliability of diagnosis

Content focus

Discuss the role of validity and reliability in diagnosis.

The presence of notions such as validity and reliability are a direct consequence of the adoption of the medical model within psychiatry. The medical model assumes abnormal behaviour can be understood in terms of having an identifiable cause (an **etiological** agent), a pathological process that can be predicted, and clear symptoms (Aboraya et al., 2005). Psychiatrists not only use diagnostic systems to identify what disorder their patients and clients have, but also to predict future behaviour and to choose an appropriate course of treatment that matches a diagnosis. Therefore, questions surrounding the correctness and stability of the diagnosis over time, place, and diagnostician are of paramount importance.

19.5.1 Validity

In basic terms, validity in psychiatry refers to the correctness of a diagnosis. There are many types of validity but **construct validity** and **content validity** can be seen as the core of psychiatry.

Construct validity refers to the extent to which a particular measure relates to other measures and is consistent with a **hypothesis** (Carmines, 1979). In addition, it asks to what extent the construct is useful (Nunnally, 1978).

Content validity refers to the degree to which an empirical measurement reflects a specific domain of content (Aboraya et al., 2005), which in psychiatry usually refers to the diagnostic criteria. A psychiatrist might ask: To what extent do my observations match the symptoms as outlined in the DSM-5 or ICD-10?

TOK What role should the patient themselves play in their diagnosis? Should they be considered an expert or a neutral observer in the same way a patient might if they are suffering from a physical illness?

In basic terms, validity in psychiatry refers to the correctness of a diagnosis.

TOK To what extent can definitive notions such as 'correctness' be applied to the human sciences?

... AND I'VE GOT A TOK QUESTION ... IF THEY'RE CALLED HUMAN SCIENCES, WHY DO WE MICE HAVE TO BE IN THE EXPERIMENTS?

Goodwin

Robins and Guze (1970) proposed five phases to achieve validity in the classification of mental disorders: clinical description, laboratory study, exclusion of other disorders, follow-up study, and family study. Therefore, in psychiatry, validity is the product of clinical research; laboratory, **epidemiological**, and other research data; and clinical experience and judgement.

In psychiatry, validity should not be seen in definitive terms. The medical model can present a definitive paradigm that creates simplicity where it might be more appropriate to acknowledge complexity and nuance. A medical doctor would not normally ask to what extent a leg is broken, because a bone is usually either broken or not. However, in psychiatry, abnormal behaviour is open to the subjective interpretation of the patient and the subjective interpretation of the clinician, as well as being relative to the culture, gender and other factors that have to be taken into consideration when considering a diagnosis. It can also be noted that effective treatments are often implemented without a clear understanding of the cause or the pathological process of the disorder (Spitzer and Williams, 1980).

Rosenhan (1973) demonstrates the problems with validity in an empirical study as he was able to show how normal and well people could be easily labelled as 'insane' and vice versa.

Rosenhan (1973) demonstrates the problems with validity in an empirical study as he was able to show how normal and well people could be easily labelled as 'insane' and vice versa. The study caused significant controversy in the psychiatric community at the time and was used by many to call for reforms. Rosenhan wanted to test whether hospitals can detect whether a person really is mentally ill or not, and then to observe how patients are treated in hospitals. He organized for colleagues and friends without any diagnosed psychological disorders to go to psychiatric hospitals and report that they had been hearing voices. These people were 'pseudopatients' and apart from questions relating to these experiences, they answered all questions honestly when asked by clinicians. Rosenhan found all of them were admitted to various hospitals and many were given a diagnosis of schizophrenia. After that, most of their behaviour was considered abnormal. For example, when taking notes about what happened in the hospital, hospital staff recorded that a patient's writing was excessive and abnormal; when they walked the corridors because they were bored they were accused of 'obsessive pacing'. Of the 12 admissions, 11 were diagnosed as schizophrenic and one with manic-depressive psychosis, which has identical symptoms. Despite their public 'show' of sanity (and the fact they were not mentally ill), the pseudopatients were never detected. It is worth noting that it was the genuine patients themselves who suspected the pseudopatients were not suffering from any mental illness but yet no hospital worker was able to do so. Each patient was eventually discharged with a diagnosis of schizophrenia 'in remission'. Length of hospitalization ranged from seven to 52 days, with an average of 19 days, although Rosenhan notes that the pseudopatients were not carefully observed.

Rosenhan came to a number of conclusions but he notes how the difference between normal and abnormal is very difficult for experts to judge and, once labelled abnormal, the label has a 'stickiness' to it that is not present in other areas of medicine. Once labelled schizophrenic, patients would always be viewed through this lens, which is why Rosenhan went to such lengths to change the names of and provide legal support for his participants.

While Rosenhan's study is used to show how the concept of normality is highly subjective, caution should be exercised when using the findings to deconstruct the entire psychiatric industry. For example, the study was conducted in the US in the early 1970s and many reforms and improvements have been put in place since then, in part due to the debate started by researchers such as Rosenhan. Furthermore, psychiatric hospitals have an ethical responsibility to investigate odd behaviour, and hearing voices is odd behaviour. Even if the hospital staff thought patients were faking, claiming to hear voices at the front desk of a psychiatric institution is odd behaviour in itself and they still had an ethical responsibility to investigate. As doctors, they had a duty to admit the pseudopatients in order to protect the community and protect the people from themselves.

Psychiatric hospitals investigate patients by admitting them to the wards, therefore the admission of the pseudopatients is not necessarily a failure in validity. The failure comes in the lack of time spent with the patients: Rosenhan estimates the pseudopatients had an overall daily contact mean of 6.8 minutes with psychiatrists, psychologists, residents, and physicians but it can also be noted the highest figure in the range was only 25.1 minutes in one of the hospitals. Therefore, the lack of 'correctness' in the diagnoses comes from the lack of time spent with the patients rather than poor judgement or a faulty diagnostic instrument.

It could be argued that, in this experiment, the failure in validity comes from a lack of resources and the lack of ability to spend time with patients; problems that plague the psychiatric industry, as mental health is often significantly underfunded.

Rosenhan followed up with a second part to his study. It was arranged at a research and teaching hospital whose staff had heard about the previous findings and doubted such errors could occur in their hospital. The staff were informed that at some time during the following three months, one or more pseudopatients would attempt to be admitted into their psychiatric hospital. Each staff member was asked to rate each patient who presented themselves at admissions or on the ward according to the likelihood that the patient was a pseudopatient. A 10-point scale was used, with a 1 and 2 reflecting high confidence that the patient was a pseudopatient.

Judgements were obtained on 193 patients who were admitted for psychiatric treatment. All staff who had had sustained contact with or primary responsibility for the patient – attendants, nurses, psychiatrists, physicians, and psychologists – were asked to make judgements. The results showed:

- forty-one patients were alleged, with high confidence, to be pseudopatients by at least one member of the staff

- twenty-three were considered suspect by at least one psychiatrist

- nineteen were suspected by one psychiatrist and one other staff member to be pseudopatients.

However, in actuality, no genuine pseudopatients presented themselves during this period. This part of the Rosenhan study demonstrates there is a lack of scientific evidence on which medical diagnoses are made and it also shows how huge mistakes can be made. However, it should also be noted many real dysfunctional patients fake their symptoms. People who fake their symptoms can still be considered abnormal and need investigation. For example, a non-depressed person who fakes being depressed can still be considered abnormal because faking being depressed is not only unusual but may be due to other personality problems.

The Rosenhan study shows that a lack of 'correctness' in the diagnoses comes from the lack of time spent with the patients rather than poor judgement or a faulty diagnostic instrument.

Caution should be exercised when using Rosenhan's insights to criticize psychiatry. Many real dysfunctional patients fake their symptoms. People who fake their symptoms can still be considered abnormal and need investigation.

Rosenhan's studies should be seen as philosophical counterweights to the dominance of the medical model within psychiatric institutions and academic thinking. They are a plea to regard psychiatry as having a special set of circumstances and considerations, such that mental illness cannot be seen as entirely comparable to physical illness.

19.5.2 Reliability

Reliability refers to the stability of the diagnosis over time, place, circumstance, and agreement between clinicians. It is really a measure of agreement and predictability over time. Reliability is achieved by asking several doctors to make a diagnosis for one patient and calculating how often they agree, and by checking to see if a patient's diagnosis stays the same for a period of time.

Two key forms of reliability are **inter-rater reliability** and **test–retest reliability**. Inter-rater reliability can be assessed by asking more than one practitioner to observe the same person and, using the same diagnostic system, attempt to make a diagnosis. If practitioners make the same decision, the system's reliability is high. Test–retest reliability is concerned with whether the same person will receive the same diagnosis if they are assessed more than once (e.g. on two different days).

Nicholls et al. (2000) asked two practitioners to use either DSM-IV, ICD-10 or the Great Ormond Street Hospital's own diagnostic system (GOS) to diagnose 81 children with eating problems who had come to a specialist clinic. This was a **correlational** study in the sense that reliability was measured based on rates of agreement between the two practitioners which were expressed as correlations. When the practitioners used ICD-10, inter-rater reliability was only 0.357, compared to 0.636 when they used DSM-IV and 0.879 for the GOS system. This shows quite clearly that for some reason the GOS system is more reliable than either of the other two. The researchers suggest that the success of the GOS system is because it is specifically designed for use with young children.

Seeman (2007) completed a literature review examining evidence relating to the reliability of diagnosis over time. She found that initial diagnoses of schizophrenia, especially in women, were susceptible to change as clinicians learned more information about their patients. It was common for a number of other conditions to cause the symptoms for which women were receiving the diagnosis of schizophrenia. This indicates the problem of test–retest reliability with schizophrenia diagnoses, although it can also be seen as a strength of the system, as it shows that clinicians are prepared to change their diagnoses if they are exposed to more information.

Aboraya et al. (2006) divides issues affecting reliability in diagnosis into two main areas: patient factors and clinician factors.

Patient factors affecting reliability in diagnosis

- The patient's psychological state: Some patients are in a state that enables them to provide useful and reliable information to the clinician. However, some patients may forget important information due to anxiety, poor concentration, poor memory, or are unable to communicate their condition in a consistently understandable way. For example, patients with disorganized thoughts are unable to provide any useful information due to their psychosis. In addition, some may not reveal information due to shame, denial, fear of legal consequences, or to

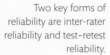

obtain or avoid particular treatments. Aboraya et al. (2006) note how patients with personality disorders may even make an effort to manipulate the clinician. This poses problems for the clinician when their role is to elicit pertinent information from the patient, assess the information, and make a rational judgement in the form of psychiatric diagnosis.

- The use of **proxy** information: For patients who are unable or unwilling to provide reliable information, the clinician must, when possible, resort to proxy information. Aboraya et al. (2006) note proxy information can be either incomplete or distorted because the individual providing it may have a vested interest in minimizing or exaggerating elements of the history for their own purposes. For example, they may want or need the patient to be taken into care and so may exaggerate symptoms, or they may be afraid of legal consequences of certain types of information (such as hearing voices) and therefore minimize it on behalf of the patient.

- Atypical presentations of psychiatric disorders: The DSM and ICD have strict assessment criteria. For example, a patient with a major depressive episode should have a two-week period of depressed mood and four of the following symptoms: weight loss, **insomnia** or **hypersomnia**, fatigue, feeling of worthlessness or guilt, poor concentration, or suicidal thoughts. Some patients have typical presentations while others with serious depressive symptoms that require clinical treatment do not fit the criteria described in the diagnostic manual and so it is difficult for different clinicians to agree on the extent to which the diagnostic criteria can be applied.

Clinician factors affecting reliability in diagnosis

- The clinician interview: Clinicians with good interviewing skills will aim to establish a therapeutic rapport with the patient and make the patient feel comfortable enough to provide pertinent information. For example, many clinicians use an open-form type of interview in routine psychiatric evaluation, but the reliability of psychiatric diagnoses using this type of interview can be low because clinicians typically focus on the most pressing presenting symptoms that are troubling the patient. It allows the patient to dominate the interview and allows potentially important symptoms to be avoided. This can lead to the clinician overlooking other important areas of inquiry.

- Clinician training, experience, and schools of thought: The background of the clinician, together with their training, may influence interpretation of symptoms. For example, one clinician with developmental training might explain the hallucinatory experience of the patient as part of post-traumatic experience of past abuse, while another clinician with a biomedical orientation might explain the same hallucinations as part of a schizophrenic process that is rooted in a brain abnormality. According to Aboraya et al. (2006), this can explain the tendency of some clinicians to overuse or underuse a particular diagnosis over time and why they might conflict with the assessment of other diagnosticians.

The influence of R.D. Laing and Thomas Szasz

Thomas Szasz and R.D. Laing are well-known critics of the diagnostic biomedical approach. However, they did not deny the existence of mental problems and they did not deny the value of treatment. Their objections were more academic, while also being rooted in trying to help people with genuine problems. Their work has helped highlight many of the complexities involved in treating abnormality as well as acting as a philosophical counterweight to the medical model.

R.D. Laing

Laing (1927–1989) is seen as one of the founders of the 'anti-psychiatry' movement. The basic premise of this movement maintains that psychiatric treatments are often damaging to the patient and do not help the patient learn to cope with their underlying problems. Furthermore, it assumes psychiatry is founded on false assumptions. For example, mental illness is diagnosed by investigating the behaviour of a patient but is then treated biologically.

Laing's work suggests diagnosis should be seen as more of a sociocultural construct rather than a medical one. Laing notes that psychiatrists do not diagnose based on a set of biological facts; this is because there are no reliable biological tests for diagnosing most psychological disorders, only guidance about categorizing behaviour, thoughts, and emotions. The process of diagnosing is full of financial, cultural, and legal considerations and can be dependent on the personal characteristics of the clinician as well as the dynamic between themselves and the patient.

Laing's work is an attempt to view diagnosis from the patients' point of view and demonstrate how many characteristics of abnormal behaviour are an understandable reaction to problems with living, rather than symptomatic of an underlying illness.

Thomas Szasz

Thomas Szasz (1920–2012) argued that mental illness is merely a metaphor for human problems in living. He assumed mental illnesses are not real in the sense that biological illness or brain diseases such as **Alzheimer's** disease are real. According to Szasz there are no objective methods for detecting the presence or absence of mental illness (Szasz, 2008). Therefore, it is wrong to use the notion of mental illness to describe behaviour that does not conform to other people's expectations of how to behave.

Szasz had libertarian political leanings and believed each person has the right to bodily and mental self-ownership. Szasz was a critic of scientism, which is the notion that science is the most authoritative worldview to the exclusion of other perspectives. Therefore, he argued psychiatry was yet another attempt by authority to impose power on individuals and was similar to religion in the sense that it imposed a hold over humankind.

Similar to Laing, he distinguished between what people 'do' (the behaviour) and what people 'had' (the disease). Given that there was very little evidence for biological causes for many mental illnesses, Laing argued social constructs surrounding human behaviour should be considered. Laing also placed importance on the use of language in how clinicians should consider behaviour. These two emphases can be seen in the following example. Religious people claim to 'take inspiration' from 'God' and may pray to 'him' to seek guidance. This is not considered abnormal. However, if people 'hear voices' and 'talk to themselves' or to 'an imaginary being' to derive comfort this may be considered abnormal.

Such an emphasis on sociocultural processes helps illuminate the constructed nature of mental illness. The medical metaphor not only influences the clinician, but Szasz also argued that it influences the thought and behavioural processes of the patient. Lacking a more valid route to express their problems with living, they resort to illness-imitation behaviour to seek sympathy and help from the establishment in the form of financial aid or access to medication.

20 Etiology of abnormal psychology

Topic focus

Discuss the etiology of one abnormal behaviour.

20.1 Explanations and prevalence rates for disorders

Content focus

Discuss explanations and prevalence rates for one disorder.

Prevalence rates are a statistical notion that refer to the number of cases of a health problem that are present in a particular population at a given time. 'Explanations' refer to causative factors that lead to abnormal behaviour. They are sometimes referred to as etiologies. In the following section, explanations for anorexia nervosa (eating disorders) and major depressive disorder (depressive disorders) will be discussed in the context of their prevalence rates for certain demographics within populations.

20.1.1 Anorexia nervosa

According to the DSM-5 criteria, to be diagnosed as having anorexia nervosa (AN) a person must display:

- persistent restriction of energy intake leading to significantly low body weight (in context of what is minimally expected for age, sex, developmental trajectory, and physical health)

- either an intense fear of gaining weight or of becoming fat, or persistent behaviour that interferes with weight gain (despite being of significantly low weight)

TOK

To what extent does the medical model help or hinder the search for explanations for abnormality?

Prevalence rates are a statistical notion that refer to the number of cases of a health problem that are present in a particular population at a given time. 'Explanations' refer to causative factors that lead to abnormal behaviour.

- disturbance in the way one's body weight or shape is experienced, undue influence of body shape and weight on self-evaluation, or persistent lack of recognition of the seriousness of the current low body weight.

The ICD-10 criteria (as outlined by the WHO) is more specific in terms of weight loss criteria and the psychological response to it. For a definite diagnosis of AN, all the following are required within ICD-10 criteria.

- Body weight is maintained at least 15 per cent below expected weight (either lost or never achieved), or **Body Mass Index** (BMI) is 17.5 or less. Pre-pubertal patients may show failure to make the expected weight gain during the period of growth.

- The weight loss is self-induced by avoidance of 'fattening foods' and one or more of the following: self-induced vomiting, self-induced purging, excessive exercise, use of appetite suppressants and/or diuretics.

- There is body image distortion in the form of a specific **psychopathology** whereby a dread of fatness persists as an intrusive, overvalued idea and the patient imposes a low weight threshold on himself or herself.

- There is **endocrine** disorder, manifesting in women as loss of periods (amenorrhoea) and in men as a loss of sexual interest and potency.

For a diagnosis of AN to be reached there is some room for interpretation and the personal judgement of the diagnosing clinician. There would also be some discussion with the patient, family, and other professionals (such as teachers, counsellors, family doctor) before a diagnosis is reached.

Eating disorders are more frequent in industrialized countries with almost all patients (95 per cent) being women (Södersten, Bergh, and Zandian, 2006). It is estimated that at least 10 per cent of school-aged girls in the developed world manifest at least some form of partial anorexic or bulimic syndromes, together with dietary, psychological, and medical problems (Steiger, Bruce, and Israël, 2003) although it should be remembered that males can also suffer from eating disorders. Much of the research does not distinguish between anorexia and other eating disorders (such as bulimia) and where possible this has been noted below.

Biological explanations

Controlled family studies have generally found increased rates of eating disorders in the biological relatives of women with anorexia compared to relatives of control groups (e.g. Strober et al., 1990). However, given that close relatives share both **genes** and environments, these studies cannot differentiate genetic versus environmental causes for the disorders. Therefore, twin studies are used to disentangle the relative etiological influence of genes versus environmental causes. They do this by comparing the similarity of identical twins (monozygotic [MZ]) and fraternal twins (dizygotic [DZ]). MZ twins share all of their genes whereas DZ twins only share about half. Overall, MZ twin correlations are approximately two times greater than DZ twin correlations for anorexia, which suggests genetic factors are involved in the disorder. It can be reasonably assumed that anorexia appears to be moderately heritable (Berrettini, 2004).

Sidebar notes:

Eating disorders are more frequent in industrialized countries with almost all patients (95 per cent) being women (Södersten, Bergh, and Zandian, 2006). It is estimated that at least 10 per cent of school-aged girls in the developed world manifest at least some form of partial anorexic or bulimic syndromes, together with dietary, psychological, and medical problems (Steiger, Bruce, and Israël, 2003), although it should be remembered that males can also suffer from eating disorders.

Overall, MZ twin correlations are approximately two times greater than DZ twin correlations for anorexia, which suggests genetic factors are involved in the disorder.

It can be reasonably assumed that anorexia appears to be moderately heritable (Berrettini, 2004).

The presence of genetic determinants for anorexia suggest there could be evolutionary benefits to the disorder as it has developed as a **Darwinian adaptation**. The **female intrasexual competition theory** assumes that eating disorders originate in the female's psychological adaptation of concern about physical attractiveness, which is an important component for female 'mate attraction' and 'mate retention' strategies (Abed, 1998).

However, this approach assumes thinness is valued as attractive because it is associated with youth and fertility. This body shape is often named 'nubile' and is seen as an indicator of youth and reproductive potential and therefore acts as a sign of attraction to males and competition to other females. An **adaptive** female reproductive strategy is to preserve the nubile shape to compete with other females, attract mates, and retain a high-ranking male. However, it can be seen as a criticism of the underlying assumption that an extreme anorexic female body actually attracts fewer males, and a female with anorexia is likely to have a reduced libido, which contradicts the basic assumption of mate attraction and retention.

The **reproductive suppression hypothesis** can be used to add nuance to this approach. This theory assumes the loss of libido and an eventual loss of fertility through anorexic symptoms can be linked to a desire to control reproduction (Frisch and Barbieri, 2002). Consequently, preferences for thinner body ideals could be beneficial for females trying to control the timing of their reproduction and allow them to manage their own reproductive cycle. This is particularly beneficial for young females where pregnancy can be a threat to health and survival.

The social attention holding power theory (Gatward, 2007) assumes individuals need to hold attention and gain investment from other members of the group (Gilbert, 1998). This basic assumption can be linked to an underlying need to belong. The survival of humans depended heavily on belonging to a group; people had to compete with others for resources and this competition could have led to the threat of exclusion. Therefore, extreme projections of thinness could elicit more caring behaviour from immediate kin members. In addition, projecting thinness to the group could elevate a lower ranking female to a higher social status because it signals control, which can be seen as a valued characteristic.

A common assumption of these theories is the notion that human females are responding to a threat (Kardum et al., 2008). The female intrasexual competition theory assumes the threat is in the form of a perceived lack of attraction or the lack of permanent male partner; the reproductive suppression hypothesis assumes the threat is in the form of a lack of control over reproductive cycles, which if they are not under control can pose a serious threat to health and survival of the young female; the social attention-holding power theory assumes the threat is in the form of group rejection or not being valued enough by the group to have adequate access to resources.

The theories are supported by the dominance of anorexia and other eating disorders in the prevalence rates of females versus males with the disorder.

According to the National Institute of Mental Health (2011), a US-based research institute:

- 0.3 per cent of men will struggle with anorexia in their lifetime

- 0.5 per cent of men will struggle with bulimia in their lifetime

The presence of genetic determinants for anorexia suggest there could be evolutionary benefits to the disorder as it has developed as a Darwinian adaptation. Researchers debate theories as to what the 'benefits' might be to the individual or the human group.

- 2 per cent of men will struggle with a binge eating disorder in their lifetime.

This can be compared with:

- 0.9 per cent of women will struggle with anorexia in their lifetime

- 1.5 per cent of women will struggle with bulimia in their lifetime

- 3.5 per cent of women will struggle with a binge eating disorder in their lifetime.

The data suggests that anorexia and eating disorders in general are still a predominantly female problem although there are indications that males are increasingly suffering as well.

Sociocultural explanations

Sociocultural explanations assume that sociocultural changes, including the proliferation of media images promoting thinness and a consumer culture dominated by globalized fashion and beauty industries, are placing individuals, especially women, at risk of developing eating disorders (EDs) (Pike and Dunne, 2015). According to this perspective, increasing exposure to 'the West' transmits a 'thin body ideal' and imparts Western notions of beauty ideals to non-Western societies, which then leads to growing body dissatisfaction, dieting, and eating disorders. The assumption is supported by the dominance of anorexia in the prevalence rates of females who live in the West or who are influenced by Western media. Macro data is difficult to develop but overall, prevalence rates in Western countries for anorexia nervosa were higher for female and male subjects compared with non-Western countries (Makino et al., 2004). Pike and Dunne (2015) note that where countries have grown more industrialized and globalized, EDs have followed, and the gap is closing between several Asian countries and the West with regards to disordered eating, weight and shape concerns, and dieting behaviours.

However, it should not be simply seen as a transmission of ideas from West to non-West with regards to beauty ideals. There are complex sociocultural considerations at play; for example, Witcomb et al. (2013) argue that the demands of an increasingly competitive environment in non-Western countries are caused by new employment opportunities as a result of globalization. Women are expected to develop a new set of skills, which can expose them to greater criticism from peers, colleagues, and society.

Witcomb et al. (2013) suggest these new social pressures outside of the family unit can prompt women to engage in more self-evaluation within the wider social scene and their physical appearance becomes one of several domains in which women 'measure' themselves against an aspirational ideal. Therefore, caution should be used when assuming eating disorders are spread solely through **'Westernization'**; other processes such as industrialization and urbanization are key causative factors. Furthermore, the notion of Westernization over-attributes the diverse changes and distinct developmental pathways of individual societies, particularly in Asia (Pike and Dunne, 2015). Individual societies do not respond uniformly to complex global shifts and pressures, nor have they passively absorbed Western templates of beauty.

Sociocultural changes that have taken place in the West may also contribute to the development and prevalence of eating disorders. Paul (2011) has highlighted how older women in the West are now becoming more susceptible to eating disorders. This

Sociocultural explanations assume that sociocultural changes, including the proliferation of media images promoting thinness and a consumer culture dominated by globalized fashion and beauty industries, are placing individuals, especially women, at risk for developing eating disorders (Pike and Dunne, 2015).

new trend could be explained by sociocultural changes in Western countries that are leading to females having fewer children and having children later in life. This is partly the result of female empowerment, which has led to more women entering careers, but also due to changes in social dynamics between men and women. Social exchange theory assumes human dynamics involve 'value' and 'commodities' that are 'traded'. Western cultural changes have led to a 'devaluation' of sex when viewed through a sexual economy lens, which potentially harms women more than men. When these changes are considered in the context of evolutionary explanations it can explain why progressively older females have to retain or recreate the nubile shape to maintain female intrasexual competition for high-quality long-term mates as they compete with younger, more nubile-shaped females (Kardum et al., 2008). This trend is reflected in the increasing prevalence of anorexia in older women. Although there is not a large amount of data (because it is a relatively new trend), the graph below shows an increase in the amount of older women with restrictive eating habits.

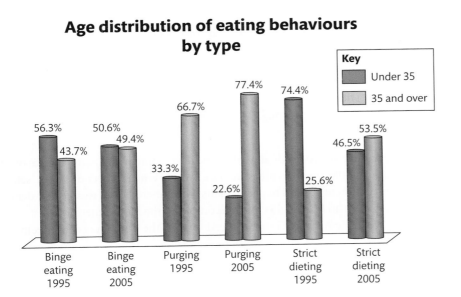

Figure 20.1 Age distribution of eating disorders (Hay et al., 2008)

Cognitive explanations

Cognitive explanations assume that impairments in cognitive processes, such as attention and perception, place individuals at more risk of developing anorexia nervosa. For example, sufferers of ED would possess elaborate and inaccurate schemata centred around their body, which would result in thoughts about body weight and shape. Therefore, it can be assumed ED would be more prevalent among people with cognitive impairments.

Attention bias (AB) refers to a tendency to over focus awareness on information in the environment that reinforces the disorder. It should be noted how such cognitive impairments are reinforced by behaviour. For example, Shafran et al. (2007) argue the frequent checking of body parts (e.g. checking weight and/or the way clothes fit; intense scrutiny of particular body parts; pinching skin to assess fatness) leads to a reinforcement of anorexia-related behaviours. Therefore, the repeated scrutiny of body parts serves as a confirmation bias in which individuals with anorexia seek out evidence to support their belief system.

Cognitive explanations assume that impairments in cognitive processes, such as attention and perception, place individuals at more risk of developing anorexia nervosa.

The dot probe task (MacLeod et al., 1986) is designed to demonstrate attention bias in anorexic patients. In this task, a probe is presented (e.g. X in the centre of the screen) prior to the presentation of another piece of stimuli. Following the initial probe, emotional and neutral stimuli are then presented on the screen, for example, the word fat. Immediately following the emotional/neutral stimuli, another probe (e.g. a single letter 'E' or 'F') is presented in either the spatial location occupied by the emotional or neutral stimuli or another spatial location. The participants are instructed to identify the probe as quickly as possible (e.g. press a key on the keyboard corresponding with the probe presented; press the 'E' key).

If the probe is displayed in the spatial location of the word/image that the person was already attending to, the response time will be faster than if the probe appears in the spatial location of the word/image they were not attending to (e.g. 'paper'). The assumption is that participants suffering from ED would look away from body-positive words and take longer to respond, but dwell on words associated with body-negative shapes, taking a shorter time to respond.

Rieger et al. (1998) found patients with eating disorders detected positive target words when they related to a thin physique. However, they detected them more quickly when they related to a large physique. Therefore, participants with EDs looked away from positive shape- and weight-related words (significant difference) and tended to look toward (trend level) negative shape- and weight-related words. This effect was not found in restrained eaters, suggesting ED sufferers paid attention to stimuli related to body size and shape.

There are other cognitive processes at work in the development and maintenance of an ED. Sassaroli et al. (2008) aimed to measure the effects of concern over mistakes, self-esteem, and perception of control in participants who suffered from eating disorders. Forty individuals with an ED and 55 controls completed the Multidimensional Perfectionism Scale, the Anxiety Control Questionnaire, the Rosenberg self-esteem scale, and the Eating Disorder Inventory to test for drives for thinness, bulimia, and body dissatisfaction.

The ED group had significantly lower perception of control and self-esteem and higher concern over mistakes, drive for thinness, bulimia, and body dissatisfaction than the control group. EDs are associated with a tendency to worry about mistakes, a low sense of self-esteem, and a low perception of control over internal feelings and external events. The results suggest that a low perception of control is an important cognitive factor in ED.

Integrative approach

Viewing approaches in isolation will mean nuances of understanding are lost. A synthesis of theories and placing them in context will lead to greater explanatory power. For example, it is likely the sociocultural pressures outlined by a sociocultural approach are filtered through (and may cause) impairments in cognitive processing. It is also reasonable to assume they have a biological underpinning rooted in evolution that have contributed to the development of the human species and there is increasing evidence that attention deficits may be due to **neurological** deficits. For example, a significant body of research on animals and humans suggests the limbic system (amygdala and insula) and prefrontal cortex are involved in the processing of threat-based stimuli (Monk, 2008).

Viewing approaches in isolation will mean nuances of understanding are lost. A synthesis of theories and placing them in context will lead to greater explanatory power.

20.1.2 Major depressive disorder

See Section 3.1.1, page 28 for an overview of major depressive disorder (MDD).

Biological explanations

There is a significant body of evidence that demonstrates MDD has its causes rooted in biology. Again, twin studies can be used to disentangle the relative etiological influence of genes versus environmental causes. Kendler et al. (2008) compared the incidence of the symptoms of depression among identical and non-identical twins. The researchers used telephone interviews to ask 42 000 twins if they and their family members had symptoms of depression. They found a significantly higher rate among MZ twins than DZ twins, suggesting a clear genetic component.

Genes manifest themselves in complex ways. It is enough to assume that they influence neurological frameworks as well as hormonal and neurotransmitter levels and sensitivity. The **monoamine hypothesis** assumes there is a lack of certain neurotransmitters which then lead to depression. For example, a lack of **serotonin** may be related to anxiety, obsessions, and compulsions. A lack of **dopamine** may be related to attention, motivation, pleasure, and reward (Nutt, 2008). Moreover, evidence comes from certain drugs that raise the levels of serotonin and dopamine and improve the mood of sufferers of MDD.

The presence of genetic determinants for MDD suggest there could be evolutionary benefits to the disorder as it has developed as a Darwinian adaptation. For example, the **conservation of resource theories** assume depression is a mechanism that leads to the inhibition of certain desires. This would be beneficial because they would enable the individual to give up unattainable goals, to conserve resources, and to redirect them to more productive tasks (Nesse, 2000). Social competition theories assume that depressed mood is an answer to a perceived descent in social hierarchy. Any descent in social hierarchy may lead to further attacks as higher ranking individuals may seek to assert their dominance over perceived lower ranking individuals. Therefore, specific behaviours accompanying depression would correspond to the loss in social rank and project messages that might serve to protect an individual from possible attacks (Price, 1998). In keeping with the notion of depression serving to regulate group dynamics, the **attachment theory of depression** assumes depressive responses serve as a distress call (Frijda, 1994) to other members of the group, as a way of signalling for help and reassurance and improving group bonds.

The presence of genetic determinants for MDD suggest there could be evolutionary benefits to the disorder as it has developed as a Darwinian adaptation.

Given the underlying assumption that depression fulfils a social projection role within group dynamics it could be assumed that rates between males and females would be approximate. However, this is not born out by the research. Kessler et al. (1994) reported that women in the USA are about two-thirds more likely than men to be depressed, with a similar trend in the UK. However, seen through an evolutionary lens, women and men have different social functions within groups as well as distinct gender roles and identities. Therefore, it could be assumed that if depression is a social projection then it might affect men and women differently. Gender differences in depression rates may be the result of genders responding to sociocultural pressures, which would mean their underlying depression symptoms manifest themselves in gender-specific ways (Nazroo, 2001). For example, men may have socialized to express depression symptoms in the form of anger, being alone, or turning to drugs, or other forms of acting out, whereas woman are more likely to talk about their feelings in social settings and peer groups, prompting them to be labelled as 'depressed' and seek help. Women may also feel more comfortable seeking help with personal problems from healthcare professionals. Studies have shown that expected gender differences in depressive disorders were balanced out by higher male rates of alcohol abuse and drug dependency (e.g. Meltzer et al., 1995), suggesting there is no underlying biological difference between men and women in experiencing these feelings, instead just differences in how they behaviourally manifest themselves.

Sociocultural explanations

Sociocultural explanations assume sociocultural processes place individuals at risk of developing major depressive disorder. Therefore, it could be assumed individuals living within challenging sociocultural processes would be at more risk of developing depression. Nicholson et al. (2008) found men who were in the lowest socioeconomic groups in Poland, Russia and the Czech Republic were five times more likely to have depression. The Brown and Harris (1978) model of depression assumes vulnerability factors such as the loss of the mother at a young age, lack of a confiding relationship, greater than three children under the age of 14 at home, and unemployment can interact with provoking agents (severe events and major difficulties) to increase the risk of depression. Their initial study surveyed 458 women in South London about their daily life and depressive episodes. Their findings were important because they viewed depression through a sociocultural lens and highlighted how it could be rooted in social class. They found the middle-class women were less likely to be depressed. It also highlighted that environmental factors could increase or alleviate provoking factors, such as the presence or absence of a supportive husband. Clearly, caution should be used when generalizing the findings to men, as only women were used, but the underlying assumption remains intact: sociocultural environments have a significant impact on depression.

Sociocultural norms can influence to what extent cultural subgroups seek help, which then influence prevalence rates. Zhang et al. (1998) found Asian Americans were more likely to feel the pressure of social stigma as only 12 per cent of Asians would mention their mental health problems to a friend or relative (versus 25 per cent of white people). This then leads to some clinicians seeing Asian Americans as 'problem free' and actually more abnormal should they seek help. This can be contrasted with African Americans, who tend to take an active approach in facing personal problems, rather than avoiding them, and being more expressive when they do so (Broman, 1996). The **normalization** of certain disorders within cultural groups can lead to more members of this group seeking treatment. For example, Levav et al. (1997) aimed to see if Jewish people in the USA are more likely than other religious groups to have depression. The researchers reviewed statistics for prevalence and lifetime rates of DSM-III major depression among Jews, Catholics, Protestants, individuals in other religious groups, and individuals with no religious affiliation in two US cities; Los Angeles and New Haven. For Jewish men, admitting being depressed and seeking help was a cultural norm within their subgroup, which inevitably shows in the prevalence rates of this group. Jewish men have higher rates of depression and the ratio between Jewish men and women for depression was 1:1. This cannot be interpreted to mean more Jewish men are depressed, it simply means more are being diagnosed.

Positive family sociocultural norms can protect against the risk of developing a mental illness. For example, supportive families and good sibling relationships can protect against the onset of mental illness (Office of the Surgeon General, USA, 2001). However, negative family cultural norms can increase the risk of developing a mental illness. For example, Dinwiddie et al. (2000) aimed to measure lifetime prevalence of psychiatric disorders among twins who reported childhood sexual abuse (CSA). They wanted to compare these rates with those among non-abused twins. Information about lifetime experiences was obtained by structured telephone interviews with 5995 Australian twins. Twins who reported a history of CSA were contrasted on lifetime psychopathology with subjects without such a history. They found a history of CSA in 5.9 per cent of the women and 2.5 per cent of the men. In the sample as a whole, those reporting CSA were more likely to receive lifetime diagnoses of major depression, conduct disorder, panic disorder, and alcoholism, and were more likely to report suicidal thoughts and a history of suicide attempts. In particular, rates of major depression, conduct disorder and **suicidal ideation** were higher if both co-twins were abused than if the respondent alone reported CSA. They concluded CSA and psychopathology arises at least in part through the influence of shared family subcultural norms, but they also concluded this influenced both the risk of experiencing CSA and the risk of developing a psychopathology later in life.

It can be assumed individuals living within sociocultural processes that mediate the effects of depression would be less at risk of developing the disorder. For example, Wu and Anthony (2000) found Hispanic communities in the USA have lower levels of depression than other communities, probably because of stronger extended family connections. This was supported by Gabilondo et al. (2010) who found depression is less common in Spain than in northern European countries, probably because family connections and communal traditions are considered more important.

Cognitive explanations

Cognitive explanations assume maladaptive cognitive processes place individuals at risk of developing MDD.

Cognitive explanations assume maladaptive cognitive processes place individuals at risk of developing major depressive disorder.

For example, Aaron Beck identified cognitive mechanisms that he linked to depression. In 1967 he outlined the notion of systematic negative bias in which faulty information processing leads to self-defeating thoughts. For example:

- arbitrary inference – drawing a negative conclusion in the absence of supporting data

- selective abstraction – focusing on the worst aspects of any situation

- magnification and minimization – problems become perceived as bigger than they really are; solutions become perceived as smaller than they really are

- personalization – negative events are interpreted through a personal paradigm where everything is the individual's fault

- dichotomous thinking – thoughts are separated into extreme black and white with little room for nuance.

Beck proposed the **cognitive triad of negative automatic thinking** (1976), which argues depressed people suffer from seemingly automatic and uncontrollable thoughts that produce negative schemas about themselves:

- the self – 'I'm worthless and ugly' or 'I wish I was different'

- the world or environment – 'No one values me' or 'People ignore me all the time'

- the future – 'I'm hopeless because things will never change' or 'Things can only get worse!'

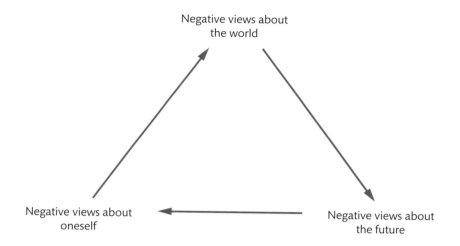

Negative views about
the world

Negative views about
oneself

Negative views about
the future

Figure 20.2 A diagram
representing Beck's cognitive
triad of negative automatic
thinking

However, a key issue with Beck's model is the lack of integration with other factors that are known to be linked to depression. Hankin and Abramson (2001) propose an integrative approach to consider depression on a wider sphere and most notably take account of negative events as well as genetic causation.

A strength of the integrative approach is that it can explain how life events as well as biological predisposition can create a causal chain of depression. Furthermore, the model also accounts for age and gender differences in depression prevalence. **Adolescence** is a period when depression becomes more widespread and Hankin and Abramson suggest this is due to a slackening of parental monitoring of social and interpersonal events. For example, children move into a period where they have to self-manage their friendship groups and therefore the amount of negative life events can increase.

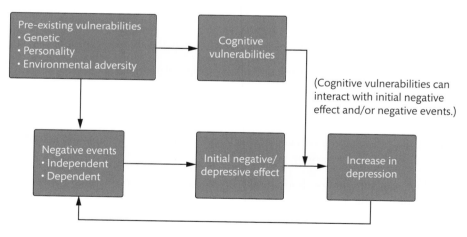

Pre-existing vulnerabilities
• Genetic
• Personality
• Environmental adversity

Cognitive
vulnerabilities

(Cognitive vulnerabilities can
interact with initial negative
effect and/or negative events.)

Negative events
• Independent
• Dependent

Initial negative/
depressive effect

Increase in
depression

Figure 20.3 The Hankin and
Abramson (2001) integrative
approach

Moreover, the model can be used to account for the greater number of girls who are depressed. Hankin and Abramson (2001) argue girls are more likely to encounter not only a greater number of negative life events, such as interpersonal problems within friendship groups, but also be more sensitive to them. Furthermore, there is evidence that girls encode life events in memory differently to boys, with girls being more prone to encode events in an emotional way and being able to recall emotional memories more quickly than boys (Davis, 1999).

However, there were also key sociocultural factors involved, with Fivush (1991b) highlighting how mothers can be more controlling of daughters than sons (adding to anxiety) and being able to discuss more sad events with their daughters than sons. In addition, girls are taught to be more bodily aware than boys starting from a younger age, leading to increased anxiety and a cycle of negative self-thoughts, although this could be linked to evolutionary processes with female physical appearance being a key trait in the human mating process (Hamida et al., 1991). Therefore, Hankin and Abramson argue biological predisposition as well as socialization effects on girls lead them to being more cognitively vulnerable to depression than boys.

EE Choose either MDD or AN. To what extent can your chosen disorder be considered an evolutionary adaptation?

21 Treatment of disorders

Topic focus

Discuss the treatment of disorders.

21.1 Biological treatments

Content focus

Evaluate the effectiveness of biological treatments for one disorder

Biological treatments assume biological interventions will either alleviate the symptoms of a disorder or be able to target and rectify a biological cause. It should be noted that the **efficacy** of biological interventions is usually tested with an experimental group who receive the treatment and then a control group who do not. However, rarely are patients given biological treatments in isolation. Even if they receive no formal counselling as an outpatient or inpatient as part of their care package, they usually have a support network of friends and family who monitor them and provide the role of an informal counselling network.

TOK How can 'cure' be measured when dealing with notions of abnormality? Does the medical model help or hinder patient care in this context?

 Biological treatments assume biological interventions will either alleviate the symptoms of a disorder or be able to target and rectify a biological cause.

21.1.1 Biological treatments for anorexia nervosa

Pharmacological treatments for AN assume pharmacological interventions can either arrest the decline of someone who is in a critical condition or aid the goal of weight maintenance after weight has been regained. However, it is extremely rare for a patient to be given a pharmacological treatment in isolation, so it is difficult to isolate the biological variable that may be either a contributory factor toward the development of AN or part of its treatment.

Tricyclic antidepressants

Tricyclic antidepressants (TCAs) are chemical compounds that are used primarily in the treatment of depression, but they can also be applied to AN. The majority of TCAs act primarily as serotonin-norepinephrine reuptake inhibitors (SNRIs), which means there is an increase in concentrations of these neurotransmitters in the brain. While being known to clinicians for their use with depression, they were tested for their efficacy in combatting AN. Clompiramine appeared to increase hunger and calorie consumption early in treatment, but did not alter outcome because it is possible the patients knew why they were feeling more hungry (Crisp et al., 1987).

Attributing their new-found hunger to a form of artificial intervention meant they could simply overcome the drive to eat with behavioural strategies (not eating) or cognitive strategies (reminding themselves they were being artificially pushed to eat). Therefore, while the drug may have been able to combat the underlying causes of AN, which is often linked to anxiety and depression, it was not able to combat the cognitive dysfunction that accompanies the illness. Furthermore, the severe side effects (see below) can often lead to patients not taking them.

SSRI antidepressants

Serotonin has been found to be low in AN patients, so there is a great deal of speculation as to what extent it could be a causal factor of the disorder. Selective serotonin reuptake inhibitors or serotonin-specific reuptake inhibitors (SSRIs) are again used primarily in the treatment of depression to tackle the low levels of serotonin. Kaye et al. (1991) performed the first of two maintenance trials of fluoxetine in AN. This study enrolled 39 outpatients who were assessed for 52 weeks. Patients were **randomized** to fluoxetine or **placebo**. However, the levels of fluoxetine were extremely varied and **psychotherapy** was optional. After one year, the majority of patients remained on fluoxetine (10/16) whereas the majority of the placebo group chose to discontinue their dose (3/19 remaining on placebo at one year). In this study, fluoxetine-treated patients had higher weights and decreased core eating disorder symptoms at one year in comparison with patients treated with a placebo. Kaye et al. (1991) judged response as good in 10, partial in 17, and poor in 4 anorexics as measured by improvements in eating behaviour, mood, and obsessional symptoms. The key characteristic of this trial is that most patients were started on fluoxetine treatment after inpatient weight restoration, which suggests fluoxetine is helpful in maintaining weight gain after it has been restored, rather than stimulating weight gain.

Mandometers

Zandian et al. (2009) developed a device called a mandometer that provides patients with feedback on their rate of eating. It is designed to help patients relearn normal eating behaviour by using a feedback device attached to a scale that tells the patient how much they should be eating and how full they should feel to achieve normal eating habits. The patient places their plate on the scale and puts their allocated food on the plate. The mandometer then registers the speed they eat and the patient puts in how full he or she is feeling throughout the meal. The system is both biologically and behaviourally based because the patient is supposed to feel rewarded when they feel full by meeting the behavioural targets set by the machine. However, while the equipment is now widely available in many countries, Van Elburg et al. (2012) found no significant benefit for the mandometer over treatment as usual.

Repetitive transcranial magnetic stimulation

Repetitive transcranial magnetic stimulation (rTMS) works on the principle of electromagnetic induction, which involves discharging a very large current (peak current: approximately 5000 amps) through the skull via capacitors. This results in the induction of a brief and pulsed magnetic field inside the cranium (Biswa et al., 2011).

Research is still in its infancy, but there appears to be a promising effect on AN patients when it is applied to the left dorsolateral prefrontal cortex. Van den Eynde et al. (2011) conducted a **pilot study** to investigate whether one session of high-frequency rTMS would reduce eating disorder-related symptoms following exposure to visual and real food stimuli. Ten right-handed people with AN underwent one session of rTMS. Subjective experiences related to the eating disorder (e.g. urge to restrict, feeling full etc.) were assessed before and after rTMS. They found rTMS was safe as well as being well-tolerated, and resulted in reduced levels of feeling full, feeling fat, and feeling anxious.

They concluded, rTMS may reduce core symptoms of AN. The results received support from McClelland et al. (2016), who had some success in replicating the basic aim of Van den Eynde et al. when they used used rTMS in comparison to a sham treatment.

21.1.2 Biological treatments for major depressive disorder

Pharmacological treatments for MDD assume pharmacological interventions can either arrest the decline of someone who is increasingly becoming depressed by stabilizing chemical imbalances or improve mood and motivation. However, it is extremely rare for a patient to be given a pharmacological treatment in isolation, therefore it is difficult to isolate the biological variable that may either be a contributory factor toward the development of depression or part of its treatment.

Pharmacological treatments for MDD assume pharmacological interventions can either arrest the decline of someone who is increasingly becoming depressed by stabilizing chemical imbalances or improve mood and motivation.

According to the US National Library of medicine (2017), when taking commonly used antidepressants such as TCAs and SSRIs:

- about 20 to 40 out of 100 people who took a placebo noticed an improvement in their symptoms within six to eight weeks
- about 40 to 60 out of 100 people who took an antidepressant noticed an improvement in their symptoms within six to eight weeks.

Therefore, antidepressants improved symptoms in about 20 more people out of 100 than a placebo. Furthermore, TCAs and SSRIs lower the risk of relapses, although it should be noted they cannot completely prevent them.

- Without preventive treatment: About 50 out of 100 people who took a placebo had a relapse within one to two years.
- With preventive treatment: About 23 out of 100 people who took an antidepressant had a relapse within one to two years.

Therefore, taking an antidepressant for a longer period successfully prevented a relapse in an average of 27 out of 100 people (US National Library of Medicine, 2017). It can also be noted that Cipriani et al. (2018) reviewed 522 trials of 21 antidepressant drugs comprising 116 477 participants to compare how effective they were in treating adults with MDD. They found all 21 antidepressants were more effective than placebo in adults with MDD. Their study was a large-scale review and supports earlier work that showed a relative improvement for patients who took antidepressants.

Tricyclic antidepressants

Tricyclic antidepressants (TCAs) are chemical compounds that are used primarily in the treatment of MDD. The majority of TCAs act primarily as serotonin-norepinephrine reuptake inhibitors (SNRIs), which means there is an increase in

TCAs are chemical compounds used primarily in the treatment of depression. The majority of TCAs act primarily as SNRIs, which means there is an increase in concentrations of these neurotransmitters in the brain.

concentrations of these neurotransmitters in the brain. Serotonin and norepinephrine have been highly implicated in depression and any increase in their activity has beneficial effects.

However, TCAs have been shown to have too many side effects, which has meant other drugs have been developed and they are now only used when other more tolerated drugs have been shown to be ineffective. Side effects of TCAs include dry mouth, dry nose, blurry vision, constipation, urinary retention, cognitive and/or memory impairment, increased body temperature, drowsiness, anxiety, **emotional blunting** (apathy/anhedonia), confusion, restlessness, dizziness, changes in appetite and weight, sweating, sexual dysfunction, muscle twitches, weakness, nausea and vomiting.

These side effects mean any upswing in mood for the patient can be offset by the behavioural and physiological changes that can take place as a result of taking TCAs. For example, a person may become apathetic while gaining weight, meaning any increase in mood will be offset by the depressive effects of having gained weight and feeling apathetic. Therefore, a patient when left to their own devices may actually stop taking the drug because of the severe side effects.

However, TCAs have been shown to be very effective in treating **melancholic depression** whereby people feel intense periods of guilt or apathy, symptoms of insomnia, loss of appetite, a relative lack of mood reactiveness to environmental circumstances. Melancholic depression is thought to be acutely biologically based and a particularly severe form of depression, which may explain why the TCAs are suited to its treatment (McGrath et al., 2008).

Monoamine oxidase inhibitors

Monoamine oxidase is a natural enzyme that breaks down serotonin, **epinephrine**, and dopamine. Monoamine oxidase inhibitors (MAOIs) block the effects of this enzyme, which results in an increase of these neurotransmitters. Too little serotonin in the brain is thought to play a role in depression, but if there is too much then it can cause **serotonin syndrome**, which is characterized by excessive nerve cell activity that causes a potentially deadly collection of symptoms. These include high body temperature, agitation, tremor, sweating, dilated pupils, and diarrhoea.

However, in a literature review on comparing the effectiveness of MAOIs with both placebo and TCAs, MAOIs were deemed to be most effective with depressed outpatients with atypical depression, and particularly those patients where other drugs had not been effective (Thase et al., 1995).

Despite its name, **atypical depression** is very common and can be contrasted with melancholic depression. Atypical depression involves symptoms of excessive oversleeping, excessive weight gain or weight loss, moods that are strongly reactive to environmental circumstances, and feeling extremely sensitive to rejection. Given the specific subset of this type of depression, any drug that can effectively treat it is welcome news for sufferers.

However, a significant problem in assessing the effectiveness of MAOIs is their declining use. Fiedorowicz and Swartz (2004) argue there is a waning physician experience, with MAOIs leading to many not actually prescribing them. For example, a 1999 survey of the Michigan Psychiatric Association found that 12 per cent of practicing psychiatrists never prescribed a MAOI, while another 27 per cent had not prescribed a MAOI in the prior three years; only 2 per cent of respondents reported frequent use of MAOIs compared with reports of approximately 25 per cent in the 1980s (Fiedorowicz and Swartz, 2004). A further problem is when MAOIs are prescribed they are often not given in adequate doses (Amsterdam and Hornig-Rohan, 1996).

21.2 Psychological treatments

Content focus

Evaluate the effectiveness of psychological treatments for one disorder.

Psychological treatments assume psychological interventions will either alleviate the symptoms of a disorder or be able to target and rectify a psychological cause that may lead to a long term definitive 'cure'. Overall, psychological treatments seek to change the way patients think and live in an effort to normalize new behaviour and thought and feeling patterns that are beneficial to the individual. However, patients often receive psychological treatments in tandem with biological treatments, therefore it is often difficult to isolate one approach and test its effectiveness in comparison to other treatments. This is particularly true when there is thought to be a specific underlying biological cause to the disorder, such as a neurotransmitter imbalance, and drugs are needed in conjunction with psychological therapy to help patients manage the new ways of feeling.

Psychological treatments seek to change the way patients think and live in an effort to normalize new behaviour and thought and feeling patterns that are beneficial to the individual.

In the following section, two psychological therapies, **cognitive-behavioural therapy** (CBT) and **interpersonal psychotherapy** (IPT), will be discussed in relation to their effectiveness in treating AN and MDD. It should be noted the separation of eating disorders is often carried out for academic and theoretical purposes rather than practical purposes. In practice, patients can suffer from AN in conjunction with other eating disorders (ED), such as **bulimia nervosa** (BN) and **binge eating disorder** (BED). Therefore research often covers a wide range of eating disorders, but where possible the following text isolates AN as a specific disorder.

21.2.1 Cognitive-behavioural therapy

CBT focuses on the development of personal coping strategies that target current problems and aim to change unhelpful patterns in cognitions (e.g. thoughts, beliefs, and attitudes), behaviours, and emotional regulation (Beck, 2011). CBT was originally designed to treat depression, but it is now used to treat a number of mental health conditions.

CBT focuses on the development of personal coping strategies that target current problems and aim to change unhelpful patterns in cognitions (e.g. thoughts, beliefs, and attitudes), behaviours, and emotional regulation (Beck, 2011).

The therapy focuses on thoughts, feelings/emotions and behaviour and assumes they can be changed by targeted interventions that focus on providing new strategies to deal with problems. The main goals are action orientated and problem focused, meaning patients are encouraged to focus on a particular problem and work to create specific actions to address them.

The cyclical and interactive nature of the assumptions can be summed up in Figure 21.1.

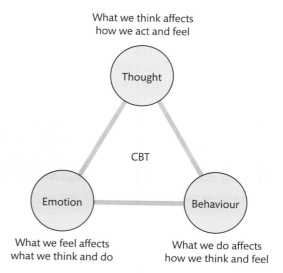

The main difference between IPT and CBT is the emphasis placed on encouraging individuals to develop social and personal skills that help create a social support network to improve their overall well-being.

21.2.2 Interpersonal psychotherapy

IPT assumes personal interaction can help a person change and overcome problems in desired ways. It focuses on an individual's well-being and mental health with the aim of resolving or reducing the impact of troublesome thoughts, feelings, and behaviour through personal relationships. The main difference between IPT and CBT is the emphasis placed on encouraging individuals to develop social and personal skills that help create a social support network to improve their overall well-being. However, the key similarities between IPT and CBT are that they both involve a qualified therapist, they are both time limited, they use homework to focus the patient, and use structured interviews and assessment tools to measure their effectiveness (Weissman et al., 2007).

21.2.3 Anorexia nervosa and CBT

CBT has been shown to be particularly effective for eating disorders. This may be due to the underlying core psychopathology of ED, which involves the over evaluation of shape and weight in conjunction with certain behaviours to restrict food intake. These are essentially cognitive and behavioural in nature. Therefore, any programme that targets underlying thought and behaviour patterns stands a good chance of success.

Questions are often asked about how the changes can become long-term changes and under what conditions CBT should be implemented to be the most effective. Bowers and Ansher (2008) aimed to assess changes in AN inpatients' core beliefs toward eating as a result of undergoing CBT. They used various measurements including a standardized Eating Attitudes Test (EAT) and Eating Disorders Inventory-2 (EDI-2) and compared the results after inpatient treatment and one-year follow-up among patients diagnosed with anorexia.

Thirty-two patients were treated for anorexia nervosa on an inpatient unit and were assessed before and after treatment. At discharge, all patients displayed significant changes in core eating disorder psychopathology and in their depressive symptoms. At the one-year follow-up, changes in some areas of core eating disorder psychopathology and depressive symptoms continued to be significantly different than from admission.

The combination of CBT and weight restoration can significantly reduce eating disorder symptoms and depression with some sustained benefit over a one-year period during inpatient hospitalization. However, while CBT was shown to be effective in this research it was conducted on hospitalized inpatients. Research on inpatients has limited generalizability to outpatient experiences because of the tight focus on attentive care that patients receive as inpatients.

It might be assumed that highly personalized treatments that focus on more complex cognitive issues might be more effective in treating outpatients with AN because they do not receive the level of attention inpatients receive, but this is not always the case.

Key study: Fairburn et al. (2008)

Aim: To test the effectiveness of enhanced cognitive therapy (CBT-E) in the UK. CBT-E creates a highly personalized psychological treatment for patients with the aim of targeting highly specific characteristics.

Procedure: Two CBT-E treatments were compared, one that focused solely on eating disorder features (CBT-Ef) and a more complex treatment that also addressed mood intolerance, clinical perfectionism, low self-esteem, or interpersonal difficulties (CBT-Eb). The researchers also tried to judge just how complex and personalized a therapy should be before it plateaus in terms of effectiveness. A total of 154 patients who had a DSM-IV eating disorder were enrolled in a two-site randomized controlled trial involving 20 weeks of treatment and a 60-week closed period of follow-up.

Findings: Patients in the two treatment conditions exhibited significant improvement when compared to the control group who received no therapy. However, there was no significant difference between the two types of CBT-E for the overall group, although the researchers noted that there was an improvement with patients who had marked mood intolerance, clinical perfectionism, low self-esteem, or interpersonal difficulties. These appeared to respond better to the more complex treatment.

Conclusion: Simpler treatments may best be viewed as the default version while the more complex treatments should be only reserved for patients who have a marked additional psychopathology such as mood intolerance and clinical perfectionism in conjunction with their ED.

21.2.4 Anorexia nervosa and IPT

Very few studies explicitly test the effectiveness of IPT in the treatment of anorexia nervosa, which limits the ability of academics and clinicians to assess the effectiveness of the treatment. Those that have been conducted have not yielded promising results.

For example, McIntosh et al. (2005) studied 56 patients who were randomized to IPT, CBT, or non-specific supportive clinical management. At the end of treatment, IPT was found to be the least effective of the three treatments. However, it can be noted at long-term follow-up (on average 6.7 years following treatment) no significant differences on any outcome measures for the three psychotherapies were found. However, patients of IPT appeared to have improved over the follow-up period. This suggests that IPT over the long term may have a beneficial effect on AN patients.

However, Champion and Power (2012) argue the findings of this study should be interpreted with caution because of the relatively small sample size and the fact that many of the patients were sub-threshold cases of anorexia nervosa with a weight above the widely used diagnostic cut-off point, meaning generalization to more severe sufferers is not possible. Consequently, given the limited amount of empirical research taken together with the findings of McIntosh et al. (2005), Champion and Power state IPT cannot be recommended as a treatment for anorexia nervosa.

Therefore, questions should be asked about why IPT may not be effective in treating AN as it intuitively appears to be an effective approach. Asking patients to use personal and social support networks with regards their AN may be superficially sound but this apparently fails in practice. The answer may lie in the mismatch between the underlying aim of the therapy and the underlying nature of the disorder. For example, Champion and Power (2012) state the most common interpersonal problem encountered in patients with eating disorders is the lack of close or satisfactory intimate relationships, romantic or otherwise. In addition, some patients describe a scarcity of interpersonal relationships and feelings of isolation. Therefore, one of the aims of IPT becomes encouraging patients to consider their own expectations and needs in relationships and to take steps to meet these before they can focus on the nature of their ED.

IPT assumes personal interaction can help a person change and overcome problems in desired ways, but if the problem itself is defined by a personal interaction deficit, then the main avenue for addressing the problem does not exist, or at least exists in a more limited way than with other disorders. Moreover, given the main demographic of AN sufferers is young females, this group often encounters transitional problems with relationships. For example, moving away from home and establishing independence from parents, starting a first job, or having a partner for the first time can cause anxiety and remove a support network that IPT would otherwise utilize to be successful.

21.2.5 Major depressive disorder and CBT

Overall, CBT is thought to be highly effective in the treatment of mild depression and may provide a viable alternative to antidepressant medications, but may be limited in the treatment of severe depression. This is because at the heart of CBT is an assumption that a patient's mood is directly related to his or her thought pattern, but if the thought patterns are too disruptive or deep seated then therapy has a limited effect. Furthermore, CBT does appear to have an enduring effect that protects against subsequent relapses following the end of active treatment, something that cannot be said for medications (Driessen and Hollon, 2010).

Initially, early studies with CBT were not promising. For example, Elkin et al. (1989) compared IPT and CBT for the treatment of outpatients with major depressive disorder. Two hundred and fifty patients were randomly assigned to one of four 16-week treatment conditions: IPT, CBT, drug treatment (imipramine hydrochloride) together with clinical management, and placebo drug plus clinical management. Patients in all treatments, including the placebo, showed significant reduction in depressive symptoms and improvement in functioning over the course of treatment. When comparing each of the psychotherapies with the placebo plus clinical management condition it was noted how there was limited evidence for the specific effectiveness of IPT and none for CBT.

However, later studies have considered the importance of the experience and competence of the clinician and sought to build this variable into the designs. For example, DeRubeis et al. (2005) considered the experience of competent clinicians who worked for research clinics at the University of Pennsylvania, Philadelphia, and Vanderbilt University, Nashville, in the USA.

Key study: DeRubeis et al. (2005)

Aim: To compare the efficacy in moderate to severe depression of antidepressant medications with cognitive therapy in a placebo-controlled trial.

Procedure: Two hundred and forty patients aged between 18 and 70 with moderate to severe MDD were randomly assigned to one of the following: 16 weeks of medication (n = 120), 16 weeks of cognitive therapy (n = 60), or eight weeks of pill placebo (n = 60).

Findings: After eight weeks, response rates in medications (50 per cent) and cognitive therapy (43 per cent) groups were both superior to the placebo (25 per cent) group.

Conclusion: The relative experience levels of the cognitive therapists as well as the patient types appear to have affected the results with different sites having different levels of success with CBT. The researchers concluded CBT can be as effective as medications for the initial treatment of moderate to severe major depression, but the degree of effectiveness may depend on a high level of therapist experience or expertise.

Driessen and Hollon (2010) note that it is not clear just how much experience and training is necessary to ensure a therapist can be considered competent, but it does appear that much of the variation in the CBT literature is related to the skill with which the therapy is implemented. They further note how differences were most apparent with the most severe and complicated patients and it is likely that therapist competence is more of an issue with these types of patients rather than being indicative of incompetence. Therefore, while CBT can be considered an effective therapy, it can fall short with patients who are difficult to interact with. Moreover, studies suggest CBT is most useful when preventing relapse rates. Vittengl et al. (2007) found relapse rates were lower following treatment termination after CBT than after drug therapy while also being lower for patients treated with combined treatment than for patients treated with drugs alone. According to Driessen and Hollon (2010), these results suggest that it is not so much the withdrawal of medication that provokes relapse in remitted patients as that prior exposure to CBT actively prevents it.

21.2.6 Major depressive disorder and IPT

Some studies have not been able to single out IPT as any more or less effective than other therapies. For example, Madelon et al. (2013) performed a systematic review describing a comparison between several standard treatments for MDD in adult outpatients, but with a focus on IPT. They focused on a range of studies between January 1970 and August 2012 in which MDD was a primary diagnosis in adult outpatients receiving individual IPT as a monotherapy and compared it to other forms of psychotherapy.

161

Eight eligible studies involved 1233 patients, out of which 854 completed treatment in outpatient facilities, and while IPT reduced symptoms better than 'usual care' or the 'wait list' condition, the differences between treatment were found to be very small and often they were not significant. Madelon et al. (2013) recommend IPT in what they term 'first-line treatments for depressed adult outpatients' but do not favour it over other treatments. They also recommend the preferences of patients should be taken into consideration when choosing a treatment.

However, a key failing of a **meta-analysis** type of approach is that it is too general and fails to properly take into account individual differences. For example, Toth et al. (2013) focused on a very specific group of socioeconomically impoverished young urban mothers in the USA (average age 25) of mixed ethnicity who were suffering from MDD but were also non-treatment seeking. They were therefore recruited from the community rather than an inpatient or outpatient facility, and to be eligible the women needed to reside at or below the local poverty level. Participants included 128 low-income urban women (aged 18–40), each with a 12-month-old infant. IPT was delivered in accord with the treatment manual (Weissman et al., 2000) and included the provision of 14 sessions of one hour each conducted on a weekly basis. Because of possible variations in literacy and reading ability, all **self-report** measures were read to participants while they followed along and marked their answers. Following confirmation of diagnostic status, women were randomized to the IPT or to the control group that did not receive IPT. However, Toth et al. (2013) argue it is not ethical to withhold treatment from people who have been identified as depressed, therefore women who were not randomized to IPT were actively offered referral to services typically available in the community. This group was labelled the enhanced community standard group (ECS). However, these women were not required to be in treatment unless they chose to do so. Overall, 66.5 per cent elected to be involved in treatment for depression, and all of these women received individual counselling or psychotherapy. Depressive symptoms were assessed before, after, and eight months post-treatment with the Beck Depression Inventory and the Revised Hamilton Rating Scale for Depression. The results showed significant decreases in depressive symptoms among the IPT group compared to the ECS group. Toth et al. note how IPT was effective in treating MDD in a population with multiple risk factors in addition to depression. Over 86.7 per cent of the women receiving IPT had significant histories of childhood maltreatment, 93.3 per cent had experienced at least one lifetime traumatic event, and 26.7 per cent met lifetime criteria for post-traumatic stress disorder. Therefore, it suggests IPT was not only effective in treating MDD but a host of other problems as well. They argue IPT is particularly well suited for impoverished mothers of infants because of the effects of strengthening and expanding their relational networks given how possible social isolation can be a main contributing factor toward MDD. Their study has implications for communities where single motherhood is a cultural norm because this demographic do not have the same level of relationship support networks that mothers who cohabitate do.

The study by Toth et al. (2013) demonstrates how targeting a specific group that would benefit from increased social support yields the most effective results with IPT. Such an approach is further supported by Mufson et al. (2004), who targeted mainly depressed adolescent Latino females in New York City to assess the effectiveness of IPT. The therapy was modified for depressed adolescents (IPT-A) and was compared with treatment as usual (TAU) in school-based mental health clinics. A 16-week randomized

A key failing of a meta-analysis type of approach to investigating human behaviour is that it is too general and fails to properly take into account individual differences.

How can individual differences be incorporated into treatment when dealing with notions of abnormality at the general population level?

clinical trial was conducted in five school-based mental health clinics in New York City with 63 adolescents who had been referred for a mental health intake visit and who met eligibility criteria for MDD. The mean age was 15 and the demographic was predominantly female and Latino. A number of measures were used to assess the outcomes, including the Hamilton Depression Rating Scale, Beck Depression Inventory, Children's Global Assessment Scale, Clinical Global Impressions Scale, and the Social Adjustment Scale–Self-Report. The results showed adolescents treated with IPT-A compared with TAU showed significantly fewer clinician-reported depression symptoms and improvement in overall functioning. Therefore, Mufson et al. (2004) concluded that IPT delivered in school-based health clinics is an effective therapy for adolescent depression and can be a practical alternative to mental health clinics.

21.3 The role of culture in treatment

Content focus

Discuss the role of culture in treatment.

Culture can be defined as a set of attitudes, behaviours, and symbols shared by a large group of people and usually communicated from one generation to the next (Shiraev and Levy, 2004). Attitudes include beliefs (for example, political, religious, and moral beliefs), values, superstitions, and stereotypes. Behaviours include norms, customs, traditions, and fashions.

Mental health treatment has a strong reliance on language, communication, and trust between patients and clinicians, many of which are culturally determined. Therefore, key elements of therapeutic success depend on the clinicians' understanding of patients' cultural identity, social supports, self-esteem, and possible reticence about treatment due to cultural stigma with the aim of building an effective rapport.

There are many areas in which cultural influences impact abnormal psychology. For example, studies that formed the empirical base for the American Psychiatric Association guidelines for depression treatment included 3860 participants, but of those only 27 identified as African American and none as being of Latino descent (US Department of Health and Human Services, 2001). Although the paucity of low-income and minority populations participating in clinical trials is beginning to change, considerably more research needs to be conducted on the efficacy of any service that is delivered to people of diverse cultures. Therefore, culture affects the treatment of disorders in a number of ways.

This section will focus on the culture of the patient and the culture of the clinician.

21.3.1 The culture of the patient

The culture of the patient can affect the treatment of their disorder because of the way they describe or present their symptoms to their clinicians. There are some well-recognized differences in symptom presentation across cultures. Cultural norms within a subgroup can influence a whole host of factors regarding mental health. Lin and Cheung (1999) argue that Asian Americans are a particular cultural group who have cultural characteristics which influence treatment as follows.

EE Choose a treatment for a specific disorder. Evaluate the extent to which it can be considered effective when contrasted with other treatments.

TOK In multicultural societies, notions of abnormality and normality are difficult to define. Should notions of standardization and generalization be abandoned and relativity and individual differences be embraced in treatment? To what extent are definitive approaches to treatment realistic?

 Culture can be defined as a set of attitudes, behaviours, and symbols shared by a large group of people and usually communicated from one generation to the next (Shiraev and Levy, 2004).

163

- Patients tend to focus more on physical discomforts than emotional symptoms, leading to an over-representation of **somatic** complaints. This is due to Asian traditions of viewing the body and mind as unitary rather than dualistic.

- Traditional practices and healing methods are frequently used to alleviate distress both before and after Asian American patients approach the conventional mental healthcare system.

- Asian Americans tend to underuse existing services except those that are culturally appropriate and linguistically compatible.

- Asian American communities place emphasis on the importance of family bonds, so treatment becomes a 'family venture'.

- Asian patients respond well to highly structured therapeutic interventions such as those used in behavioural, cognitive, and interpersonal models.

Culture influences the 'meaning' of disorders to the patient, which influences their likelihood of seeking treatment and their experiences within it. Native Americans and Alaska Natives can express emotional distress in ways that are inconsistent with the diagnostic categories of the DSM, so they may conceptualize mental health differently to how it appears in diagnostic criteria.

Key study: Manson et al. (1985)

Aim: To investigate the cultural representations of depression in North American Hopi Indians.

Procedure: Semi-structured interviews were conducted with 36 Hopi Indians in the USA. The interviewer was a bilingual member of a Hopi community and was therefore able to access the cultural nuances of this particular subculture.

Findings: 'Depression' could not be translated into a single concept for the Hopi participants because they held a multifaceted understanding of the feelings associated with depression and no single translation of depression could be found. Furthermore, they had a very distinct understanding of 'the soul', which is not represented in mental health criteria. The Hopi have five different sicknesses that were in some way connected with the DSM-IV symptoms for depression: worry sickness, unhappiness, heartbreak, drunken-like craziness, and disappointment. Therefore the DSM symptoms for major depression did not match with any disorder that the Hopi were aware of. Instead, it seems that there are different ways of responding to the problems of life among the Hopi.

Conclusion: Different cultural groups have different ways of approaching depression. This may help explain differences in prevalence and the likelihood of members of this cultural subgroup seeking treatment because the categories of Western manuals that influence treatment do not match the experiences of individuals within certain cultural groups.

If those who seek treatment come up against a clinician as well as diagnostic criteria that views their experiences through a different cultural lens than their own, they may find less value in the treatment. This has consequences for other members of the cultural group who may also seek help. It may be necessary to create treatment that is more in line with the cultural expectations of the subgroup. Beals et al. (2005) found a greater percentage of Native Americans were more likely to actively seek services than the general US population, especially when a traditional healing approach was included. Traditional healing systems focus on balancing mind, body, and spirit within a community context. For many Native American groups such a holistic approach to healing involves a sense of connectedness with place and land and rather than isolating one part of the person and attempting to heal it, they focus on the whole person (Beals et al., 2005). Consequently, cultural subgroups will seek out treatment services that match their understanding of their illness. For example, seeking help from traditional healers is common among Native Americans, with those who meet the criteria for depression/anxiety or substance abuse being significantly more likely to seek help from traditional/spiritual healers than from specialty or other medical sources (Walls et al., 2006).

Culture influences the progression of treatment because of subcultural norms relating to personal expression. For example, Asian American groups tend not to dwell on upsetting thoughts and believe reticence or avoidance is better than outward expression, which means they are less likely to express their negative emotions and thoughts (Office of the Surgeon General, USA, 2001). They place a higher emphasis on suppression of emotions while relying on themselves to cope with distress (Narikiyo and Kameoka, 1992).

The way a patient expresses themselves helps the clinician decide on the validity of diagnosis and treatment and allows them to make changes where necessary, which means any patient who is less likely to express their negative thoughts and feelings makes treatment and diagnosis more challenging. These are rooted in cultural norms of expression. For example, McCarty et al. (1999) compared children living in Thailand and children living in the USA. Thailand has an influential Buddhist religion that encourages self-control, emotional restraint, and social inhibition: Thai children were two times more likely than American children to report reliance on covert coping methods such as 'not talking back,' than on overt coping methods such as 'screaming' and 'running away'.

Moreover, culture influences the progression of treatment because of the way patients interpret their symptoms and experiences and then present them to the clinician as the treatment unfolds. For example, the appearance and behaviour of the patient can be misinterpreted by the clinician if they have not taken the time to become familiar with the cultural nuances of the individual's culture. For example, many Native Americans avoid eye contact as a sign of respect, many dress informally, they are 'cooperative' rather than 'competitive', they are open, humble, and live by few rules, which can be compared with the rule-centric approach of many Western cultures.

Furthermore, the distinction between mind and body that is common among individuals in industrialized Western nations is not shared throughout the world. For example, Somervell et al. (1993) sampled 120 adult Native Americans belonging to a single Northwest coast tribe using the Center for Epidemiologic Studies Depression Scale. They found somatic complaints and emotional distress were not well differentiated from each other in this population.

21.3.2 The culture of the clinician

A group of professionals can be said to have a 'culture' if they have a shared set of beliefs, norms, and values (Office of the Surgeon General, USA, 2001). The culture is then reflected in the jargon or language norms that members of the group use, the orientation

Culture influences the progression of treatment because of the way patients interpret their symptoms and experiences and then present them to the clinician as the treatment unfolds.

Research the 'Rudali' concept in India. To what extent are emotional expressions culturally relative? How much should this be taken into account by researchers and diagnosticians?

Modern Western psychiatry can trace its ideological roots to two major European milestones: the development of biological psychiatry in the mid-19th century and the advent of psychotherapy (or 'talk therapy') near the end of that century. These assumptions have led to the dominance of pharmacological therapy and psychotherapy in the treatment of mental illness in the 20th and 21st centuries. Western clinicians working in mental health are rooted in the notions that underpin Western medicine, which emphasize the primacy of the human body in disease.

and emphasis in their measuring instruments, and in their way of looking at the world. However, such trends do not occur in isolation as it can also be noted that clinicians often reflect the attitudes and discriminatory practices of their society (Whaley, 1998).

Western clinicians working in mental health are rooted in the notions that underpin Western medicine, which emphasize the primacy of the human body in disease. Furthermore, Western medicine emphasizes the acquisition of knowledge through scientific and empirical methods, which hold objectivity paramount in the overall aim of uncovering universal truths about diseases, their causation, diagnosis, and treatment (Office of the Surgeon General, USA, 2001). According to Shorter (1997), modern Western psychiatry can trace its ideological roots to two major European milestones: the development of biological psychiatry in the mid-19th century and the advent of psychotherapy (or 'talk therapy') near the end of that century. These assumptions have led to the dominance of pharmacological therapy and psychotherapy in the treatment of mental illness in the 20th and 21st centuries.

The culture of the clinician can cause problems if they and the patient do not come from the same cultural background. In these circumstances, which can occur in multicultural populations, there is greater potential for differences to emerge and clinicians may be more likely to ignore symptoms that the patient deems important, or less likely to understand the patient's fears, concerns, and needs (Office of the Surgeon General, USA, 2001).

However, if the overall aim of any clinician is to help the patient then clinicians should be mindful of imposing a 'God's Eye' perspective on their disorder. Cultural sensitivity is therefore essential if the clinician is to understand the patient's perspective and increase the chances of the treatment being effective, because unless the therapist is aware of the cultural norms of the various groups they interact with, the behaviours and interpretations of the patients may be misinterpreted. For example, the Native American norm of avoiding eye contact and being cooperative rather than competitive can be interpreted as a lack of interest or laziness and apathy (Richardson, 2012).

Therefore, there is a responsibility of the clinician to become culturally competent (Sue and Sue, 2013). Cultural competence refers to the notion that mental healthcare providers should engage in actions or create conditions that maximize the optimal development of treatment for the patient (Sue and Torino, 2005). Sue and Sue (2013) made a number of explicit recommendations for clinicians working within multicultural communities who want to become culturally competent.

The clinician should:

- be aware of their own biases and cultural influences that form their worldview. This is important because very little training is given to clinicians that asks them to consider how their own cultural heritage may influence diagnoses and patient management.

- be encouraged to undertake cultural role-taking where there is a cognitive empathy for the worldview of the patient. The clinician should not necessarily take on the worldview of the patient as their own but should make an effort to understand how the patient views the world.

- use strategies, techniques, and treatments that are consistent with the life experiences of the patient.

These recommendations can be seen in practice in the following example. The following recommendations have been given to clinicians working with Native American traditional healers in the USA.

The clinician should:

- develop background knowledge of the traditional beliefs and practices in the community in which they are working by becoming a serious student of healing practices of the American Indian culture

- actively seek an opportunity for collaboration rather than impose a top down, objectivized worldview on the patient, which may come through clinical care, employment, or personal relationships

- develop a trusting relationship with a community member who has knowledge of traditional healing practices, and is connected with healers in the community

- identify collaboration as major goal of ongoing relationships.

Adopted from Shore and Manson (2009), cited in Richardson (2012).

21.4 Assessing the effectiveness of treatment(s)

Content focus

Discuss how the effectiveness of treatments can be assessed.

As has been discussed earlier, whenever the effectiveness of a treatment of a disorder is measured, questions about the sociocultural background of the patient should be considered. Patients will have their own expectations of what it means to be ill and undergo treatment. Consequently, they will have their own conceptions of what it means to be 'cured'.

Siewert et al. (1999) have argued that mental illness cannot be separated from the individual's social and cultural context, and culture plays an important role in the perception of mental illness. Therefore, it also plays an important role in the perception of what might be considered effective treatment. For example, success in treatment often means living with an illness rather than being completely free of it and many doctors may aim to move toward a position where the patient can live more comfortably with the illness. This may not be acceptable to some patients, who expect a definitive end to their suffering, but being free of mental suffering in traditional medical terms is often unrealistic.

Within Western cultures, a definitive concept of 'cure' is appealing because of the dominance of the medical model within the medical establishment. Many physical ailments have a definitive end point when the person can be said to be free or 'cured' of the illness. However, psychological illnesses are often very personal and relative to the individual or their cultural worldview.

Furthermore, assessing the effectiveness of treatments raises a number of questions about what can be considered an effective measurement. Nation states that provide healthcare to their citizens through tax-funded services (such as the UK) have a

Create a set of ethics for clinicians and place them on a ten-point scale. Which are more important than others?

Choose a culture. Explore the limitations of the medical model or Western medicine in healing people from within that culture who have a particular disorder. To what extent is the medical model suitable for treating your chosen cultural group?

Can all human experience be fully measured, then generalized to larger populations?

responsibility to measure whether those services are effective. Nation states that allow private healthcare providers to offer services also have a moral responsibility to ensure those services meet the needs of the client base. Governments and centralized bodies may wish to measure the effectiveness of treatment on a regional or national level of analysis. However, individual hospitals and clinicians may wish to assess their effectiveness on a more local individual level of analysis in terms of a particular therapy or therapist. In the following section, both levels of analysis are considered.

21.4.1 Assessing the effectiveness of treatments: macro level of analysis

Donabedian (1980; cited in Kilbourne et al., 2010) published an assessment framework for assessing mental healthcare on a macro level of analysis that is still influential today. This framework incorporates three domains of quality measurement: structure, process, and outcomes.

Structure measures refer to resources and policies that can inform processes of care provided by clinicians. For example, how many mental healthcare facilities are available in a region? How many doctors are available in a given mental health facility? Structure measures are relatively simple to assess because they can be easily quantified and measured through easily obtainable resources. However, they can also be subject to **response bias**, for example, programme leaders can sometimes over-report resources or over-idealize clinic operations such as working hours. Moreover, structure measures do not indicate whether good care happened, but only if a particular region or site has a capacity to provide good care.

Process measures refer to interactions between patients and the structural elements of the healthcare system. For example, are patients able to access the services? Are they aware of the services? While these may appear relatively straightforward to measure, they can be seen as being overly dependent on patients who have sought and received care. Accessing potential patients who need treatment but are not being cared for is a relatively difficult exercise for professionals interested in measuring the effectiveness of treatments.

Outcome measures refer to the results of these interactions for patients, including day-to-day functioning, mortality, and perceptions of quality of life (Lim et al., 2008), as well as overall patient satisfaction. For example, is the care making a difference for the individual patient and society? While this is a natural focus for any assessment of the effectiveness of treatment, in private insurance systems such as the USA, it can often lead to healthcare providers finding ways to avoid taking on particularly sick patients knowing their chances of improvement are slim. Furthermore, there is such a large range of outcome measuring scales available, achieving reliability across them is very difficult. For example, for measuring outcomes in depression there is the Hamilton Depression Rating Scale, Beck Depression Inventory, Children's Global Assessment Scale, Clinical Global Impressions Scale, and the Social Adjustment Scale–Self-Report.

A macro level of analysis may consider the effectiveness of a particular therapy. For example, on earlier pages therapies such as CBT and IPT have been discussed. A more general patient-centric and cooperative approach might involve developing an instrument that could be applied to all healthcare settings. For example, Hunter et al. (2015) aimed to explore whether patient-reported outcome measures (PROMs)

A macro level of analysis measures the effectiveness of treatment on a regional or national level.

could be developed to measure key attributes of all long-term conditions (LTCs) care in England and not just within mental health boundaries. They wanted to assess the potential value of a single generic measure that could be applied to patient experiences, which had actually been developed by patients themselves. They used a **qualitative** semi-structured interview method and found there was broad support for a single PROM that could be used to measure outcomes for patients. Interviewees identified three desired uses for a PROM: to improve the quality of individual care; to increase people's engagement in their own care; and to monitor the performance of services. Furthermore, interviewees felt that a PROM could also incorporate notions of functioning, empowerment, and social participation, and be co-designed with patients and professionals alike.

21.4.2 Assessing the effectiveness of treatments: Micro level of analysis

Mental health clinicians have been found to be assessing progress of their patients through unstructured interactions. These yield unquantified results that cannot be subjected to traditional measures of reliability and validity (Zimmerman, 2017). For example, some clinicians ask only broad, global questions such as 'How are you feeling?' or 'How are you doing?', which encourages the patient to respond with global responses such as 'Okay' or 'Fine'. However, these responses often do not accurately reflect the patient's clinical status.

Therefore, incorporating standardized scales into clinical practice to assess the effectiveness of treatments should be an essential first step. One obstacle to assessing the effectiveness of treatments is convincing individual clinicians to engage in consistent and regular measuring practices. Gilbody et al. (2002) conducted a survey with 500 psychiatrists in the UK and found that among the 340 who responded, 58 per cent never used a scale to measure clinical change of depression and anxiety. Finding a common measure and encouraging clinicians to use it is therefore a key goal of mental health researchers and care providers.

A micro level of analysis measures the effectiveness of treatment on an individual hospital and clinician level. Finding a common measure and encouraging clinicians to use it is a key goal of mental health researchers and care providers.

An example of a standardized system of measurement is a self-report questionnaire. These are often used where the patients themselves are asked to consider the effectiveness of their own treatment. The advantages of self-report questionnaires mean they do not require clinician time for administration and can be free from clinician bias, however they can result in an overestimation of patient improvement. Moreover, a self-report questionnaire may be more effective in assessing the internal mental states of patients more validly than clinician rating scales. However, this may be offset by the patient tendency to over-report symptom severity. Furthermore, an assessment scale needs to be replicable and open to standardized measuring practices. Therefore, language would need to be standardized across the measuring instrument, but this would still mean it would not be able to be completed by some individuals due to illiteracy. The key drawback of self-report questionnaires in assessing the effectiveness of treatment is that patients have compromised cognitive or emotional functioning and may be unable or unwilling to accurately report the condition of their internal mental state.

An effective approach is to develop focused scales that measure distinct illnesses that have agreed boundaries within accepted classification systems such as the DSM-IV and DSM-5 and the ICD-10. For example, depression is a common disorder and attempts to measure the effectiveness of treatments have attracted a great deal of attention. *The Practitioner's Guide to Empirically Based Measures of Depression* by Nezu et al. (2000) is a compendium that summarizes all of the scales available to measure depression. It aims to guide clinicians and researchers in choosing practical tools relevant for clinical assessment. There are several scales assessing the DSM-IV criteria of MDD that have been developed and are considered reliable and valid measures.

Beck Depression Inventory-II (BDI-II)

The original version of the BDI was published in 1961 and the current BDI-II contains 21 multiple-choice items assessing symptoms of depression. It has been found that the BDI-II correlates highly with clinician assessments of depression severity. A key strength of BDI-II is that it provides a quantitative assessment of the intensity of depression. Furthermore, it is quick and easy to use and is written in deliberately accessible language. Moreover, it acknowledges and separates MDD into affective components and cognitive components. For example, patients are asked to respond to the following questions about how they approach a work situation.

- **0:** I can work about as well as before.
- **1:** It takes an extra effort to get started at doing something.
- **2:** I have to push myself very hard to do anything.
- **3:** I can't do any work at all.

There are also statements that relate to the affective components of MDD.

- **0:** I do not feel sad.
- **1:** I feel sad.
- **2:** I am sad all the time and I can't snap out of it.
- **3:** I am so sad and unhappy that I can't stand it.

However, a key limitation of the BDI-II, which it shares with other self-assessment scales, is that scores can be easily exaggerated or minimized by the person completing them.

22 Research methods: abnormal psychology

Learning focus

Discuss approaches to research in abnormal psychology.

Abnormal psychology creates a number of special considerations for researchers. Research in abnormal psychology usually aims to measure patient or clinician experiences so improvements or adjustments can be made to the treatment of people who suffer from a mental illness. Therefore, patients and clinicians are often at the core of research. This means researchers have to carefully consider how they approach their designs to achieve validity and avoid bias. They must be confident the treatment they are interested in has the effect that they and the clinicians claim.

22.1 The use of control groups

Research in abnormal psychology is often intertwined with treatment or care-related programmes. Working with people who either implement treatment or are patients means researchers have to think very carefully about the methods they use for gathering data and what their research aims are. Often, when mental health researchers collect data they do so in a fashion that means they can be said to compare a treatment with the lack of a treatment, or a treatment compared to another treatment. However, in abnormal psychology the individuals collecting the data have a deep interest in the patients or the care-related programme and this will influence their decisions about what kinds of treatment their participants receive.

For example, Toth et al. (2013) wanted to test the effectiveness of IPT on socioeconomically impoverished young urban mothers in the USA (average age 25). These were of mixed ethnicity who were suffering from MDD but who were also non-treatment seeking – therefore they were recruited from the community rather than an inpatient or outpatient facility. A normal research design may involve a 'treatment group' and a 'non-treatment group', but Toth et al. (2013) argued that it was not ethical to withhold treatment from people who have been identified as depressed, therefore women who were not randomized to IPT were actively offered services that were typically available in the community, which was labelled the enhanced community standard group (ECS). The ECS women were not required to be in treatment unless they chose to do so and the treatment they received was not monitored or controlled by the researchers.

The decision to offer treatment to the control group, but not monitor or control it, meant they were comparing two types of treatment but without the control of the ECS group. This should be considered when the results are analyzed and the effectiveness of IPT is considered.

As Toth et al. shows, interventions rarely operate in isolation. They take place in complex sociocultural places where patients live their lives in ways that are difficult to quantify and explain.

For example, Kaye et al. (1991) was interested in the effects of fluoxetine on 31 patients with DSM-III-R anorexia nervosa (AN). Most anorexics were started on fluoxetine treatment, but after inpatient weight restoration they were discharged from the hospital and followed up as outpatients. Every patient will have a different outpatient experience and while the researchers could be fairly confident about who was taking the drug and how much, this in itself is open to error as they could not account for the experiences the outpatients were having on a day-to-day basis, for example, the extent to which family and friends supported them. They were able to conclude that fluoxetine may help patients with AN to maintain a healthy body weight as outpatients but the reasons for the positive effects of fluoxetine were uncertain and it was not clear how the drug was able to interact with environmental factors to help recovery.

Therefore, the researchers could not be certain of the efficacy of fluoxetine and they urged caution and argued that fluoxetine should not be used as the sole treatment for AN. Such vagaries are not the fault of the researchers, they are a natural outcome of working with real patients in the real world.

Often when mental health researchers collect data, they do so in a fashion that means they can be said to compare a treatment with the lack of a treatment, or a treatment compared to another treatment.

22.2 Being aware of participant expectations

One of the more important factors to consider in abnormal-related research is that the participants are less likely to respond passively to the research process, but are intimately engaged in it because the issues relate to their own personal experiences and needs. Researchers need to be aware that mental health research is an active process that requires reflection and dynamic interrogation of the data, the participant who is sometimes also a patient, and the research context, but it may also lead to participant expectations (also called **reactivity**).

Participant expectations are an issue for all types of social science research but are particularly prescient in mental health related research because of the vested interest participants or the clinician may have in the outcome of the study. Participants may try and guess the nature of the research or programme and influence the results. Therefore, if the participant feels they have to behave in certain ways in order to please the researcher, this will affect the value of the data in a negative way. One way to address participant expectations is to use placebos and **sham treatments**.

One way to address participant expectations is to use placebos and sham treatments.

22.3 The use of placebos or sham treatments

An alternative to allowing participants access to treatment the researcher does not control is to use a sham treatment. These are analogous to a placebo, where an apparent treatment is given to a control group of subjects to enable the effects of the supposedly 'active' treatment to be assessed, but in the sham treatment the procedure is not active.

For example, McClelland et al. (2016) wanted to test the effectiveness of rTMS on treating AN. One group received the rTMS while the other group went through a similar procedure but did not receive the magnetic stimulation. They found individuals who received rTMS had reduced symptoms post-rTMS and at the 24-hour follow-up, relative to those who received the sham stimulation. Therefore, the study was able to provide modest evidence that rTMS reduces core symptoms of AN.

However, sham treatments are only appropriate in certain settings. For example, with an rTMS device it is possible to fake treatment. However, with any interpersonal type therapy where the therapist interacts with the patient on a personal level to undercover their anxieties and thoughts etc., a sham approach is not suitable because it is impossible to fake this type of interaction.

22.4 The use of pilot studies

Researchers have to be cautious about pronouncing the relative efficacy of treatments they have investigated. Research with real patients needs to be deemed safe and appropriate before it can go ahead in earnest. Moreover, effective research usually costs time and money and will take up the time and resources of hospitals, clinicians, and patients.

Therefore, researchers often use pilot studies to help them address these issues. Pilot studies are usually small in scale and are a preliminary study to evaluate feasibility, time, cost, adverse events, etc. in an attempt to predict an appropriate sample size and improve the design before a full-scale study can be developed.

For example, Van den Eynde et al. (2011) conducted a pilot study to investigate whether one session of high-frequency rTMS would reduce eating disorder-related symptoms following exposure to visual and real food stimuli. Safety and tolerability were also assessed. They used a relatively small sample of ten right-handed people with AN who underwent one session of rTMS and resulted in reduced levels of feeling full, feeling fat, and feeling anxious. They concluded rTMS may reduce core symptoms of AN in the small sample, but further research was needed.

22.5 The use of meta-analysis

Rather than conduct a trial with real patients in real clinic settings, researchers often chose to perform a meta-analysis of others' work so they can reach broad conclusions. A meta-analysis allows a large-scale review of work in the same area so conclusions can be drawn. This approach has the advantage of being able to collate the results from many studies, although researchers conducting meta-analysis need to be sure they include studies that have similar methodologies so appropriate comparisons can be made. For example, Von Wolff et al. (2013) wanted to assess the efficacy of SSRIs and TCA in the treatment of depression. They conducted a systematic search of a number of databases including CENTRAL, MEDLINE, EMBASE, ISI Web of Science, BIOSIS, and PsycINFO. They only considered randomized, controlled trials. However, while the methodological quality of the primary studies was evaluated as unclear in many cases and they argue more evidence is needed to assess the efficacy of SSRIs and TCAs in patients suffering from chronic forms of depression other than **dysthymia**, they were able to claim both SSRIs and TCAs are effective in the treatment of chronic depression.

A meta-analysis allows a large-scale review of work in the same area so conclusions can be drawn.

22.6 The importance of reflexivity

One way to minimize the effect of participant expectations and researcher bias is by demonstrating **reflexivity** throughout the research process. Reflexivity is a process that occurs throughout the research and is based on the assumption that it is important the researcher is aware of his or her own contribution to the construction of meaning in the research process and then makes the reader of their research aware of this. Such an approach allows the researcher to reflect on ways in which bias may occur by acknowledging that his or her own background and beliefs can influence the way the research is conducted. This line of thinking argues that researchers should provide sufficient details about issues that may potentially bias the investigation. For example, revealing where they stand in terms of certain treatments of cultural groups or political issues such as funding for mental healthcare.

22.7 The issue of generalization

Generalization refers to the extent to which results are relevant outside the context of the study. Mental health researchers have to carefully consider the extent to which they want their findings to apply to people other than those who participate in a study. Generalizing findings from a study means that the results are relevant outside the context of the study itself. According to Lewis and Ritchie (2003), it is useful to consider the following forms of generalization.

- Representational generalization means findings from research can be applied to populations outside the specific population of the study. A typical question could be if findings from a drug treatment for depression are representative of all people who suffer from MDD in general. This could have implications for the development of MDD treatment programmes. If a researcher has used small samples that are not selected to be statistically representative, and other non-standardized methods may be used (such as interviews), it makes it difficult to generalize findings to other populations. Furthermore, researchers often target highly specific populations. For example, Toth et al. (2013) tested the effectiveness of IPT on socioeconomically impoverished young urban mothers in the USA whose average age was 25. Therefore, considerations of the uniqueness of certain populations have to be built into mental health-related research and researchers need to be cautious about generalizing outside of these groups.

- Theoretical generalization means theoretical concepts derived from the study can be used to develop further theory. The findings from a study might lead to inferences about what could be effective policies to design MDD treatment programmes for other populations. Therefore, the findings from the study may contribute to wider therapeutic development.

23 Ethical considerations: abnormal psychology

Learning focus

Discuss ethical considerations in abnormal psychology.

Abnormal psychology creates a number of special considerations for researchers. Research in abnormal psychology usually aims to measure patient or clinician experiences so improvements or adjustments can be made. Therefore, patients are often at the core of research. This means researchers have to carefully consider ethics in their research designs and respect the **autonomy** and **dignity** of people they are researching, even those who may not fully understand the research that is taking place around them.

23.1 Research Ethics Committee

Most respected academic institutions should have some form of **Research Ethics Committee** (REC) consisting of a multidisciplinary team of professional researchers and/or experienced academics with a balance of gender and cultural backgrounds.

A REC is normally responsible for (based on the BPS Ethical guidelines 2010):

- reviewing all research involving human participants conducted by individuals employed within or by that institution

- ensuring that the ethics review is independent, competent, and timely

- protecting the dignity, rights, and welfare of research participants

- considering the safety of the researcher(s)

- considering the legitimate interests of other stakeholders

- making informed judgements of the scientific merit of proposals

- making informed recommendations to the researcher if the proposal is found to be wanting in some respect.

Abnormal psychology raises some particular ethical considerations that any REC would have to consider before approving research. For example, researchers:

- often deal with people who are suffering from a major mental health issue and can therefore be classed as 'patients' as well as 'participants' in a study

- may be trying to find out why people are suffering from a mental health issue

- may be measuring the effectiveness of a treatment programme

- may want to generalize their findings to wider populations if the efficacy of a treatment is established.

Therefore, researchers may well deal with very sensitive data regarding the experiences of their participants, who may also be patients.

23.2 Intervention

Mental health researchers often collect data in a fashion that means they can be said to compare a treatment with the lack of a treatment, or a treatment compared to another treatment. Therefore the researchers collecting the data will have a deep interest in the patients or the care-related programme and this will influence their decisions about what kinds of treatment their participants receive.

Most respected academic institutions should have some form of REC consisting of a multidisciplinary team of professional researchers and/or experienced academics with a balance of gender and cultural backgrounds.

For example, Toth et al. (2013) wanted to test the effectiveness of IPT on socioeconomically impoverished young urban mothers in the USA (average age 25). Patients were women of mixed ethnicity who were suffering from MDD but were also non-treatment seeking – therefore they were recruited from the community rather than an inpatient or outpatient facility. A normal research design may involve a 'treatment group' and a 'non-treatment group', but Toth et al. (2013) argued that it was not ethical to withhold treatment from people who have been identified as depressed. This decision was made despite the fact that the women themselves were non-treatment seeking.

Therefore, the women who were not randomized to the active experimental group were actively offered services typically available in the community. Overall, 66.5 per cent elected to be involved in treatment for depression, and all of these women received individual counselling or psychotherapy.

Other researchers may decide isolating the effectiveness of the treatment given to people they have identified as depressed has more long term ethical advantages than any short-term ethical considerations. In such a scenario, traditional treatment versus placebo designs are used.

> Researchers may decide isolating the effectiveness of the treatment has more long-term ethical advantages than any short-term ethical considerations.

For example, DeRubeis et al. (2005) aimed to compare the efficacy of antidepressant medications with cognitive therapy in a placebo-controlled trial. They randomly assigned 240 patients aged between 18 and 70 with moderate to severe major depressive disorder to one of the following: 16 weeks of medications (n = 120), 16 weeks of cognitive therapy (n = 60), or eight weeks of pill placebo (n = 60). They found after eight weeks, response rates in medications (50 per cent) and cognitive therapy (43 per cent) groups were both superior to the placebo (25 per cent) group.

Because of the effective use of a non-treatment placebo group they were able to conclude that CBT can be as effective as medications for the initial treatment of moderate to severe major depression. They would not have been able to make such cause-effect conclusions if they had allowed the placebo group access to the same form of treatment.

23.3 Cultural competence

For clinicians who deal with people from varied cultural backgrounds there is a responsibility for them to become culturally competent (Sue and Sue, 2013). **Cultural competence** refers to the notion that mental healthcare providers should engage in actions or create conditions that maximize the optimal development of treatment for the patient (Sue and Torino, 2005). Sue and Sue made a number of explicit recommendations for clinicians working within multicultural communities who want to become culturally competent, but the same approach can be applied to all mental health researchers as all communities have varied cultural norms within them.

> Cultural competence refers to the notion that mental healthcare providers should engage in actions or create conditions that maximize the optimal development of treatment for the patient (Sue and Torino, 2005).

The mental health researcher should:

- be aware of their own biases and cultural influences that form their worldview. This is important because it asks them to consider how their own cultural heritage may influence their expectations for treatment and outcomes.

- be encouraged to undertake cultural role-taking where there is a cognitive empathy for the worldview of the patient. The researcher should not necessarily take on the worldview of the patient-participant but should make an effort to understand how the patient views the world.

- use strategies, techniques, and approaches to research that are consistent with the life experiences of the patient-participant.

23.4 Patient's psychological state

Some patients are in a state that enables them to provide useful and reliable information to the researcher. However, some patients may be in a state of anxiety, have poor concentration, poor memory, or are unable to word their experiences in a consistently understandable way.

For example, patients with disorganized thoughts are unable to provide any useful information due to their psychosis. In addition, some may not reveal information due to shame, denial or fear of legal consequences to obtain or avoid particular treatments.

Aboraya et al. (2006) note how patients with personality disorders may even make an effort to manipulate the clinician, which can also apply to the researcher. This poses problems for the researcher when their role is to elicit pertinent information from the patient, assess the information, and make a rational judgement in the form of assessing the effectiveness of an intervention. Therefore, researchers need to consider how much they are able to involve patients in the research, which means considerations are given to the patient's mental state. The researchers need to consider how much the patient-participant is able to give **informed consent**.

23.5 Informed consent

As a starting point, participants should know that participation in mental health research is voluntary. This is particularly important if the research is conducted by people who have some kind of relation to members of the sample (for example, a clinician), since participation could then be motivated by feelings of obligation. The researcher must provide participants with sufficient information about the study, such as who funded the study, who will conduct the study, how the data will be used, the time commitment needed from participants, and the topics the study will address. It should also be made clear that consent can always be renegotiated. In cases where children aged under 16 years are involved, consent must be obtained from parents or legal guardians. The rule is that informed consent should always be obtained. This is stressed in all guidelines on ethical conduct in research. However, in some cases, where it would not otherwise be possible to study a phenomenon (e.g. patients who use illegal drugs to self-medicate), ethics committees may offer dispensation from the rule because the goal of the research is to obtain knowledge that may eventually lead to the drug being seen as effective therapy. However, this rarely happens.

Participants should know that participation in mental health research is voluntary and the researcher must provide the participants with sufficient information about the study.

23.6 Protecting participants from harm

Researchers should take preventive action in all research to avoid harming the participants. This is particularly true in sensitive research topics, such as mental health issues. Due to the nature of certain methods (e.g. qualitative methods such as in-depth interviews), participants may disclose very private information that they have never shared with anyone before. This can happen because the interview situation seems like a friendly encounter where the participant may feel comfortable and safe with an individual who cares about them. However, the participant may regret such revelations and feel upset after the interview when the interviewer has gone. This situation should be avoided.

Prior to the research, and before they agree to participate, participants should have a clear understanding of the topics to be addressed. Researchers must approach sensitive issues through clear and direct questions, so that participants are not drawn into irrelevant and sensitive details by mistake. If participants show signs of discomfort, the researcher should be empathetic and consider stopping the research. If the research has dealt with emotional and sensitive issues, the researcher should try to return to less sensitive topics toward the end. It is not advised that the researcher should provide advice or counsel the participant, but he or she might provide useful information about where to find help if this is necessary. The mental health researcher has to decide what they will do in these situations and present their intentions to the REC.

23.7 Anonymity and confidentiality

Anonymity and **confidentiality** are a key part of psychological research. Usually, the identity of participants should not be known outside the research team and not usually be identifiable to each other. Potential mental health researchers have to show their RECs how they will guarantee that participants remain anonymous and how the data will be held securely. At no point should any reader of the eventual report be able to guess the identity of the participants.

Confidentiality means that research data will not be known to anyone outside the study. The researcher may have to change minor details in the report to avoid the possibility of participants being recognized. Confidentiality also relates to the way data is stored after the research. If interviews or observations have been video recorded and archived, it can be difficult to guarantee total anonymity, so these should be destroyed when transcripts have been made.

In addition, ethical issues in terms of anonymity may arise in case studies or in research designs with a small number of participants, because of the risk that they may be identified in research reports, as it is difficult to lose people in a small qualitative crowd. If the researcher finds it necessary to archive non-anonymized data, or the researcher will be using extensive quotes from their sample, the participant should give written informed consent.

Researchers should take preventive action in all research to avoid harming participants. This is particularly true in sensitive research topics, such as mental health issues. Due to the nature of certain methods (e.g. qualitative methods such as in-depth interviews), participants may disclose very private information that they have never shared with anyone before.

Anonymity and confidentiality are a key part of psychological research. Usually, the identity of participants should not be known outside the research team and not usually be identifiable to each other.

Research different ethical guidelines from different psychology sources. For example, REC committees; academic specifications such as the IBO Diploma Psychology course. Create Venn diagrams showing where they have similarities and differences.

Activity

Find all of the new words or expressions from this chapter and write them into a document with their definitions and explanations next to them. Be creative and use diagrams or boxes to help make your personal glossary unique and effective.

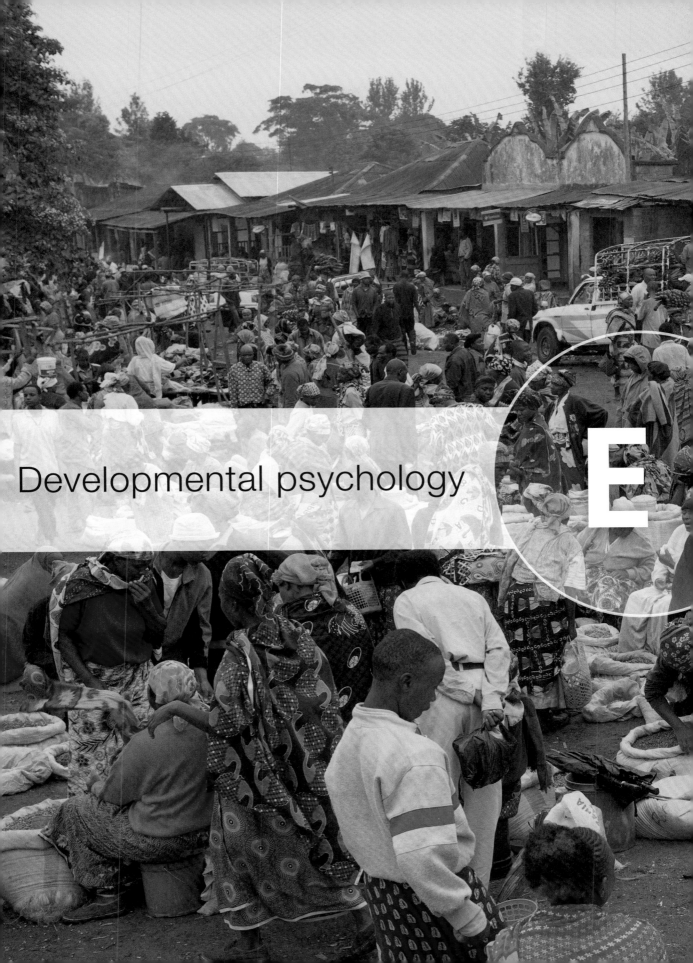

Developmental psychology

E

Developmental psychology is the study of how and why people's behaviour and thinking changes over time. The three topics in this option are:

- influences on **cognitive** and **social development**

- developing an identity

- developing as a learner.

Knowledge about the influence of biological, social, and cultural factors in the development of an individual is helpful not only for families, but also in childcare and education to create opportunities for children and young people all over the world.

Developmental psychology focuses on how development can be supported or undermined. It is important to gain an understanding of the extent to which early experience may influence later development and whether there are critical periods in development. Ideas centred around **resilience** are relevant in this option and may help explain why some people are more affected by their experiences than others.

Write a timeline featuring all the developmental stages you can think of throughout your life. Include emotional and cognitive milestones.

24 Influences on cognitive and social development

Topic focus

Discuss influences on cognitive and social development.

24.1 The role of peers and play

Content focus

Discuss the role of peers and play on cognitive and social development.

A child's peers can be defined as a group with whom they interact who are of a similar age and developmental level.

A child's **peers** can be defined as a group with whom they interact who are of a similar age and developmental level. Some definitions also include levels of education and/ or social status or 'class'. Peers are of interest to developmental researchers because in many cultures children significantly interact with their peers, and are therefore influenced by them from a young age.

Play can be defined as a range of activities the child is motivated to be involved in and which provide pleasure. It usually involves imagination, role-play, the involvement of their peers, and an engagement with toys or props.

24.1.1 The role of peers in social development

Social development begins at a very young age. Most infants and toddlers meet their peers on a regular basis, and some experience long-lasting relationships with particular peers that start at birth (Hay et al., 1999). By the age of 6 months, infants communicate with other infants by smiling, touching, and babbling. In the second year of life, they can show both **prosocial** and aggressive behaviour with their peers, with some toddlers clearly being more aggressive than others (Rubin et al., 2003). By early childhood, the actual time spent interacting with age peers surpasses the time spent with parents (Ellis et al., 1981).

During early and middle childhood, **gender** seems to be the most consistent characteristic to organize peer group affiliation. This reflects the importance of reinforcing values and **norms** associated with one's gender identity even at a young age (Fagot and Rodgers, 1998), as well the different types of play the two genders engage in.

An important part of social development is the acceptance and rejection of peers. This process can be quite ruthless and is determined by group dynamics as well as by the child's behaviour. For example, studies show that highly aggressive children are not accepted by their peers (Crick et al., 1997), although this does not affect both genders equally, as boys can be socially rewarded for overtly aggressive behaviour (Coie and Kupersmidt, 1983).

However, it is inaccurate to blame peer rejection on perceived negative behaviour. It may actually be the absence of prosocial behaviour, not the presence of aggression, that leads to peer rejection (Denham et al., 1990). For example, shy children who lack social skills can experience problems gaining acceptance in their peer groups (Cooper and Eke, 1999).

It is assumed by social development researchers that peer acceptance in early childhood is a predictor of later peer relations. There have been links made between children who are isolated from their peer groups in early childhood and problems later in childhood. However, like many social psychological phenomena it is difficult to pinpoint a singular cause for this process or isolate the mechanisms that lead to it. Social interaction is a complex process and children who are socially isolated may choose to isolate themselves and come from homes where this is the norm. Parents who do not encourage social mixing or the development of social skills in their children will model behaviours their children will imitate.

However, some **generalizations** can be made about the short- and medium-term effects of socializing in young children. For example, researchers found that toddlers who were able to engage in complex play with their peers were more socially competent in dealing with other children in the preschool years and in middle childhood (Ladd and Troop-Gordon, 2003). Furthermore, children who did not have friends in preschool continued to have problems dealing with peers by the age of 10 (Woodward and Fergusson, 2000).

Peer rejection is associated with educational underachievement, even when many other probable **causal** influences (such as parental influences) are taken into account (Criss et al., 2002). Furthermore, links have been made between having friends in early childhood and protection against the development of psychological problems later in childhood (Criss et al., 2002).

24.1.2 Peer contagion and antisocial behaviour

Peer influence can have a negative impact on social development. **Peer contagion** describes a mutual influence process occurring between an individual and a peer (Dishion and Tipsord, 2011). Peer contagion includes behaviours and emotions that potentially undermine the individuals' own development or cause harm to others.

During early and middle childhood, gender seems to be the most consistent characteristic to organize peer group affiliation. This reflects the importance of reinforcing values and norms associated with one's gender identity even at a young age, as well the different types of play the two genders engage in.

It is assumed by social development researchers that peer acceptance in early childhood is a predictor of later peer relations. There have been links made between children who are isolated from their peer groups and problems later in childhood.

Peer contagion includes behaviours and emotions that potentially undermine the individuals' own development or cause harm to others, e.g. aggression, bullying, weapon carrying, disordered eating, drug use, and depression.

Examples of peer contagion include aggression, bullying, weapon carrying, disordered eating, drug use, and depression. It should be noted that participants may not intend to influence their peers in a negative way, but they engage in behaviours that satisfy immediate needs, such as the need for an audience or companionship, or to feel empowered.

Antisocial behaviour of individuals can also influence the social development of those around them. Snyder et al. (2005) randomly selected preschool children from their classrooms and video recorded them playing. They coded the content of the children's play (what they talked about) and the process (laughter, anger, etc.) they engaged in when they spoke. They found that many children at age five mimicked 'deviant' behaviour that occurred in adults.

Snyder et al. (2005) found that when this behaviour was received positively by randomly selected peers, the child was more likely to commit forms of antisocial behaviour during the subsequent two years, as reported by parents. This finding suggests that peer interactions in the preschool playgroup also affects the home environment. The key mechanism at work was **social conditioning** positively rewarding antisocial behaviour.

Children may collectively learn aggression in peer contexts in which 'winning' a fight is their main problem-solving strategy, and this in turn increases the likelihood of future aggression.

In a later study by Snyder et al. (2008), children who were observed using aggressive behaviour to assert themselves in peer interactions (such as an escape condition in play situations) were assessed by parents and teachers on **covert** (e.g. stealing, lying) and **overt** (e.g. aggression) antisocial behaviour over three years from ages five through to eight years old. The results suggest children may collectively learn aggression in peer contexts in which 'winning' a fight is their main problem-solving strategy, and this in turn increases the likelihood of future aggression.

Furthermore, aggressive children are often found to be central to the core social cliques in the classroom, and this occurs even when they are socially rejected by classmates. This is particularly true for boys who value and reward aggressive behaviour among their peers more than girls (Coie and Kupersmidt, 1983).

24.1.3 The role of play on cognitive development

Cognitive development refers to the development of mental processing such as problem solving, language ability, and abstract thinking skills.

Animal studies show how enriched environments have a significant impact on brain development.

Animal studies show how enriched environments have a significant impact on brain development. For example, Diamond et al. (1972) manipulated the richness of rats' environments by either giving them or not giving them interesting toys to play with for a period of 30 days. The **dependent variable** (DV) was the weight of the **frontal lobe**, measured after the rats had been euthanized. Researchers found the frontal lobe was heavier in the rats that had been in the stimulating environment.

This experiment could never be conducted on humans for ethical reasons, but it shows a clear link between the role of play and the brains of social animals. Further research has confirmed these results. For example, rats raised in stimulating environments had bigger brains and were able to find their way through mazes more quickly (Greenough and Black, 1992).

Humans are influenced by the type of play they engage in. For example, unstructured breaks where children are free to play without direction from adults appears to benefit them more than structured play such as a PE lesson (Bjorkland and Pellegrini, 2000; Pellegrini and Holmes, 2006). This may be due to PE classes relying too heavily on adult-imposed rules.

Fisher (1992) performed a **meta-analysis** of six published studies on the cognitive benefits of play and concluded 'sociodramatic play' (social pretend play) results in improved performances in both cognitive-linguistic and social emotional domains. Chinese and Japanese students, who are traditionally academic high achievers, attend schools that provide short breaks for play and socializing every 50 minutes (Stevenson and Lee, 1990).

Lewis et al. (2000) measured children's ability to play in a symbolic way. Children aged between 1 and 6 years old were asked to perform symbolic tasks such as substituting a teddy bear for an absent object. They found children who scored higher on a test of symbolic play had better language skills, both in terms of what they understood and what they could express.

The types of problems presented during play influence the problem-solving abilities of children. For example, Pepler and Ross (1981) measured the effects of **convergent** and **divergent** play materials on children's problem-solving abilities. Convergent problems have a single correct solution or answer. Divergent problems present many solutions. Some children were given materials for convergent play (puzzle pieces) while others were given materials for divergent play (blocks). They were then tested on their ability to solve problems.

Children who had been given divergent play materials performed better on divergent problems, showing more creativity in their attempts to solve the problems (Pepler and Ross, 1981). This was supported by Wyver and Spence (1999), who found children who were given training in pretend-play showed an increased ability to solve divergent-type problems.

> **TOK**
>
> How should psychologists measure observable human behaviour? Should notions of standardization and generalization be applied to the human sciences to the same extent as they are applied in the natural sciences?

Spatial ability

Spatial ability is a skill associated with being able to understand, manipulate, and remember objects and their relationship with space. It can be assumed that spatial ability increases as children engage more in playing with LEGO®, blocks, and jigsaw puzzles (Hegarty and Waller, 2005).

This assumption is supported by empirical research. For example, Caldera et al. (1999) observed the construction activities of 51 preschoolers and found that children who showed more interest in construction and built more sophisticated structures performed better on a **standardized** test of spatial intelligence.

Building structures allows a child to practise and test spatial relationships. In doing so, they mentally rotate objects, which provides them with knowledge and confidence in spatial awareness.

Spatial ability is a skill associated with being able to understand, manipulate, reason, and remember objects and their relationship with space.

> ### Key study: Oostermeijer et al. (2014)
>
> **Aim:** To measure how free time in construction play influences test scores on mathematical word problems.
>
> **Procedure:** Parents or caregivers of 128 sixth-grade students (64 boys and 64 girls) from eight elementary schools in the Netherlands provided written informed consent based on printed information about the purpose of the study. A short **self-report** questionnaire was forwarded to the parents or caregivers. They were asked to indicate on a 4-point **Likert scale** (1 = never, 4 = often) to what extent their child engaged in constructive play activities (e.g. playing with LEGO®, blocks, and jigsaw puzzles).
>
> The researchers then measured mathematical word problem-solving performance using the Mathematical Processing Instrument (MPI), which was translated to Dutch. Children were allowed to solve each word problem in a maximum of three minutes and during this time the researcher did not speak to the child.
>
> The number of mathematical word problems solved correctly was used as the DV in the analysis.
>
> **Findings:** The results of this study showed children who frequently engaged in constructive play had better spatial skills and showed a higher performance on mathematical word problems.
>
> **Evaluation:** Only one task was used in the analysis to measure spatial ability (i.e. mental rotation of an object). Ideally, more spatial tasks should have been applied to draw broad conclusions.
>
> Furthermore, the study is only **correlational**, which made it impossible to draw conclusions about any causal relationships among constructive play, spatial ability, and mathematical word problem-solving performance. The results of this study only showed that these variables were associated with each other, but the researchers were very cautious about drawing broader conclusions.
>
> Finally, a third party (i.e. the parents/caregivers) filled out the questionnaires regarding the extent to which children showed constructive play behaviour. Although parents may be able to provide a reliable image of the constructive play activities in which their children are involved within their household, because the researchers themselves did not report on the levels of constructive play, it makes it difficult to generalize within the group as to what extent constructive play was similar.

What is the role of peers and play on the cognitive development of young children?

Trauma can be defined as a deeply distressing experience that has an effect on the thoughts, feelings, and behaviour of an individual. Resilience can be defined as the process of avoiding problematic outcomes or doing better than expected when confronted with problems.

24.2 Childhood trauma and resilience

Content focus

Discuss the role of childhood trauma and resilience on cognitive development.

24.2.1 Trauma

Trauma can be defined as any deeply distressing experience that has an effect on the thoughts, feelings, and behaviour of an individual. Distressing experiences children may experience include the following.

- Poverty and disadvantage: Growing up in poverty is associated with increased levels of family stress, less effective parenting, and higher risk of separation and divorce.

- **Social exclusion** from the mainstream of society: Living in places where services (e.g. schools, playgrounds, housing) are in a poor state and the norms of the mainstream (e.g. having social skills and not committing crime) are missing.

- Serious abuse: Sexual, physical, or emotional abuse causes high levels of stress in children as well as creating dysfunctional and harmful norms.

- Neglect: Children who are neglected are not provided with day-to-day needs such as healthy food, clean clothes, and consistent bedtimes, as well as lacking emotional needs such as love and attention.

It should be noted: poverty does not automatically mean children will do poorly in life or that it will impair their cognitive development.

Children who suffer serious abuse and neglect often have strong desires to feel power and control, and this can lead to criminal and immoral behaviour (Britton, 1997). However, there is an interaction between biological factors and **sociocultural** factors in this response. The **orchid-dandelion hypothesis** suggests some people have **genes** that make them more or less likely to succeed in challenging environments (Dobbs, 2009).

Dobbs uses a flower metaphor, describing some people as dandelions (able to take root and survive almost anywhere) and others as orchids (fragile but capable of doing well if given good care). He argues that orchid children have a **genetic** predisposition to vulnerability and this can be magnified positively or negatively depending on the environment the child is raised in. In a poor environment and with poor parenting, orchid children can end up depressed, drug-addicted, or in jail, but with the right environment and good parenting, they can grow up to be society's most creative, successful, and happy people.

This is supported by research into genes. Poulton et al. (2015) conducted a **longitudinal** case study over 26 years with 1037 children born in New Zealand in 1972. They found children were much more likely to grow up to be aggressive and antisocial if they had inherited a 'short' version of a gene called MAOA. However, they noted carriers only became antisocial if they had experienced an abusive upbringing. This clearly shows how the environment interacts with genes to affect later development.

This assumption is supported by animal research. In an experiment, Maestripieri (2009) took non-**neurotic**, high-scoring monkeys from nurturing mothers and had them raised by abusive, non-nurturing mothers. This setting produced extremely nervous monkeys. This study again shows that environment has a clear impact on behaviour.

It would be highly unethical for researchers to deliberately manipulate the environment of children to test the effects of trauma. Therefore, researchers conduct longitudinal human studies over time to observe the effects of different environments.

Rutter et al. (2001) followed two types of institutionally reared children. One group were Romanians who were exclusively reared in Romanian institutions and then adopted into the UK; the other group were British who had been raised in UK institutions and then adopted within the UK.

The orchid-dandelion hypothesis suggests some people have genes that make them more or less likely to succeed in challenging environments (Dobbs, 2009). There is a genetic predisposition to vulnerability and this can be magnified positively or negatively depending on the environment the child is raised in.

TOK

To what extent do animal models help or hinder knowledge creation in developmental psychology?

Longitudinal studies have high validity but low generalizability because of the uniqueness of the settings.

The key difference was the initial institution (Romanian versus British). Romanian orphanages are characterized by large numbers of children to very few caring adults.

Three differences were noted.

- The Romanian children had **attachment** problems (e.g. they would not identify their new parents as carers and would go with strangers easily; they did not go to their new parents for comfort). This is known as **disinhibited attachment** – they had learned to seek comfort where they could find it.

- The Romanian children were overactive and less cognitively developed.

- The Romanian children had emotional expression problems and showed 'near **autistic** features'.

Rutter et al. concluded the age of adoption was important and the reason why the Romanian children were different was the time they had spent in an unloving environment. Rutter et al. also argued some children showed natural resilience (the process of avoiding problematic outcomes or doing better than expected when confronted with problems). Despite their emotional and physical deprivation (and in some cases sexual and physical abuse), some children were able to overcome their initial deprivation.

Saigh et al. (2006) aimed to measure the effect of trauma on IQ scores. They asked Bellevue Hospital clinics in the USA to refer youths who reportedly experienced, witnessed, or were confronted with events (e.g. sexual assaults, physical assaults, or accidents) that could lead to **post-traumatic stress disorder** (PTSD). A **control** group consisting of children and **adolescents** without a reported history involving trauma exposure was also recruited. Child assent and the written **consent** from one of the parents or legal guardians were obtained prior to participation.

Participating children and adolescents received two independent **clinical** interviews and two independent administrations of the Children's PTSD Inventory. Participants were excluded if they had a significantly low IQ score (70 and below); had experienced head injury; could not speak fluent English or were addicted to drugs. The final sample consisted of 26 PTSD participants and 37 non-traumatized controls. The Wechsler Intelligence Scale for Children (WISC–III) was used to measure IQ performance.

Research local government programmes that support families in the community. What are the advantages and disadvantages?

Saigh et al. (2006) determined that youths with PTSD had significantly lower scores on discrete measures of verbal intelligence than non-traumatized controls. It was also noted that children who had been exposed to trauma but were not diagnosed with PTSD showed no significant difference with the control group, suggesting trauma has to be severe enough to trigger PTSD symptoms to have an effect on IQ scores. It was also noted that this difference only occurred with verbal measures of intelligence, suggesting an effect on specific centres of the brain.

24.2.2 Resilience

Resilience can be defined as the process of avoiding problematic outcomes or doing better than expected when confronted with problems. There are strategies that can be constructed in the environment to build resilience.

Community programmes

Strong community programmes, such as **postnatal** care visits for new parents and after-school programmes for at-risk children, can build resilience because they offer outside support at a vulnerable time for individuals.

Home visits for new parents occur in most developed countries. These are aimed at providing new parents and their children with access to a well-rounded social and educational support network. Government workers (usually social workers) visit families to check children are being cared for and to act as a source of support after children have just been born. They serve a practical purpose – increasing access to healthcare – but they also lower rates of maternal depression and help the relationship between mother and baby. They also remind parents that it is their job to care for the child, and make them aware of a wider social interest in their parenting skills.

Britner and Reppucci (1997) found that groups for teenage mothers provided support and reduced social isolation and depression. The programme also involved the extended family in the baby's care, providing a wider social support network for new mothers.

When children become older but not old enough to attend school, high-quality and affordable childcare (e.g. daycare, nursery, preschool) allows children to develop in a social environment and not just with their parent. It also allows parents to find and maintain a job. Maintaining employment acts as a social learning role model for the child.

Employment programmes allow parents to find work and/or re-train. Examples are apprenticeship schemes and adult education classes.

Schools are the centre of many communities and are a place where children not only learn academic subjects but also learn social skills and meet role models. Schools teach values and create norms for children – this is sometimes referred to as the 'hidden curriculum' because what is taught is implicit rather than explicit.

According to Sagor (1996) and Wang et al. (1995), schools can build resilience by having the school culture focus on five themes:

1. competency (feeling successful)

2. belonging (feeling valued)

3. usefulness (feeling needed)

4. potency (feeling empowered)

5. optimism (feeling encouraged and hopeful).

Ackerman (1997) argues that schools can also be more explicit in developing resilience in children through classroom meetings, **counselling**, and play therapy. Schools can improve resilience in children by providing after-school programmes in all high-risk communities where teachers work with students outside of school hours to complete homework and play sports. If schools become centres where children feel safe, receive support for their educational needs, and feel individually known by teachers, this produces resilience in children.

Resilience can be defined as the process of avoiding problematic outcomes or doing better than expected when confronted with problems. There are strategies that can be constructed in the environment to build resilience.

Mahoney et al. (2005) carried out a longitudinal study of the effect of after-school programmes on the school success and motivation for disadvantaged children. They found a full year's after-school programme achieved better test scores, reading achievement, and overall motivation for the students who took part.

Supportive home life

Children should have a close relationship with at least one parent figure, and even children who suffer from extreme early deprivation can be resilient as long as their home environment is loving and supportive. Successful children of parents employed in unskilled jobs or living in rented and overcrowded conditions were still more likely to have experienced a supportive family environment, and to have parents who showed an interest in their education (Schoon and Bartley, 2008). A supportive family environment was defined as: parents who read to their child, who took an active interest in their education, who fed their children regular healthy meals, and who took their children out for family activities such as holidays and days out.

Elder and Conger (2000) looked at data in the USA after a farm crisis in the 1980s and 1990s. The farm crisis put people out of work and their homes. They found a large number of young people had been protected and were on paths to successful academic development and were law abiding despite the awful events. The characteristics the families of the successful children had in common were:

- strong bonds between parents and children

- children who were raised with non-material goals (e.g. it is better to be a good person rather than have a nice car)

- positive connections with the wider community (e.g. church, school, and community projects); close relationship with grandparents.

The sense of community and family bonds provided the resilience needed to overcome crises.

A further longitudinal study (Koluchova, 1976) followed Czech twin boys born in 1960. The twins had been placed into an institution after their mother had died. Their father remarried and reclaimed the boys when they were 11 months old, only to allow his new wife to deprive and abuse them. They were forced to live in a cellar, were seriously undernourished, and they were not exposed to any stimulation or love apart from the contact they had with each other. They were rescued at the age of 7 and were placed in foster care, then adopted by two caring women who were sisters.

The boys' IQ scores were around 40 when they were rescued, but with a supportive and loving environment they had risen to over 100 and around 90 respectively by the time they were 14. School performance was good, and they became motivated. They got married and now live functional normal lives.

The deprivation they suffered caused cognitive and emotional dysfunction/lack of development, but their recovery supports Dobbs (2009), who argues that with the right environment and good parenting even seriously abused children can grow up to be society's most creative, successful, and happy people.

The Koluchova (1976) study has high **validity** but lacks generalizability because it is rare and extreme. However, extreme cases can be used to show how single variables such as deprivation can have singular outcomes, such as emotional and cognitive dysfunction.

Limitations to resilience-building initiatives

There are wider sociocultural and political factors at work in areas of childhood trauma. Governments can provide social workers and daycare centres as well as cheap childcare for parents who want to work, but these depend on taxation and political will.

Governments are also responsible for providing an economic landscape suitable for work. For example:

- An individual might want to find work but if government policies shut down factories and other places for good jobs then it will be difficult.

- Parents may want their children to do well in school but if the school does not have good teachers or good facilities and has overcrowded classes with multilingual children, this will also be a problem.

Any government initiative is dependent on the will of parents to achieve and take care of their families.

There is also the notion of individual willpower or '**agency**'. In psychology, agency refers to the capacity of individuals to act independently and make their own free choices while limiting or resisting structural factors that might inhibit their free choices, such as **socioeconomic** status, religion, gender expectations, ethnicity, cultural norms, etc. People have to be willing to help themselves and get involved in the community to do well and put in place measures that can resist or limit factors that might cause problems.

Agency refers to the capacity of individuals to act independently and make their own free choices while limiting or resisting structural factors that might inhibit their free choices, such as socioeconomic status, religion, gender expectations, ethnicity, cultural norms, etc.

However, it is difficult to protect children from the wider norms of the community. They may have good family values with parents who teach them right from wrong, but if the local community has high crime rates, poor housing, a prevalence of inappropriate role models (such as drug dealers, car thieves and gangsters who establish negative subcultural norms), poor schooling, and unsupportive police then it can be very difficult for family and individual strategies to succeed in building resilience.

This can also be seen as ethnically relative. For example, research from the Equality and Human Rights Commission (EHRC) looked at police stop powers in the UK, where officers do not require suspicion of involvement in crime to stop and search people. These are known as Section 60 stops. The EHRC found police forces are up to 28 times more likely to use stop-and-search powers against black people than white people. Therefore, black people have a different experience of the same community than white people. This can undermine community cohesion, make certain groups suspicious of authority and undermine the ability of the individual to succeed or be resilient in what they perceive as a hostile environment filled with hostile forces outside of their control.

24.3 Poverty and socioeconomic status

Content focus

Discuss the role of poverty on cognitive development.

Poverty can be defined in absolute terms, relative terms, or by a measure of social exclusion.

Absolute poverty is defined as the lack of sufficient resources with which to live. It can be measured using a definitive paradigm and applied globally. However, it does not take individual experiences relative to the society in which individuals live into account. For example, a 'poor' person in the UK may have access to clean water, free education, healthcare, and housing, but if their experiences are significantly different from the societal norm then despite being materially richer than many people worldwide, the measure of poverty will not help to explain why they think, feel and act the way they do.

Relative poverty defines income or resources in relation to a national or regional average. Social sciences researchers often use relative poverty because it is concerned with the absence of the material needs to participate fully in accepted daily life within a given society. Therefore, it takes account of the facilities, material goods, and experiences that are available to individuals, and measures to what extent people have access to them.

Social exclusion is an extension of relative poverty. It can refer to unemployment, poor skills, low income, poor housing, high crime environments, bad health, and family breakdown.

Socioeconomic status is linked to the notion of social exclusion. It can be defined as total measure of a person's social and economic position, based on income, occupation, education and how much power/autonomy they have over their own lives.

24.3.1 Poverty

Experiences of relative poverty can create ongoing feelings of stress as a result of the experiences of living within relatively poor conditions. For example, Pilyoung et al. (2013) used functional magnetic resonance imaging (fMRI), which detects blood flow in various areas of the brain as a reflection of brain activity to study the regulation of emotions in young adults who were part of a longitudinal poverty study.

They compared a participant's family income at age 9 (based on survey data collected at the time) with his or her current **neural** activity in different brain regions. They found that those who grew up in poverty showed increased activity in the **amygdala** (believed to be involved in anxiety, fear, and emotional disorders) and decreased activity in the **prefrontal cortex** (which limits the influence of the amygdala, putting long-term decision making over impulse) when shown emotionally upsetting images.

The researchers suggest a range of **chronic** stresses that can accompany growing up in poverty, such as overcrowding, noise, violence, family turmoil or separation, and these impact the development of the brain in childhood and adolescence.

Sidebar notes:

Poverty can be defined in absolute terms, relative terms, or by a measure of social exclusion.

As the world becomes more globalized and interconnected, should universal understandings be more applicable in understanding human thoughts, feelings, and behaviour? Can there be any universal laws of human behaviour?

TOK

Experiences of relative poverty can create ongoing feelings of stress as a result of the experiences of living with poor conditions.

Family trauma, or the mere absence of consistent nurturing, can impact brain development. Luby et al. (2013) studied the relationship between poverty during childhood, parental nurturing skills and the growth of brain tissue in 145 children between the ages of six and 12 using an MRI. Children whose parents had poor nurturing skills had slowed growth in white matter, grey matter and the volumes of several different areas of the brain involved with learning skills and coping with stress.

Based on the differing growth rates between children who resembled each other in terms of other key factors, it seemed as though the experience of growing up with adults with poor nurturing skills effectively set back their cognitive development.

It is assumed any impact on brain development will impact cognitive ability. Dickerson and Popli (2014) analysed data on over 8700 members of the Millennium Cohort Study, which follows the lives of children born in the UK in 2000–2001. The researchers looked at whether the children were in poverty at ages nine months, three years, five years and seven years. Children were said to be in persistent poverty if their families were poor at the current and all previous surveys. They found seven-year-olds who have lived in poverty since infancy performed substantially worse in a range of cognitive ability tests than those who had never been poor, even when family circumstances and parenting skills were taken into consideration. On a scale from 0 to 100, a child who has been in persistent poverty ranks ten levels below a similar child who has no early experience of poverty.

It is assumed any impact on brain development will impact cognitive ability. Children were said to be in persistent poverty if their families were poor at the current and all previous surveys. They found seven-year-olds who have lived in poverty since infancy perform substantially worse in a range of cognitive ability tests than those who have never been poor, even when family circumstances and parenting skills are taken into consideration.

However, it can be noted that the effects of socioeconomic status on development can be overcome. For example, parents of high-achieving students were found to set higher standards for their children's educational activities compared to parents of low-achieving students from similar socioeconomic circumstances (MDE, 2001). The Michigan Department of Education (MDE) states that when parents set high expectations students have higher grades and graduation rates. The department found families whose children do well in school exhibit the following positive investment characteristics.

- They have an established daily family routine, such as providing time and a quiet place to read, being firm about bedtime, and having dinner together.

- They model the value of learning, self-discipline, and hard work. For example, they read books themselves and take an interest in what the child is reading.

- They encourage children's development/progress in school, such as by maintaining a warm and supportive home, helping with homework, and staying in touch with teachers and school staff.

- They encourage reading, writing, and discussions among family.

Therefore, the quality of parenting skills and investment are important for children's development and can overcome the effects of poverty.

However, Dickerson and Popli (2014) argue that poverty adversely affects parental investments, especially in the very early years, which makes it more difficult for parents to invest positively in their children. This may be due to a lack of:

- time due to work commitments

- ability and confidence due to their own educational attainments

- suitable environments for completing homework, etc.

Therefore, poverty influences the cognitive development of the child through direct means, but also indirect means by significantly limiting the ability of the parents to positively invest in the upbringing of their children.

24.3.2 Diet

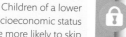

Diet is an **environmental variable** because food is consumed based on environmental norms, but it is also a biological variable because nutrition (or lack thereof) influences brain and body growth, which in turn influence thoughts, feelings, and behaviour.

Raloff (1989) carried out a longitudinal study over the course of a year with children from lower socioeconomic backgrounds. He studied 1023 sixth-grade children and found those who were given free school breakfasts improved their maths and science scores. A meta-analysis of breakfast programme studies by the Food Research Action Centre (FRAC) in the USA concluded that:

- children who skip breakfast have slower memory recall

- children experiencing hunger have lower maths scores

- children who were given free school breakfasts improved their maths and science scores.

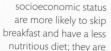

Skipping breakfast and being hungry are likely to be part of wider problems. For example, children of a lower socioeconomic status are more likely to skip breakfast and have a less nutritious diet (Keski-Rahkonen et al., 2003).

Parents who fail to feed their children breakfast may fail in other positive investment behaviours such as:

- not reading to their children

- not checking homework

- not buying books or taking them to the library

- feeding them unhealthy food.

Children of such parents may also lack social and emotional skills, which will also affect their school scores and emotional life in the community. Therefore, researchers need to be cautious when attributing isolated variables to inhibited cognitive and social development.

Breastfeeding infants has been shown to positively impact a child's development. However, the rate of breastfeeding is influenced by socioeconomic status. In a survey conducted for the New York City Department of Health, it was found that women who lived in wealthier neighbourhoods were more likely to breastfeed their babies and do so for longer than women in low-income areas (Summers et al., 2009). This has long-term implications for development.

Kramer et al. (2008) investigated the effect of breastfeeding on IQ and school performance with a large sample of 17 000 Belarusian babies that were followed for six years in a longitudinal study. The experimental group were breastfed, while the control group were not. They found the experimental group had significantly higher means

Diet is an environmental variable because food is consumed based on environmental norms but it is also a biological variable because nutrition (or lack thereof) influences brain and body growth which in turn influence thoughts, feelings and behaviour.

Children of a lower socioeconomic status are more likely to skip breakfast and have a less nutritious diet; they are less likely to be breastfed and they are more likely to experience trauma and disruption at home.

on all of the Wechsler Abbreviated Scales of Intelligence measures (e.g. verbal IQ and performance IQ).

This was a large **randomized** trial in the area of human lactation and it provides strong evidence that prolonged and exclusive breastfeeding improves children's cognitive development. It should be noted however, that Belarus is a relatively poor country. Some children who were not breastfed may have been undernourished. Therefore some of the results may be explained by the undernourishment of the non-breastfed group rather than the effects of breast milk.

It is thought poorer women face barriers that discourage them from breastfeeding, such as hospital policies and practices; the marketing of infant formula; and the lack of education for poorer women who might be more swayed by advertising messages. There are also socioeconomic pressures such as the need to return to work early after maternity leave and an unsupportive work environment when they get there.

TOK

To what extent can definitive measurements be established for all cultures? For example, can one measure of poverty be applied to different cultural settings? What are the difficulties of gathering and analyzing data in different socioeconomic settings?

Key study: Bhoomika et al. (2008)

Aim: To measure the effect of malnutrition on cognitive performance.

Procedure: Twenty poor and malnourished children in India were compared with one control group who were adequately nourished. They recorded daily nutrition and measured their attention, working memory (visual-spatial ability and executive functioning), comprehension, learning and general memory ability, and some physical tests (e.g. motorspeed and coordination).

Findings: Malnourished children scored lower on cognitive tests (but not on physical tasks) and the older children showed less cognitive improvement over time.

The effects of undernourishment on cognitive development are further supported by Whaley et al. (2003). They investigated the effects of food supplements on school performance in children from rural Kenya. This was a longitudinal study conducted over 21 months with 555 first-grade children who were put into four groups, receiving one of the following:

- meat supplements

- milk supplements

- energy supplements

- no supplements (control).

The children were asked to perform cognitive tests throughout the 21-month period. Children who were given animal-sourced supplements or energy supplements outperformed children in the control group during arithmetic and other tests.

While these studies are culturally specific to Kenya and India, they do show the effects of poverty and diet on an undernourished population. However, given the brain is a biological organ, it is reasonable to conclude that diet will have a clear effect on its development and this will impact cognitive development.

To what extent does poverty impair cognitive development in Western children?

It is difficult for researchers to measure cognitive development in Western children without focusing on school achievement. However, school achievement is influenced by many factors that cannot be isolated from each other.

25 Developing an identity

Topic focus

Discuss how identity develops.

25.1 Attachment

Content focus

To what extent does attachment in childhood influence adult identity?

Attachment is a deep and enduring emotional bond that connects one person to another across time and space and can be seen as a 'lasting psychological connectedness between human beings'.

Attachment is a deep and enduring emotional bond that connects one person to another across time and space (Bowlby, 1969; Ainsworth, 1973). Bowlby further defined attachment as a 'lasting psychological connectedness between human beings' (1969, p. 194). Infants have a universal need to seek close proximity with their caregiver when under stress or threatened (Prior and Glaser, 2006).

In humans, attachment can be characterized by specific behaviours in children, such as seeking proximity with the attachment figure when upset or threatened (Bowlby, 1969). Attachment behaviour in adults toward a child includes responding sensitively and appropriately to the child's needs. Such behaviour appears universal across cultures, suggesting powerful biological drives that are the result of **evolutionary** processes.

25.1.1 Assumptions of attachment research and models

There are key sociocultural assumptions made about attachment.

Assumption 1: attachment patterns are constant within families

However, attachment patterns differ from one family to the next, and even between children from the same parents. These differences are due to personality differences, dynamics and sociocultural influences.

Assumption 2: a child's individual personality is not as important as an attachment

Are there constants in human behaviour that research can make use of? On what basis can researchers generalize to a larger population?

However, Kagan (1982) states that differences in children's temperaments influence how they interact with the environment and therefore greatly affect how they attach to adults in their environment. He also argues that a child's temperament is stable over time and can predict future behaviour. Different children respond differently to the same family dynamics.

Assumption 3: circumstances remain constant within families

However, a family is not always a stable, unchanging unit over time and setting. Events intervene, such as poverty, deaths, and house moving, and the child may not receive the same type of support all of the time. This will affect attachment development. There are so many sociocultural variables interacting inside and outside of a family unit that it is difficult to pinpoint exactly how attachment will affect future behaviour.

25.1.2 Attachment theory

Attachment theory provides an explanation of how the parent–child relationship emerges and influences subsequent development. Bowlby and Robertson (1952) observed that children experienced intense distress when separated from their mothers, and even when children were fed by other caregivers, this did not reduce the child's anxiety. These findings contradicted the dominant behavioural theory of attachment (Dollard and Miller, 1950), which stated that the child becomes attached to the mother because she fed the infant.

Bowlby's attachment theory

Bowlby's attachment theory was first published in 1951 but has been adapted and improved many times since then by Bowlby and other researchers.

The basic assumptions are:

1. Between 6 and about 30 months, children are likely to form emotional attachments to familiar caregivers, usually the mother, especially if the adults are sensitive and responsive to child communications, such as facial expressions, hand gestures, crying, laughing, and so on.

2. The emotional attachments of children are shown in their preferences for familiar people; they seek to be close to those people, especially in times of distress, and then use the familiar adults as a base to explore the environment.

3. Events that interfere with attachment, such as separation or an unresponsive carer, have short- and long-term consequences for the child.

Bowlby's theory (1951) has a key biological assumption because it assumes attachment can be understood within an evolutionary context, in that the caregiver provides safety and security for the infant. Attachment is seen as **adaptive** as it enhances the infant's chances of surviving and thriving.

There is strong evolutionary support for a biological explanation of attachment; babies who are attached to a loving caregiver are more likely to survive and be better adjusted. Attachment acts as a cohesive force in human dynamics, sticking humans together to create a unified team within a **symbiotic** relationship.

The model also has a key cognitive component: the formation of a **schema** known as the internal working model. The internal working model provides a schema for future behaviour for both the child and caregivers. The key underlying assumption of Bowlby's theory is that the bonds created between the child and caregiver will be repeated with other people into adulthood as a result of a stable schema.

Attachment theory provides an explanation of how the parent–child relationship emerges and influences subsequent development.

Bowlby's theory has a key biological assumption because it assumes attachment can be understood within an evolutionary context, in that the caregiver provides safety and security for the infant. Attachment is seen as adaptive as it enhances the infant's chances of surviving and thriving.

195

The internal working model provides a schema for future behaviour for both the child and caregivers. It is relatively stable over time, which is why it can be used to predict and explain future adult relationships.

While the motivation to form attachment is biological, the schema is cognitive and relatively stable – although it can be changed by ongoing experience moderated by the environment. For example, if a child receives consistent love from their caregiver, they will develop a schema through reinforcement where they believe they are worthy of love. The child will develop confidence and be able to provide love to others in the future. If a child experiences a negative environment they will assume they are worthy of such treatment and will not develop confidence.

Attachment theories assume attachment behaviour influences later adult relationships. Adjusted children able to give and receive love will grow into adjusted adults able to give and receive love – greatly increasing the chances of offspring survival.

Ainsworth et al. (1979) identified three distinct patterns of infant attachment from observations of infants.

- **Secure:** Securely attached infants seek proximity and welcome their caregivers' return from absence, seeking comfort during times of distress.

- **Anxious–resistant:** These infants tend to show ambivalent behaviour toward caregivers and are resistant to the comforting behaviours of caregivers if distressed.

- **Avoidant:** Infants classified with an avoidant attachment style avoid proximity or interaction with the caretaker on reunion.

Researchers can then question to what extent such attachment styles lead to problematic outcomes in later life. For example, Bifulco et al. (2006) investigated the relationship between childhood adverse experiences and adult disorders. They used standardized interview methods to assess the attachment style of 154 women from high-risk communities. They then followed up four years later with a standardized Structured Clinical Interview (for DSM-IV depression and anxiety disorders) to test the role of insecure attachment styles in predicting new episodes of anxiety and/or major depressive disorder.

They found 'markedly' or 'moderately' insecure attachment styles could predict both major depression and anxiety over time, although attachment styles were unrelated to **panic disorder** and **agoraphobia**. They concluded that attachment theory provides a framework for explaining how dysfunctional interpersonal styles arising from early childhood can lead to an increased vulnerability to affective disorders in adulthood.

It could be argued that these childhood experiences provided a negative framework for **self-identity**. Therefore a schemata of self-worth associated with a positive identity was not developed.

Hazan and Shaver (1987) developed Bowlby and Ainsworth's work on infant–caregiver attachment to include attachment styles within adult romantic love relationships. They argued that adult romantic love can be categorized as secure, avoidant, and anxious (or anxious–ambivalent).

- Secure: Adults with a secure attachment style are comfortable depending on others and find it easy to become close to others.

- Avoidant: Adults with an avoidant attachment style are uncomfortable with close proximity with others and can have trust issues.

- Anxious: Adults with an anxious attachment style see others as reluctant to get close to them while being overly dependent on others.

25.1.3 Animal studies

Attachment is a personal and emotional topic and researchers have to meet exacting ethical standards when researching it in humans. There are also strict ethical considerations when working with animals, but animal studies allow for greater flexibility and re-testing than in studies with humans. Animal attachment studies have many advantages.

- They allow variables to be isolated, manipulated, and then measured.

- They allow empirical data to be collected in the form of experiments.

- Experiments allow cause and effect to be established and then re-tested using controlled conditions.

Lorenz and the geese

A key use of animals in attachment research is Lorenz's work with geese (1935). He took a large clutch of goose eggs and kept them until they were about to hatch. Half of the eggs were then placed under a goose mother, while Lorenz kept the other half beside him for several hours. When the geese hatched, Lorenz imitated a mother goose's quacking sound, which made the young birds regard him as their mother and follow him accordingly. The other group followed the mother goose.

Lorenz found that geese follow the first moving object they see during a 12- to 17-hour critical period after hatching. This process is known as **imprinting** and suggests that attachment is innate and programmed genetically. To ensure imprinting had occurred, Lorenz put all the goslings together under an upturned box and allowed them to mix. When the box was removed, the two groups separated to go to their respective 'mothers' – half to the mother goose, and half to Lorenz.

Imprinting does not appear to be active immediately after hatching, but there seems to be a critical period in which imprinting can occur. Hess (1958) showed that although the imprinting process could occur as early as one hour after hatching, the strongest responses occurred between 12 and 17 hours after hatching, and that after 32 hours the response was unlikely to occur at all.

Lorenz and Hess believed that once imprinting has occurred it cannot be reversed, nor can a gosling imprint on anything else.

Imprinting has consequences, both for short- and long-term survival. It is assumed imprinting helps form internal templates (schemas) for later relationships and that it occurs without any feeding taking place. If no attachment has developed within 32 hours, it's unlikely any attachment will ever develop and the chances of the individual surviving and thriving are rapidly diminished.

It would be ethically impossible to replicate this study on human babies. Therefore the use of animals in this study is crucial to help social scientists understand a key process that impacts survival. However, studies with animals lack the nuances of human attachment processes. For example, Segal and Jaffre (2007) emphasize that the non-verbal skills learned in childhood are essential for adult attachment relationships. Newborn infants cannot talk, reason or plan, yet they are able to communicate with a caregiver who understands and meets their physical and emotional needs. Segal and Jaffre argue that the learning and practising of non-verbal cues deeply impact our later love relationships.

Suomi and Harlow and the pit of despair (vertical chamber apparatus)

During the 1960s and 1970s, Suomi and Harlow aimed to disrupt attachment in rhesus monkeys and then observe their behaviour as they developed. They designed a steel cage that denied the monkeys any connection with the outside world or any other living organism. Baby monkeys were placed in these steel cages.

After 30 days the monkeys were found to be 'enormously disturbed'. The monkeys barely moved after one year. They did not explore or play and were found unable to have sexual relations. Two moneys starved to death after refusing to eat.

When the isolated monkeys became parents, they were unable to parent their offspring. Having no social experiences themselves, they were incapable of engaging in positive social interaction with others – including their own offspring, with many mothers ignoring their offspring completely. In fact, one mother chewed off her baby's feet and fingers while another crushed her baby's head.

The researchers were able to claim the pit of despair demonstrates the importance of love and nurturing during development in later life.

The work has been heavily criticized from an ethical perspective. Harlow was criticized for deliberately designing the apparatus to cause shock from his colleagues. He probably did this to generate controversy – naming his apparatus the way he did ('the pit of despair') and avoiding technical language are both examples of this. Furthermore, monkeys are very social animals, so when placed in isolation they emerge badly damaged (Blum, 2002). With this experiment, Harlow did nothing but demonstrate 'common sense'. It could be argued that social science should reach beyond demonstrating the higher wisdom of common sense and instead create new knowledge.

However, it should be noted during the 1960s and 1970s it was normal in Western cultures to advise parents to limit bodily contact to avoid too much emotional stimulation of the child, which was seen as spoiling the child. Harlow clearly demonstrates how important love and contact is in development and his shocking experiments were widely publicized and helped generate public debate on the issue.

Generalizing animal findings to humans should always be carried out cautiously, but it seems reasonable to argue that depriving human youngsters of a loving environment will produce adults who are less well-adjusted.

What is the role of childhood attachment on later adult identity for romantic love?

EE

25.2 Gender identity and social roles

Content focus

To what extent can gender identity and social roles be explained by sociocultural, cognitive, and biological processes?

Identity is a form of self-concept that answers the question, 'Who am I?' It is a collection of beliefs about oneself and how one relates to the wider world. It can be seen as a cognitive process influenced by social and biological factors.

Gender identity refers to a person's experiences of masculinity or femininity and to what extent they identify with the roles associated with being male or female. Gender identity is usually linked to biological sex organs, but this is not always the case. Some women adopt a more masculine identity and some men adopt a more feminine identity, as well as many personal interpretations in between.

Sex refers to the biological architecture a person is born with – either male or female. Social scientists have been at the forefront of distinguishing between sex, gender identity, and gender roles. These areas are interlinked but it is also true that not all individuals are easily defined.

Social roles are behavioural projections that are influenced by social, cognitive, and biological elements. Social roles in the context of gender refers to the sets of behaviours, rights, and duties of being male or female (Bee, 1995).

Gender has its own separate branch of academia (gender studies). It is a complicated subject, and can be a deeply personal, evoking many emotions. However, some generalizations can be made.

- Gender has elements that are clearly **socially constructed** as shown by the diversity of gender-specific behaviours across cultures.

- Gender has elements that are clearly biologically determined as shown by the universality of gender-specific behaviours across cultures and because of the usefulness gender and social roles have had to the evolution and success of the human species.

- Most people either identify as male or female and only a tiny minority question their identity in this regard.

- The academic focus on the minority of people who do not identify as male or female has helped develop new insights into gender, while also reducing prejudice toward people who do not identify as either male or female.

The role of the psychology academic is to determine to what extent biology, cognition, and sociocultural processes interact to produce different thoughts, feelings, and behaviours with regards to gender identity and social roles.

TOK

Psychology is a human science. Therefore psychology can sometimes be seen as biased toward sociocultural explanations for human behaviour. It could be argued this inbuilt bias of the human sciences has undermined the validity of biological explanations in the social narrative regarding gender identity and social roles.

Gender identity refers to a person's experiences of masculinity and femininity and to what extent they identify with the roles associated with being male or female. Social roles are behavioural projections that are influenced by social, cognitive, and biological elements. Social roles in the context of gender refers to the sets of behaviours, rights and, duties of being male or female (Bee, 1995).

25.2.1 Sociocultural factors that explain the formation of gender identity and roles

Sociocultural approaches assume thoughts, feelings, and behaviour are the result of sociocultural mechanisms. Social factors that explain the formation of gender roles include processes in the environment such as **modelling** and **conditioning** that shape gender roles through reward and punishment.

Reinforcement can be direct, for example, 'You look like a girl in that hat' (said to a boy) or, 'Girls don't wear football kits' (said to a girl). Reinforcement can also be indirect, for example, seeing characters dress and act in gender-specific ways on TV shows.

Leary et al. (1982) found children who were frequent television watchers were more likely to hold **stereotyped** ideas about gender. This suggests the importance of modelling from the media. Lewis (1972) observed parent–child interaction and found boys were encouraged to be active and independent and girls were encouraged to be passive and dependent.

A clear example of social conditioning for the different genders is the dominance penalty for women (Anderson, 2015). When a woman displays characteristics of traditional leadership – like decisiveness and strength – for which a man would be rewarded and respected, she often has to deal with being disliked more than men. This dislike is projected by both men and women. Consequently, women have to exert more effort by showing warmth and compassion to offset any penalties they receive for transgressing expected social roles.

It could be argued that it suits a liberal political agenda to assume gender role variations are caused by sociocultural factors. If gender roles are socially constructed, then changing social circumstances can 'liberate' women from 'oppression'. This can potentially be seen as a noble aim. However, we need to be extremely cautious about assuming all gender-related behaviour is **culturally constructed**.

Research suggests the more liberated a culture and the more choice people have, the more likely women and men are to choose traditional social roles according to their gender. In countries with high levels of poverty, there are more women in traditionally 'male' occupations because women have less choice when it comes to earning a living and choose those occupations out of necessity.

Cultural construction of gender roles

The cultural construction of gender roles was demonstrated by Mead (1935). This work had a significant impact on debates surrounding gender identity and social roles. Mead researched tribes in Papua New Guinea. She claimed to find the Tchambuli tribe where men showed some 'feminine' behaviour (being passive) and women showed some 'masculine' behaviour (being dominant, shaving their heads, taking control of trading relationships).

Mead's work became well known because:

- it argued that gender differences are culturally constructed

- it had a noble cause, which was to promote the notion of freedom and choice for gender role adoption

> Sociocultural approaches to explaining gender identity and social roles assume thoughts, feelings, and behaviour are the result of sociocultural mechanisms such as modelling and conditioning that shape gender roles through reward and punishment.

- it influenced the sexual revolution of the 1960s. This was a social movement that challenged traditional gender and sexuality norms in the West.

However, it could be argued that the validity of Mead's findings with the Tchambuli has been exaggerated because of the nobility of the cause that adopted it. Showing that gender is socially constructed has helped liberate women from constraining role expectations. However, Mead's work has been heavily criticized and her methods largely dismissed by modern anthropologists.

For example, Gewertz (1984) studied the Tchambuli in 1974–1975 and met many who had been interviewed by Mead. She comprehensively criticized Mead's findings and her methods. Some points to note:

- Mead admitted that she wanted to make her gender findings relevant to a Western audience.

- Mead observed aggressive women, but Gewertz observed women who socialized in female groups, laughed and joked about men and were independent of men in some areas of their lives. For example, they would organize night dances without the permission of men. These shaven-headed women engaging in night dances may have appeared 'aggressive' to a Western woman living through the 1930s, but were not considered aggressive to the Tchambuli.

- During Mead's 1930s research, 52 per cent of Tchambuli men were away working. Those who remained were busy rebuilding houses that had been destroyed during a recent war with a rival tribe. Women adopted roles traditionally performed by men (e.g. management of trade) because of the shortage of male labour. Therefore, the masculine gender roles Mead saw women adopting were not being permanently adopted through choice, but temporarily adopted by necessity.

- Mead correctly reported how Tchambuli men were warlike and territorial. However, these findings have been largely forgotten by Western writers, perhaps because they do not fit the narrative that the gender roles were 'inverted' for these tribes. Moreover, Gewertz found evidence that the tribe was heavily patriarchal in nature.

Mead's assumptions and those of others who focus on the cultural construction of gender roles should not be entirely dismissed. Clearly, mechanisms such as modelling and conditioning encourage and discourage individuals and groups from undertaking certain roles regarding gender.

For example, in the Aka Pygmy there is an absence of negative social consequences for male 'breastfeeding', so it occurs (Hewlett, 1991). It should be noted that male breastfeeding does not involve the giving of milk through the male nipples, which is why it has been written here in inverted commas. The nipples are used to pacify the child because they are a cleaner part of the body when compared to fingers or objects on the ground. Furthermore, nipples will be familiar to the baby because they are breastfed (with milk) by their mothers.

Mead had a noble cause to show how female roles could be changed and women had choice in their lives. To what extent should the intentions behind research be taken into consideration when assessing the validity of explanations?

TOK

According to Hewlett, Aka fathers are within reach of their infants 47 per cent of the time – apparently more than fathers in any other cultural group. Male and female gender roles are virtually interchangeable. While the women hunt, the men mind the children; while the men cook, the women decide where to set up the next camp. Therefore, Aka fathers will slip into roles usually occupied by mothers without any loss of status.

However, it should be noted:

- There is still a gender division of labour in the Aka community – women, for example, are the primary caregivers but there is a significant level of flexibility.

- While tasks and decision making were largely shared activities, there is an Aka 'glass ceiling'. Top jobs in the tribe invariably go to men: the *kombeti* (leader), the *tuma* (elephant hunter) and the *nganga* (top healer) in the community are all male.

The male and female bodies are significantly different to one another in many areas, such as hormones, neurotransmitters, brain structure, and physicality. It is reasonable to assume these biological predispositions have an impact on how males and females think, feel, and behave.

Hewlett showed how cultural **stigmas** encourage different genders to fulfil different roles. When stigmas are downplayed or are absent, roles become more interchangeable. For example, there is no negative social consequence for male breastfeeding, so it occurs. However, this should not be taken to mean there are no underlying biological determinants for gender roles. The male and female bodies are significantly different to one another in many areas, such as hormones, **neurotransmitters**, brain structure, and physicality. It is reasonable to assume these biological predispositions have an impact on how males and females think, feel, and behave.

25.2.2 Cognitive factors that explain the formation of gender identity and roles

A cognitive approach assumes thoughts, feelings, and behaviour are the result of cognitive mechanisms. Cognitive factors such as motivation and perception affect how a child develops an identity in the social environment. Kohlberg (1966) argued that children acquire a gender concept and then seek information from members of the same gender for clues on how to behave. Once they understand gender is fixed and they are to be a boy or a girl forever, they become increasingly motivated to find information on the 'correct' behaviour.

Understanding that gender is fixed is called **gender constancy**. Gender constancy occurs between four-and-a-half and seven years old and is similar to the Piagetian notion of conservation, as the child understands gender as fixed despite surface changes like hair length. (For further information on Piaget, see page 210).

Slaby and Frey (1975) divided children aged between two and five into two groups; one group was considered to have high gender constancy, and the other group was considered to have low gender constancy. This was established after asking them if they knew if they were a boy or a girl or if they had always been a boy or a girl. The researchers showed a film with a split screen, one side had male models doing a task, the other side had female models doing a task. The results showed children with high gender constancy watched the same-sex side of the screen more than children with low gender constancy. It shows they had more same-sex bias in their attention. This shows children actively look for, then respond to, the 'correct' gender models.

Gender schema theory (GST) argues that children form mental guides for action and then find information that supports their schema and forget information that does not. In this way, ideas become fixed and stereotypes form. Liben and Signorella (1993) found children who were shown pictures of adults in less traditional gender roles (e.g. male nurse; female car mechanic) forgot the information. This suggests children only select information that supports their schema of gender-appropriate behaviour.

A cognitive approach to explaining gender identity and social roles assumes thoughts, feelings, and behaviour are the result of cognitive mechanisms such as motivation and perception. GST argues children form mental guides for action and then find information that supports their schema and forget information that does not.

Furthermore, social environments can also enforce cognitive expectations about role and identity. For example, Fagot (1985) observed teachers and found they positively reinforce female behaviour stereotypes (sedentary, quiet, calm behaviour). However, Fagot also noted teachers can negatively reinforce male behaviour (impulsive, physical) and yet boys still display male characteristics. Fagot argues this is due to the strength of the male schema the boys have as well as their biological need to play in a certain way.

25.2.3 Biological factors that explain the formation of gender identity and social roles

The biological approach assumes thoughts, feelings and behaviour are the result of biological determinants. Like many evolutionary psychologists, Campbell (2010) argues that gender role division has been essential to the success of humans and many other species, and can therefore be considered to have powerful biological determinants caused by evolution. She argues it is reasonable to assume that clear biological differences seen in the bodies of different genders would also lead to clear psychological and emotional differences in the different genders.

The biological approach to explaining gender identity and social roles assumes thoughts, feelings, and behaviour are the result of evolutionary pressures.

An example of behaviour differences between the different genders is rough and tumble (R&T) play. R&T play is found in most male mammals and in particular in chimpanzees, orangutans, humans (Braggio et al., 1978), and even squirrels (Biben, 1998). It is action orientated and involves mock aggression such as wrestling, running, and pretend battles.

R&T play is thought to be the result of hormonal changes in males. It is clearly observable as a common behavioural trait in preschool human males (Maccoby and Jacklin, 1980; Parke and Slaby, 1983). The early onset suggests powerful biological differences between the genders as it occurs before any meaningful socialization has taken place.

A meta-analysis of aggression studies has shown there is a greater sex difference in aggressive behaviour in younger children than older children, showing the effect of socialization is to reduce the aggressive tendencies of boys rather than exacerbate them further. This suggests aggressive tendencies have biological origins because they appear at a young age in males from all cultures (Hyde, 1986).

Aggression is also a key part of young boys' fantasy lives, suggesting a clear relationship between biology and cognition. For example, Nicolopuolou (1997) collected 495 stories from preschool children and found aggression and violent themes were present in 87 per cent of boys' stories compared to 17 per cent of girls' stories. Furthermore, the girls' stories focused on interpersonal relationships with a concept of 'home' being a centering locale. The girls' stories often dealt with maintaining those relationships and restoring any discord that may have occurred.

Jarvis (2006) performed an observation study on children in a primary school in northern England and concluded that boys show a clear preference for R&T play. She puts forward an evolutionary argument to explain this: boys need to learn how to compete with other boys for resources and access to female mates, and those who are more practised are more likely to be successful. Females occupy a caring role and do not 'need' to engage in R&T play.

Marsh (2000) observed preschool children in a nursery and supports Jarvis (2006). She asked the children to play in a 'batcave'. She told them both boys and girls could play and be 'batmen' or 'batwomen'. She found the batwomen were more likely to be 'caring' and rescue people in need; the batmen chased and captured villains.

Links between male hormones and male behaviour have also been found in female participants. For example, congenital adrenal hyperplasia (CAH) is a condition in children resulting from accidental exposure to male hormones while still a foetus. Berenbaum and Snyder (1995) found girls with CAH showed more preference for boys' toys. Beach (1974) found female dogs who were exposed to male hormones were more likely to urinate like male dogs.

There are also key structural differences in the brain between the genders, and recent studies have shown gender differences in identity development can be linked to brain differences. Lenroot et al. (2007) used evidence from 829 MRI scans taken from 387 subjects, aged between 3 and 27 years. They argued brain development differences between males and females are significant. MRI scans suggest young women reach full brain developmental maturity between 21 and 22 years of age; young men reach full brain developmental maturity at 30 years of age.

There are key structural differences in the brain between the genders and recent studies have shown gender differences in identity development can be linked to brain differences.

Spalek et al. (2015) found gender-specific differences in information processing: 3398 test subjects were scanned using fMRIs and it was found that women considered emotional events more emotionally stimulating than men. Women showed stronger appraisal of negative emotional images and had increased brain activity in motoric regions. This suggests there are biological causes for what humans find interesting and how we process the information. This will affect how memories are created and how schemas are formed.

Baron-Cohen (2005) argues the existence of an 'extreme male brain' clearly demonstrates biological differences. He shows how, on a population level, females are stronger empathizers and males are stronger systemizers. The 'extreme male brain' theory argues that the more **testosterone** a prenatal (in the womb) baby has:

- the less likely the child will make eye contact

- the slower the language development will be

- the more inclined the child will be toward 'systems' rather than people (measured using quantified data using Empathy Quotient (EQ) testing and Systemizing Quotient (SQ) testing).

This is also true for females (with female genitalia) who experienced increased testosterone while prenatal. The theory has been used to explain why autism is predominantly a male disorder. Autism represents an extreme of the male pattern because it includes impaired empathizing and enhanced systemizing.

The evidence clearly shows there are key brain and bodily differences between the two genders. It is reasonable to assume these differences will manifest themselves in different thoughts, feelings, and behaviours. The question is always to what extent can they cause psychological and behavioural differences, and to what extent are these differences moderated by sociocultural processes?

Furthermore, while there are some cross-cultural differences in how males and females are expected to behave, one might argue that these are minor. Despite all of the different cultures that exist, there are still many cross-cultural similarities in how males and females actually behave. Cross-cultural universal behaviour suggests powerful biological causes of gender role behaviour.

For example, Lippa (2002; 2005; 2010) has documented significant cross-cultural gender similarities in areas such as aggression and occupational choice. Using the BBC (a British secular liberal broadcaster), 200 000 participants were surveyed from 53 nations. Lippa found that females were less aggressive and gravitated toward social or caring occupations; men were more aggressive and gravitated toward technical occupations. There were still significant gender role differences in 'modern' countries where equality was actively promoted, such as Norway. In other words, despite active and well-funded attempts to increase the number of male nurses and female engineers over many decades, these occupations were significantly filled by the traditional genders. This suggests a biological mechanism for gender role differences as people in these developed countries have more choice over their preferred professions.

However, a purely social, cognitive, or biological approach to explain the formation and development of gender roles is unrealistic. Gender identity and roles are probably the result of a combination of all three.

What can transgenderism teach us about the origins of gender identity and social roles?

Caitlyn Marie Jenner (born 28 October 1949) was formerly known as Bruce Jenner. She is a US television personality and retired Olympic gold medal-winning

The evidence clearly shows there are key brain and bodily differences between the two genders. It is reasonable to assume these differences will manifest themselves in different thoughts, feelings, and behaviours. The question is always to what extent can they cause psychological and behavioural differences, and to what extent are these differences moderated by sociocultural processes?

Despite all of the different cultures that exist, there are still many cross-cultural similarities in how males and females actually behave. Cross-cultural universal behaviour suggests powerful biological causes of gender role behaviour.

 TOK

If identity is fluid and personal, can people change identity at will? Can other identifiers also become fluid and open to social influence? For example, can white people claim a 'black' identity and vice versa? Who decides and how is identity measured?

Research Laxmi Narayan Tripathi and her work 'Me Hijra Me Laxmi'.

205

How might a research programme be influenced by gender? What is the role of objectivity in psychology?

To what extent can transgenderism offer insight into the origins of gender roles?

Empathy requires an understanding of someone else's mental or emotional state and a sharing of the emotional experience of the other person. ToM is the ability to attribute mental states to oneself and others. For example, to understand that others have their own beliefs, desires, intentions, and perspectives that are different from one's own (Premack and Woodruff, 1978).

Are theories based on empirical foundations more valid than theories based on theoretical foundations? What is the relationship between empirical and theoretical constructions in human science?

decathlete. In 2015, Jenner transitioned from a male identity to a female identity. She has stated life as a woman is primarily a matter of mental state and lifestyle. She remains sexually attracted to women.

Like many **transgender** people, Jenner suffered from **gender dysphoria** since her youth and had powerful feelings she was in the 'wrong body'. She has stated she feels like she has always had the 'soul' of a female.

Such stories suggest gender identity is a powerful internal drive that is largely immune from sociocultural influences. Similar to gay people, transgender people often have to face prejudice and discrimination from hostile groups, and it is an extremely brave decision to transition from one gender to another. If a person decides to transition, they may have to undergo years of difficult hormone and surgical procedures, and yet their own desires and deep-seated instinct that they are in the wrong body often compels them to endure these. As a result of intensive hormonal treatment, they will begin to think, feel, and act differently, which suggests the powerful influence hormones have on gender-related behaviours. More research is needed with transgender people, but their experiences offer insight into gender.

25.3 Development of empathy and theory of mind

Content focus

Discuss explanations of empathy.

Empathy requires an understanding of someone else's mental or emotional state and a sharing of the emotional experience of the other person (Decety and Jackson, 2004; Singer, 2006). For example, observing someone else's sadness causing sadness in the observer, and this internal experience enabling the observer to understand the other person's emotional experience (Levenson et al., 1990).

Empathy is seen as essential for healthy relationships and overall well-being. **Affective empathy** is the emotional response to others' distress and can take two forms: personal distress or empathic concern (Cassels et al., 2010).

Theory of mind (ToM) is the ability to attribute mental states to oneself and others. For example, to understand that others have their own beliefs, desires, intentions, and perspectives that are different from one's own (Premack and Woodruff, 1978). It is called a theory in a nod to the philosophical underpinnings of the approach: it is theoretically assumed others have a mind, but this assumption is theoretical as noone has direct access to the mind of another.

25.3.1 Mentalization

A key factor in ToM is the notion of mentalization. Mentalization refers to a type of imaginative mental ability that allows us to perceive and interpret human behaviour in terms of intentional mental states (e.g. needs, desires, feelings, beliefs, goals, purposes, and reasons) (Fonagy et al., 2002). Mentalization is developmental and becomes increasingly complex over time. It allows us to answer questions about why we and others behave the way we do. Wallin (2009) describes it as a process of 'thinking about thinking'.

Mentalization has implications for attachment theory and **self-development**. Fonagy and Bateman (2006) argue that mentalization:

- emerges through interaction with the caregiver, in the context of an attachment relationship

- may be inhibited (decoupled) temporarily or more extensively in response to interpersonal conflicts, **acute** stress, or trauma in vulnerable individuals

- is procedural and mostly non-conscious

- is inexact but central to understanding and regulating emotions.

According to Fonagy and Bateman, the degree and type of attachment interactions an individual has partially determines their capacity to mentalize. Individuals without proper attachment (due, for example, to physical, psychological, or sexual abuse) can have greater difficulty developing mentalization abilities.

In this way, mentalization can be seen as similar to Bowlby's basic assumption – that a secure attachment environment in childhood creates cognitive structures that allow secure attachment thoughts, feelings, and behaviours into adulthood. Securely attached individuals tend to have had a primary caregiver that has more complex and sophisticated mentalizing abilities. These children have more robust capacities to understand the states of their own and other people's minds. Furthermore, the secure attachment allows the child to form a positive schema about themselves and their place in the world.

Mentalization could be seen as a largely cognitive process, with empathy making up an additional affective component. Mentalization is essential to being able to empathize, however both require knowledge of the 'other'. Mentalizing skills require the integration of both knowledge about beliefs and knowledge about emotions, which then allow people to empathize (Shamay-Tsoory et al., 2003, 2004).

There are many instances when another person's emotional response is not observable, and therefore has to be inferred or imagined. These aspects of 'affective mentalizing' (or 'affective ToM') have not been adequately studied (Hooker et al., 2008). However, it could be reasonably assumed that the more vividly the future emotional response is imagined, the more it can help motivate prosocial behaviour (Batson, 1991; Hooker et al., 2008).

25.3.2 Biological determinants of mentalization and empathy

The term '**social brain**' refers to the network of brain regions that are involved in understanding others (Blakemore, 2008). The **social information processing network** (SIPN) model (Nelson et al., 2005) argues that social information processing occurs by way of three interacting neural 'nodes': the 'detection node', the 'affective node' and the 'cognitive-regulatory node'.

Mentalization refers to a type of imaginative mental ability that allows us to perceive and interpret human behaviour in terms of intentional mental states (e.g. needs, desires, feelings, beliefs, goals, purposes, and reasons) (Fonagy et al., 2002).

Securely attached individuals tend to have had a primary caregiver that has more complex and sophisticated mentalizing abilities. Therefore these children have more robust capacities to understand the states of their own and other people's minds.

The term 'social brain' refers to the network of brain regions that are involved in understanding others (Blakemore, 2008).

The detection node, comprising areas including the temporal and occipital regions, deciphers the social properties of a stimulus, such as movement in the environment.

The affective node, comprising areas including the limbic areas of the brain (such as the amygdala, ventral striatum, hypothalamus and orbitofrontal cortex), is thought to process the emotional significance of a social stimulus.

The cognitive-regulatory node, consisting of much of the prefrontal cortex, is responsible for mentalizing, impulse inhibition, and goal-directed behaviour. This is the area responsible for 'thinking about thinking'.

Nelson et al. (2005) argue there is a mismatch in the maturation development of the different nodes. For example, they propose the development of the cognitive-regulatory node lags behind the development of the other nodes. This maturation deficit may explain why adolescents can suffer from mood and anxiety disorders.

Hooker et al. (2008) were able to isolate neural regions involved in predicting the emotional response of another person. Participants were given a questionnaire to measure their levels of empathy in daily life by answering questions on a five-point scale. They were then given an emotion recognition task in which they were asked to identify what emotion a character (indicated by a fixation symbol) was feeling in various pictured scenes while they were scanned using fMRIs.

For their primary condition (the emotion prediction of what they termed 'the False Belief Character'), the additional information sometimes causes the False Belief Character to change from a positive to a negative emotion (e.g. the parent who is blissfully unaware of his son's failing grade but will be angry when he finds out) and sometimes causes the emotion to change from a negative to positive emotion (e.g. a person believes they are being held-up at gun point, but it is really a friend using the end of a banana to play a trick on him).

Participants were asked to judge what a character was feeling and then asked to predict what they would feel when a better understanding of the situation became apparent. The researchers found more activity in primarily emotion-related regions, particularly the bilateral thalamus, when predicting a new emotional state, and this was related to more self-reported empathy in daily life. Therefore, there was a connection between the strength of emotion-related neural activity and empathy in daily life.

The researchers suggest that when people predict an emotional response in someone else, they generate an internal affective representation of the predicted emotional response. Therefore there is a clear cognitive and biological element to feeling and acting on empathetic feelings. The stronger the affective representation, the more likely they were to experience empathy.

In Western cultures, high empathic concern and low personal distress have been implicated in increased prosocial behaviour (Eisenberg et al., 1989). This is in turn related to better emotion management as well as better peer relations (Eisenberg and Fabes, 1998).

25.3.3 Sociocultural determinants of mentalization and empathy

In Western cultures, high empathic concern and low personal distress have been implicated in increased prosocial behaviour (Eisenberg et al., 1989). This is in turn related to better emotion management as well as better peer relations (Eisenberg and Fabes, 1998). However, previous work suggests cultural differences in personal distress and levels of empathetic concern. For example, Trommsdorff (1999) has argued children from East Asian cultures experience greater personal distress but less empathic concern than children from Western cultures.

This has been supported by other researchers. For example, Cassels et al. (2010) focused on empathic concern and personal distress and compared East Asian and European-Canadian young adults. They used a predominantly female sample of 190 school and university undergraduate students from the Vancouver area who clearly identified as East Asian or European-Canadian. Potential participants who did not clearly identify as either were excluded.

They used Davis's (1980) Interpersonal Reactivity Index (IRI) to measure empathy and personal distress. The index has 28 items answered on a five-point Likert scale ranging from 'Does not describe me well' to 'Describes me very well', and produces quantifiable data easily replicated across different groups. It is one of the most widely used self-report measures of empathy in circulation and has both good internal and external validity.

Cassels et al. (2010) found Westerners reported more empathic concern (the tendency to feel sympathy and/or concern for others in negative situations), but less personal distress (the tendency to experience distress and/or discomfort in response to another person's distress) than East Asians.

Trommsdorff et al. (2007) observed preschool children responding to a sad event (an adult having her balloon popped). They compared four different cultural groups (children from Germany, Israel, Indonesia, and Malaysia). They found children from other-oriented cultural groups (Indonesia and Malaysia) displayed more self-focused distress than children from individual-oriented cultural groups (Germany and Israel).

However, Ma-Kellams and Blascovich (2012) highlight an important moderator of cultural differences in empathy. They argue that empathy is influenced by whether the observed target is a stranger or a close-other. They found East Asians were able to infer the emotions of close-others more accurately than European Americans. However, European American participants inferred the emotions of strangers more accurately than East Asian participants.

De Greck et al. (2011; cited in Atkins, 2014) asked participants to intentionally empathize with a familiar face displaying an angry expression, a familiar face displaying a neutral expression or an unfamiliar face displaying a neutral expression. They found stronger dorsolateral prefrontal cortex (DLPFC) responses among Chinese participants compared to German participants when intentionally empathizing with a familiar face displaying anger.

The DLPFC region has been linked to emotional regulation strategies, suggesting the Chinese group reflects greater emotional regulation of anger emotions. It could be that interpersonal harmony is highly valued in Eastern cultures when compared to Western cultures (Markus and Kitayama, 1991) and therefore people from Eastern cultures have developed better regulation of their anger responses to maintain harmony (de Greck et al., 2011).

Mind-blindness

Mind-blindness is seen as a cognitive disorder where an individual is unable to attribute mental states to the self and others (Gallagher and Frith, 2003). People with this disorder lack the ability to mentalize. Consequently, they may be unaware of others' mental and emotional states.

Mind-blindness theory assumes children with mind-blindness are delayed in developing a ToM, which normally allows developing children to imagine what it is like to be in the position of another (Baron-Cohen, 1990). Baron-Cohen argues that any individual who suffers from mind-blindness would find the world a confusing and frightening place, which increases their chances of withdrawing from society.

26 Developing as a learner

Topic focus

Discuss how individuals develop as learners.

26.1 Cognitive development

Content focus

Evaluate two theories of cognitive development.

TOK

Piaget used his own experiences as a parent to help formulate his ideas. To what extent should researchers use their own experiences in their research? How should this be acknowledged in research? What are the implications for notions of validity and reliability?

Piaget assumed cognitive development is under genetic control and develops in the form of predisposed stages; children do not passively receive knowledge; they are curious, self-motivated and seek out information to construct their own understanding of the environment – they are active learners; children construct schemas to help shape their understanding of the world.

Cognitive development can be defined as the increasingly advanced thought and problem-solving ability that occurs over time from infancy to adulthood.

There are two main approaches to explaining cognitive development. The first approach is an explicit attempt to link cognitive development to biological maturation over time. This is best illustrated by **Piaget's theory**, which links cognitive stages to biological development (the 'ages and stages' approach). The second approach links cognitive development to the social and emotional surroundings a child experiences. This is best illustrated by **Vygotsky's theory**, which links language and culture to cognitive development. The theories are not necessarily at odds with one another and can be seen as complementary explanations of the same phenomena.

26.1.1 Piaget's theory of cognitive development

Piaget's assumptions (e.g. Piaget, 1977):

- Cognitive development is under genetic control and develops in the form of predisposed stages.

- Children do not passively receive knowledge; they are curious, self-motivated and seek out information to construct their own understanding of the environment – they are active learners.

- Over time, children construct their view of the world through mental frameworks of understanding called schemas. Schemas are mental representations of the world and all children are born with a range of schemas, such as a schema for sucking, reaching, and gripping. These are modified as a result of experience and Piaget called this process modification adaptation.

There are two types of adaptation:

Assimilation: Occurs when new events (such as objects, experiences, ideas, and situations) can be fitted into existing schemas of what the child already understands about the world. An example of this is when a child calls the family German shepherd a 'doggie', then points at the neighbour's labrador and also call it a 'doggie'. This shows he has understood the parameters of his existing schema (furry, playful, four legs) and fitted the image into it.

Accommodation: Occurs when new events do not fit existing schemas, so a new schema is created or an existing one is modified to allow the new worldview. For example, a child points at a small horse and calls it a 'doggie'. He would be corrected and told it is a 'horse' and he would have to create a new schema (with new parameters) in order to understand all future encounters with horses. Accommodation is therefore the creation of new knowledge and the rejection or adaption of existing schemas.

Piaget's four stages of cognitive development

Sensorimotor stage (0 to 2 years): Characterized by the infant having no formal schema for the world or itself other than their basic survival schemas for eating and receiving attention. The infant can only know the world via his or her immediate senses and the motor or movement actions he or she performs. This stage is illustrated by profound **egocentrism** as the infant cannot distinguish between self and the environment because he or she has no real knowledge of the world around him or her. Egocentrism is illustrated by a lack of object permanence: when an infant cannot see an object then it effectively ceases to exist for the child.

Pre-operational stage (2 to 7 years): The stage begins with the establishment of object permanence and ends with the emergence of concrete operations (rules they can apply to other objects in the real or concrete world). The stage is still dominated by the cognitive limiting effects of egocentrism as the child has a limited ability to see, think, feel, or imagine the world from another's point of view. Egocentrism is demonstrated by the three mountain experiment (Piaget and Inhelder, 1956) in which 4-year-olds, when shown a mountain scene, tended to fail when asked to describe the same scene from a doll's point of view placed on the other side.

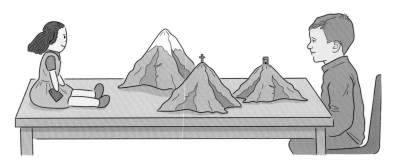

Figure 26.1 The three mountain experiment

211

During this stage, children have a lack of conservation – the realization that objects can remain the same despite a change in appearance. To demonstrate this, Piaget used two rows of different coloured beads and spread one row out. The pre-operational child does not understand that spreading the beads out does not increase the number of beads present.

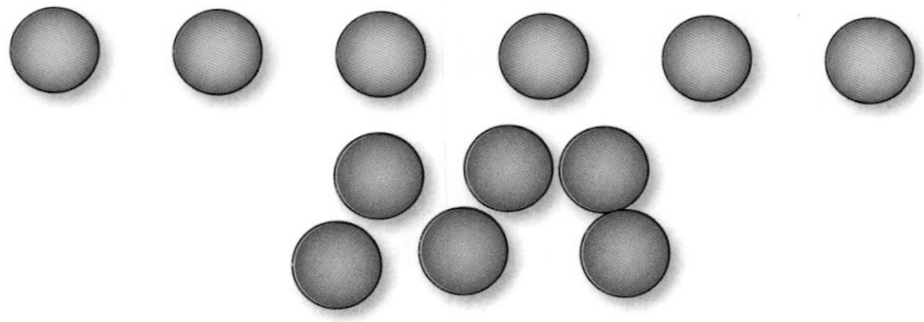

Figure 26.2 In the pre-operational stage, children are egocentric and lack conservation.

Concrete operational stage (7 to 11 years): Characterized by a development of definitive rules or schemas for ordering the world and the development of conservation.

Formal operational stage (11 years onwards): The child's mental structures are well developed. Problems can be manipulated in the head without the need for physical objects. Children can think about possible occurrences and imagine themselves in different roles without the need for dolls or play acting.

Positive evaluation of Piaget's theory

Piaget produced the first comprehensive theory of child cognitive development, which has generated debate and stimulated research. Before this theory was proposed, children were not treated as independent thinkers by researchers.

Piaget modified his theory to take into account criticisms, and envisaged it constantly changing as new evidence came to light. For example, Piaget was the first to investigate whether biological maturation drove cognitive development, and his vision of a child as having cognitive changes regulated by their biology is now widely accepted and supported by cross-cultural research.

His vision of children being determined, dynamic thinkers who are anxious to achieve coherence and test theories through assimilation and accommodation ('little scientists') significantly influenced the education profession. There is now an emphasis on child-centric classrooms with opportunities for intellectual exploration and children are expected to actively participate in their own learning. Classrooms have become places where children 'do' things rather than passively receive knowledge.

Negative evaluation

Bower (1982) showed that object permanence is not as rigid as envisioned in the sensorimotor stage. He showed an infant an object and then placed a screen between it and the infant. The object was then removed and the screen taken away and the child showed surprise. This shows the child may have been expecting to see the object and does not lack the concept of object permanence as stated by Piaget.

The pre-operational stage has been criticized for being negative in tone. Piaget focuses on what the child cannot do rather than what they can achieve. Field et al. (1982) found children aged 4 to 5 can spend as much as 20 per cent of their playtime constructing sophisticated roles for different objects above and beyond their intended use (e.g. blocks become trucks, brooms become horses with names and personalities), as well as being capable of imitating and discriminating between emotions in faces they see.

Taylor et al. (1993) demonstrated how pre-operational children can develop imaginary companions with complex personalities and engage in conversation with them, suggesting a lack of egocentrism.

Children are egocentric but Piaget probably exaggerated the amount of egocentrism, and his methods are not child friendly enough to access the nuances of the children's understanding. When methodologies are changed, fewer children make egocentric mistakes, suggesting Piaget's 'ages and stages' paradigm is less rigid than he envisioned.

Piaget has also been criticized for underestimating the role of social development. The three mountain experiment is a presentation of a social scene, and yet Piaget focused on it as a mental problem. When the approach was changed to a more child-friendly format, more children were able to understand the different views.

This is because children fail to see it as an abstract problem and see only the literal question. If the adult says, 'What can I see?' then the child may think, *They can see the whole scene because they are bigger than me and this is their experiment so of course they have seen everything*. If the adult says, 'What can the doll see?' then the child may think, *The doll is not real so they can see whatever they want because this is a game*. Either way, the child fails to understand the abstract nature of the task, but this does not mean they are egocentric.

Piaget's theory assumes cognitive development as largely the same for both genders. However, there is some evidence that male and female brains develop in different ways and at different rates. For example, Cooke and Woolley (2005) found structural differences in the amygdala in male brains when compared to female brains. Some of these differences include size (men have a larger amygdala than women) and the rate of development over time.

Frings et al. (2006) studied hippocampi differences in males versus females. Activation of the hippocampus is more dominant on the left side in females, while it is more dominant on the right side in males. This in turn influences cognitive reasoning; women verbalize strategies more than men when performing a task that requires cognitive thinking. Therefore, it cannot be assumed both genders cognitively develop in the same way at the same rate. However, this technology was not available to Piaget when he was developing his theory.

26.1.2 Vygotsky's theory of cognitive development

Vygotsky focused on the importance of social interaction and culture on a child's cognitive development. In his model, a child makes sense of the world through shared meaning with others, whereas the Piagetian child makes sense of the world as the result of biological processes that drive cognitive development.

Vygotsky thought of culture as a body of knowledge held by persons of greater knowledge who transmitted ideas through language – hence the importance he placed on language development as part of overall cognitive development. In summary, his theory proposed that language and culture drive cognitive development. Note that Vygotsky lived between 1896–1934, but many citations of his work (e.g. Vygotsky,

1978) are from after this period and represent translations or anthologies not endorsed by Vygotsky.

Language for children is primarily a way to produce change in others, but when language becomes internalized it converges with thought, and eventually we are able to direct and control our thinking with the use of language. Piaget saw this as 'egocentric speech', whereas Vygotsky sees it as the precursor to internalized thought.

We develop an inner voice for thinking and a more complex, vocabulary-rich voice for communication with others.

Vygotsky articulated the importance of culture through his **zone of proximal development (ZPD)**. Instruction from an expert wakens a series of embryonic functions that can be extended under supervision from an expert (usually an adult). These abilities would lie dormant and unused if they were left untutored. This illustrates the difference between the Piagetian individual-construction approach and the importance of social construction put forward by Vygotsky. Vygotsky believed that learning comes before development. Development occurs when a new task is just out of reach of a child's current developmental ability. Development occurs as the child reaches for it. Piaget believed that development comes before learning.

Wood et al. (1976) introduced the notion of scaffolding as development of the ZPD, where the disorganized and spontaneous thoughts presented by the child are responded to with the more systematic, logical, and rational concepts of a more knowledgeable (usually adult) helper.

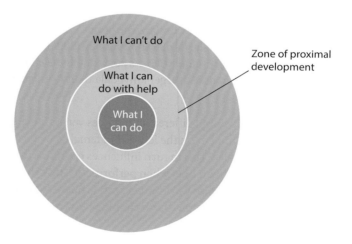

Figure 26.3 Vygotsky's three stages of language development

Vygotsky's three stages of language development

Pre-intellectual social speech (0 to 3 years): Thought is not constructed using language and speech is only used to enact social change. For example, asking for and receiving objects from a parent.

Egocentric speech (3 to 7 years): Language helps to control the child's own behaviour and it is spoken out loud. For example, when children play games they often verbalize their actions.

Inner speech (7+ years): The child uses speech silently to develop their thinking and publicly for social communication.

Positive evaluation

Vygotsky placed importance on a child's inner speech, which has a common-sense value because thought and language are interconnected. He argued that the inner voice was a key part of learning and cognitive development.

Emphasis on inner speech has empirical support. For example, Behrend et al. (1992) quantified inner speech by observing the amount of whispering and lip-reading children engaged in when given a task. They found children who used the greatest amount of inner speech tended to perform better in tasks.

There are methodological and practical applications for this theory. For example, scaffolding has been useful from a teaching perspective (both in terms of organizing thoughts and emotions). Conner et al. (1997) argued that the quality of the scaffolding provided by a mother and father could predict the success of the child in the classroom, arguing that children who are socially and intellectually supported at home will be more confident in the classroom.

Negative evaluation

There is a lack of empirical support for Vygotsky's ideas, but this can be largely explained by his emphasis on inner emotional and cognitive processes rather than outcomes (which Piaget emphasized), and processes are harder to test for. For example, inner speech is difficult to test for and quantify. Vygotsky's ideas are theoretical, and his theory can be criticized for being too vague in its outline of social influence.

Rogoff (1990) dismisses the idea that Vygotsky's ideas are culturally universal and instead states the concept of scaffolding – which is heavily dependent on verbal instruction – may not be equally useful in all cultures for all types of learning. Indeed, in some instances, observation and practice may be more effective ways of learning certain skills. However, even though verbal instruction may vary from culture to culture, emotional scaffolding in some form takes place in all cultures.

It should be noted that Vygotsky died at the age of 38; his work as a cognitive developmental researcher was still in its infancy and had he lived longer he would have advanced his theories and been able to respond to **peer review**.

26.2 Brain development

Content focus

To what extent is the brain influenced by environmental factors?

26.2.1 Maturation and development of the brain

Animal studies have been used to clearly show how specific regions of the brain mature at different ages. For example, Zehr et al. (2008) showed hippocampal function, including spatial cognition and stress response, matures during adolescence in Syrian hamsters. They also showed how these are dependent on sex differences as maturity changes taking place in the brain also respond differently to the different sex hormones. These changes are likely related to the adolescent development of cognitive functions such as learning and memory, as well as the mediation of stress (Zehr et al., 2008).

TOK How are the boundaries of academic subjects determined and maintained? As technology improves, researchers are able to link thoughts, feelings, and behaviours to specific brain areas. Where does psychology begin and where does biology end? Do the improvements in technology eventually mean psychology will become obsolete? Can human experience be captured and explained using purely biological explanations?

Piaget's theory assumes cognitive development as largely complete by the age of 11. This can be challenged, as it could be argued that cognitive development and its decline is a lifelong process. For example, Johnson et al. (2009) argue that brain development continues into the twenties and thirties and this has a significant impact on cognitive reasoning and emotional maturity. This is particularly apparent for males as the process of 'adolescence' does not end until 25 in brain development terms.

26.2.2 Brain plasticity

The brain is a dynamic system that interacts with the environment. The brain is physically sculpted by experience. Not only can the brain determine and change behaviour, but behaviour and environment can change the brain.

Before the 1960s, the brain was thought to be influenced only by genetics, and therefore it was considered unchangeable. However, researchers such as Hubel and Wiesel (1965) demonstrated that the brain could change in response to environmental input. These results were based on laboratory experiments with rats, but it has now become generally accepted that environmental enrichment can modify the brain, especially the cerebral cortex, which is the area of higher cognitive functioning. It seems that the brain is constantly changing as a result of experience throughout the lifespan.

> The brain is a dynamic system that interacts with the environment and the brain is physically sculpted by experience. Not only can the brain determine and change behaviour, but behaviour and environment can change the brain.

Key study: Luby et al. (2012)

Aim: To measure the effect of parental nurturing on the growth of the hippocampus. The hippocampus is essential for learning because it is involved in long-term memory function. Long-term memory function provides storage for information and allows new information to be assimilated and organized ready for use. Humans would not be such successful creatures had they not been able to learn complex information and call upon it when needed.

Procedure: Magnetic resonance imaging (MRI) was used to scan 92 children's brains. An experiment was conducted when the children were between 3 and 6 years old. The children were put into a frustrating situation where they and their mothers were left in a room with a brightly wrapped gift. The children were not allowed to open the gift and they were told to wait while the mother filled out a series of forms. Researchers observed how the children and mothers handled this situation, which was meant to replicate the typical **stressors** of daily parenting. Mothers who offered reassurance and support that helped their child control their impulses were rated as being nurturing. Mothers who either ignored the child or harshly scolded the child were rated as non-nurturing.

Findings: After four years, when the children were between 7 and 10 years old, Luby performed MRI brain scans on them. She found children with the nurturing mothers had a hippocampus that was 10 per cent larger than the hippocampi of children who had mothers that were non-nurturing.

Conclusion: Nurturing mothers impact brain development on children.

Evaluation: This was a tightly controlled **natural experiment** with a large sample size offering common-sense insight into a real-world problem. However, not all variables could be controlled and the variable of 'nurturing' is very broad. For example, non-nurturing mothers may also neglect to feed their children healthily (the hippocampus is a biological entity in the brain that is influenced by diet) or read to them regularly, which may also impact their children's brain development. There may be other factors such as a lack of sleep, drug use during pregnancy, smoking, and drinking, which may all have impacted the children. Therefore, it is difficult to infer causation from one variable onto another.

However, it should be noted that Luby and her colleagues were building on knowledge gained by experiments conducted with animals such as Kozorovitskiy et al. (2005), who studied how experience induces structural and biochemical changes in the adult primate brain by placing primates in either a complex environment or a simple environment for a month. The results showed the structure of the adult primate brain is highly sensitive even to modest levels of experiential complexity.

Rats provide a biological research platform and allow clear manipulations and measurements of variables that would not be possible in humans. For example, it is possible to manipulate the environment to pinpoint the exact variable and the extent to which it can shape brain development.

Diamond et al. (1972) wanted to test the effect of a physically enriched environment on the frontal lobe. The frontal lobe is essential for learning because it is involved in many important cognitive skills in humans, such as emotional expression, problem solving, memory, language, and basic judgement through reasoning. Diamond et al. placed rats into one of two environments – one enriched and one deprived. The richness of the environment was **operationalized** by being surrounded by interesting toys. The dependent variable was the effect on the frontal lobe and was operationalized by measuring the thickness of the frontal lobe. The rats spent 30 or 60 days in their respective environments and then they were euthanized.

Post-mortem studies of their brains showed that rats that had been in the stimulating environment had an increased **cortical** thickness. The frontal lobe, which is associated with thinking, planning, and decision making, was heavier in the rats that had been in the stimulating environment. Similar research studies have constantly demonstrated that cortical thickness increases even further if the rats are placed with other rats. The combination of having company and many interesting toys created the best conditions for developing cerebral thickness.

This was a tightly controlled study with a clear **independent variable** (IV) and clear, quantifiable DV, therefore clear causation can be inferred that would not be possible with human subjects. Although this was an animal study and caution should be used when generalizing the results to humans, the experiment followed the correct guidelines for ethical treatment of animals. It should be remembered that the rats are bred for experimental purposes and were used sparingly.

26.2.3 Learning to be social

Humans are an intensely social species. They have to learn a varied repertoire of social skills to survive and thrive in a complex social environment: from quickly and automatically detecting the presence of another human in their environment, to

Humans are an intensely social species. They have to learn a varied repertoire of social skills to survive and thrive in a complex social environment.

making inferences about another's emotions, beliefs, and enduring character traits, and using this knowledge to guide future behaviour (Frith and Frith, 2010).

Social cognition refers to the collection of cognitive processes that are required to understand and interact with others. Evidence suggests many social cognitive functions develop during adolescence as the brain continues to develop. Consequently, there are clear age differences in **sociocognitive** abilities such as face processing, mental state inference and responding to peer influence and social evaluation. These are linked to the 'social brain', which refers to the network of brain regions that underlies these processes (Burnett et al., 2010). New research indicates the social brain undergoes structural development, including **synaptic** reorganization, during adolescence (Blakemore, 2008).

There are many aspects to social learning. For example, learning to interpret others' emotional expressions, learning to make strategic social decisions – which can be tested using behavioural economic games (e.g. Binmore, 2007) – and learning to deal with social rejection – with many accounts showing a clear gender difference in sensitivity to group exclusion (e.g. Kloep, 1999). Furthermore, learning to understand the intended meaning of a remark beyond what is explicitly stated is a necessary skill for social success. It can be considered an integral part of mentalizing.

Wang et al. (2006) compared the neural circuitry underlying the interpretation of communicative intent in children and adults using an MRI scanner. They used irony comprehension as a test case. Participants viewed cartoon drawings while listening to short scenarios ending with a potentially ironic remark and were asked to decide whether the speaker was being sincere or ironic. It was a relatively small sample (12 adults and 12 children) and all were right-handed, with the exception of one left-handed boy. They performed all analyses both with and without the left-handed participant but the pattern of results did not change when he was excluded.

The researchers found that children engaged the medial prefrontal cortex and left inferior frontal gyrus (located in the frontal regions of the brain) more strongly than adults. Adults used the fusiform gyrus, extrastriate areas and the amygdala (located in the posterior of the brain) more strongly than children. This developmental shift from a reliance on frontal regions to posterior regions of the brain may reflect the automatization of basic reasoning about mental states in social situations as the social learner develops with age.

27 Approaches to research: developmental psychology

Learning focus

Discuss approaches to research in developmental psychology.

> Research in developmental psychology usually aims to measure the experiences of people over long periods of time.

Developmental psychology creates a number of special considerations for researchers. Research in developmental psychology usually aims to measure the experiences of people over long periods of time. Therefore, children as well as professionals who work with them are often at the core of research.

27.1 Working with young children

Working with children means developmental psychologists have to think very carefully about the methods they use for gathering data. For example, Piaget's methods have been criticized as being too formal for children, resulting in key misunderstandings. When his methods were changed to show more 'child sense', children understood what was being asked of them and showed cognitive ability outside of their age-appropriate stage.

For example, in Piaget's conservation of beads experiment, an adult would ask, 'Which has more beads?' and the child would be under stress to provide a 'correct' answer, one that supports the 'logical' direction of the test: 'Are these the same?', 'Yes.' The beads are then changed. 'Are these the same?' The 'logical' answer is that they are not the same because they have been changed.

Children may assume they are being tricked or the adult wants a particular answer and the results showed that fewer children could conserve. This was interpreted to mean children could not conserve until much later. However, when researchers made the methodology more age-appropriate they got different results.

For their conservation of beads experiment, McGarrigle and Donaldson (1974) used a glove puppet, known as Naughty Teddy, to 'accidentally' transform the beads. They found 63 per cent of 4–6-year-old children could successfully 'conserve', as they recognized the number of beads remained the same. By using a 'naughty teddy' the beads may not have been 'changed', but 'messed around with' as a result of a naughty interloper. Therefore, while things appeared to change, there is a greater possibility they were the same: naughty teddies are not necessarily good at providing correct answers, so the child feels freer and less pressured.

The notion of a naughty teddy is important because children understand the concept of being naughty. It implies something bad has happened that does not necessarily change reality. They are more able to contradict naughty teddy than the adult.

Researchers have to be clear their methodology means the same to the child as it means to the researcher. One way to check this is to perform **pilot studies** to ensure the methods make sense to the child. For example, Oostermeijer et al. (2014) conducted a study in the Netherlands with 128 sixth-grade students where they focused on measured mathematical word problem-solving performance using the Mathematical Processing Instrument (MPI). They fixed a time limit of three minutes to solve each word problem, but only after conducting a pilot study with five sixth-grade students. This showed every child was able to solve each of the 14 items of the MPI within the required three minutes and so they were able to eliminate 'time' as an extraneous variable that may have impacted the results.

27.2 Longitudinal studies

Longitudinal studies are useful for developmental psychologists because they show change over time. If variables are identified, and in some cases held constant, the extent to which they influence an effect can be measured and debated. For example, Mahoney et al. (2005) carried out a longitudinal study of the effect of after-school programmes

Working with children means developmental psychologists have to think very carefully about the methods they use for gathering data.

Longitudinal studies are useful for developmental psychologists because they show change over time. If variables are identified, and in some cases held constant, the extent to which they influence an effect can be measured and debated.

219

on the school success and motivation for disadvantaged children. They found a full year's after-school programme resulted in better test scores, reading achievement, and overall motivation for the students who took part. They were only able to reach these conclusions because they studied the children over the course of a full year.

Similarly, Dickerson and Popli (2014) analysed data on over 8700 members of the Millennium Cohort Study, which follows the lives of children born in the UK in 2000–2001 (see p. 191 for details). As a result of the longitudinal nature of the study they found 7-year-olds who have lived in poverty since infancy perform substantially worse in a range of cognitive-ability tests than those who have never been poor – even when family circumstances and parenting skills were taken into consideration.

TOK

To what extent should 'common sense' be a part of explanations for human behaviour? Should every aspect of human experience be tested empirically before it is accepted as a fact?

27.3 Correlations versus experiments

Experiment is the only method that can produce **cause-and-effect** with certainty. However, experiments lack **ecological validity** because so many variables need to be controlled. The isolation and control of variables produces an artificial setting that can make children behave differently. Therefore, experiments in developmental psychology are often not as tightly controlled as they might be.

Oostermeijer et al. (2014) conducted a study in the Netherlands with 128 sixth-grade students. They found those who spent more free time in construction play performed better on a test of mathematical word problems (see p. 184 for details). However, the study was only correlational, which made it impossible to draw conclusions about any causal relationships among constructive play, spatial ability, and mathematical word problem-solving performance.

For causality to be established, tight control over variables needs to occur. For example, in a study sponsored by the toy maker Mega Bloks®, researchers gave toy blocks to middle- and low-income toddlers (Christakis et al., 2007). The children ranged in age from 1.5 to 2.5 years, and were randomly assigned to experience two conditions:

- Children in the treatment group got two sets of toy Mega Bloks®: 80 plastic interlocking blocks and a set of specialty blocks, including cars and people. The parents of these toddlers were given instructions for encouraging block play.

- Children in the control group did not get blocks until the end of the study. The parents of these children received no instructions about block play.

Parents in both groups were not told the real purpose of the study but were asked to keep time diaries of their children's activities. After six months, each parent completed a follow-up interview that included an assessment of the child's verbal ability using the MacArthur-Bates Communicative Development Inventories.

The results showed children in the experimental group scored higher on parent-reported tests of vocabulary, grammar, and verbal comprehension and showed a trend toward watching less TV (although this was not significant).

The deliberate manipulation of the variable (presence or absence of playing blocks) made it possible for the researchers to infer a cause-effect relationship that was not present in the equivalent correlational study performed by Oostermeijer et al. (2014).

27.4 The use of technology to monitor cognition

Modern technology is now extensively used in developmental **neuropsychology** because it provides an opportunity to study the active brain. This allows developmental researchers to see where specific brain processes take place and enable them to study localization of function in the living human brain as it changes over time.

The key problem with using technology in brain research is that it can lead to **reductionist** arguments about the causes of behaviour. It is important to always consider wider considerations for the causes of behaviour. Overall, the technology allows researchers to pinpoint key areas and speculate on their function and development during maturation.

Hooker et al. (2008) were able to investigate areas of the brain involved in empathy. They were able to isolate neural regions involved in predicting the emotional response of another person using fMRIs (see p. 207 for details). Therefore, they were able to pinpoint and speculate as to what extent areas of the brain were responsible for feelings of empathy.

Lenroot et al. (2007) used evidence from MRI scans to argue that differences in brain development between males and females are significant (see p. 204 for details) and Spalek et al. (2015) used MRI scans to find gender-specific differences in information processing, suggesting there are biological causes for what humans find interesting and how we process the information (see p. 204 for details).

Luby et al. (2012) showed how parental nurturing can influence the growth of the hippocampus. Luby et al. used MRIs to scan 92 children's brains. They found that children with nurturing mothers had a hippocampus that was 10 percent larger than the hippocampi of children who had mothers that were non-nurturing. Luby et al. therefore concluded that nurturing mothers impact on brain development in children (see p. 11 for details).

27.4.1 Technology use for mass surveys

Technology allows developmental researchers to focus on large populations. For example, Lippa (2002; 2005; 2010) used the BBC (a secular liberal broadcaster) to access 200 000 participants from 53 nations in order to document significant cross-cultural gender similarities in areas such as aggression and occupational choice (see p. 205 for details). He was able to access such a large sample due to the worldwide nature of the BBC and the ability to conduct research online. **Quantitative** data collected from large-scale surveys allows psychologists to draw broad conclusions about behaviour across cultures. While it does not reveal personal nuances about individual behaviour, it does allow developmental psychologists to see trends over time and place.

Modern technology is now extensively used in developmental neuropsychology because it provides an opportunity to study the active brain. This allows developmental researchers to see where specific brain processes take place and enable them to study localization of function in the living human brain as it changes over time.

28 Ethical considerations: developmental psychology

Learning focus

Discuss ethical considerations in developmental psychology.

Look back at section 23.1, page 175, which looked at Research Ethics Committees (RECs) and what they are responsible for.

TOK To what extent do ethical boundaries help or hinder knowledge creation in developmental psychology?

Most respected academic institutions should have some form of REC consisting of a multidisciplinary team of professional researchers and/or experienced academics with a balance of gender and cultural backgrounds.

28.1 Working with children

Developmental psychologists often deal with children and they must abide by clear guidelines for collecting data from young people. The key notion of the power dynamic between the researcher and the researched has to be acknowledged and considered by the researcher. This is especially important when working with children. For example, the British Psychological Society (BPS) has the following ethical guidelines regarding the use of children in research.

- Children under the age of 16 need a parent/guardian to give consent.

- Parents/guardians should be informed about the nature of the study and reminded they can withdraw their child at any point of the research process if they wish.

- If research is taking place in a school or institutional setting, the appropriate supervisor can give consent as long as the research falls within the range of usual curriculum or other institutional activities.

- Very young children should be regularly monitored for any signs, verbal or non-verbal, that they are not wholly willing to continue with the data collection.

- The language should be clear and accessible to people with limited literacy, using short words and sentences, written in the active voice, and avoiding the use of technical terms.

28.2 Guaranteeing anonymity

Anonymity and confidentiality is a key part of psychological research. Potential researchers have to show their review boards how they will guarantee that participants remain anonymous and the data will be held securely. At no point should any reader of the end report be able to guess the identity of the participants.

Anonymity and **confidentiality** are a key part of psychological research. Potential researchers have to show their review boards how they will guarantee that participants will remain anonymous and the data will be held securely. At no point should any reader of the end report be able to guess the identity of the participants.

This is especially true when working with young people as is often the case with developmental researchers. Researchers can be hampered by notoriety that they did not predict when carrying out the initial research. An example of anonymity being violated is the case of Czech twin boys born in 1960 and researched by Koluchova (1976). Koluchova publicly and widely documented the twins' progress over a number of years during the 1970s in order to study the effects of deprivation on cognitive and emotional development (see p. 188 for details). However, they were named as 'Andrei' and 'Vanya' and were said to be identical twin boys born in 1960. The country, type of relationship between the participants, age, and circumstance were all revealed, making their anonymity difficult to guarantee. It is unlikely such details would be allowed to be released today.

The boys became something of a cause celebre within the psychological community and were clearly not able to give informed consent about their treatment or about how their situation became public knowledge. This was due both to their age (they were under the age of 16), the lack of a caring family guardian, and their cognitive impairment as a result of the abuse they suffered.

28.3 The use of animals

Using animals in studies of developmental psychology has many advantages.

- It allows variables to be isolated, manipulated, and then measured.

- It allows empirical data to be collected in the form of experiments.

- Experiments allow cause and effect to be established and then re-tested using controlled conditions.

Researchers do not have the same level of moral obligation toward animals as they do toward humans. However, there are still strict guidelines that have to be followed. The British Society of Animal Science wrote a set of ethical guidelines for the use of animals in research experimentation that they refer to as the 3Rs:

- Refinement: Any animal science research undertaken should be as focused as possible and have realistic and achievable aims of increasing knowledge of the species of interest in relation to our understanding of its functioning, performance, health, or welfare.

- Replacement: Researchers must consider all available options to replace animals with other techniques that will fulfil the research objectives. Researchers should always actively look for non-animal methods of investigation (e.g. computer models).

- Reduction: There is a scientific, moral and legal requirement to expose as few animals to pain, suffering, and distress as possible.

A key example of what can be achieved with animals and not with humans is Lorenz's attachment experiments with geese (1935). Attachment is a personal and emotional topic and researchers have to meet exact ethical standards when researching with humans. Lorenz instead used geese and found that they followed the first moving object they see during a critical period after hatching – a process known as imprinting (see p. 197 for details). The results suggest that attachment is innate and programmed genetically. Such a high degree of manipulation and control would not be possible for human subjects.

Another example of this is the study conducted by Suomi and Harlow and their pit of despair (vertical chamber apparatus). During the 1960s and 1970s Suomi and

Attachment is a personal and emotional topic and researchers have to meet exact ethical standards when researching with humans. While there are strict ethical considerations when working with animals, they allow for greater flexibility, isolation, and manipulation of variables, as well as re-testing than what would be possible with humans.

Harlow aimed to disrupt attachment in Rhesus monkeys and then observe their behaviour as they developed. They designed a steel cage that denied the monkeys any connection with the outside world or any other living organism (see p. 198 for details). The researchers were able to claim the pit of despair demonstrates the importance of love and nurturing on later life. The work has been heavily criticized from an ethical perspective and it is highly unlikely these experiments would be allowed to happen today.

Activity

Find all of the new words or expressions from this chapter and write them into a document with their definitions and explanations next to them. Be creative and use diagrams or boxes to help make your personal glossary unique and effective.

Health psychology

F

Health psychology is the study of psychological and behavioural processes in health, illness, and healthcare (Johnston, 1994). Health psychologists research how social, psychological, and cultural processes impact issues surrounding health. Many health issues are the result of lifestyle, either imposed on individuals or chosen by individuals, and often despite well-publicized risks. An understanding of health psychology is important in the development of prevention strategies and fosters a more positive perception of healthy choices.

The three topics in this option are:

- determinants of health

- health issues

- promoting health.

It is important for health psychologists to take differences in attitudes toward health-related behaviour into account, as well as variations in the incidence of health problems when trying to help individuals or consider ways to promote health. In addition, factors such as lifestyle and social context may influence health and illness, making one of the goals of health psychology to promote an understanding of behaviour that leads to a healthier lifestyle.

29 Determinants of health

Topic focus

Discuss determinants of health.

29.1 Biopsychosocial model of health and well-being

Content focus

Evaluate the biopsychosocial model of health and well-being.

TOK
To what extent do models of human behaviour help or hinder knowledge creation in health psychology?

Engel (1977) argued that the way physicians approach patients is influenced by the conceptual models around which their knowledge is organized. He argued that physicians are largely unaware of the power such models exert on their perceptions and behaviour toward patients. In a series of academic papers, he outlined an approach to patient care that incorporated elements of medicine, psychology, and **sociology**. He called this the **biopsychosocial** model, and while it can be seen as a criticism of the dominant **biomedical model**, it provides a new and positive framework through which to view patients and their care.

The biopsychosocial model has two main assumptions.

- The biomedical model is too narrow in its approach to patients and their care.

- A 'systems approach' is the most effective way to explain health and well-being via acknowledging the interaction of **biological factors** (genetic, biochemical, etc), **psychological factors** (mood, personality, behaviour, etc.), and **social factors** (cultural, familial, socioeconomic, medical, etc.) that impact health and patient care (Santrock, 2007).

The biopsychosocial model explains health and well-being via acknowledging the intricate interaction of biological, psychological, and social factors that impact health and patient care.

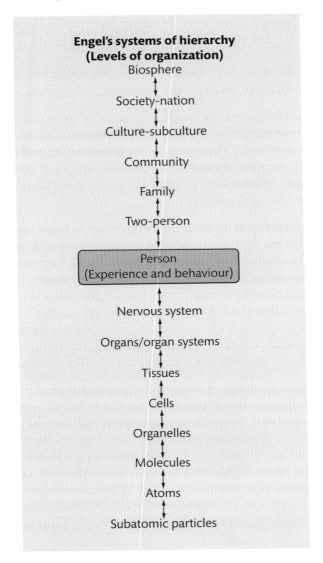

Figure 29.1 A representation of George Engel's hierarchy of natural systems (1980)

29.1.1 The biomedical model

One of the main aims of the biopsychosocial model was to counter the biomedical model, which explains health and well-being via only biological factors, such as viruses, **genes**, or **somatic** abnormalities (Engel, 1977). The biomedical model was criticized for reducing human health to purely physico-chemical terms (Engel, 1980), although it is the dominant model for healthcare professionals in developed countries.

Engel saw the biomedical model as being too **reductionist** and believed it led doctors to ignore the wider dimensions of human care. He saw the model as failing to take the attributes the patient has 'as a person' into account. He argued that how the patient behaves, how they perceive their care, what they believe about their health and care, and what their friends and family believe will all influence the care the patient receives and the outcomes of the care itself.

Example of a biomedical approach to treating stress

The biomedical approach to treatment assumes problems are based on biological malfunctioning, therefore any problem should be addressed from a primarily biological perspective. This usually means drugs should be used to 'correct' the biological system or alleviate symptoms. However, the problem with a purely biomedical approach is that not all patients respond in the same way to the same drug.

Most health-related drugs typically operate by affecting transmission in the nervous system of **neurotransmitters** such as dopamine, **serotonin**, noradrenalin, or GABA (Gamma-Aminobutyric acid). Depending on which neurotransmitter the drugs affect, and whether they enhance or diminish its effectiveness, drugs can have calming or energizing effects on different kinds of behaviour. The methods of action of drugs vary and they produce different side effects.

For example, **antidepressant** drugs are used to improve the mood of people suffering from stress, anxiety, and depression. The most common group of drugs to treat stress are **selective serotonin reuptake inhibitors** (SSRIs). They increase the level of serotonin by preventing its reuptake in the synaptic gap. The most common SSRI is fluoxetine, better known by its brand name, Prozac®, which is now one of the most widely used antidepressant drugs. SSRIs are effective and they are relatively safe. However, there can be side effects such as vomiting, nausea, **insomnia**, sexual dysfunction, or headaches. Some researchers, such as Lacasse and Leo (2005) and Kirsch et al. (2008), are very critical of what they call the 'over-prescription' of SSRIs.

Generally, antidepressant drugs are an effective way to treat depression in the short term, significantly helping 60 to 80 per cent of people who use them (Bernstein et al., 1994). A controversial study by Kirsch and Sapirstein (1998) analysed the results from 19 studies, covering 2318 patients who had been treated with Prozac®. They found that antidepressants were only 25 per cent more effective than **placebos**, and no more effective than other kinds of drugs, such as tranquillizers. Moreover, Leuchter et al. (2002) found that depressive patients receiving drug treatments improved just as well as patients receiving a placebo, and Blumenthal et al. (1999) found exercise was just as effective as SSRIs in treating depression in an elderly group of patients.

29.1.2 A systems approach to explaining and treating health

The biopsychosocial model utilizes a systems approach to addressing health issues. A systems approach provides a conceptual framework within which organized whole and component parts can be studied. The biopsychosocial model views the patient as a whole human being who interacts in a social environment; as someone who has beliefs and perceptions about their own well-being and about their health that will influence their health and recovery. Therefore, the approach to patients and their care should incorporate elements of medicine, psychology, and sociology.

The biomedical approach to treatment assumes problems are based on biological malfunctioning, therefore any problem should be addressed from a primarily biological perspective. This approach was criticized for reducing human health to purely physico-chemical terms (Engel, 1980), although it is the dominant model for healthcare professionals in developed countries.

The biopsychosocial model utilizes a systems approach to addressing health issues. It views the patient as a whole human being who interacts in a social environment; as someone who has beliefs and perceptions about their own well-being and about their health that influence their health and recovery.

Systems approaches have been described as a 'common-sense' approach (Weiss, 1959) because nature is organized according to distinct hierarchies, with larger, more complex, units superordinate to smaller, less complex, units.

A systems approach to health reveals that each level is part of a higher system. Systems theory compels health professionals to:

- view individuals as part of a stable configuration (the 'system')

- treat individuals as part of a system of interacting influences

- understand the importance of the 'two-person' system to the patient and to the care of the patient.

According to the model, nothing exists in isolation, whether the cell, a person, or a community. Everything is influenced by the configuration of the system of which it is part.

The biopsychosocial model provides a useful conceptual framework for healthcare professionals through which to think, feel, and act. It can be contrasted with the biomedical approach in the sense that it is far more complex and socially astute. It is designed to challenge the **dogma** of the biomedical model where a patient is reduced to a list of biological symptoms and causes.

It encourages health professionals to think and act more rationally and become more informed and skilful in the psychosocial areas of a patient's life. The biopsychosocial model is an attempt to move away from reductionism and introduce **holism** into patient care, seeing as patients are parts of complex systems that need to be considered for effective care to be offered.

Systems theory compels health professionals to:
- view individuals as part of a stable configuration (the 'system')
- treat individuals as part of a system of interacting influences
- understand the importance of the 'two-person' system to the patient and to the care of the patient.

Take one health issue and draw a mind map to show how it is connected to as many different factors as possible.

Engel's example patient

Engel (1980) uses an example patient to demonstrate how the assumptions of the biopsychosocial model can be applied to health and well-being.

Mr Glover (a pseudonym) is a 55-year-old property salesman. Mr Glover experiences chest pain while at work. He worries it is another heart attack but responds by denying that possibility because he has a conscientious nature and wants to finish his work – he tries to 'work it off' but also tries to get his affairs in order because he worries about his family; he avoids his colleagues and sits and worries alone, afraid and anxious that he is ill once more. His female employer convinces him after some negotiation to go to the hospital and reassures him it is in his best interests.

As a consequence of this 'care' by his employer, he arrives at hospital calmer and with less chest discomfort. His employer's involvement has enabled him to accept the need for further care and during examinations he has a heart attack.

However, during interviews after the event it is revealed that Glover had become distressed during an attempt by medical staff to effect an 'arterial puncture'. He sensed they were incompetent and they ignored him. The situation challenged his personal sense of 'mastery' and 'need to be in control' of the situation. He felt angry and victimized. Over a short space of time he felt hot, flushed, and frustrated because he could not bring himself to protest (being polite and conscientious). It was during this rising tide of frustration and anger that he passed out and suffered the heart attack.

While Glover was almost certainly saved because he was in the care of the hospital, Engel points out that the medical team focused solely on a reductionist approach to treat Glover's heart condition rather than seeing Glover as a patient in a social situation.

The biopsychosocial model encourages the medical team to take into account biological, psychological, and social factors. Therefore it is acknowledged:

- Glover's medical history was considered

- Glover and his doctor form a 'two-person' system that focused on his care

- Glover's personality was considered (it was noted his employer was the one who convinced him to go to hospital)

- Glover's unique personal response added to the strain placed on his heart.

What can health professionals learn from the Mr Glover example?

His employer was effective in intervening and calming Glover down – she became part of a two-person system. It was determined his employer had been successful because she appealed to the conscientious side of Glover's personality (praising him for being diligent; reassuring him that his affairs had been left in order and he was not causing any problems for other employees; reminding him about his responsibility to his family). Engel notes that his employer intuitively respected 'this man's need to see himself as responsible and in control, and sensed his deep fear of being weak and helpless'. She calmed him down and encouraged him to go to hospital. This demonstrates:

- the personality of the patient influences how they perceive care, which in turn influences how they react to care

- people who know the patient (the employer; the family) can reveal details about the personality and circumstances of the patient that are pertinent to how the patient should be treated by the medical team

- two-person relationships are important for good care. For example, the doctor enters into a two-person system with the patient and even when the doctor is not present they are still deferred to.

With this approach, health professionals do not reduce the care of the patient to a biological level. Instead they use intuition, knowledge about the patient and their circumstances, common sense, personal self-reference, tradition, customs, compassion, social and self-awareness, and bring it to bear on the approach to the patient.

There are some well-established criticisms of the biopsychosocial model (based partly on Ghaemi, 2011). For example:

- It creates ambiguity, which makes linear explanations for health and well-being more difficult to achieve.

- It lacks philosophical coherence to the extent that it is difficult to rigorously teach, apply, and test as a model.

- It creates an expectation that as much information about the patient as possible should be gathered when many clinicians will want to focus on key factors they specialize in.

- It does not allow for reductionist explanations or analytical understanding. Explanations that have been broken down into intelligible frames allow for research and analysis built upon established academic norms, such as **peer review** and empirical reliability.

- Physical ailments are often the result of physical causes and any model that makes these **causations** more difficult or time-consuming to identify adds a burden to the clinician. When applied, it creates practical problems for clinicians. Clinicians are often tired, overworked, and stressed, and the biopsychosocial model provides a framework for understanding their patients which cannot often be realistically fulfilled in a normal medical setting.

- The 'eclectic freedom' the model offers for clinicians can be interpreted as 'do whatever one wants', which has led to a lack of standardized responses to patient care in the name of seeking wider **psychosocial** information.

The deliberate lack of dogma that is built into the model means there is no one 'correct' way to approach patient care. Clinicians can place different emphases on the 'bio' or the 'psycho' or the 'social' depending on their own **biases** or experiences. While this may seem like a superficial strength, it has led to claims that the biopsychosocial model has meant patient care has become less standardized. Standardization is essential when dealing with health matters for a large population as governments and institutions have to set policies, train clinicians, measure outcomes, and set budgets based on medical events.

Draw a table labelled advantages and disadvantages. Answer the question: Is it reasonable for medical doctors to take into consideration the personality and sociological factors associated with the health of the patient in front of them?

EE To what extent is the biopsychosocial model of health and well-being an effective way to help patients with health problems?

29.2 Dispositional factors and health beliefs

Content focus

To what extent do health beliefs act as determinants of health?

Health beliefs refer to the attitudes and beliefs of an individual and how they influence issues regarding their health. Dispositional factors refer to the notion that thoughts, feelings, and behaviour regarding health can be influenced by the internal factors of the individual.

Health beliefs are the attitudes and beliefs of an individual that influence issues regarding their health. **Dispositional factors** are the internal factors of the individual that influence thoughts, feelings, and behaviour regarding health. Examples of dispositional factors are personality traits, temperament, and genetics. Dispositional factors can be contrasted with **situational factors**, which are **environmental factors** that influence thoughts, feelings, and behaviour of the individual regarding their health. Examples of situational factors are cultural **norms** and media approaches to health issues.

Dispositional, situational, and health belief factors should not be seen in isolation to one another as they all interact to create thoughts, feelings, and behavioural outcomes for the individual. These can be positive or negative but taken together they are a useful paradigm for both understanding health-related behaviour and as a prediction tool for future behaviour.

In the following section, dispositional factors and health beliefs will be discussed in the context of alcohol addiction.

29.2.1 What is addiction?

An individual is said to be addicted when they cannot function properly (such as in employment or relationships) as a result of substance abuse. It can be argued that people do not become addicted to a substance, but rather the chemical reaction of the body to that substance. This may seem like a moot point, but it is important when considering how to approach and treat people with addictions.

The American Society of Addiction Medicine was founded in 1954. It is a widely respected professional society representing over 4000 physicians, clinicians, and associated professionals who work in the field of addiction medicine. In 2011 it published the following assumptions about **addiction**.

- Addiction is characterized by ABCDE:

  - inability to consistently **A**bstain

  - an impairment in **B**ehavioural control

  - **C**raving; or increased 'hunger' for drugs or rewarding experiences

  - a **D**iminished recognition of significant problems with one's behaviours and interpersonal relationships

  - dysfunctional **E**motional response.

- Addiction is a primary, **chronic** disease of brain reward, motivation, memory, and related circuitry. Dysfunction in these circuits leads to characteristic biological, psychological, social, and spiritual manifestations. This is reflected in an individual pursuing reward and/or relief by substance use and other behaviours, regardless of the consequences.

- Addiction often involves cycles of relapse and remission.

- Addiction is **progressive** and can result in disability or premature death.

- Genetic factors account for about half of the likelihood that an individual will develop addiction.

Viewing addictive behaviour as a 'disease' and primarily as an issue of 'brain reward' is not without controversy. However, creating paradigms through which to view personal and societal issues regarding health is one of the roles of health professionals. Acknowledging the strengths and weaknesses of such paradigms is one of the roles of academics who work in the field.

Substance abuse is the dependence on a drug that has negative effects on the individual's physical and mental health, or the welfare of others (Nutt et al, 2007). An example of a substance that is addictive (and can therefore be abused) is alcohol. **Alcoholism** is a compulsive need for alcohol. It leads to negative effects on the drinker's physical and psychological health.

29.2.2 Dispositional and situational factors

Alcoholism has a clear connection to dispositional factors.

Family: Alcoholism runs in families. This suggests a clear biological link. However, this may be due to environmental factors, as well as modelling from other people.

Gender: Men are more likely to misuse alcohol and then maintain and persist in an alcohol misuse diagnosis than women (Knight et al., 2002). This may be partly due to the female body, as women have lower rates of alcohol gastric **metabolism**, with females metabolizing alcohol at a rate of about 80 per cent of men, therefore they cannot consume alcohol at the same rate (Wechsler et al., 1995). Addiction is linked to risk-taking behaviour, which is more common in men than women. Men are twice as likely as women to be alcoholics.

Perception: Perception can be gender specific. Minugh et al. (1998) found that differences in perceived risks and behaviours exist between women and men, with men perceiving a lower risk of alcohol addiction. This approach to gender-related alcohol problems quickly became outdated as 'binge drinking' among Western women gathered pace in the early 21st century, and now the gender gap in terms of the difference between male and female alcohol misuse is rapidly closing (White et al., 2015).

Ethnicity: Caucasian university students have the heaviest drinking rates and African American students have the lowest drinking rates (O'Malley and Johnston, 2002).

Personality: The personality traits of impulsivity and sensation seeking have been **correlated** with alcohol misuse. Higher levels of impulsivity and sensation seeking are consistently related to greater alcohol use and risk (LaBrie et al., 2014).

Viewing addictive behaviour as a 'disease' and primarily as an issue of 'brain reward' is not without controversy. However, creating paradigms through which to view personal and societal issues regarding health is one of the roles of health professionals. Acknowledging the strengths and weaknesses of such paradigms is one of the roles of academics who work in the field.

Dispositional factors are the internal traits of the individual that influence thoughts, feelings, and behaviour regarding health.

Gene evidence: Family, twin, and adoption studies have convincingly demonstrated that genes contribute to the development of alcohol dependence, with **heritability** estimates ranging from 50 to 60 per cent for both men and women (McGue, 1999).

Brain structure: PET scans have found that alcoholics have fewer GABA (gamma-aminobutyric acid) receptors in their **frontal lobes**. GABA is a neurotransmitter that is involved in calming the body. Fewer GABA receptors might suggest a greater chance of anxiety and therefore an increased likelihood of alcoholism (Lingford-Hughes et al., 2005). It is not clear if the brain differences cause alcoholism or are a consequence of it.

There needs to be some caution when associating addiction with dispositional factors. There is strong evidence that certain biological factors may mean an individual is more likely to be an alcoholic, but they do not mean it is certain they will become one. Furthermore, gene research is still in its infancy and discovering a genetic pattern that can determine an individual's likelihood of becoming an alcoholic is still a long way off (Ducci and Goldman, 2008).

A different set of genes seems to influence the level of alcohol consumption than those associated with alcohol dependency (Tabakoff et al., 2009). For example, people with genes that predispose them to drink only moderate amounts of alcohol may still have the genetic predisposition to lose control over their drinking behaviour and become addicted, whereas other people may be able to drink large amounts of alcohol and not become addicted.

There are also a great number of **sociocultural** factors that increase the chances of an individual becoming addicted to alcohol. Western society, for example, can be seen to aggressively promote alcohol use as a cultural norm: pubs are a central part of some UK communities; bars are a central part of many US communities; cafés that sell alcohol are a central part of many European communities; and commercials by alcohol companies have a significant influence, particularly on young people (Snyder et al., 2006), meaning alcohol can be seen as an effective way to achieve social and sexual success (Dring and Hope, 2001). This creates an environment where alcohol is difficult to avoid.

Moreover, there are different gender expectations for men and women. For example, males may be **socialized** to externalize stress, which manifests itself by drinking more, and women may be more risk aware when it comes to drinking because the consequences of drinking too much (such as the risks associated with sexual behaviour) are more severe for them (Ham and Hope, 2003).

These factors make it difficult for researchers and academics to decide how much behaviour is caused by dispositional factors and how much is caused by sociocultural norms. Overall, it can be concluded that there is strong evidence to suggest certain biological factors and/or cultural norms mean certain individuals are more likely to become alcoholics.

29.2.3 Health beliefs

Health beliefs are the attitudes and beliefs of an individual that influence issues regarding their health. The belief system regarding alcohol addiction is important for both the start and continuance of addictive behaviour, and the extent to which eventual treatment will be effective. For example, if alcohol addiction is seen as a

To what extent is reductionism helpful or helpful in explaining complex human behaviour in health psychology?

TOK

Health beliefs are the attitudes and beliefs of an individual that influence issues regarding their health.

treatable disease, this will influence whether an individual seeks treatment and how they respond to treatment when they receive it.

There is an established link between beliefs about alcohol and any resulting negative consequences (Champion, 2012). For example, people often see alcohol as a vehicle for friendship, social success, and sexual opportunity (Cashin et al., 1998), which may influence how much they drink and how seriously they view any side effects.

The health belief model

The health belief model (HBM) was first developed by Rosenstock (1966). It is a psychological model that attempts to explain and predict health-related behaviours. It focuses on the attitudes and beliefs of individuals. The HBM assumes the following:

- People are rational thinkers, which means they are capable of making and following choices that are in their best interests. The greater the risk of a health problem, the more a person will engage in behaviours to decrease the risk.

- Different people have different perceptions of the same health risks. For example, drinking heavily may be perceived as 'social' or 'beneficial' by an individual who has grown up with alcohol as a family or community norm. This perception influences their behaviour.

Using the basic tenets of the HBM, Bardsley and Beckmen (1988) found the more severe people perceived their problem to be, the more likely they were to enter treatment.

Compensatory health belief model

The **hedonistic principle** assumes that humans like to achieve maximum pleasure for minimal disadvantage. However, the interaction and constant mediation between desire and health goals can lead to internal conflict or dissonance (Gleitman et al., 2011). Dissonance is thought to generate a state of pressure, which requires self-regulatory processes to deal with the negative state associated with it (Rabiau et al., 2006).

The **compensatory health belief** (CHB) model assumes dissonance can be diminished using compensatory beliefs which then motivate compensatory behaviour. Compensatory beliefs are thought processes that justify unhealthy behaviour by offsetting the cost with the benefits of future planned behaviour, which will compensate for the negative effects. For example: 'I will drink this beer because tomorrow I will go for a run.'

Problems occur with this sort of thinking when people do not carry out the compensatory behaviour. If this becomes the norm, the **cognitive** dissonance becomes less over time and the motivation to engage in healthy compensatory behaviour becomes less **acute**.

Hein (2014) used an online questionnaire to investigate 113 psychology students of University Twente in Holland (mean age 22; 79 per cent female). She gave them standardized questionnaires about their belief system and their behaviour regarding alcohol consumption. She found that people use compensatory health beliefs to compensate for a generally higher consumption of alcohol but do not necessarily engage in compensatory behaviour after consumption. This supports the notion that compensatory health beliefs serve as a masking factor for the dissonance created by beliefs and behaviour, and can be used as a prediction for future alcohol-related behaviour.

29.3 Risk and protective factors

Content focus

To what extent do risk and protective factors act as determinants of health?

A **risk factor** is any phenomenon that increases the chance of someone becoming ill relative to the overall population. A **protective factor** is any phenomenon that decreases the chance of someone becoming ill relative to the overall population. In the following section, risk and protective factors will be discussed in the context of stress.

Stress is a failure to respond appropriately to emotional or physical threats (Selye, 1956). It is a subjective experience and what is stressful for one person is not necessarily stressful for another. For example, tight deadlines in a workplace may be enjoyed by one type of employee as stimulator for hard work while other employees may find them stressful. A '**stressor**' is any event (real or imagined) that leads to stress.

Stress has three main components.

- Physiological – the body reacts, for example, the heart rate increases when an individual is presented with a deadline.

- Cognitive – the person then either perceives the deadline as stressful or they are motivated to use it as an opportunity to impress the boss. The key idea being that different people perceive the same event in different ways and have different motives for doing so.

- Behavioural – the person responds to how they perceive the event. For example, they may procrastinate (causing more stress) or not sleep well (causing yet more stress).

29.3.1 Risk factors

There are biological factors that affect how stress is experienced by the individual, as detailed below.

Gender: The different genders have different physiological aspects of stress. Frankenhauser et al. (1976) found males have **adrenaline** rushes in exams that take longer to return to normal. Females have a gentler, lower increase of adrenaline that returns to normal much more quickly.

Situational: Children who have had significant stress in their home life (such as abuse) have growth problems due to low levels of growth hormones (Powell et al., 1967).

Mood: There is a correlation between a change in mood and a change in the amount of **antibodies** in the body, suggesting that good moods contribute to a healthy immune

Sidebar notes:

A risk factor is any phenomenon that increases the chance of someone becoming ill relative to the overall population. A protective factor is any phenomenon that decreases the chance of someone becoming ill relative to the overall population.

Stress has three main components: physiological, cognitive, and behavioural.

TOK: What does it mean for notions of validity and reliability if health psychology researchers cannot agree on definitive boundaries and definitions for disorders and health problems?

system (Stone et al., 1987). Therefore, stress can lead to an increased likelihood of developing illness.

For example, Cohen et al. (1991) gave 394 participants nasal drops containing a mild cold virus after completing questionnaires assessing degrees of psychological stress. Those who had negative life events in the weeks before were twice as likely to develop colds than participants who reported lower levels of stress.

Gross (1996) argues that people often catch colds soon after periods of high stress, such as exams, suggesting a clear biological connection between stress and the body's response to it. Goetsch and Fuller (1995) show less activity of white blood cells that fight illness among medical students during their final exams. Therefore, positive life experiences with low stress improve physical health while negative life experiences with high stress negatively affect physical health.

Sociocultural factors that increase the risk of stress include when, how, and where people work and how well they feel they fit into their occupation. For example, people spend a lot of time in the workplace away from their families, which leads to feelings of isolation and guilt. When social environments lead to disruptions in social life or mean being away from familiar social partners, this leads to stress (Levine, 1993).

Furthermore, stress occurs when there is a poor match between job demands and personal skills. If a person is not suited to a particular job they may not complete it to a sufficient standard, which may cause stress if the person is conscientious (The National Institute for Occupational Safety and Health (NIOSH), 1999).

Moreover, there has been a move away from the physical labour of the industrial revolution toward a workplace where people have to enhance, suppress, and fake their emotions to meet the needs of employers and customers (Hochschild, 1983). The new type of labour has been termed 'emotional labour' as workers have to manipulate their emotions to serve a particular need (Hochschild, 1983). This causes stress and leads to:

Alienation: People faking their emotions so they feel their workplace is not genuine.

Emotional autonomy: Employers insist on certain emotions (e.g. smiles and asking 'How are you today?'). Employees feel a lack of control over their emotional lives, which leads to stress.

Exploitation: People who have to fake their emotions feel exploited. For example, employees who have to smile at customers and ask questions about them ('How are you today?') often receive unwanted attention in return. This is especially true for young/inexperienced employees working in supermarkets or fast food restaurants where customers do not understand the emotion is faked. The employee has to deal with the behaviour of the customer and this leads to stress (Grandey, 2000).

De-individuation: People lose their identity because they spend a long time faking their emotions (Perrow, 1984). Foegen (1988) called for hypocrisy pay for people who work in these organizations.

29.3.2 Biological consequences of stress

It is now assumed some environmental events induce biological consequences that may have long-term effects. Such interactions are now being shown in human

Growing up in a poor home or neighbourhood can give rise to toxic stress, which in itself is a response to adverse childhood experiences. It is now assumed stress can reform the architecture of a child's developing brain, particularly in the prefrontal cortex (differentiating between good and bad) and the hippocampus (memories and learning) (Bassett, 2016).

research, particularly with the effect of poverty on children. It is now assumed stress can re-form the architecture of a child's developing brain, particularly in the **prefrontal cortex** (responsible for differentiating between good and bad) and the hippocampus (responsible for memories and learning) (Bassett, 2016). It has been documented that poor children experience significantly higher levels of family turmoil, family separation, violence, and significantly lower levels of structure and routine in their daily lives (Evans et al., 2011). The key element appears to be the amount of risk factors and the frequency of exposure that stack up and pose an accumulative risk to children (e.g. Evans and English, 2002).

There are now concerted efforts to demonstrate **cause-and-effect** between risk and stress using animal models. For example, Gilles et al. (1996) aimed to create an animal model to show the effects of continuous chronic stress on **corticosterone** secretion in response to an acute environmental stressor. Previous studies used an absence of the mother in rats to induce stress, but the researchers wanted a model that could be comparable with human experiences.

In this study, stress was induced by placing newborn rats into an environment with their mothers that featured either good or limited bedding. The group with limited bedding manifested increased corticosterone.

Gilles et al. were able to suggest the experiences they had created in the laboratory approximated the human situation of chronically stressed, neglected infants. The research is important because corticosterone secretion has a profound effect on the structure, development, and function of the hippocampus, particularly via **dendritic retraction**. Dendritic retraction is a form of **neuroplasticity** where the brain can physically adapt to various influences. It involves reductions in dendritic length and reduced branch numbers and can be related to **spatial** memory deficits (Conrad, 2006).

Other studies have shown the effects of environmental stress on the development of the hippocampus can be reversed when maternal care is reintroduced after an absence, showing further how environmental change can cause neuroplasticity (Edwards and Burnham, 2001).

For an event or a situation to be stressful for humans, it must be cognitively appraised as such by the person who is experiencing it (Lazarus, 1966). What one person considers stressful another person might not. Therefore, psychologists must consider individual interpretations of stressors in any given environment when conducting research or assessing patients.

29.3.3 Protective factors for coping with stress

The following two models show how cognition is a risk factor in developing a health-related problem and how, consequently, changes to cognition can act as protective factors against developing a health problem.

The transactional model of stress

The **transactional model of stress** and coping (Lazarus and Folkman, 1984) provides a framework for understanding how certain factors may serve as protective factors in the experience of stress by the individual.

The basic premise of the theory is that stressful experiences are construed as transactions between the environment and the individual. The transactional process is the flow of events between a constantly changing environment and the individual's emotional reaction to them. The shift in emotions reflects changes in the meaning of the relationship.

- The environmental factors of the transaction emphasize environmental events, or stressors, which result in significant demands that require a response from the individual.

- The individual factors of the transaction emphasize the individual's appraisal of the potential threat posed by the stressor, as well as the availability of coping resources perceived by the individual to meet the demands of the stressor.

- Stress is experienced if the individual perceives the environmental demands as threatening and feels they do not have the coping resources available to meet those demands (Dolbier et al., 2007).

Therefore, for **therapy** to be effective it must consider both environmental and individual factors, with an emphasis placed on how the individual perceives their environment. If the transactional model of stress is used as an assumption behind therapy, the aim becomes attuned to the individual with their environment. This model assumes stress reactions and coping are relative and change for different types of encounters, as the encounter unfolds, and when experienced at different times. Effective therapy centres on an individual's emotions and their vulnerabilities and coping mechanisms (Lazarus and Folkman, 1984).

Stress inoculation training

The aim of **stress inoculation training** is to alter the way a person perceives potential stressors. It is a cognitive approach to stress regulation, with the aim of changing the way people perceive situations and stressors to enable them to develop protection for health-related problems.

Where the transactional model of stress looks at stress as a past event, stress inoculation training looks forward. The model was developed by Meichenbaum in the 1970s. He argued that training should come before the onset of stress, not after, in the same way that medical inoculation is given before a patient gets sick, not after.

According to Meichenbaum (1993), there are four distinct phases to stress inoculation training:

- Conceptualization (how to view a problem): A good relationship is established between the client and the therapist. The client is educated about stress. Clients are encouraged to see stressful events as problems to be solved.

- Re-conceptualization (the problem is then seen in a different way): During talks, a new way of looking at the problem is agreed between client and therapist. It must be hopeful and helpful for the client.

- Rehearsal: Skills for coping with stress, such as breathing techniques, relaxation training, social and communication skills training, attention diversion procedures

If the transactional model of stress is used as an assumption behind therapy, the aim becomes attuned to the individual with their environment. Effective therapy centres on an individual's emotions and their vulnerabilities and coping mechanisms (Lazarus and Folkman, 1984).

The aim of stress inoculation training is to alter the way the person perceives potential stressors. This is a cognitive approach to stress regulation with the aim of changing the way people perceive situations and stressors to enable them to develop protection for health-related problems.

(e.g. thinking about something else or going for a walk), and using family and friends, are rehearsed.

- Application: Clients imagine stressful events and apply the skills they have learned. This involves role playing/acting with the therapist.

Stress inoculation training is very specific to the needs of the person suffering stress. An underlying assumption of the training is that it accepts the stress an individual can experience is often unavoidable (for example, a work environment). Because stress is accepted as unavoidable, the role of the training is to manage it. This is a very realistic position and when coupled with the active cooperation of the client, it can be very effective.

Furthermore, stress inoculation training promotes equality between client and therapist and encourages the individual to take control of their stress management, resulting in feelings of empowerment that act as further steps toward managing stress.

There are, however, some problems with stress inoculation training. For example, while the therapy tries to empower the individual, it must be recognized that some people are simply not suited to certain work or social environments and stress inoculation training may not recognize that. Success with this approach requires high levels of motivation and clients must talk about inner feelings and personal thoughts. This is not suited to people from cultures where this is not the sociocultural norm.

Key study: Dolbier et al. (2007)

Aim: To uncover protective factors in the context of work-related stress.

Procedure: The researchers focused on two Fortune 500 companies in the USA and used **convenience samples** from both. They asked participants to fill out questionnaires on the following protective factors.

- Supervisor support – the level and type of support from a supervisor. This was deemed important because supervisors are responsible for evaluating an employee's performance. To measure this, participants had to respond to statements such as, 'Supervisors usually compliment an employee who does something well', by stating how 'true' these were on a scale.
- Individual protective factors – specific dispositions from the participants that could be correlated with coping with stress. Researchers drew conclusions from the inherent characteristics stated by the participants (e.g. gender) and correlated them with their responses to the other questions.
- Hardiness – a constellation of hardiness characteristics that serve as a resistance resource when the individual encounters stressful situations. Three basic elements comprise hardiness.
  - Challenge: the extent to which people perceive change as normal and natural and an opportunity for personal growth.
  - Commitment: the extent to which people have a sense of purpose or meaningfulness in their lives.
  - Control: the extent to which people believe they are capable of impacting their own lives.

To measure this, participants responded to statements such as, 'Changes in routine are interesting to me', and, 'By working hard you can always achieve your goals'.

- Coping style – an individual's preferred behavioural and cognitive processes that remain stable over time and circumstance. To measure this, participants had to respond to various coping strategies on a four-point **Likert scale** ranging from 'I usually don't do this at all' (1) to 'I usually do this a lot' (4).

Findings: Supervisor support helps protect against work-related stress, but this is dependent on the relationship between the worker and the supervisor as well as the quality of support offered. It also influences the perception of available coping resources at work and reduces the likelihood of appraising work demands as threatening.

Increased levels of hardiness were found to be associated with lower levels of stress and fewer symptoms of illness.

Females reported significantly greater levels of stress and symptoms of illness.

Participants who perceived events and factors to be stressful while also perceiving low levels of control were more likely to be stressed at work.

To what extent is yoga effective in protecting against stress?

Yoga is an ancient discipline that involves physical positions or postures (these help with flexibility), meditation (a focus on inner thoughts), energy control (usually associated with breathing), and a focus on pure desire. As a practice, it can be said to improve quality of life (Cohen, 2006) because it promotes a holistic approach to living, taking into account as many lifestyle choices as possible, such as diet and exercise.

Yoga offers many sensible ways to take control of one's life, because its broad aim is to encourage people to be more peaceful and healthy and to give them strategies to achieve these goals. It also provides exercise, there is a focus on relaxation and a focus on the self. All of these things are good, common-sense approaches to reducing stress.

Hartfiel et al. (2010) aimed to determine the efficacy of yoga in stress reduction by placing 48 workers either in a yoga group or a **control** group. The yoga group was offered six weeks of yoga, which consisted of one hour-long lunchtime class per week for six weeks. The control group received nothing. Participants were given psychological tests measuring mood before and after the six-week period. They found the yoga group had significant improvements in mood, satisfaction, and confidence, and lower levels of stress.

However, the extent to which yoga can be seen in itself as a protective force against stress is debatable. For example, just being with a group of like-minded people means a person is being social and experiencing stress reduction as well as listening to how other people cope with stressful events. Social interaction and talking about problems helps reduce stress.

List the ways that studying for the IB Diploma causes stress. List the physical, emotional, and cognitive consequences of being in a stressed state.

Furthermore, Lasater (1995) argues that we stand or sit most of the day, which is not natural or healthy for the body. By exercising in certain ways, blood flow is improved and made more natural by 'washing' the organs in fresh blood; increasing oxygen flow and getting rid of waste. Therefore, the habits of mind and body as well as the social and personal routines associated with yoga are what make yoga so effective in protecting against stress and can be replicated by non-yoga related exercises.

30 Health problems

Topic focus

Discuss issues relating to health problems.

30.1 Explanations of health problems

Content focus

To what extent can biological, cognitive, and sociocultural factors explain health problems?

'Explanations' refers to causative factors that lead to health problems. In the following section, explanations of health problems will be discussed in the context of obesity.

Obesity is a medical condition in which excess body fat has an adverse effect on health. It occurs when an individual eats more food energy than they use. Obesity is commonly measured using the body mass index (BMI).

Obesity is a medical condition in which excess body fat has an adverse effect on health. It occurs when an individual eats more food energy than he or she uses. Obesity is commonly measured using the **body mass index** (BMI). The BMI is a weight-for-height ratio, defined as a person's weight in kilograms divided by the square of their height in meters (kg/m^2) (WHO, 2016).

For adults, the World Health Organization (2016) defines overweight and obesity as follows:

- overweight is a BMI greater than or equal to 25

- obesity is a BMI greater than or equal to 30.

BMI provides the most useful population-level measure of overweight and obesity as it is the same for both sexes and for all ages of adults. However, it should only be considered a 'rough guide' because some people have naturally more muscle, which increases their weight.

30.1.1 Biological factors

Only a small number of obesity cases are caused by biological abnormalities. Most cases of obesity are caused by poor diet and a lack of exercise or a sedentary lifestyle.

Genes

The American Academy of Child and Adolescent Psychiatry (2008) states if one parent that is obese, there is a 40 per cent chance children will also be obese; when both parents are obese, children will have an 80 per cent chance of being obese. The chances of an underweight parent having an overweight child are only 7 per cent (Garn et al., 1981), which may superficially suggest a genetic cause for obesity. However, parents are also usually responsible for feeding and setting healthy examples for their children. Therefore, researchers need to be cautious when assuming a specific genetic link.

The US Centers for Disease Control and Prevention (2010) states that genes can directly cause obesity through disorders such as **Prader-Willi syndrome**, which causes feelings of constant hunger. These disorders are rare but their existence does show a genetic link to obesity.

Animal studies show genetic transmission of obesity and poor health in general. For example, Fang Ng et al. (2010) hypothesized that the poor diet of rats would negatively impact the offspring. They focused on male rats because the results were so pronounced in male to offspring transmission. The **independent variable** (IV) was poor diet, **operationalized** by giving 40 per cent more calories to one group of rats compared to the control rats, making them 'fat'. The **dependent variable** (DV) was the extent to which it would biologically affect the offspring and was operationalized by **glucose intolerance** and **insulin** secretion. Insulin is a hormone that regulates the metabolism of protein, fats, and carbohydrates. Glucose intolerance is any condition that results in too much blood sugar, which is considered a serious health issue.

The rats became obese and began developing **diabetes**, including glucose intolerance and high resting levels of insulin. After the rats were mated, researchers analysed the offspring. They noted the female offspring were more sensitive to the effects of their father's diet so the team focused on female offspring. By 6 weeks old, the young female rats were glucose intolerant. By 12 weeks of age, they had impaired insulin secretion.

243

While it should be remembered that this study used animals and so caution should be used when **generalizing** the results to humans, this was a tightly controlled experiment with clear IVs and DVs. Therefore, a clear cause-effect relationship can be established, which would not be possible with humans. This study is important because it shows how genetic transmission can impair insulin secretion and the lack of insulin is thought to contribute to the development of obesity (Kahn and Flier, 2000).

Human studies have shown a correlation between genes and obesity. For example, Lombard et al. (2012) used a longitudinal method to study 990 black South Africans. BMI was used to assess how obese the participants were and their genetic history was mapped out. The results showed a significant association between four genes and obesity. Each risk gene was associated with an estimated average increase of 2.5 per cent in BMI. While this is a very culturally specific study, so caution should be used when generalizing/transferring to other cultures, it seems reasonable to assume that genes do play some role in weight gain and loss. However, because the study only uses correlational evidence, caution should be used when assuming genes cause the effect of obesity. The only way to be sure of a cause-effect relationship is to carry out an experiment, and this is not ethically possible while investigating genes and obesity in humans.

The evidence is weak for innate predetermined factors within the individual to explain the obesity epidemic in wider society. There have always been different body styles in human history, but never has the human body been so overweight on such a scale before. Biological factors cannot solely account for the rapid number growth of obesity in society.

There will always be biological variations in energy intake for individuals, for example the basal metabolic rate may well be under genetic influence (although definitive studies do not yet exist). Other bodily processes – such as the rates of carbohydrate-to-fat oxidation, and the degree of insulin sensitivity, which are closely involved in energy balance and therefore body weight (Ravussin, 1993) – may also play a part. But they cannot solely account for the rapid growth of obesity in society. There have always been different body styles in human history, but never has the human body been so overweight on such a scale before.

But while evidence is weak for innate predetermined factors within the individual to explain the obesity epidemic, that does not mean food cannot be designed to influence physiological mechanisms to make us eat more.

Why do humans like fat?

Human beings appear to like fat, and there are many explanations as to why this is the case (Drewnowski, 1997). Several physiological mechanisms have been proposed, most of which take an evolutionary approach to explaining the phenomenon: early humans would have encountered fat very rarely and when they did it would have been beneficial for them to consume it.

Fat has a high energy density and humans experience feelings of satiety when they eat it. This natural liking for fat is used by processed- and fast-food manufacturers, who engineer food in a way to encourage consumers to buy more of it and to buy it regularly.

David Kessler is a former commissioner of the FDA (the US Food and Drug Administration) and in an article for the *Guardian* newspaper (March, 2010) he argues that people are becoming conditioned hyper-eaters; conditioned because food intake becomes an automatic response to widely available food, 'hyper' because the eating is excessive and hard to control. He made the following points.

- Higher sugar, fat, and salt actually make the individual want to eat more as these elements make the intake of food compelling for the brain. They stimulate **neurons** and release **dopamine**, a chemical that has been linked with making people want to eat more. Food manufacturers understand this and deliberately engineer food to be 'compelling'.

- People reach a **bliss point** with food and it is here they get the greatest pleasure from sugar, fat, or salt as they become part of a physiological feedback loop.

Kessler interviewed industry insiders who detailed how corporations deliberately design food to create a bliss point, making a product indulgent or high in hedonic value, maximizing the chances of the consumer eating more as well as receiving positive rewards for eating the product. The sugar, fat, and salt releases dopamine, which is involved in **endorphin** release. The person is rewarded for eating the food and wants to eat more.

Food itself has been deliberately changed in terms of its chemical composition: sugar, fat, and salt are either loaded into a core ingredient (such as meat, vegetables, potato, or bread), layered on top of it, or both. Deep-fried tortilla chips are an example of loading – the fat is contained in the chip itself. When it is smothered in cheese, sour cream, and sauce, it then becomes layered. When this level of engineered complexity is built into food, the effect becomes more powerful.

Sweetness is another example of food reward, but it does not account for the full impact of a fizzy drink – its temperature and tingle, resulting from the stimulation of the trigeminal nerve by carbonation and acid, are essential in creating bliss points and hedonic value for money. If a product is high in hedonic value then it increases palatability (Moss, 2013).

Food itself has changed in terms of its physical texture. Kessler interviewed an industry insider who argued that coleslaw composition has been altered to make it more palatable and therefore more desirable as a product. When its ingredients are chopped roughly, it requires time and energy to chew. However, when cabbage and carrots are softened in a high-fat dressing, coleslaw becomes liquidized and will be guzzled by the consumer and the high fat content makes it more appealing for the brain.

30.1.2 Cognitive factors

It has already been noted that humans have a preference for fat. This preference is manipulated by food manufacturers to create tastes and textures that humans perceive as pleasurable (Drewnowski and Almiron-Roig, 2010). This perception almost certainly has an innate evolutionary beneficial reason underlying it. However, the ways and extent to which fat is deliberately used to manipulate perception in humans is worth discussing further.

For example, studies of food texture have shown consumer preferences for yogurts and other dairy products are determined by the perception of smooth or creamy textures that are dependent on fat content (Folkenberg and Martens, 2003). Consequently, fat is a useful tool in making food more palatable and therefore more desirable. Fat also contributes to crispiness or crunchiness in pastries and cookies, which is perceived to be pleasant and it can also suggest freshness and moisture by binding it with water

Studies of food texture have shown consumer preferences for yogurts and other dairy products are determined by the perception of smooth or creamy textures that are dependent on fat content (Folkenberg and Martens, 2003). Consequently, fat is a useful tool in making food more palatable and therefore more desirable.

molecules (Cooper, 1987). It should also be noted that the perception of texture could also involve both sight and hearing when the consumer interacts with food (Engelen and Van der Bilt, 2008).

However, too much fat can make the food unpalatable without consumers knowing why. Food manufacturers combat this by adding more sugar, because the perception of fat content decreases as sugar content increases (Drewnowski and Schwartz, 1990).

Drewnowski et al. (1989) compared the ability of 25 young men and women to rate the sweetness, creaminess, and fat content of solid and liquid foods. The participants were able to accurately estimate the sweetness intensity for both solid and liquid samples, but they were unable to track the increasing fat content of the solid foods. Hedonic preferences for high-fat food samples remained high despite difficulties in estimating how much fat was in the food (Drewnowski et al., 1989). This suggests preferences for fat may be independent on the conscious ability to detect or perceive the fat content of solid foods (Drewnowski and Almiron-Roig, 2010), which means humans can desire fat because of what it does to the taste and texture of the food, without actually realizing it is the presence of fat that is making them desire the food.

There are further cognitive factors that influence how an individual approaches food. Eating healthily and exercising regularly takes self-discipline and motivation. It also requires that people educate themselves about the effects of food and their lifestyle. If an individual feels hopeless, this can demotivate them to reduce or maintain weight (Byrne, 2002). Gaining weight can be seen as a problem that needs to be approached and solved. According to the Malaysian Association for the Study of Obesity (MASO, 2009), poor problem-solving skills usually lead to negative coping mechanisms, which leads to weight gain.

TOK How can willpower and self-discipline be defined so that they can be operationalized and measured?

30.1.3 Sociocultural factors

Social learning theory (SLT) assumes humans learn behaviour through observation. This involves observing models and imitating their behaviour, and learning to associate a certain response with a specific stimulus. Factors that influence whether or not the observer decides to imitate and learn are consistency, identification with the model, the level of rewards/punishment, and association.

Consistency

If the model behaves in a way that is consistent across situations – for example, always eating healthy food – then the observer will be more likely to imitate them. Tibbs et al. (2001) gave parents questionnaires to find out how often they model dietary behaviours for their children. They found inconsistent and low levels of modelling for healthy snacks and eating fruit and vegetables in families with overweight children.

Identification with the model

Parental modelling has been shown with smoking, seatbelt use, and physical activity, and suggests that observational learning is in part responsible for the transmission of health promoting (eating healthily) or risky behaviour (eating unhealthily) in children (Tinsley, 2003).

Parental modelling for early **adolescents** (aged 9 to 13) and physical activity was lower than with young children or older adolescents (Duncan et al., 2005). This is because early adolescents may look to their **peers** as role models rather than their parents.

Rewards/punishment

Encouragement, help with transport, payment of fees, and money to buy equipment (for example, football boots) can all be seen as rewards for physical activity. There is a correlation between parents who do this and higher activity levels in their children (Sallis et al., 2000).

Punishment can come in the form of price increases. Khan et al. (2012) looked at the correlations between fast food consumption in preschool children and the price of the food. They found a 10 per cent increase in the price of fast food resulted in a 5.7 per cent reduction in children eating it. This suggests 'fat taxes' would work to a certain degree as a negative consequence of unhealthy behaviour. Other studies show a high taxation rate but only a small effect on behaviour.

For example, $0.45 tax per soft drink was calculated to lead to a 26 per cent decline in sales. Therefore, a 20 per cent tax on sugary drinks in the USA would only reduce obesity levels by 3.5 per cent from 33.5 per cent to 30 per cent among adults (Mytton et al., 2012).

Association

People associate fast food with positive experiences. This is particularly true for children. Companies know this and associate themselves with characters that invoke positive feelings in children. For example, Pepsi® licensed the rights to Yoda, the Star Wars® creature, to allow it to be associated with its products (McCarthy, 2005).

A UK consumer advice group, Which?, found 38 per cent of 8–11-year-olds preferred McDonald's® as their favourite restaurant because of the toy and Happy Meal® the company marketed to them (Which?, 2010). Which? expressed concern over the use of the toys with fast food, arguing they contributed to pester power, where children nag parents to be taken to the restaurant.

List the ways food manufacturers target children. Research how national laws regulate corporate food advertisements to children.

In the USA in 2003, Coca-Cola® spent $184 million on promotional activities, including sponsoring sports events (*Advertising Age*, 2004). Associating their products with fashionable athletes and athletic events is a long-standing tradition for fast food and soft drink manufacturers as it allows consumers to see healthy people associated with their product.

Schlosser (2001) outlines how soft drink manufacturers deliberately target school children as they are still developing their taste preferences and habits. Establishing brand loyalty by positive association at a young age increases the chances of those children becoming adult consumers of the product over their lifetime.

Companies pay US school districts for exclusive marketing rights. For example, Coca-Cola® had a ten-year exclusive contract with the Colorado Springs district that was worth between $8 million and $11 million (Kaufman, 1999). Again, this demonstrates a deliberate targeting of children.

McDonald's® operates more playgrounds designed specifically to attract children and their parents to its restaurants than any other private entity in the USA (Schlosser, 2001). The playgrounds and high sugar content of the products provide positive associations with the industry and corporation (Schlosser, 2001).

Learned lifestyles

The immediate environment of a child is the home and it seems reasonable to assume many food habits are learned there. It can be assumed parents who eat healthily will pass that knowledge onto the child, and that the opposite is also true. Having two obese parents increases the chances of the offspring being obese by 80 per cent and by 40 per cent with one obese parent. This phenomenon has become known as 'second-hand obesity'. In this way, obesity is being passed on via the cultural equivalent of the gene, known as a '**meme**'. Memes are ideas, symbols or behavioural practices that are transmitted from one mind to another through writing, speech, gestures, cultural or family rituals, or other imitable phenomena.

The term was first coined by Richard Dawkins in his book *The Selfish Gene* (1976). Memetic transmission of obesity is more likely than genetic transmission, as the recent exponential increase in obese people points to an environmental change and a shift in how humans interact in their environment rather than an inherent genetic alteration. Clearly, body type is inherited, but lifestyle choices are the key. Children who are overweight stand more chance of being overweight as an adult (Freedman et al., 2005) as they will develop certain eating habits, but they will also be biologically primed to carry more fat cells that they will take into adulthood. It should also be noted: children are not born with a predisposition to eat processed food and avoid exercise.

Memetic transmission of obesity is more likely than genetic transmission, as the recent exponential increase in obese people points to an environmental change and a shift in how humans interact in their environment rather than an inherent genetic alteration.

SLT assumes humans learn behaviour through observation. This involves observing models and imitating their behaviour, and learning to associate a certain response with a specific stimulus. Factors that influence whether or not the observer decides to imitate and learn are consistency, identification with the model, the level of reward/punishment, and association.

30.2 Prevalence rates of health problems

Content focus

Discuss the prevalence rates of a health-related problem.

Prevalence rates are a statistical notion referring to the number of cases of a health problem that are present in a particular population at a given time. In the following section, prevalence rates of health problems will be discussed in the context of obesity.

- Worldwide obesity has more than doubled since 1980.

- In 2014, more than 1.9 billion adults, 18 years and older, were overweight. Of these, over 600 million were obese.

- Thirty-nine per cent of adults aged 18 years and over were overweight in 2014 and 13 per cent were obese.

- Most of the world's population live in a country where being overweight or obese kills more people than being underweight.

- Forty-one million children under the age of 5 were overweight or obese in 2016.

Cited from WHO (2016)

Obesity has been a growing problem in developed countries. For example, in the UK in the 1970s 10 per cent of people were obese, while in 2010 it was 25 per cent (Kessler, 2010). Furthermore, obesity was at one point the largest single cause for the discharge of uniformed personnel in the US military (Basu, 2004).

Data from the National Health and Nutrition Examination Survey in the US for the period 2009–2010 (Flegal et al., 2012) stated:

- more than 2 in 3 adults are considered to be either overweight or obese

- more than 1 in 20 adults are considered to have extreme obesity

- about 1 in 3 children and adolescents aged 6 to 19 are considered to be either overweight or obese.

The pie chart below shows adult rates of obesity in the USA in 2009–2010.

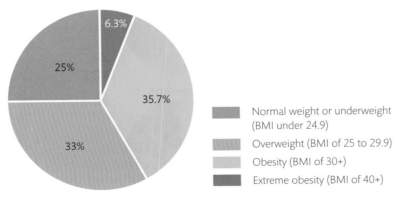

Normal weight or underweight (BMI under 24.9)

Overweight (BMI of 25 to 29.9)

Obesity (BMI of 30+)

Extreme obesity (BMI of 40+)

Source: NHANES, 2009–2010

TOK The human sciences work with large populations and attempt to explain behaviours via generalizations. To what extent should 'individual agency' be an integral part of psychology studies and how can that be researched?

EE To what extent can obesity be explained by sociocultural factors alone?

TOK In what sense does psychology depend on both reasons and causes to explain behaviour?

🔒 Worldwide obesity has more than doubled since 1980 and most of the world's population live in a country where being overweight or obese kills more people than being underweight.

Figure 30.1 Overweight and obesity among adults age 20 and older, USA, 2009–2010, estimated percentage by BMI

The figure below shows the estimated percentage of overweight and obese adults by sex in the USA in 2009–2010.

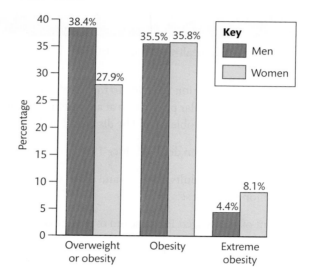

Figure 30.2 Estimated percentage of overweight and obesity by sex, USA, 2009–2010

Source: NHANES, 2009–2010

The prevalence rates suggest that in Western countries people are getting more overweight. The prevalence rates can be linked to some of the explanations discussed in the previous section. For example, while obesity is becoming a global phenomenon, it is most prevalent within countries who adopt Western-style fast-food diets. The food is characterized by being processed, high in fat, high in sugar, and high in carbohydrates. It is marketed in a way that creates associations with a positive image and is advertised by role models. The effects of this diet are augmented by an increasingly sedentary lifestyle that has been in partly brought about by a growth in car and motorcycle ownership as well as the shift from agrarian (agricultural) labour-focused work to factory and office work for the working-age population.

The figure below shows a projected prevalence of overweight men and women aged 30 years or more in China.

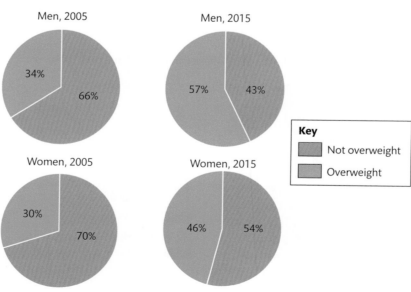

Figure 30.3 Projected prevalence of overweight men and women aged 30 years or more in China

An e-bike on the streets of China. Low-cost travel but without the benefit of exercise.

It can be noted that within one generation in China the percentage of obese children has increased from 5 per cent to 20 per cent (Luo, 2015). This is almost exclusively confined to cities where children have access to Western fast food.

In China the problem is compounded by the sociocultural issue of the one-child policy. Although it has recently been relaxed, this policy has meant that many children are the only child in their family and are doted on by two parents and four grandparents who want to give them the benefits of an economic boom that they themselves never experienced. These older generations experienced near-starvation levels of food shortages and may lack knowledge regarding processed foods, products which are relatively new to China (Macleod, 2007). They want to reward grandchildren with copious amounts of food that are heavily advertised while also being quite novel or new to the Chinese cultural landscape.

The problem can also be demonstrated in India. For example, there were fewer than 800 000 obese women in India and 400 000 obese men in 1975. However, by 2014 that figure had jumped to 20 million obese women and 9.8 million obese men (Lancet, 2016, cited in Bhattacharya, 2016) as people adopt new lifestyles and new ways of thinking and living become social norms.

The increase in obesity rates in China can also be linked to the increase of e-bike usage. China has a cultural norm of using bicycles for daily transport, but increasingly pedal-powered bicycles are being replaced by e-bikes. E-bikes are low-cost electrically driven bicycles charged with a normal mains electricity supply. In 2016 there were 200 million e-bikes from 700 manufacturers in China and that number is growing at a rate of over 35 million each year (Shepard, 2016). These bikes either do not have pedals or they allow for human power to be enhanced with electric power. They allow relatively poor people a greater range on their daily commute, but the switch from a traditional bike to an e-bike means users burn significantly fewer calories each day, which may not be factored into their daily diet.

31 Promoting health

Topic focus

Discuss issues relating to health promotion.

31.1 Health promotion

Content focus

Contrast two models of health promotion.

Health promotion is any technique that encourages behaviour believed to be good for society. Health promotion is usually conducted on a population level and involves generalizations and patterns.

Health promotion is any technique that encourages behaviour believed to be good for society. Health promotion is usually conducted on a population level and involves generalizations and patterns.

Governments have to consider how people think and why they choose the behaviours they do. For behaviour to change, beliefs, thought processes, and feelings usually have to change. Therefore, human science researchers make social cognition models to analyse why and how people behave in the way they do. These models serve as templates for research and action, as well as starting points to predict future behaviour.

In the following section, health promotion will be discussed in the context of sexual health. In the past few decades, there has been an increase in research, programme and policy attention given to factors that influence sexual health (WHO, 2010). Sexual health is a complex topic that includes gender roles and sexual orientation, and is influenced by the interaction of biological, psychological, cognitive, social, political, cultural, ethical, legal, historical, religious, and spiritual factors (WHO, 2006).

Because of the risks associated with sexual activity, any approach to sexual health requires a positive, responsible attitude to sexuality and sexual relationships as well as pleasurable, safe sexual experiences that are free from coercion, discrimination, or violence (WHO, 2006).

The two models of health promotion examined here are the health belief model and the theory of reasoned action.

31.1.1 The health belief model

The HBM was first developed by Rosenstock (1966). It assumes people will respond best to messages about health promotion when the following conditions apply:

- the person believes that he or she is at risk of a specific condition

- the person believes that the risk is serious

- the person believes that the risk will be reduced by a specific behaviour change

- the person believes that barriers to the behaviour change can be overcome and managed.

TOK

On what basis should decisions about human behaviour in multicultural societies be established?

Therefore, health professionals have to focus on people's beliefs about their health problems, their beliefs about the perceived benefits if action is taken, their beliefs about any barriers to action, and their beliefs about their **self-efficacy**. This belief system can be used to explain why people engage (or do not engage) in health-promoting behaviour. There is a focus on perception as the key process that influences beliefs.

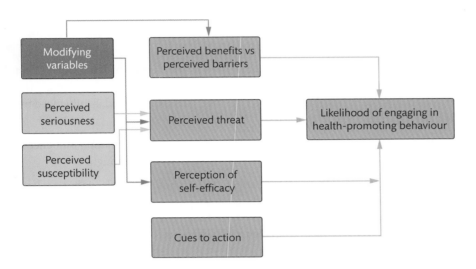

Figure 31.1 The health belief model, showing the factors that influence whether people engage in health-promoting behaviour.

The HBM assumes health professionals have to focus on people's beliefs about their health problems; their beliefs about the perceived benefits if action is taken; their beliefs about any barriers to action; their beliefs about their self-efficacy. This belief system can be used to explain why people engage (or do not engage) in health-promoting behaviour.

Application of HBM

Khajehkazemi et al. (2013) investigated perceptions of HIV in Iranian females. They gave a questionnaire to 180 female students from three schools in Yazd, Iran. They found the students' beliefs about HIV and how it was spread were linked to the students' perception of their risk status. They perceived themselves as not at risk as they did not see themselves as 'typical' of HIV at-risk groups.

This misperception resulted in problems: students believed they were not at risk and so actually engaged in risky behaviours and actually put themselves at risk.

Furthermore, Khajehkazemi et al. (2013) showed that people who do believe they are at risk (for example, prisoners who use drugs) actually decreased their HIV high-risk behaviours by, for instance, using clean syringes. However, this only occurred when they believed in the effectiveness of strategies.

Khajehkazemi et al. (2013) demonstrate how each subcultural group will have its own perceptual nuances regarding health-related behaviour. Therefore, health promotion strategies should target the belief system of subgroups (for example, female students or prisoners) and not offer one general message to many demographics.

Health promotion strategies should target the belief system of subgroups and not offer one general message to many demographics.

There is a key problem with the HBM – it assumes people are rational – but people know certain behaviours put them at risk and yet still engage in them. For example, they know unprotected sex leaves them at risk of contracting HIV and yet they will still engage in it. This may be partly due to positive illusions (Taylor and Brown, 1988) where people want to be optimistic about the world rather than negative. Positive illusions are an example of **optimism bias** (see p. 127) where people are over-optimistic about their health-risking behaviour.

Positive illusions and health apathy can explain why people engage in behaviour that they know to be unhealthy.

Furthermore, the HBM assumes that people care about their health or the health of those they care for; it underestimates the impact of **health apathy**. Health apathy is a lack of concern toward personal health or to the health of someone in your care. It can explain why people still engage in unhealthy behaviour such as eating unhealthy food when they are obese and feeding it to those who are also obese.

31.1.2 The theory of reasoned action and the theory of planned behaviour

Some of the problems of the HBM are addressed by the **theory of reasoned action** (TRA) developed by Fishbein and Ajzen (1975). The assumptions of the TRA are that people's behaviour is not always in line with their stated beliefs and is influenced by their attitudes and subjective norms.

TRA assumes that people's behaviour is not always in line with their stated beliefs and is influenced by their attitudes and subjective norms. A simple presentation of facts is not enough.

- Attitudes – people's beliefs based on interpretations of information influence how they make decisions. A simple presentation of facts is not enough.

- Subjective norms – the beliefs of people's friends and family also influence how they make decisions. These carry different weights. For example, a work colleague asking you to exercise will carry less weight than a wife or husband. These lead to intention and this is the best predictor of behaviour.

Therefore, a person's attitude, combined with the attitudes of others, forms their behavioural intention.

Ajzen later modified the theory into the **theory of planned behaviour** (TPB) (1985) by adding '**perceived behavioural control**', which refers to how much control people think they have over their own actions. This was influenced by the **self-efficacy theory** (SET) put forward by Bandura (1977). Self-efficacy is the belief that one can successfully engage in a behaviour to produce desired outcomes (e.g. eat healthily and exercise regularly to lose weight). Bandura argued motivation, performance, and feelings of frustration will all affect how an individual approaches a problem.

Bandura argues that people with a strong sense of self-efficacy:

- view challenging problems as something to be overcome – they have a positive view of them

- develop deeper interest in the activities in which they participate

- recover quickly from setbacks and disappointments.

People with a weak sense of self-efficacy:

- avoid challenging tasks because they have a fear of failure

- focus on personal failings and negative outcomes

- quickly lose confidence in personal abilities.

According to Bandura, self-efficacy is the most important factor that will lead to behavioural change. The TRA assumes that social norms, attitudes, and the attitudes of others influence the actions of individuals. However, the theory lacks a clear affective component to explain the interaction between cognition and emotions. Health is a personal and therefore emotional area and so some consideration of this should be given when certain health choices are being promoted. Furthermore, key cultural nuances need to be considered when applying the TRA to health promotion.

Key study: Tlou (2009)

Aim: To apply the theory of reasoned action (TRA) and the theory of planned behaviour (TPB) to the design of workplace HIV/**AIDS** health promotion programmes in South Africa. The AIDS Foundation Africa report cites the UNAIDS 2000 Global Report, which rated South Africa as having the sixth highest prevalence of HIV in the world, with 18.8 per cent of the population estimated to be infected with HIV.

Procedure: A longitudinal, **quasi-experimental** study of 170 government employees was divided into two groups; Group 1 comprised 92 employees who participated in a HIV/AIDS health promotion workshop based on the theories of reasoned action and planned behaviour. The workshop was aimed at enabling the participants to explore, understand, question, and reformulate their attitudes, subjective norms, and perceived behavioural control in relation to condom use, HIV testing, and **monogamy** with cognitive behavioural techniques. Group 2 comprised 78 employees who took part in an educational information session about HIV/AIDS but did not receive any attempt to target their attitudes and behaviour. Both groups of participants were measured on HIV/AIDS health behaviour intentions and HIV/AIDS health behaviour (for example, condom use, seeking HIV testing, monogamy) over a period of six months.

Findings: There was no significant health behaviour change and no health behaviour differences between the two intervention conditions at one month and six months post-intervention measurements.

Conclusion: The theoretical models formulated in the developed world (such as the TRA and TRB) may not apply in certain cultural contexts for health promotion.

The theory of reasoned action has been criticized for being focused exclusively on individuals and neglecting the social groups of which those individuals are members (Dutta-Bergman, 2005). This focus on the individual, according to Kippax and Crawford (1993), means that the theory neglects the collective nature of certain behaviours. For example, sexual behaviour occurs within an interpersonal and cultural **milieu**, not in isolation.

Mphahlele (2002) argues that people in African contexts find fulfilment in those around them. Therefore, they will always use others as a cue to guide their behaviour, whereas participants in Tlou's study completed questionnaires with questions directed at an individual person. Furthermore, the intervention workshop in the study placed emphasis on individual responsibility in changing risky sexual behaviour. Therefore, Tlou cites Adams and Salter (2007) to conclude that health psychology in African settings needs to complement a wider explanation of health, where the focus of intervention is still the individual person with his or her beliefs, but also incorporates behaviours and physiological processes within a more holistic approach that recognises connectedness to other people, places, and spiritual worlds.

The theory of reasoned action has been criticized for being focused exclusively on individuals and neglecting the social groups of which those individuals are members (Dutta-Bergman, 2005). This exclusive focus on the individual, according to Kippax and Crawford (1993), means that the theory neglects the collective nature of certain behaviours.

31.2 Effectiveness of health promotion programmes

Content focus

Evaluate the effectiveness of health promotion programmes.

TOK

How can 'effectiveness' of health promotion programmes be translated into necessary and sufficient conditions for well-being?

Health promotion programmes can be defined as a coordinated set of activities or services that are aimed at addressing a particular health issue in a defined population. There is a clear need to make them measurable to decide how effective they are.

In the following section, the effectiveness of health promotion programmes will be discussed in the context of sexual health and drug addiction.

31.2.1 What is a health promotion programme?

Health promotion programmes can be defined as a coordinated set of activities or services that are aimed at addressing a particular health issue in a defined population. Particular groups in any given community can experience significantly poorer health and lower overall life expectancy than other groups (Hall, 2006). Governments usually want to encourage behaviour within these groups that they believe will improve health outcomes and might also benefit society overall. Health promotion programmes can potentially be large and unwieldy and involve many disciplines such as health, geography, psychology, sociology, and economics. They can be expensive and they often use public money. Therefore, there is a clear need to make them measurable to decide how effective they are.

HIV awareness campaign poster

However, measuring success is often complex and open to interpretation. For example, the overall goal of reducing the spread of HIV is appropriate and desirable from a macrosocial perspective, but it may not be adequate as an evaluation objective for a health promotion programme (Coyle et al., 1991). 'Reducing the spread of HIV' could be seen as too general, as it does not specify how the spread of HIV will be reduced by specific interventions among specific populations and in specific contexts. Futhermore, focusing on HIV alone can be misleading in some contexts. For example, in a community that begins with zero HIV prevalence, an outcome of zero prevalence following an intervention cannot be taken as evidence of the intervention's effectiveness (Coyle et al., 1991).

Deciding how to measure the effectiveness of health promotion programmes is a key question for health professionals. Some considerations for measuring the effectiveness of health promotion programmes are as follows.

- Health status should be measureable and measured before an intervention is carried out.

- The intervention itself should be measurable.

- The health status should be measured again after the intervention.

There are two main ways to create and then measure the effectiveness of health promotion programmes: the measurement of outcomes approach and the population health approach. These should not be seen in isolation to one another and elements of each can be used by health professionals to plan, implement, and then measure the effectiveness of health promotion programmes.

31.2.2 Considering populations

For health promotion programmes to be effective they need to consider which population they want to target and how they will measure the population's response. A population health approach (PHA) aims to improve the health of an entire population and to reduce health inequities between population subgroups. It is a mental framework for thinking about why some populations are healthier than others and aims to improve the health of those populations that are less healthy. A PHA uses specific strategies that are focused on the needs of those populations.

For health promotion programmes to be effective they need to consider which population they want to target and how they will measure the population's response.

This approach is effective because different populations may have:

- different attitudes to health

- different education levels

- different ways of viewing messages and different opinions of government messages

- different incomes.

A population health approach assumes health is embedded within social, economic, and physical environmental factors that influence particular populations in unique ways.

A population health approach assumes that health is embedded within social, economic, and physical environmental factors that influence particular populations in unique ways.

For example, HIV rates can be high in certain gay male communities, but the widespread availability of **antiretroviral therapy** has contributed to a relapse to unsafe sexual practices among gay men, a phenomenon known as **'treatment optimism'**. HIV has become seen as a treatable chronic condition (as opposed to a fatal one), which has led to a relaxation in certain behaviours among this population that had, in the past, lowered their risk. This view is not shared by other specific populations and is unique to this particular group.

257

Overall, macro community-level HIV prevention targeting has been relatively effective in staving off unsafe sexual behaviours (Kegeles et al., 2002), but Lee et al. (2011) wanted to find out which particular strategies are the most effective for a specific population. They used a **meta-review** of the medical literature on HIV reduction in gay male communities and found gay men in Australia, the UK and the USA were experiencing safe sex 'fatigue'. Condom use was in decline and instead, gay men were making their own rules about their main relationships in order to prevent HIV infection. For example, any sexual partners outside of the relationship were asked to prove HIV-negative status and condoms were used with someone who the men did not know very well.

This approach is known as **negotiated safety**. Lee et al. concluded that the notion of negotiated safety, if used properly and consistently, can be effective in reducing HIV infection rates in gay men despite it going against the more general advice to 'always wear a condom'.

Negotiated safety is a particular behaviour unique to a particular population. Health campaigns targeted at gay men should still promote condom use, as this the best way to reduce HIV rates, but they can also promote negotiated safety strategies as a way of making the campaigns realistic and relevant to the target population's lifestyle choices.

One way of targeting specific populations for health promotion campaigns is **social marketing**. Social marketing involves applying marketing principles to promote social goods. It involves audience segmentation and then repeatedly exposing specific groups to prevention messages. In the context of health behaviour, it has been used successfully to reduce alcohol-related car crashes, smoking among youths, and malaria transmission, among other goals.

Key study: Gibson et al. (2010)

Aim: To measure the effects of social marketing on 479 injection drug users (IDUs) in the USA. They evaluated a community-based social marketing campaign to reduce injection risk behaviour among an estimated 7000 heroin users in Sacramento, California.

Procedure: A quasi-experimental design comparing two cities (Sacramento and San Diego), where one city's population would be exposed to the campaign and the other would not. The four components of the campaign included convenience advertising or 'narrowcasting', which involved the placement of small posters with HIV prevention messages in venues frequented by injection drug users, newsletters, a TV documentary and a small free gift (a stress grip, which is a small sponge designed to be squeezed) with health messages written on the side of it. The social marketing campaign was evaluated by the use of surveys and interviews, which each took six to nine months to complete. The surveys were conducted in street settings (a mobile van, parks, coffee houses, and other places) and used **targeted sampling** techniques.

Findings: Analysis of follow-up data from Sacramento indicated that 56 per cent of a sample of 479 IDUs had seen a prevention-related poster, 45 per cent had seen two or more copies of the newsletter, 29 per cent had seen the television show, and 41 per cent had seen the stress grip.

Conclusion: Exposure to the narrowcasting posters and IDU newsletter significantly increased the chances of users adopting low-risk behaviours for drug injection and there was a trend in HIV risk reduction for those who were exposed to the TV show.

Such subcultural nuances can be further illustrated with UK government anti-drug campaigns (Advisory Council on the Misuse of Drugs, 1984). For example, the UK Advisory Council on the Misuse of Drugs (1984) argued that government anti-drug campaigns were not effective after researching drug use among the target population of young people. The campaigns mainly used scare tactics aimed at shocking young people about how dangerous drugs were. However, certain types of young people were more likely to try drugs because:

- governments specifically told them not to

- the scare campaigns made the drugs look mysterious

- the anti-drug campaigns made drug users look rebellious.

The solution was to make anti-drug campaigns more subtle. Over time, anti-drug campaigns were changed. For example, facts were presented coldly and maturely; scary, dramatic tactics were toned down; government symbols were removed; and personal responsibility was emphasized, which has led to a greater reduction in drug use (Slater et al., 2011). Therefore, targeted campaigns do work as long as the at-risk group is exposed enough and the message is communicated in a way that makes sense to the at-risk group.

31.2.3 Considering outcomes

For health promotion programmes to be effective they also need to consider which outcomes they want to see achieved and how these will be measured.

A measurement of outcomes approach (MOA) aims to discover if any change in health can be directly related to the intervention. With regards to personal health matters, controlled **randomized**, lab-based trials are often not realistic as people live in the real world rather than a laboratory. Furthermore, medical practitioners use their individual experiences with treatments, which are subjective and not based on evidence from large-scale realistic studies. An MOA approach aims to use statistically significant data to show an effect of a health promotion programme while still retaining a realistic setting. To achieve this, an MOA approach has to:

- standardize the measurement of health

- standardize the measurement of treatments

- use an evidence-based approach to evaluating the effectiveness of interventions.

An MOA approach has many advantages because it focuses on **outcomes** rather than **outputs**. Outcomes refers to an improvement in health in realistic and everyday settings. Outputs refers to any 'thing' that makes the outcome happen. An example would be a health service that has to reduce HIV rates in a local community. The output is the intervention they decide on, such as 'giving out free condoms'.

Research anti-drug messages from different cultures. What do they have in common? How are they different?

For health promotion programmes to be effective they also need to consider which outcomes they want to see achieved and how these will be measured.

What variables of human behaviour are most difficult to measure?

An outputs approach would just focus on the amount of free condoms that were given out, whereas an MOA approach would ask: Has there been a reduction in HIV rates? Are people actually using the free condoms?

There are some disadvantages to an MOA approach. It requires a clearly defined population and a reasonable control of variables within it, which is often unrealistic. In addition, many non-measureable, or hard-to-measure variables, such as cultural norms, perception, and self-belief, also affect health outcomes in complex and subtle ways. Coyle et al. (1991) discuss the challenges facing researchers who wish to assess the effectiveness of health promotion programmes from an outcomes point of view. They suggest biological, behavioural, and psychological outcome variables as a focus for assessment for the effectiveness of HIV prevention programmes.

Biological outcomes

Biological outcomes are variables associated with the body.

Biological outcomes are variables associated with the body. HIV infection rates are seen as the most informative biological outcome variable to indicate the spread of the disease among adults or adolescents. Infection rates can be measured by **seroconversion**, which is the period of time during which HIV antibodies develop and become detectable. The variable is quite appealing as an outcome measure because it relates directly to the overarching goal of HIV prevention programmes. If reliable data from representative samples of the target populations can be collected, HIV infection rates might prove to be useful indicators of a programme's effectiveness.

Furthermore, rates of other sexually transmitted diseases (STDs) may also be useful, as they should respond to changes in sexual behaviours that risk HIV transmission. Coyle et al. (1991) state that HIV infection rates as the primary outcome of an evaluation effort seems intuitively appealing because HIV infection is exactly what any programme wants to reduce and prevent. In addition, the approach to evaluation using HIV infections as the outcome variable of interest seems straightforward because if there are fewer new cases of infection among people involved in an intervention programme, compared with an equivalent group of people who were not involved, then it is reasonable to conclude the prevention campaign was effective.

However, the emphasis placed on statistical analysis can cause problems when researchers try to determine the effectiveness of a programme's success. For example, on a population level (even those within an 'at-risk' population), HIV seroconversion rates are relatively small and therefore any evaluation requires extremely large samples and long intervals of time before there are enough occurrences of the event to conduct statistical tests of programme effectiveness.

Although the goal of HIV prevention efforts is to keep as many people as possible uninfected, a significant factor of a person remaining HIV negative involves the behaviour of people who are infected with HIV, such as sexual partners and peers. Therefore, prevention assessment for HIV infection should not be limited only to the uninfected, but should include all members of a wider population.

Behavioural outcomes

Behavioural outcomes refer to variables associated with explicit, expressive behaviour.

Behavioural outcomes are variables associated with explicit, expressive behaviour. People's behaviour directly affects their chances of contracting HIV infection.

Consequently, it is not necessary to rely on HIV seroconversion rates as the primary outcome of evaluation studies of HIV prevention programmes because specific behaviours can be targeted for assessment.

Certain types of behaviour put people more or less at risk of HIV infection. For example, the rates of extramarital intercourse, needle sharing, and condom use for a person can be used to assess the extent of their risk and the effectiveness of a health promotion programme that was put in place to help them.

Studies that rely on behavioural outcomes can be conducted more quickly and cheaply than those based on biological outcomes because they do not need to carry out the extensive screening required in seroconversion studies over a long period of time. This also avoids the problem of the reluctance of some people to be tested for HIV seroconversion.

Psychological variables

Psychological variables are largely cognitive in nature. They include the level of awareness of AIDS and HIV and of the gravity of the problems they pose in society; awareness of personal risk regarding HIV infection; knowledge of AIDS and HIV transmission; and **stigmatization** and **stereotyping** of individuals who have AIDS or who are infected with HIV.

Behavioural outcomes refer to variables associated with explicit, expressive behaviour.

Coyle et al. argue that behavioural change is unlikely to occur without knowledge and awareness of the AIDS problem and the means of HIV transmission, and they state that one of the most important public health goals should be to maintain the current high level of knowledge and awareness that exists in Western populations about the risk of HIV transmission by sexual contact and the sharing of infected drug equipment.

From a research standpoint, psychological variables are also relatively straightforward to assess, as people can be quickly surveyed using standardized measurement techniques such as questionnaires.

What makes a health promotion programme effective?

Using either a strictly PHA or a strictly MOA approach to measure the effectiveness of health promotion programmes is unrealistic and potentially restricting. Both approaches assume health promotion programmes can be implemented in a largely fixed state and then measured.

Health promotion programmes are complex and can be expensive, using public money. It is essential that health professionals can plan, implement, and then measure the effectiveness of health promotion campaigns. However, programmes involve many variables that interact in subtle and hard-to-measure ways. Variables such as perception, attention, motivation, and personal and cultural nuances influence the effect of health promotion programmes on individuals and populations, as well as the ability of any assessor to measure their effectiveness. However, some broad conclusions can be made. To be effective, health promotion programmes should:

- consider cultural and subcultural nuances of the populations they hope to reach

- focus on outcomes rather than outputs and consider the extent to which an intervention has affected a population

- standardize the measurement of the health issue

- standardize the measurement of treatments

- use an evidence-based approach to evaluate the effectiveness of interventions that is agreed upon by all researchers and health professionals

- be viewed as active living systems embedded within sociocultural contexts that should evolve to meet the needs of the population they are addressing.

A systems approach may pose challenges to attempts to standardize interventions, measurements, treatments, and effectiveness, but these challenges are an inherent part of performing complex health work in the public sphere.

To what extent is a population health approach an effective way to measure health-related programmes in the context of sexual health of a chosen subgroup?

32 Approaches to research: health psychology

Learning focus

Discuss approaches to research in health psychology.

Health psychology creates a number of special considerations for researchers. Research in health psychology usually aims to measure the experiences of people with health problems so improvements or adjustments can be made to processes in the public sphere that will impact people on an individual level. Therefore, people with health problems, as well as professionals who address these problems, are often at the core of research.

Research in health psychology usually aims to measure the experiences of people with health problems so improvements or adjustments can be made to processes in the public sphere that will impact people on an individual level.

32.1 Researcher bias

Health psychology research is often intertwined with health promotion programmes. Working with people who may have health issues means health psychologists have to think very carefully about the methods they use for gathering data and what their research aims are. They have to ask questions about whether or not they want to collect data and/or conduct a health-related programme.

Often when human scientists collect data they will do so in a way that means they cannot be said to be interfering with the results. However, health psychology can be seen as unique because data is often collected in conjunction with a health promotion programme. Therefore, the individuals that collect the data on the programme's effectiveness can sometimes be the same individuals who implement the programme.

For example, Gibson et al. (2010) wanted to study the effects of social marketing on injection drug users (IDUs) in the USA while also implementing a programme to reduce injection risk behaviour. They found largely positive results about their work and were able to demonstrate how certain techniques can be used to target specific groups. However, researcher bias could be an issue for any researcher who evaluates the implementation of their own health promotion programme.

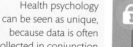

Health psychology can be seen as unique, because data is often collected in conjunction with a health promotion programme. Therefore, the individuals who collect the data on the programme's effectiveness can sometimes be the same individuals who implement the programme. Researchers need to be aware of this potential and their own biases, and put in place clear methodologies that can account for this to address issues of credibility.

Researcher bias may occur because there could be a strong desire to see positive results related to a health issue. Researchers need to be aware of this potential and their own biases, and then put in place clear methodologies that can account for this to address issues of **credibility**.

Researcher bias can be explained as the researcher not paying enough attention to the participants, so it is the researcher's own beliefs that determine the direction and outcome of the research process. It is imperative in health-related research that participants' perceptions and beliefs in the understanding of health-related processes are given priority over the researcher's own.

However, there is a balance to be struck between health researchers and the research participants.

A researcher's experience can add richness and insight to the data. For example, Tlou (2009) assessed his own health promotion programme. He applied the theory of reasoned action (TRA) and the theory of planned behaviour (TPB) to the design of workplace HIV/AIDS health promotion programmes in South Africa (see page 257 for details). Tlou was therefore occupying two roles: a health promoter and an evaluator of health promotion that he himself had designed. His results showed there was no significant health behaviour change and no health behaviour differences based on his programmes. It could also be argued that because he is a South African who cares a great deal about the health of his fellow South Africans, this inherent subjectivity and 'lived experience' may be seen to contribute to the validity of his findings.

Potvin et al. (2001) argue that evaluating effectiveness should become an inherent part of any health-related programme, a subproject within a project that constantly assesses whether the programme is achieving change and responds enough to the needs of the population. Such a view can turn health promotion campaigners into human scientists who are assessors of their own work, or human scientists into health promotion campaigners. Either way, it raises questions of objectivity and **confirmation bias**.

Another view might be that due to the inherent morality of health-related research (an attempt to improve the health of people while measuring the effectiveness of a health promotion programme), a researcher should not avoid connecting with participants and should immerse themselves in the population and the health issue being studied.

32.2 Participant expectations

One of the more important factors to consider in health-related research is that the participants are less likely to respond passively to the research process. They are intimately engaged in it and its findings because the issues relate to their own personal health. Researchers need to be aware that health research is an active process that requires reflection and interrogation of the data, the participant, and the research context, but it may also lead to participant expectations (also called **reactivity**).

Participant expectations are an issue for all types of human science research, but are particularly prescient in health-related research. Participants may try and guess the nature of the research or programme and influence the results. If the participant feels

TOK How should researcher bias be acknowledged and to what extent does it help or hinder knowledge production? Should 'subjectivity' be accepted as an inherent part of the human sciences?

 Participants are less likely to respond passively to the research process but are intimately engaged in it and its findings because the issues relate to their own personal health.

they have to behave in certain ways in order to please the researcher, this will affect the value of the data in a negative way.

Therefore, it can be assumed that 'reality' in a research study is a multiple and co-constructed entity and researchers should be aware that participants who are asked to comment on the researcher's interpretation of the data will not necessarily have the same conclusions as the researcher. One way to minimize the effect of participant expectations and researcher bias is **reflexivity** throughout the research process.

32.3 The importance of reflexivity

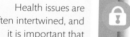

Reflexivity is based on the assumption that it is important the researcher is aware of his or her own contribution to the construction of meaning in the research process and then makes the reader of their research aware.

Reflexivity is a process that occurs throughout the research and is based on the assumption that it is important the researcher is aware of his or her own contribution to the construction of meaning in the research process and then makes the reader of their research aware. Such an approach allows the health researcher to reflect on ways in which bias may occur, by acknowledging that his or her own background and beliefs can influence the way the research is conducted. This line of thinking argues that health researchers should provide sufficient details about issues that may potentially bias the investigation – for example, revealing where they stand in terms of political ideology if this could be important.

32.4 Choosing an appropriate methodology

Health issues are often intertwined, and it is important that researchers do not apply one method as a definitive approach to researching complex issues. It is likely that a combination of qualitative and quantitative mixed methods is appropriate, with triangulation of different data sources.

Health issues are often intertwined (for example, drug addiction, needle use, and sexual health are connected) and it is important that researchers do not apply one method as a definitive approach to researching complex issues. It is likely that a combination of **qualitative** and **quantitative** mixed methods is appropriate, with **triangulation** of different data sources.

32.4.1 Triangulation

Triangulation is the validation of data through cross-verification from two or more sources. The sources are usually theoretical and/or methodological, and collected using different methods (e.g. interviews plus observations, questionnaires and diary analysis).

Theoretical triangulation is the search for evidence or approaches that could contradict a particular interpretation (e.g. a feminist lens; a behaviourist lens; a collectivist lens).

Researcher triangulation is the use of other researchers who would bring different perspectives and experience that might challenge the findings of a report.

For example, Gibson et al. (2010) used a quasi-experimental design comparing two cities (Sacramento and San Diego). It was evaluated by the use of surveys and interviews that each took six to nine months to complete.

32.4.2 Measurement

The issue of measurement poses problems for health researchers. Health is a complex issue and researchers may be tempted to measure the psychological aspects of health as they can be readily investigated using traditional methods such as questionnaires, surveys, and **self-reports**. Nonetheless, according to Coyle et al. (1991), who discuss the challenges facing researchers who wish to assess the effectiveness of health promotion programmes, the development of specific questions must be carefully considered. Questions involving knowledge and attitudes must be sensitively crafted, as well as clearly worded in the type of language used by the target population to avoid introducing bias and error. For example, questions involving personal drug use and sexual relationships will mean different things to different populations. Questions should therefore be suited to specific populations who may have their own understanding of certain words, as well as their own slang term for drugs and sexual conduct. However, this may in turn present a problem of consistency, reliability, and generalization across populations.

Furthermore, research based on self-reports involves respondents accurately remembering specific events and behaviours. In addition, health-related behaviour is time dependent, and if personal nuances are not explored in depth it can cause distortion in the date. For example, a participant who reports **celibacy** or monogamy for a week is describing a different behaviour from one who reports celibacy or monogamy for a year and one will be remembered more accurately than the other (Coyle et al., 1991). It may also be tempting to under report the amount of celibacy or monogamy due to negative perceptions surrounding a lack of sexual encounters.

Researchers may also have to contend with low rates of occurrence of a particular health issue. For example, while issues such as obesity are quite widespread in Western societies, HIV seroconversion rates are still relatively low. Therefore, any study on HIV seroconversion rates requires extremely large samples and long intervals of time before there are enough occurrences of the event to conduct statistical tests. Such an approach may require the screening of thousands of individuals to assemble a sufficiently large cohort, a process that requires great time and expense. These tasks are highly labour intensive, and they will be very expensive and time-consuming if sample sizes are large (Coyle et al., 1991).

Researchers have to consider how their methodology will be interpreted by the population they are studying.

32.5 The issue of generalization

Generalization refers to the extent to which results are relevant outside the context of the study, although the term '**transferability**' is used for generalizing qualitative results. Health researchers have to carefully consider the extent to which they want their findings to apply to people other than those who participate in a particular study. According to Lewis and Ritchie (2003), it is useful to consider the following forms of generalization.

- **Representational generalization:** findings from research can be applied to populations outside the specific population of study. For example, if findings from interviews with people in a study on HIV risk are representative of all people in general, this could have implications for the development of HIV prevention programmes. But if a researcher has used small samples that are not selected to be statistically representative, and other non-standardized methods have been used (such as interviews), it makes it difficult to generalize findings to other populations. Therefore, considerations of the uniqueness of certain populations have to be built into health-related research.

- **Theoretical generalization:** theoretical concepts derived from the study can be used to develop further theory. The findings from a study might lead to inferences about what could be effective policies to design HIV prevention programmes for other populations. Therefore, the findings from the study may contribute to wider social theory.

32.6 The problem of cause and effect

Health psychology researchers like to connect potential causes to health effects. For example, it can be assumed an environmental event may induce a biological consequence that may have long-term effects on the health of individuals. However, it is not ethical, practical, or desirable to deliberately induce negative events on humans and test for cause and effect.

However, such interactions are thought to occur with the effect of poverty on children. For example, growing up in a poor home or neighbourhood can give rise to toxic stress, which in itself is a response to adverse childhood experiences (ACEs). It is now assumed stress can reform the architecture of a child's developing brain, particularly in the prefrontal cortex (differentiating between good and bad), and the hippocampus (memories and learning) (Bassett, 2016).

It is now assumed that environmental events induce a biological consequence that may have long-term effects on the health of individuals. However, it is not ethical, practical, or desirable to deliberately induce negative events on humans and test for cause and effect.

GRIMACING MOUSE COMES UP AGAINST THE PROBLEM OF GENERALIZATION IN HEALTH RESEARCH.

There are now concerted efforts to demonstrate cause and effect by using animal models. For example, Gilles et al. (1996) aimed to create an animal model to show the effects of continuous chronic stress on corticosterone secretion in response to an acute environmental stressor. Previous studies had used an absence of the mother in rats to induce stress, but the researchers wanted a model that could be comparable with human experiences. Therefore, stress was induced by placing newborn rats into an environment with their mothers that featured good or limited bedding before being killed. The group with limited bedding manifested increased corticosterone. Gilles et al. were able to suggest the experiences they had created in the laboratory were approximate to the human situation of chronically stressed, neglected infants. However, caution should always be used when generalizing to humans, but it seems reasonable to assume that negative environmental experiences can influence biological events.

33 Ethical considerations: health psychology

Learning focus

Discuss ethical considerations in health psychology.

Look back at section 23.1, page 175, which looked at **Research Ethics Committees** (RECs) and what they are responsible for.

Health psychology raises some particular ethical considerations that any REC would have to consider before approving research. For example:

- researchers often deal with people who are suffering from a major health issue and can therefore be classed as 'patients' as well as 'participants' in a study

- researchers may be trying to find out why people are suffering from a health issue

- researchers may be measuring the effectiveness of a health intervention or health promotion programme

- researchers may want to generalize their findings to wider populations to promote a health programme or prevent health problems.

Therefore, researchers may well deal with very sensitive data regarding lifestyle choices of their participants.

Kaptein (2014) assumes health psychologists should adhere to the four basic principles of medical ethics.

- **Autonomy** – people have a right to control what happens to their bodies.

- **Beneficence** – all healthcare providers must strive to improve their patient's health, and do the most good for the patient in every situation.

- **Non-maleficence** – in every situation, healthcare providers should avoid causing harm to their patients.

TOK
Does morality necessarily involve action, or can it involve thoughts and attitudes alone?

Most respected academic institutions should have some form of REC consisting of a multidisciplinary team of professional researchers and/or experienced academics with a balance of gender and cultural backgrounds.

- Justice – researchers and healthcare providers should try to be as fair as possible when offering treatments to patients and allocating scarce medical resources (Runzheimer and Larson, 2010, cited in Kaptein, 2014).

However, Belar and McIntyre (2004) argue that health psychologists should have a special set of ethical guidelines because of the particular nature of health psychology work. They offer the following ethical considerations to be taken into account by health psychologists.

- Knowledge – relating to knowledge of health, diagnosis, disease and patient response, the role of other healthcare professionals, legal and ethical issues. Health psychologists should ask to what extent they possess adequate knowledge in their field of interest.

- Multicultural competence – relating to the relationship between culture and ethnicity and the implications these have on health issues.

- Professional responsibility – relating to being aware of responsibilities regarding communicating knowledge to patients/participants and follow-up procedures.

- Respect for rights and dignity – relating to being aware of differences of language, attitudes and health beliefs of different populations and incorporating those nuances into a framework of understanding for the patient/participant.

- Confidentiality – relating to the nature of health work and how communication that might otherwise be confidential in traditional research settings often circulates quickly and widely in settings where health psychology research is practiced.

33.1 Informed consent

Participants should know that participation in health research is voluntary and the researcher must provide participants with sufficient information about the study.

As a starting point, participants should know that participation in health research is voluntary and the researcher must provide participants with sufficient information about the study. This is particularly important if the research is conducted by people who have some kind of relation to members of the sample (for example, a health worker, a social worker, or a doctor), since participation could then be motivated by feelings of obligation.

Sufficient information about the study could include who funded the study, who will conduct the study, how the data will be used, and what the research requires of the participants (for example, in terms of time and the topics the study will address). It should also be made clear that **consent** can always be renegotiated. In cases where children aged under 16 years are involved, consent must be obtained from parents or legal guardians.

The rule is that **informed consent** should always be obtained. This is stressed in all guidelines on ethical conduct in research. However, in some rare cases, where it would not otherwise be possible to study a phenomenon (e.g. the use of a particular harmful illegal street drug), ethics committees may offer dispensation from the rule because the goal of the research is to obtain knowledge that may eventually lead to the drug being targeted by the police.

Gibson et al. (2010) studied the effects of social marketing on injection drug users (IDUs) in California and had their research approved by the institutional review board of the University of California. Even though there were particularly large numbers in the study (479), they were able to show that all participants provided written informed consent.

33.2 Protecting participants from (psychological or emotional) harm

Researchers should take preventive action in all research to avoid harming the participants. This is particularly true in sensitive research topics, such as drug abuse, alcoholism, and risky sexual behaviour. Due to the nature of certain methods, such as in-depth interviews, participants may disclose very private information that they have never shared with anyone before. This can happen because the interview situation seems like a friendly encounter, where the participant may feel comfortable and safe with an individual who cares about them. However, the participant may regret such revelations and feel upset after the interview when the interviewer has gone. This situation should be avoided.

Prior to the research, and before they agree to participate, the participants should have a clear understanding of the topics to be addressed. The researchers must approach sensitive issues through clear and direct questions so that participants are not drawn into sharing irrelevant and sensitive details by mistake. If the participants show signs of discomfort, the researcher should be empathetic and consider stopping the research. If the research has dealt with emotional and sensitive issues, the researcher should try to return to less sensitive topics toward the end.

It is not advised that the researcher should provide advice or counsel the participant, but he or she might provide useful information about where to find help if necessary. This is often difficult in health research because the researcher may actually be a health worker. The health researcher has to decide what they will do in these situations and present their intentions to the REC.

For example, Tlou (2009) applied the theory of reasoned action (TRA) and the theory of planned behaviour (TPB) to the design of a workplace HIV/AIDS health promotion programme in South Africa and not only did he obtain informed consent, but he also made himself available for 'follow-up consultations' in case there was an issue that participants wanted to discuss further.

33.3 Anonymity and confidentiality

Anonymity and **confidentiality** are key parts of psychological research. Usually, the identity of the participants should not be known outside the research team and participants should not be identifiable to each other. Potential health researchers have to show their RECs how they will guarantee that their participants will remain anonymous and how the data will be held securely. At no point should any reader of the eventual report be able to guess the identity of the participants.

Researchers should take preventive action in all research to avoid harming the participants. This is particularly true in sensitive research topics, such as drug abuse, alcoholism, and risky sexual behaviour. Due to the nature of certain methods, such as in-depth interviews, participants may disclose very private information that they have never shared with anyone before.

Potential health researchers have to show their RECs how they will guarantee that their participants will remain anonymous and how the data will be held securely.

As noted above, Belar and McIntyre (2004) argue that health psychology has a particular responsibility toward data and participants because of the sensitive and personal nature of the work.

Furthermore, health research has the potential to collect data of an immoral or illegal nature (drug dealing and use, sex without protection, etc.). Therefore, participants should be informed about the issues surrounding anonymity and confidentiality. The identity of participants should not be known outside the research team, but in cases where sampling has involved a third party (e.g. managers, friends, teachers, health workers), this cannot be done, and in this case the participants should be informed.

Confidentiality means that research data will not be known to anyone outside the study. The researcher may have to change minor details in the report to avoid the possibility of participants being recognized. Confidentiality also relates to the way data is stored after the research. If interviews or observations have been recorded and archived, it can be difficult to guarantee total anonymity, so these should be destroyed when transcripts have been made. If the researcher finds it necessary to archive non-anonymized data or to use extensive quotes from their sample, the participant should give written informed consent.

In addition, ethical issues in terms of anonymity may arise in case studies or in research designs with a small number of participants because of the risk that they may be identified in research reports – it is difficult to lose people in a small qualitative crowd.

Activity

Find all of the new words or expressions from this chapter and write them into a document with their definitions and explanations next to them. Be creative and use diagrams or boxes to help make your personal glossary unique and effective.

Psychology of human relationships

G

Humans are **social** animals dependent on others for their well-being. Human relationship psychology is a social psychology option that focuses on relationships between individuals and groups.

The three topics in this option are:

- personal relationships

- group dynamics

- social responsibility.

Studying human relationships has its challenges and it is tempting to oversimplify complex social and psychological issues. One approach to the study of human relationships concentrates on the role of hormones and **genetics**. However, this gives a limited understanding of how relationships develop. **Cognitive** theorists have also contributed to the understanding of relationships by applying **schema theory**, while social psychologists have focused on beliefs, **social identity theory** and the role of **culture**. The notion of an **ingroup** ('us') being contrasted with an **outgroup** ('them' or 'the other') is a key notion underpinning social psychology (see p. 88 for more details).

However, it should be noted that groups are dynamic and represent social and personal **constructions**. For instance, an individual may perceive someone as belonging to several groups (e.g. 'black', 'female', 'lesbian' or 'white', 'male', '**heterosexual**'), whereas the individual may not consider themselves to be identified with those groups or may have a different understanding of what those group labels mean. Overall, the key goals of social psychologists are to understand the complexities of relationships, improve interpersonal relationships, promote social responsibility, and reduce violence. As such, notions such as credibility and trustworthiness, as well as a consideration of ethics are important throughout.

TOK

If several of the goals of social psychology are to improve the world, how might these goals influence research and the acceptance of results?

34 Personal relationships

Topic focus

Discuss factors influencing personal relationships.

34.1 Formation of personal relationships

Content focus

Discuss the role of sociocultural, biological, and cognitive factors in the formation of personal relationships.

In the following section, personal relationships will be discussed in the context of romantic love and romantic relationships. Lindholm (2006) has defined romantic love as an intense attraction that involves the idealization of the other.

Lindholm has defined romantic love as an intense attraction that involves the idealization of the other.

34.1.1 The role of sociocultural factors in the formation of relationships

A **sociocultural** approach to relationship formation assumes that sociocultural events influence who people want to form relationships with. Culture can be defined as a set of attitudes, behaviours, and symbols shared by a large group of people and usually communicated from one generation to the next (Shiraev and Levy, 2004). Attitudes include beliefs (for example, political, religious, and moral beliefs), values, superstitions, and **stereotypes**. Behaviours include **norms**, customs, traditions, and fashions.

The norms and values of a culture affect relationship formation by influencing the perception of romantic love and what people find attractive in another person. In addition, cultural norms can guide who individuals can expect to enter into a relationship with, when they are allowed to start romantic relations, and what characteristics make a good partner.

A sociocultural approach to relationship formation assumes sociocultural events such as cultural norms regarding attraction and marriage influence who people want to form relationships with.

Attraction

One assumption when studying romantic relationship formation is that attraction is culturally specific. For example, Cunningham et al. (1995) found a major difference in the perception of attractive bodies between cultures. African American men found larger women more attractive than white men did. Swami et al. (2006) compared female physical attributes in the UK and Japan and found many cross-cultural differences occur between British and Japanese perceptions of an attractive female body. The Japanese preferred images of women with significantly lower **body mass indexes** (BMI) than Britons, were more reliant on body shape, and accepted less variation in what was considered attractive in body shape than the Britons. Swami and Tovee (2005) asked 682 participants from the UK and Malaysia to rate a set of images of real women with a known BMI. The results showed that BMI is the primary determinant of female physical attractiveness in both cultures. However, there were significant differences in preferences for physical attractiveness along a gradient of **socioeconomic** development, with **urban** participants preferring images of women with significantly lower BMIs than their **rural** counterparts.

Buss (1994) gave questionnaires to 10 000 people from 37 cultures to investigate which factors were important in relationship formation. He found significant **universals**, such as men preferring younger mates and women preferring older mates, but there were cultural differences in the value of various characteristics. For example, people from mainland China and those from Taiwan placed tremendous value on virginity, as did participants who lived in India and Iran, while those from Finland, Denmark, Sweden, France, and Germany placed much less importance on chastity. Nevertheless, research suggests that men universally value sexual fidelity in a mate more than women. It was noted that cultural specifics were underpinned by biological universals. For example, while there are cultural variations in expressions of wealth, women found the ability to create wealth (industriousness, ambition, social status) as universally attractive.

Love is seen as a clear **cultural construct** not found universally. For example, Buss found that in the USA, love ranked first when measuring what people find important about relationship formation, whereas in Nigeria love ranked fourth. Zulus ranked love seventh (emotional stability and dependability were first in Zulu culture).

This suggests the more rural the community, where survival pressures take over, the less important love becomes.

Love may even be seen as a Western 'luxury', but there is a clear link between culture and relationship formation as culture can dictate what is considered important in attraction. Lindholm (2006) has argued that romantic love is neither a universal nor an entirely Western construct, although the notion of romantic love appears to be spreading worldwide as other cultures adopt the 'Western' approach to their relationships. This phenomenon may be partly the result of increasing integration driven by **globalization**.

Marriage

The notion of passionate love as a reason to form a serious relationship can be seen as culturally specific. Goodwin (1995) argues that passionate love is largely a Western construct rather than a universal one, and more traditional societies love the person they marry; not marry the person they love.

Arranged marriages are a sociocultural norm in several cultures and usually mean that the people who get married did not choose their partner alone. Normally the parents make the decision or, in some cases, find a range of possible partners for their child and let them make the decision. In some cases, the person who gets married has no choice at all about the partner or the marriage.

Arranged marriages are seen as unions between two families, with family honour at stake and community involvement in the marriage. Such arrangements are viewed as a 'partnership' to raise children and provide social support for the partners (Dion and Dion, 1993).

Epstein (2012) interviewed 70 couples and also performed a **meta-analysis** of studies of arranged marriages. He concluded that:

- arranged marriages last longer and are happier because feelings of love in arranged marriages tend to gradually increase as time goes on in the relationship

- arranged marriages usually have the advice of a third party (e.g. parents), and so feelings are not the only factor involved; there is an intellectual element

- 'love marriages', where attraction is based on passionate emotions, are less stable, as passion decreases over time by as much as 50 per cent after only 18 to 24 months of marriage.

The success of arranged marriages may partly explain why this method of relationship formation is the accepted norm in many cultures.

Housing

Social and economic policies often mean people have little choice about where and how they live. This can impact relationship formation because of who people interact with and how they interact with each other.

Nahemow and Lawton (1975) aimed to test if more friendships were found among people who live near them. They asked residents in Manhattan, New York, who their three best friends were in the housing area and gathered information about how far

---

Investigate the Swayamvara system in ancient India.

Social and economic policies often mean people have little choice in where and how they live. This can impact relationship formation because of who people interact with and how they interact with each other.

away most friendships were based. They found that 88 per cent of the people named a person living in the same building as their first best friend, and nearly half lived on the same floor. Similarly, Bossard (1931) found couples in Chicago who lived within one block of each other were more likely to get married than those who lived two blocks apart and Clarke (1951) found 50% of people marrying in Columbus, Ohio lived within walking distance of each other.

Kerckoff (1974) referred to this phenomenon as the 'field of availables': people have to be geographically close to each other to reward each other. Being geographically close also allows increased exposure, which leads to familiarity, and people who live near us are more likely to share our social class, values, norms, etc.

However, these decades-old studies have limited **generalizability** to contemporary society because of digital technology and multiculturalism. For instance, people can now reward and 'meet' each other without the need for social proximity, which means that physical geography no longer determines emotional 'proximity'. Furthermore, in modern multicultural societies geographical proximity does not necessarily mean those living close together share the same values.

Sharing the same physical space usually means an increase in the likelihood that people will encounter each other. Zajonc (1971) states the '**mere exposure effect**' assumes mere interaction can produce feelings of attraction, which increases the likelihood people will form relationships. Sixty-four male undergraduates and 64 female undergraduates took part in the study. They were shown four black and white pictures of different male undergraduate students and asked to rate them out of seven on a **Likert**-type scale based on attractiveness.

The results showed that interpersonal attraction varied positively with the frequency of prior encounters, even when those encounters did not entail social interaction. Repeated exposure was found to enhance subjects' feelings of attraction toward the people represented in the stimulus material. People who are encountered more frequently seem to elicit greater feelings of attraction even though little or no social interaction has actually taken place. This suggests that mere interaction can influence attraction under a variety of conditions. It is possible, however, that mere exposure may increase perceived similarity or a reduction of perceived difference, which leads to feelings of greater comfort.

Social cues

Social cues are visual characteristics in an environment that cause people to think, feel, and behave in a certain way. Examples of social cues include body language and facial expression.

Key study: Hill and Buss (2008)

Aim: To measure the extent to which men and women use the presence of members of their sex to inform desirability assessments of potential mates. The study assumes men and women are influenced differently by social cues when making desirability assessments.

Procedure: The participants of this study included over 1200 undergraduate heterosexual women and 369 undergraduate heterosexual men. Participants were shown pictures of ten people. They were either depicted alone, surrounded by others of the same gender, or surrounded by others of the opposite gender. The participants were then asked to rate the people in the photographs on a ten-point rating scale on five different characteristics.

Findings: Men were more likely to find a woman desirable or attractive if she was surrounded by the same sex or by herself, compared to being surrounded by the opposite sex. However, women were more likely to find males more attractive if they were surrounded by the opposite sex compared to being alone or surrounded by the same sex.

Conclusion: These findings suggest men and women may use the same social cues in **qualitatively** different ways, based on the different evolutionary significance of the cue to each sex. For women, seeing men surrounded by other women gave a '**social proof**' that they had been vetted and deemed attractive by other women. For men, seeing women surrounded by other women also suggests social proofing is important, but it may also suggest the woman in the picture is not promiscuous with men.

34.1.2 The role of biological factors in the formation of relationships

A biological approach to relationship formation assumes biological events influence who people want to form relationships with. Furthermore, it assumes relationships between heterosexual couples serve a survival purpose (that is, passing on the best possible genetic combination to eventual offspring). There are also evolutionary arguments for the presence of homosexuality as a trait in humans, but this section will only focus on heterosexual relationships. From a genetic point of view, attraction is the product of evolution and is therefore an adaptive function.

> A biological approach to relationship formation assumes biological events influence who people want to form relationships with. There are also evolutionary arguments for the presence of homosexuality as a trait in humans.

This is shown by:

- males and females finding different characteristics attractive

- males generally preferring younger women and paying attention to physical details such as teeth and lip colour, hair length and shine, hip size and skin smoothness, which are female characteristics that represent the ability to produce offspring

- females generally preferring older men and paying attention to ambition, wealth, intelligence, social status, energy levels, and good health, which are male characteristics that represent the ability to provide for offspring.

It can be noted that there are some similarities between males and females. For example, females also pay attention to the appearance of a potential mate, and both sexes value 'kindness' and 'intelligence'. However, the gender differences listed above represent generalizations and have theoretical support in the form of the theory of evolution and empirical support in the form of large-scale cross-cultural surveys (e.g. Buss, 1994; 1995).

MHC genes

A biological approach to relationship formation assumes that attraction occurs between two people because the combination of their **genes** would result in healthy offspring. Evidence for this assumption can be found in the attraction to **pheromones** carried in sweat that contain information about a person's **immune system**. It is assumed that genetically different immune systems complement each other and the mixture of two complementary immune systems should produce a child with a good immune system.

Major histocompatibility complex (MHC) genes control the immunological self/non-self discrimination, and subsequently tissue rejection and immune recognition of infectious diseases. Therefore, MHC genes are involved in making sure people stay healthy. It is assumed that MHC genes are the product of **sexual selection** to improve the immune system of offspring and avoid inbreeding. Studies in house mice indicate that both males and females prefer MHC-dissimilar mates, which they apparently recognize by odour cues. Studies in humans have also found MHC-associated odour and mating preferences (Wedekind and Penn, 2000).

Wedekind et al. (1995) aimed to test if a woman will rate a sweaty t-shirt as more attractive if it is from a man with different immune system genes to her own. Forty-nine female and 44 male students were tested to see what type of immune system genes they had. The males were then asked to wear a plain white t-shirt for two days. The worn t-shirts were put in closed boxes until the females were asked to smell them and rate the shirts for pleasantness and sexiness.

The women rated the t-shirts as more pleasant and sexy if they came from a man with a different set of MHC genes. Therefore, Wedekind et al. concluded that people are motivated to find a mate with different immune system genes so their offspring will have stronger immune systems.

Facial symmetry

Facial symmetry is an indication a person has experienced fewer genetic and environmental disturbances, such as diseases, toxins, **malnutrition**, or genetic mutations while growing. It also is suggestive of greater cognitive health, with symmetry indexing the reliability or precision of **developmental** processes (Penke et al., 2009). Linking both cognitive and physical processes supports the **bodily integrity hypothesis** that assumes scoring well on cognitive ability tests might be an indicator of a more general tendency for complex systems in the body to be efficient and healthy (Deary, 2012).

Although the causes of these associations are not understood, bodily cues such as facial symmetry may indicate good cognitive health and better physical health. It has been suggested facial symmetry can be linked with the mathematical equation known as the 'golden ratio', which refers to pleasing, harmonious proportions that conform to a mathematical equation.

Achieving symmetry is a difficult task during human growth, requiring billions of cell reproductions while maintaining a parallel structure. Therefore, achieving symmetry is a visible signal of genetic health.

MHC genes control the immunological self/non-self discrimination, and subsequently tissue rejection and immune recognition of infectious diseases. Therefore, MHC genes are involved in making sure people stay healthy.

TOK When Pythagoras said that 'all is number', could he have meant that even love or beauty has a mathematical formulation?

Perceiving symmetry has a clear cognitive element and is cross-cultural, suggesting it has biological origins. However, it should be noted there are also cross-cultural differences in what is considered beautiful.

Ovulation

Ovulation is thought to influence what characteristics women find attractive in men as well as their own physical appearance, which influences their attractiveness to prospective partners.

Key study: Puts (2005)

Aim: To measure the effect of ovulation on perceived attractiveness of male voices. The study assumed females' perception of 'attraction' changes as they move through their ovulation cycle.

Procedure: Puts obtained voice recordings of 30 men attempting to persuade a woman to go out on a romantic date. Then 142 heterosexual women listened to the recordings and rated each man's attractiveness for a short-term sexual encounter and a long-term committed relationship.

Findings: Women said the deeper voices were more attractive in both mating contexts, but deeper voices were particularly preferred when considering them as prospects for sexual, short-term encounters. Women in the **fertile** phase of their ovulation cycle showed the strongest attraction to men with deep voices.

Conclusion: There is a clear link between ovulation cycles and the perception of attractive characteristics in prospective mates.

Puts et al. (2012) aimed to investigate the impact of woman's cycle on **fertility cues**. They assumed female hormonal shifts may cause facial and vocal changes in women (known as fertility cues) that rendered them more attractive during the most fertile stage of their **menstrual cycle**. They **operationalized** fertility by measuring when **progesterone** levels were at their lowest and **estrogen** levels were at their highest.

At two points in their menstrual cycles Puts et al. took:

- photographs of 202 women's faces

- voice recordings of the women's speaking voices

- saliva samples to measure hormone levels during both sampling sessions.

Five hundred men rated the attractiveness of the women's faces and voices from one of the two sessions. The ratings from the first session were averaged for each woman and compared with ratings for her second session. Puts et al. found that men rate women as more attractive when they are at the most fertile phase of their ovulation cycle.

They also tested female participants and asked 500 women to rate other women's attractiveness across their cycles. They scored the photographs and vocal recordings based on two measures: flirtatiousness and perceived attractiveness to men. They found the female participants also rated the subjects higher on both measures when the subjects were in their more fertile phase.

Ovulation is thought to influence what characteristics women find attractive in men as well as own their physical appearance, which influences their attractiveness to prospective partners. However, caution should be used when assuming such fertility cues are a clear advert for fertility.

Puts et al. concluded the ovulation cycle influences fertility cues for women that are perceived by both men and other women. It suggests facial changes over a woman's cycle could make her appear more or less attractive and could be the result of blood flow, causing colour changes in the face, changes in acne, or changes in puffiness due to water retention.

However, caution should be used when assuming such fertility cues are a clear advert for fertility. It can be assumed cyclic changes of the fertility cues are 'leaked' rather than an explicit advertisement of fertility. Therefore, they are a by-product of female reproductive biology rather than traits that evolved to advertise fertility.

It is thought that unlike female chimps and other mammals, human females conceal their ovulation, giving them more control over their reproduction. Concealing ovulation afforded female ancestors the ability to cheat on their mates, because their mates could not concentrate '**mate guarding**' activities near ovulation if they could not tell when it occurred. This allowed females to obtain the best genes for their offspring (Puts et al., 2012).

The notion of control would suggest females are conscious of the effect their fertility cues have on other people. Haselton et al. (2007) aimed to determine whether female ovulation could be marked by observable changes in **overt** behaviour such as levels of ornamentation and dress style. Thirty partnered women were invited to be photographed during high- and low-fertility cycle phases while wearing dresses and ornamentation. Fifty-nine point five per cent of the women were in a high-fertility phase and 40.5 per cent were in a low-fertility phase.

Forty-two participants were shown the images of the women and asked to rate which women were trying to look more attractive. It was found that the closer a woman was to her fertility phase the more the participants thought she dressed more attractively. This was determined through the amount of ornamentation women wore and how their clothes were perceived.

34.1.3 The role of cognitive factors in the formation of relationships

A cognitive approach to relationship formation assumes cognitive processes influence who people form relationships with.

Physiological arousal

Physiological arousal is a biological phenomenon; however, it has to be interpreted before a person can act. For example, Dutton and Aron (1974) aimed to test if physiological arousal can influence attraction. The researchers selected two bridges in Canada; one bridge was higher and shakier than the other and therefore more frightening. A female interviewer stood on these bridges and stopped men aged between 18 and 35 years old to ask them various questions. She then asked the men to write a story connected with a picture she gave them. She then gave them the telephone number of the psychology department and told them they could call if they wanted to talk further. She told participants a different name depending on which bridge they were on.

TOK Does the presence of underlying biological universals help or hinder explanations of the human experience in human relationship psychology? What is the future for psychology as an academic subject if human behaviour can be reduced to biological determinants?

279

The **independent variables** in this study were the levels of fear and arousal, operationalized by type of bridge (shaky and high or not). The **dependent variable** was the levels of attraction, operationalized by the number of phone calls received by the psychology department (which produced **quantitative** data), as well as the levels of sexual content in stories the participants were asked to write. Therefore, the results were both quantitative and qualitative in nature.

The results showed only two of the 16 men from the regular bridge called the phone number, compared with nine out of 18 from the frightening bridge. In addition, there was more sexual content in the stories from the frightening bridge. They concluded that attraction is stronger when there is more physiological arousal from the danger of the bridge. The researchers suggest that attraction occurs when physiological arousal is interpreted as sexual excitement.

Perception of attraction

Perception influences how people think, feel, and behave. For example, Dion (1972) asked women to read reports of severe classroom disruptions by school children. In some cases the report was accompanied by a photograph of an 'attractive' child, while in other cases the photo was of an 'unattractive' child. The subjects tended to blame the disruptive behaviour on the 'unattractive' children, saying that it was easy to see that they were 'brats'. Alternatively, when the photo was of an 'attractive' child, the women were more likely to excuse him or her.

This study is **gender** specific but it suggests perceived physical attractiveness influences thoughts, feelings, and behaviour even when the 'attraction' is non-sexual in nature. The **halo effect** is the false correlation of positive characteristics such as the assumption that someone who has a few positive characteristics has many. A halo effect is sometimes associated with physical attractiveness, i.e. people tend to assume that physically attractive people have other positive characteristics. Verhulst et al. (2010) found attractiveness and familiarity to be strong predictors for selecting people for leadership roles.

Similarity and attraction

Markey and Markey (2007) investigated the extent to which perceived similarity is a factor in the way people choose partners. They recruited 103 female and 66 male single undergraduate students through advertisements to participate in their study. The participants first completed a questionnaire where they rated their own personality in terms of values and attitudes, and then described the personality of their romantic ideal also in terms of values and attitudes. They also completed filler questionnaires that disguised the true purpose of this study. Their perception of their own values was similar to their perception of their ideal partner's values and attitudes and provides empirical support for the notion that people are attracted to partners they perceive to be similar to themselves.

Self-esteem

Kiesler and Baral (1970) aimed to test whether boosting the feelings of **self-esteem** in male participants would increase their chances of talking to an attractive woman. They issued a fake **IQ** test that was given to male participants. They were then given

Cognitive factors such as interpretations of physiological changes, perceptions of attraction, and similarity and self-esteem influence relationship formation.

280

fake scores that were either high or low. The men were asked to wait in a room and an 'attractive' female entered. They found that the men who had been given high IQ scores were quicker to talk to the woman. Kiesler and Baral (1970) concluded that self-esteem influences the chances of individuals interacting.

Aronson and Linder (1965) aimed to test how a specific series of 'accidentally' overheard compliments would affect male attraction toward women. The participant 'accidentally' overheard the experimenter describe them in one of four ways: all positive, all negative, initially negative but becoming positive, or initially positive but becoming negative. They were then asked to rate the experimenter for attractiveness. The participants liked the experimenter when the evaluation was completely positive; they liked the experimenter even more when the evaluation was initially negative but became positive.

Aronson and Linder (1965) concluded that males prefer a situation when they feel they have overcome an obstacle by changing from unattractive to attractive. Winning people over is more rewarding and boosts self-esteem. Although it should be noted that the difference in participants' initial level of self-esteem before the experiment began may have affected the results. For example, participants with higher self-esteem may not have been affected greatly by negative comments.

34.2 Role of communication in personal relationships

Content focus

Discuss the role of communication in personal relationships.

Interpersonal communication refers to the exchange of information between two or more people using direct or indirect methods. The focus of the study of interpersonal communication is not only on the message itself but also whether the receiver understands the message.

34.2.1 Communicating openness and assurance

Openness means talking about shared history and telling your partner things about yourself that they do not know. It can be viewed as a form of reciprocation where people give the gift of 'sharing' valuable information in a social exchange. Giving assurances means offering comfort and showing an interest in their emotional well-being.

Fitzpatrick and Ritchie (1994) argued that people have internalized ideologies that act as marital **schemata**. These are internal cognitive models which then frame their actions and perceptions regarding communication. For example, those who saw themselves as 'traditional couples' viewed themselves as more dependent on each other, which led them to have high levels of **assurance** but low levels of openness. 'Independent couples' communicated more in highly expressive styles, with unconventional values and moderate levels of interdependence. It could be argued that 'traditional' couples wanted to avoid conflict and so were less open, whereas

To what extent can attraction be explained by evolutionary pressures?

Interpersonal communication refers to the exchange of information between two or more people using direct or indirect methods.

How can complex and deeply personal phenomena such as communication be measured in the human sciences? Researchers may focus on elements they can quantify to allow for statistical analysis to take place and to allow their research be replicated by others.

'independent' couples wanted to solve problems rather than avoid them. Therefore, communication plays different roles in different relationships.

34.2.2 Managing negativity

Gottman (2000; 2003) argues there are four major emotional reactions that are destructive within relationships and can be used to predict **divorce**: criticism, defensiveness, stonewalling, and contempt. Among these four, Gottman considers contempt the most potent. Couples who avoid these emotions in their relationships will have more successful couplings, but it should be noted that the presence of negative emotions does not mean there is a problem in the relationship.

According to Gottman, anger does not necessarily have to have a negative impact on relationships. Happy couples can be as frequently angry as unhappy couples and if anger is communicated appropriately it can actually help maintain relationships.

Furthermore, living with an unresolved conflict can be a normal and healthy part of relationship maintenance. Gladwell (2005) found that 69 per cent of happy couples still have the very same unresolved conflicts after ten years, yet remain happy because they do not get gridlocked in the conflict and manage to work around it.

> John Gottman argues there are four major emotional reactions that are destructive within relationships and can be used to predict divorce: criticism, defensiveness, stonewalling, and contempt.

Key study: Gottman (2003)

Aim: To test whether older married couples and younger married couples have different approaches to managing conflict, and to test if these different approaches can be correlated with unhappiness in the marriage.

Procedure: In a highly controlled setting, 156 married couples came to a laboratory after not talking to each other for eight hours. In the laboratory, they were observed discussing three topics, and physiological measurements such as heart rate were also taken. The couples discussed what events had happened that day and agreed on one pleasant topic and another topic that they knew they would disagree about. The discussions were video recorded and different emotions were observed.

Findings: The older couples, with longer marriages, communicated more affection to their partner during the discussions, but middle-aged married couples displayed more negative emotion. Couples in unhappy marriages expressed more negative emotions.

Conclusion: Couples in happy marriages were better able to manage their emotional displays to show more positive emotions while withholding negative emotions. Therefore, in successful relationships, people communicate with their partner in a way that avoids negative results.

34.2.3 The role of listening

Ahmad and Reid (2008) argue it is necessary for partners to practise listening to understand how their partner feels and respond in a way that shows they have actually understood what has been communicated. They came to this conclusion while researching traditional roles within marriage as they wanted to test whether couples who believe in traditional roles in a marriage have less satisfaction.

They asked 114 married people of South Asian descent living in Canada to complete a questionnaire. Only one partner completed the questionnaire, and the researchers used a **snowball method** to contact participants: the first participants were given copies of the questionnaire to give to friends and family. The questionnaire contained questions about their attitudes toward marriage; their communication style in the marriage, and their marital satisfaction.

They found traditional role beliefs did not result in lower satisfaction. However, there was a connection between satisfaction and the listening style in the relationship. Those who had traditional beliefs and did not listen to understand their partner were less likely to be satisfied. What is insightful about this particular study is the use of the arranged marriage sample. Despite having less choice in their partner, listening played a key role in producing satisfaction in the relationship. Therefore, arranged marriages with traditional role beliefs can be satisfying, but it is necessary for the partners to practise listening to understand how their partner feels. This is important because it suggests that communication may have a stronger role in maintaining happy relationships than the cultural factors that cause people to marry.

34.2.4 Gender differences in communication styles

Understanding gender differences in communication styles may help to maintain relationships (although this is probably most relevant to heterosexual relationships). Lakoff (1975) argued that women have a less 'powerful' form of speech, meaning they tend to swear less, speak more politely, and use more **tag questions** and **intensifiers**. An intensifier serves to enhance and give additional emotional context to the word it modifies. According to Lakoff, women are more likely to use words such as 'so', 'really' and 'very', which bring an extra emotional component to conversations that are not always positive. However, Lakoff was writing in 1975 so, while it may still offer some insight, this statement is open to question in modern Western settings.

Flora and Segrin (2003) carried out a **longitudinal study** and found negative feelings of women toward men could predict problems for the marriage. However, it was reported that the women may not actually realize how harmful their negative messages can be, suggesting men and women may perceive negative messages differently.

In addition, women appear to **self-disclose** more than men. Self-disclosure refers to sharing facts about oneself, usually of an intimate nature. A meta-analysis of self-disclosure studies by Collins and Miller (1994) found people who self-disclose more are more liked and they are more likely to self-disclose to people who they also like, creating a loop of self-disclosure that increases intimacy and being liked. Women may expect the same level of self-disclosure from their male partners that they are accustomed to with their female friends, but men appear to be less interested in this method of communication. For example, Thelwall et al. (2009) compared emotional comments between males and females on MySpace®. Females were more likely to give and receive positive comments than men.

Tannen (1990) also studied communication differences in men and women. She found:

* women are more likely to respond to another person's negative feelings with understanding and acceptance ('It is okay to feel like that, sometimes I feel that way too.')

Lakoff (1975), argued that women have a less 'powerful' form of speech, meaning they tend to swear less, speak more politely, and use more tag questions and intensifiers. An intensifier serves to enhance and give additional emotional context to the word it modifies.

- men see negative feelings as a complaint about a problem and so set about trying to solve it. For example, a woman may complain about weight gain during pregnancy. Another woman would say, 'It feels bad because you feel like you have lost control of your body.' A man might say, 'Don't worry. You can join a gym.' In this scenario, the woman feels like her feelings have not been dealt with, whereas the man feels like he has solved a problem and cannot understand why his solution is not appreciated.

- women use more language 'tags' (yup, uh huh, right, yeah). This happens in conjunction with the main speaker, serving as 'support' in the form of overlapping speech. So, when a man says, 'I want to buy a new motorbike,' and the wife says, 'uh huh,' he hears consent, but she was just showing she was listening.

- men interrupt and change the topic more frequently, perhaps because men are competitive and combative and prefer 'banter', which is a teasing and playful exchange of remarks

- women tend to be more inclusive and seek other people's opinion.

West and Zimmerman (1987) investigated the tendency of the different genders to interrupt and use silence in conversation. Through quantitative counting they found that all overlaps and most interruptions during conversations between different genders were made by males.

Count how many times males interrupt a conversation compared with females. Are the findings of West and Zimmerman (1987) supported?

It could be concluded that frequent interruption and overlaps by males is due to the males wanting to 'compete' for conversational advantage and expecting others to do the same. However, caution should be used when assuming this is a universal trait. For example, Ueno (2004) explored the differences between interaction styles of Japanese men and women and found Japanese women were slightly more likely to interrupt the conversation than Japanese men.

34.3 Why relationships change or end

Content focus

Discuss explanations for why relationships change or end.

34.3.1 Communication changes

Knapp et al. (2014) proposed a model (See Figure 34.1) to describe the stages that people go through from the beginning to the end of a relationship. For example: at the start, people become closer by using 'we' instead of 'I' when talking to other people, in order to emphasize their status as a partner. In the later stages, there is less communication between the partners and the 'I' is used more often. This is a sign that the relationship might end.

Stage	Typical events and behaviour
Coming together – growth of the relationship	
Initiation	• first meeting and brief interaction • first impressions are formed
Experimenting	• small talk, testing the other person, and searching for common ground intensifies • relationship becomes friendship • personal disclosures become common, especially regarding feelings about the relationship
Integrating	• the two lives become more connected and partners consider each other in making plans • those outside the relationship become more aware of the couple • use of 'we' becomes more frequent
Bonding	• some form of commitment is made, often ritualized, like engagement, marriage, cohabitation, or friendship rituals
Coming apart – decline of the relationship	
Differentiating	• differences become more obvious and partners desire independence • some arguments over this may begin • more use of 'I' and 'my'
Circumscribing	• partners avoid difficult topics in conversation as communication is restricted, but public appearances are maintained
Stagnating	• further restrictions in conversation; partners 'know' what the other will say and prefer not to start talking • may stay together in order to avoid greater pain of breaking up
Avoiding	• one or both partners choose to avoid contact, through lateness or alternate commitments, or direct expressions of disinterest
Terminating	• physical distancing and disassociation as partners prepare to be individuals

Figure 34.1 Knapp and Vangelisti model for change in relationships

There is an emphasis on communication in the Knapp and Vangelisti (1996) model. According to the model, couples begin their relationship actively seeking ways to communicate with each other and a change occurs when the relationship begins to end and they actively seek ways to avoid communicating.

The model explains how this change occurs, but does not fully explain *why* it does. The lack of why in the model means it has low **predictive validity** as it cannot be used to predict which couples will have problems in their relationship. It does have *some* predictive validity, as it can show what the next steps might be.

People in a relationship have a choice about how they communicate their thoughts and feelings. '**Patterns of accommodation**' refers to the process where people respond to their partner's negative behaviour with a certain type of accommodation. These can be divided into constructive accommodations and destructive accommodations.

Constructive accommodations are behaviours such as discussing problems openly; showing and feeling forgiveness and being patient enough to wait for problems to subside. **Destructive accommodations** are behaviours such as giving the 'silent treatment', referring to past failures and physical avoidance. Relationships change for the negative or end when partners adopt greater destructive accommodations than constructive accommodations.

34.3.2 Cognitive change

Attribution changes

When we try to explain other people's behaviour we do not do so in a logical way. We give explanations or attributions for behaviour we see in our environment. Attributions can be dependent on how we feel about the person whose behaviour we are explaining.

Bradbury and Fincham (1990) investigated whether marriage quality was affected by attributions by conducting a meta-analysis of studies. They concluded that successful marriages had **positive biases** to the partner: positive behaviours were seen as the consequence of **dispositional** attributions; negative behaviours were seen as the consequence of **situational** factors. Therefore, if a partner did something negative it was attributed to situational rather than dispositional factors and vice versa.

For unsuccessful marriages the effect was reversed: positive behaviours were seen as the consequence of situational attributions; negative behaviours were seen as the consequence of dispositional factors and vice versa. Therefore, relationships can change negatively or end when there is an increase in negative attributions between the couple.

Perceptions of benefits and rewards

Social exchange theory (SET) assumes relationships are maintained through a constant **cost-benefit analysis** and the costs must not outweigh the benefits (Thibaut and Kelley, 1959). The more one invests in a relationship the more one expects in return. A further assumption of SET is balance. It argues that balance must be maintained over the long term with regards to partners' investment and returns: relationships change for the worse or end when there is an imbalance in investment and returns.

SET assumes relationships are maintained through a constant cost-benefit analysis and the costs must not outweigh the benefits (Thibaut and Kelley, 1959).

However, it is more accurate to talk of perception of imbalances and inequality because each is dependent on an individual's point of view. In addition, the theory cannot be tested rigorously because it is difficult to quantify costs and benefits in a relationship, particularly when they are so open to individual differences and perceptions.

Carlson et al. (2014) analysed data on housework and sex from the 2006 Marital and Relationship Survey on a representative sample of 600 married and cohabiting low to moderate-income couples with children. They found that couples who shared the routine housework equally had the most sex (7.74 times a month). They reported the highest level of satisfaction with that frequency compared to the other couples, and also the highest quality of the sexual relationship. Therefore, when men are expected to take part in the housework and share in the upbringing of children, and perceive this as fair within a cost-benefit analysis, it can lead to increased intimacy in Western societies.

However, cost-benefit analysis is dependent on perception and expectation. If a marriage is built on traditional expectations then the perception of costs/rewards will be different to one built on non-traditional expectations. 'Traditional marriage' may refer to a model where the man focuses on providing economically for the family (the breadwinner) and the woman focuses on taking care of the home and being the main care provider for the children.

Despite Norway having high levels of gender equality, divorce rates for the couples who did equal housework is approximately 50 per cent higher than that of the more traditional couples, where the woman does it all (Hansen and Slagsvold, 2012). This could be interpreted as traditional roles providing clear rules for each person where cost-benefits are also clear, and suggests relationships are more likely to be maintained when agreed roles match the expectations for each partner and each partner feels as though they are being fairly treated within a cost-benefit **paradigm**.

34.3.3 Sociocultural change

Empowerment and financial independence of women

Changes in cultural norms in the West and increasingly in other non-Western countries mean women are more involved in the paid workforce and are actively developing careers. The employment rate of women aged 16 to 64 rose from 53 per cent in 1971 to 66 per cent in 2012, and during the same time period there has been falling employment for men (Office for National Statistics, 2013).

One possible factor is the rise of the service sector and decline of heavy industry beginning in the 1960s, which advantages women and disadvantages men. There are many advantages, both for women and for society as a whole, when women enter paid employment but it also influences relationships. Careers take time and energy to develop, and there is evidence that serious or long-term relationships are being delayed because of this, which puts women under pressure as their fertility declines. The man in the relationship who is also developing a career may feel less pressure to commit as he is not under the same biological time pressure as his fertility does not decline. Therefore, in the early stages of a serious relationship women may feel more pressure because they increasingly have to manage a career and their desire to have children. However, in later relationship stages, women have become more financially independent as well as building up their own financial capital such as investing equally in the family property. Therefore, women are now more able to support themselves outside of marriage than they were in the past, and this, coupled with easier and cheaper divorce options, allows them more freedom of choice if they feel their relationship has broken down.

Less stigma for divorce in Western cultures

UK statistics suggest that divorces are becoming more socially acceptable and are easier to arrange in Western societies.

Year	Number of divorces per 1000 men over 60	Number of divorces per 1000 women over 60
1991	1.6	1.2
2011	2.3	1.6

Research the top ten reasons for divorce in your own culture. Compare with another group or student who has a different culture. Does one gender initiate divorce more than the other? What might be the reasons for this?

Figure 34.2 UK divorce statistics in 1991 and 2011 (Office for National Statistics, 2011)

No-fault divorce became an option in some US states in the 1950s. With this change to the law, couples no longer needed to prove that one person was at fault in order to file for divorce; they could simply say the marriage had broken down. By 1970, almost all US states had laws allowing no-fault divorces. From 1940 to 1965, the divorce rate remained near ten divorces for every 1000 married women. By 1979, the rate was 20 for every 1000 married women.

Furthermore, religion has declined in Western societies as a major influence on people's decisions in relationships. This, coupled with legal relaxations, has meant couples are more likely to seek a way out when relationships become problematic.

Ageing and active population

Overall, people in the West are living longer, healthier lives as a result of better healthcare and better education about living healthy lifestyles. While there have been some concerns about levels of obesity and sedentary lifestyles, life expectancy is increasing in most Western developed economies.

Figure 34.3 Graph showing the number of people aged over 60 in Canada

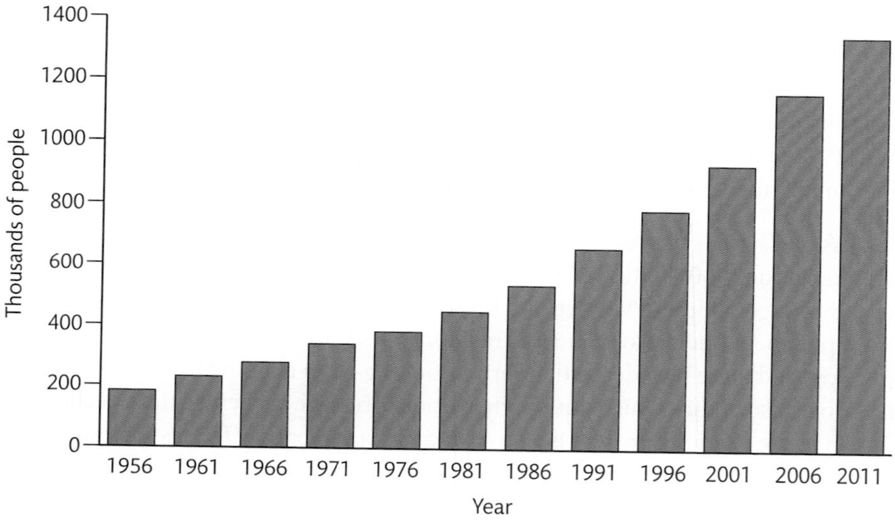

In the past, couples would reach late middle age and know their lives would soon be over. However, people now increasingly look to start second major relationships as they move through their elongated life cycles. In 2011, the total number of divorces in the UK was 118 000. Of these, 9500 were granted to men aged 60 – a 73 per cent rise from 1991. The figures suggest that people increasingly choose to end relationships as they get older, because they have more healthy years ahead of them.

Figures suggest people increasingly choose to end relationships as they get older because they have healthier, longer lives ahead of them.

This is being reflected in **sexually transmitted disease** (STD) rates as people end long-term relationships and embark on new sexual liaisons. For example, in 2013, people aged 55 and older accounted for more than one-quarter (26 per cent) of the estimated 1.2 million people living with diagnosed or undiagnosed HIV infection in the USA (Centers for Disease Control and Prevention, 2017). Furthermore, new trends in medicine have given older men medications for erectile dysfunction, which have enabled more of them to engage in sexual activity throughout their older years. However, older men tend to be less educated about STD risk and actually perceive themselves to be at a low risk, which helps explain the STD figures in this age group.

35 Group dynamics

Topic focus

Discuss factors influencing group dynamics.

35.1 Theoretical foundations

35.1.1 Biological influences

Inclusive fitness refers to the ability of an individual organism to pass on its genes to the next generation. The notion takes into account the direct descendants of the individual as well as the shared genes of close relatives. It can be used to explain how a gene can increase its chances of evolutionary success by indirectly promoting the reproduction and survival of other individuals who share the same genes.

Inclusive fitness can be used to explain why individuals engage in behaviour that helps their ingroup (sometimes at a cost to themselves) while competing with their outgroup. It is the main assumption underpinning kin selection theory, which suggests **intragroup** cooperation behaviour is an adaptation as organisms are motivated to help others who are genetically similar to themselves.

However, it can also be assumed that intergroup competitiveness can be considered an adaptation. For example, non-human primates appear to be sensitive and react to the rankings of other individuals within groups (Sapolsky, 2005) as well as to social category fault lines, distinguishing between the ingroup and outgroups (Bergman et al., 2003). However, competitiveness can also be seen in more primitive species who appear sensitive to situational factors, such as the number of potential competitors. This has been shown in beetle larvae (Smiseth and Moore, 2004) and cockroaches (Zajonc et al., 1969).

35.1.2 Social identity theory

SIT was developed by Tajfel and his colleagues (e.g. Tajfel and Turner, 1979) and assumes that humans naturally divide the social environment into ingroups, to which an individual belongs ('us'), and outgroups, to which the individual does not belong ('them' or 'the other').

Social categorization reduces perceived differences within the ingroup (we are similar to one another); reduces perceived differences in the outgroup (they are all the same) and increases perceived differences between the ingroup and the outgroup (we are different from them). The exaggeration of ingroup and outgroup differences and intragroup similarities is called the **category accentuation effect**. Individuals usually belong to many groups at the same time and, depending on the group with which they are associating, their behaviour is likely to change to match the group's behaviour.

Social identity refers to the process of how people perceive themselves according to their membership of social groups. It is separate from personal identity, which is how they perceive themselves according to how they perceive their personality traits

Inclusive fitness refers to the ability of an individual organism to pass on its genes to the next generation. The notion takes into account the direct descendants of the individual as well as the shared genes of close relatives. It can be used to explain why individuals engage in behaviour that helps their ingroup (sometimes at a cost to themselves) while competing with their outgroup.

TOK Perceptions of the 'other' are often a mechanism used in the arts to generate tension and drama. To what extent are other areas of knowledge an equally valid way of investigating the human condition?

(Turner, 1982). People tend to assimilate into their group by adopting the group's identity by behaving in the same ways that the group members behave. The group becomes the person's ingroup.

Social comparison refers to the process of how people categorize themselves within a group and so identify themselves as members of the group. They then tend to compare their group (their ingroup) with respect to another group (their outgroup). To improve their self-esteem, group members see their group in a positive light and other groups in a negative light. People also tend to perceive the people in other groups (outgroups) negatively. This is known as **positive distinctiveness** and leads to **prejudicial** thinking and **discriminatory** acts.

SIT can be used to explain **ethnocentrism**, which refers to **ingroup-serving bias** and involves:

- positive behaviours by ingroup members being attributed to dispositional factors

- negative behaviours of ingroup members being attributed to situational factors

- positive behaviours of outgroup members being attributed to situational factors

- negative behaviours by outgroup members being attributed to dispositional factors.

In summary, if we do good things it is because we are good and if we misbehave that is due to external factors. The reverse applies to 'them'.

SIT can also be used to explain stereotyping, which refers to fixed and oversimplified images of an individual or group. Stereotyping of individuals usually occurs because they are perceived to be members of an outgroup and it is assumed they possess the characteristics of the other group members. Therefore, the categorization process that underlies stereotyping implies that members of an outgroup share common attributes, which means they are seen as more similar to each other than they are to other groups' members. SIT shows that perceptions of group **homogeneity**, of both ingroups and outgroups, are linked to social identity processes. Therefore, stereotypes cannot be understood by considering them solely as cognitive devices to simplify thinking, but also the product of sociocultural processes that are ongoing and affect people's thinking.

Group dynamics refer to a system of behaviours and psychological processes that occur within a social ingroup (intragroup dynamics) or between social outgroups (intergroup dynamics). Ingroups and outgroups are defined in terms of comparisons and contrasts with outgroups (Yuki, 2003). The study of group dynamics can be useful in understanding **prosocial** behaviour, prejudice, discrimination, and violence.

35.2 Cooperation and competition

Content focus

Contrast cooperation and competition in relation to group dynamics.

Cooperation refers to a prosocial process of individuals working or acting in a way that leads to mutual benefit. Competition is the direct opposite of cooperation where

---

Cooperation refers to a prosocial process of individuals working or acting in a way that leads to mutual benefit. Competition is the direct opposite of cooperation where individuals work toward a selfish goal that cannot be shared by the competing parties. Cooperation usually occurs within ingroups as an intragroup process; competition usually occurs between outgroups as an intergroup process.

individuals work toward a selfish goal that cannot be shared by the competing parties. Cooperation usually occurs within ingroups as an *intra*group process; competition usually occurs between outgroups as an *inter*group process.

35.2.1 Cooperation

Mere knowledge of shared **group identity** increases cooperative behaviour (Brewer, 2008). The viability of organized groups is increased when their members behave in ways that help the group to function more effectively (Tyler and Blader, 2000).

Tyler and Blader (2001) identified three types of cooperation within ingroups:

* the following of group rules

* conducting work on behalf of the group

* an intention to stay within the group.

However, while intention is primarily cognitive in nature, there is also a social element. If intention is not signalled clearly enough, it might be assumed that the individual lacks motivation to cooperate within the group.

They also distinguish between two types of basic cooperative behaviour:

* mandatory (or required) behaviours, which are specified to be part of particular roles in a group; they originate in the group or from the group leader.

* discretionary (or non-required) behaviours, which go beyond what is required; they originate in a group member, not the group.

SIT can be used to explain ingroup cooperation. For example, it can be assumed people are willing to cooperate with their group as long as it provides them with a positive social identity. When this is not the case, and people are offered the possibility of changing group membership, they will be tempted to do so (Doosje et al., 1999).

This involves a clear ongoing cognitive process as the individual constantly measures the perceived quality of the group as well as the extent to which they are considered a member of it. Both will reflect on the individual's sense of self-worth relative to the group, because the group's success can bring about benefits for their self-identity. Therefore, there is a clear link between the success of the group and the maintenance of a positive sense of self.

Tyler and Blader (2001) argue the extent to which an individual identifies with the group will directly affect ingroup cooperation. **Identification** refers to the degree to which people cognitively merge their sense of self and the group. It can be expected that when people identify more with their group, they will be more willing to act cooperatively. For example, they will invest more time and energy in working toward the group succeeding, in terms of mandatory but also discretionary behaviour. The stronger the identification with the group, the more important it is to the individual for the group to succeed.

Key study: Tyler and Blader (2001)

Aim: To measure the influence of identification on the degree to which people cooperate with groups.

Procedure: Researchers defined identification as the individual's cognitive intermingling of self and group. They asked participants (404 employees (50:50 male to female ratio) with an average age of 30, who worked in a variety of settings chosen to maximize variation in the level of instrumental investment in the work environment) to complete a questionnaire **anonymously**, assessing on a scale of 1–6 the extent to which they defined themselves in terms of their work group membership. For example, they were asked to respond to statements such as: 'My work is important to the way I think of myself as a person', 'When someone praises the accomplishments of my work organization, it feels like a personal compliment to me', 'When I talk about where I work I usually say "we" rather than "they"'. Cooperative behaviour was investigated by **self-report** and was measured according to levels of compliance, deference, and discretionary behaviour. For example, participants were asked how much they thought they followed the rules, implemented their supervisor's directives even when unobserved, exerted 'full effort' in their roles, volunteered to help others, helped their supervisor, and the extent to which they were considering leaving their place of work. They were also **reverse scored** on the extent to which they thought they completed substandard work and hindered their supervisor.

Findings: People's identification with their group has an important role in shaping their behaviours within that group. Identification is a strong and significant predictor of compliance, deference, and discretionary behaviour. Extra-role behaviour shows an especially strong effect for identification.

Conclusion: People who identify most with their group are more likely to cooperate, less likely to engage in uncooperative behaviours and more likely to engage in discretionary behaviours, even when they are not being observed.

Identity itself is also influenced by perception. For example, the perceived status of the group will influence the degree to which people receive a positive social identity as a result of being a member of a group. If groups serve an important function in the creation and maintenance of a positive social identity, then members of groups perceived as having high status should cooperate more because the person will want to maintain their close connection with the group and therefore maintain the group's existence. The higher the status of the group, the more important it is to the individual for the group to succeed to maintain their positive self-identity.

35.2.2 Competition

The mere existence of socially comparative groups leads to competitive behaviour (Festinger, 1954). According to social comparison theory, individuals are propelled by a basic drive to improve their performance and minimize discrepancies between their and other individuals' performance. Thus, competitiveness is one manifestation of the social comparison process.

The mere existence of socially comparative groups leads to competitive behaviour (Festinger, 1954).

Garcia et al. (2013) argue that **comparison concerns** are the prime motivator for competitive behaviour. These are defined as the desire to achieve or maintain a 'superior relative position'. However, it can be noted that their notion has a definitive quality to it and it is more accurate to state the *perception* of a superior relative position rather than an absolute relative position.

Comparison concerns are dependent on:

- the relevance of a performance dimension to the individual (Tesser, 1988), meaning competitiveness increases the more relevant the activity is to the individual

- the degree of the individual's similarity to the target (Kilduff et al., 2010), meaning competitiveness increases the more similar the individual is to their rival

- the degree of the individual's closeness to the target (Pleban and Tesser 1981), meaning competitiveness increases the closer the individual is to their rival.

Key study: Taylor and Moriarty (1987)

Aim: To measure the extent to which competition and physical distinctiveness play a critical role in **interracial** conflict. It was predicted that the tendency to favour the ingroup over the outgroup is enhanced when groups are competitive rather than interdependent, and when groups are racially dissimilar rather than racially similar.

Procedure: Fifty-six white female college students who were enrolled in a psychology course at the University of Maryland (USA) participated in return for extra course credit. As each participant arrived for a session they were given a numbered card in a seemingly random fashion. However, by prearrangement, the numbers assigned to the participants were always even (two and four) while those for **confederates** were always odd (one and three). They were told that the purpose of the study was to investigate the efficiency and performance of small working groups. They were then informed that for the first part of the study they would be divided into two small groups, each of which would work on identical tasks for the same amount of time. The researcher then announced that participants holding even numbers (**naive** subjects) would be members of one small group, while those holding odd numbers (confederates) would be members of the other small group. Thus, it was possible to ensure that the ingroup was always white while the outgroup was either white (similar-race condition) or black (dissimilar-race condition). It was determined in pre-tests that participants were equally likely to believe in the randomness of their partnership assignments whether the outgroup was white or black. The relationship (interdependent or competitive) between the two small groups was then manipulated.
Interdependent conditions: Participants were told that any solutions to a problem devised by each small group would be combined in such a way as to provide the best overall solution to the task. If this combined solution met a predetermined standard, members of both groups could win a prize. It was emphasized that both groups could win.
Competition conditions: Participants were told that any solutions devised by each small group would be compared in order to determine which solution came closest to meeting a predetermined standard. The members of the group with the better

solution would win a prize. It was emphasized that one group would win and one group would lose.

The problems to solve were 'reading a case history of a delinquent **adolescent** and recommending an approach to his rehabilitation' and 'writing an advertising slogan for a new brand of toothpaste'. Participants were then asked to rate their mood toward their ingroup and outgroup. The questions were designed to disguise the true purpose of the experiment.

Findings:

- Significant ingroup bias occurred under all conditions.
- Participants exhibited greater ingroup bias in competition conditions than in interdependent conditions.
- Participants in competitive conditions exhibited both increased ingroup attraction and decreased outgroup attraction.
- Participants' attraction for both the ingroup and the outgroup was influenced by competition.

Conclusion: Weak identity can produce ingroup bias. For example, merely telling two strangers that they were members of one small problem-solving group led to significant ingroup preference in all inter-group conditions. However, an element of competition can enhance ingroup bias and lead to decreased outgroup attraction.

Evaluation: The female and Western-centric nature of the participant group mean caution should be used when generalizing the findings. Furthermore, Western societies have become more multi-ethnic since 1987, which means people may identify less with their ethnicities, which would mean the impact on intergroup competition would be less. However, the study does put a difficult subject on a secure empirical foundation. There have been previous studies that have also shown the phenomena of physical distinctiveness affecting intergroup competition. For example, Worchel et al. (1978) operationalized physical distinctiveness as differences in dress, so participants in two groups either dressed similarly (both groups wore white lab coats) or dressed dissimilarly (participants in one group wore white lab coats while subjects in a second group wore red lab coats). It was found that distinctive groups in a competitive relationship were least attracted to each other. Therefore, competition decreases ratings of attractiveness between groups who are seen as physically distinctive.

35.3 Prejudice and discrimination

Content focus

Discuss prejudice and discrimination in relation to group dynamics.

Prejudice refers to unjustified (usually negative) thoughts and feelings toward an individual or group based solely on the individual's perceived membership of a social group. Discrimination refers to behaviour (usually negative) toward an individual or group for being a perceived member of a social group.

Prejudice has effective as well as cognitive components, whereas discrimination is the behavioural extension of these. An individual can hold prejudicial views but these do not always manifest themselves in behaviour. Therefore, prejudice and discrimination are very difficult for psychology researchers to study.

People are usually aware of how socially unattractive prejudice and discrimination can be, and can be prone to the **social desirability bias**. Moreover, groups are not static, they are dynamic and represent social and personal constructions. An individual may perceive someone else as belonging to several groups, whereas the individual themselves may not consider themselves to be identifiable with those groups or may have completely different understandings of what those group labels mean.

35.3.1 Prejudice

Taylor and Moriarty (1987) demonstrated the extent to which competition and physical distinctiveness play a critical role in interracial conflict. They demonstrated how ingroup favouritism over the outgroup is enhanced when groups are competitive rather than interdependent, and when groups are racially dissimilar rather than racially similar. Therefore, physical distinctiveness as well as real or perceived competition leads to prejudicial thinking.

The **stereotype content model** (SCM) aims to identify the fundamental underlying dimensions that explain some ingroup/outgroup perceptions (Fiske et al., 2002). Fiske argues that thoughts and feelings regarding prejudice can be distilled into two fundamental dimensions of social perception: feelings of warmth and perceptions of competence. However, binary distinctions of high warmth and high competence toward the ingroup and low warmth and low competence toward the outgroup are not always possible or accurate. Frequent mixed clusters combine high warmth with low competence or high competence with low warmth. Furthermore, there are distinct emotions (pity, envy, admiration, contempt) that further differentiate the four competence–warmth combinations.

Therefore, feelings and perceptions toward outgroups are mixed, either pitying (low competence, high warmth) or envying (high competence, low warmth). Stereotypically, the 'status' of members of the outgroup usually predicted high competence and any perceived competition with an outgroup usually predicted low warmth. Consequently, it is too simplistic to assume ingroup perceptions of outgroups are characterized by antipathy. Ingroup perceptions of outgroups often include a mix of feelings and perceptions.

Key study: Fiske et al. (2002)

Aim: To measure the extent to which outgroups are defined by mixed perceptions and feelings.

Procedure: A number of studies were conducted using a questionnaire that was given to undergraduate students from the University of Massachusetts who were recruited from various psychology courses. They were asked to rate proposed outgroups on a five-point scale on the basis of how the groups are viewed by US society. Participants rated these groups on scales reflecting warmth, competence, perceived status, and perceived competition.
The instruction read, 'We are not interested in your personal beliefs, but in how you think they are viewed by others.' The instruction was intended to reduce social desirability concerns and to tap perceived cultural stereotypes. The outgroups were suggested by the researchers and chosen because they were seen as important for the US cultural scene (for example black people, 'blue-collar Southerners', elderly people, gay men, 'sexy' women, welfare recipients, Arabs, Asians, feminists, rich people).

Findings: Perceived status was highly correlated with perceived competence. Perceived competition negatively correlated with perceived lack of warmth.

Conclusion: Perceptions of outgroup members include mixed ascriptions of competence and warmth, as defined by low ratings on one dimension coupled with high ratings on the other. Moreover, stereotypes depict outgroups as competent to the extent that they are also perceived as powerful and high status; stereotypes depict outgroups as relatively warm and nice to the extent that they do not compete with others.

Evaluation: Fiske et al. make a number of relevant criticisms of their own work. For example, they state that outgroups were selected by the researchers and not by the participants. This allowed for **standardization** and measurement across numerous studies, but it also means the methodology is open to criticism that researchers chose the outgroups to fit their **hypothesis**.

Secondly, they state the trait scale was modified slightly across the various studies to address the issue of participant fatigue, which they argue was becoming a problem. This means caution should be used when generalizing from one study to another because they did not use standardized scales throughout the entire research.

Thirdly, the participants were University of Massachusetts undergraduates, so they may have accorded some positive attributes to any given outgroup because of their potential liberal political orientation, 'North-East American subcultural norms' or because of an adherence to the college ethos of **egalitarianism**.

Finally, Fiske et al. argue their own stereotype perceptions may not have been shared with the participants. For example, for 'sexy women' they had 'brainless bimbo' as a referencing image, whereas they state some of their own respondents may have been thinking 'villainous vamp'. However, this final criticism by Fiske et al. is in itself a fairly narrow-minded stereotype, as many people would have other stereotypes in mind when presented with the phrase 'sexy woman' rather than the two listed here.

It is too simplistic to assume ingroup perceptions of outgroups are characterized by antipathy. Ingroup perceptions of outgroups often include a mix of feelings and perceptions.

TOK How can prejudice and discrimination be measured in a reliable and valid way?

EE To what extent does prejudice and discrimination play a role in family relationships?

35.3.2 Discrimination

The behavioural element of discrimination means there has to be an appropriate sociocultural landscape for discriminatory behaviour to manifest. In order for behaviour to be projected into an environment, there has to be either a perceived positive consequence for those discriminating or a perceived lack of negative consequence. In this way, discrimination can become established and self-sustaining.

Etieyibo and Omiegbe (2016) explored the extent to which culture and religion are contributory factors in the discrimination against people with disabilities in Nigeria. Culture can be defined as a shared set of attitudes, beliefs, values, goals and practices that characterizes an institution, an organization, or a group (Uwagie-Eroet et al., 1998). Religion can be seen as part of culture and may be defined as a belief in the existence of a deity or a supernatural power, a being that created and controls the universe and who is worshipped on the basis of such belief (Etieyibo and Omiegbe, 2016).

The behavioural element of discrimination means there has to be an appropriate sociocultural landscape for discriminatory behaviour to manifest. In order for behaviour to be projected into an environment, there has to be either a perceived positive consequence for those discriminating or a perceived lack of negative consequence.

Discrimination against people with disabilities (and **albinism**) in Nigeria involves serious human rights abuses and can take the following forms:

- the burning of women who are thought to be witches because witches are believed to be evil

- the raping of women with mental illness because it is believed being intimate with them could bring wealth or prolong an individual's life

- the killing of people with albinism for rituals because it is believed their body parts could be used for potions that could bring wealth or prolong an individual's life (Oji, 2010). The body parts are then trafficked and sold.

Oliver (1990) argues that disability is a cultural construct and therefore discriminatory practices against persons with disabilities should be seen from this point of view. It is not only the case that people with disabilities are killed on the basis of disability beliefs (e.g. superstition), but these killings are also ritualized, suggesting perpetrators discriminate against disabled persons (and kill them) because they either believe that doing so would make them rich and successful or believe it is part of some ceremony rituals (Etieyibo and Omiegbe, 2016). Therefore, people with disabilities are targeted for their social, personal, and economic benefits, that is, killed for their **utility** value, which is sustained by belief systems embedded in culture (Abang, 1988).

As Etieyibo and Omiegbe (2016) conclude, both religion and culture exert powerful influence on many Nigerians, not only when it comes to negative attitudes toward people with disabilities, but also in their engagement in highly discriminatory practices against them.

It should be noted that the problem is not confined to Nigeria. Throughout history people with disabilities have been subjected to a large number of oppressive social attitudes, which have included hostility, distrust, pity, overprotection, and patronizing and discriminatory behaviour (Barton, 1993).

TOK

Can cultural norms be placed on a hierarchy that can be measured and moderated by a definitive ethical framework? On what basis can that ethical framework be explained and defended? Given the nature of culturally laden perceptions, how reliable is the research of a non-native observer?

35.4 Origins of conflict and conflict resolution

Content focus

Discuss the origins of conflict and conflict resolution.

Peace psychology is an academic field that focuses on peace and group conflict. The overall aim is to work toward sustainable peace through non-violent methods. This section will focus on the psychological dynamics of groups. However, it should be noted that peace psychology also encompasses politics and diplomacy; military and economic considerations; and sociocultural, international, and national structures that promote or undermine peace.

Peace psychology is an academic field that focuses on peace and group conflict. The overall aim is to work toward sustainable peace through non-violent methods.

Conflict is an ever-present hazard in many cultures around the world.

35.4.1 Origins of conflict

The previous pages have demonstrated how the origins of conflict between groups can be explained from biological, sociocultural, and cognitive perspectives. They are not mutually exclusive to one another. They can be summarized as follows.

- Evolutionary explanations such as inclusive fitness and kin selection theory show how individuals are instinctively driven to favour ingroups at the expense of outgroups. Therefore, intergroup competition and intragroup cooperation can be seen as adaptations.

- SIT was developed by Tajfel and his colleagues and assumes humans naturally divide the social environment into ingroups, to which an individual belongs, and outgroups, to which the individual does not belong.

- Social categorization reduces perceived differences within the ingroup (we are similar to one another); reduces perceived differences in the outgroup (they are all the same) and increases perceived differences between the ingroup and the outgroup (we are different from them). The exaggeration of in- and outgroup differences and intragroup similarities is called the category accentuation effect.

- Social identity is how people perceive themselves according to their membership of social groups.

- Social comparison means people improve their self-esteem by perceiving their ingroup in a positive light and other groups in a negative light. Social comparison can lead to competitive behaviour with social outgroups. Taylor and Moriarty (1987) demonstrate how physical distinctiveness along racial lines plays a critical role in the origins of conflict.

- SIT can be used to explain ethnocentrism, which refers to an ingroup-serving bias.

- The SCM (Fiske et al., 2002; Fiske, 2012) demonstrates how perceived status of outgroups is highly correlated with perceived competence and perceived competition is negatively correlated with perceived lack of warmth, which means that outgroups are perceived as relatively warm and nice to the extent that they do not compete with ingroups.

- Discrimination needs an appropriate sociocultural landscape for it to manifest. Etieyibo and Omiegbe (2016) demonstrate how culture and religion are contributory factors in the discrimination against outgroups.

TOK

To what extent are personality types measureable?

- Furthermore, **social dominance orientation** (SDO) is a personality trait where individuals have a preference for maintaining and/or increasing the differences between groups, as well as individual group members. Typically, they have personality characteristics of being driven, 'tough', dominant, and relatively uncaring seekers of power. Therefore, SDO is a measure for an individual's preference for **hierarchies** within social systems. Hierarchies provide dominance over lower-status groups both inside groups (intragroup dynamics) and between groups (intergroup dynamics).

The origins of conflict and obstacles to conflict resolution can be summarized as (Fuchs, 2004):

- the presence of identifiable ingroups and outgroups

- the presence and promotion of ethnocentricity, where the ingroup is deemed to be superior than the outgroup

- the **dehumanization** of the outgroup

- the legitimization of violence toward the outgroup

- the promotion of 'enemy images' of the outgroup

- the presence of an education system that creates values that promote power differentials between groups such as **authoritarianism** and SDO.

Research two conflicts that have either been resolved or are in the process of being resolved. What are the similarities and differences in the processes? Can we establish conflict resolution universals that apply to all situations?

35.4.2 Approaches to resolving conflict

For conflict to be resolved the following needs to occur.

- There needs to be an understanding that group allegiance can lead to intergroup conflict.

- Group identity is a powerful force (sometimes referred to as the 'collective self') that needs to be accepted and understood by group members before peace resolution can be attempted.

- Structures that promote peace and social responsibility need to be built, maintained, and respected. This can happen in a literal way, such as the building of schools and community centres, but also in a figurative way, such as the building of cultural norms regarding how groups are addressed and described in the media and cultural spaces.

Endogenous court system in post-conflict Rwanda

Rwanda is dominated by two main groups of people: Hutus and Tutsis. These two groups have grievances and perceived differences stretching back over hundreds of years, and each group has vied for dominance over the other through political, military, cultural, and economic struggles. These differences were exploited by European colonial powers for their own ends in the 19th and 20th centuries.

The Rwandan **genocide**, also known as the 'genocide against the Tutsi', was a mass slaughter of the Tutsi people by the Hutu people in a 100-day period from 7 April to mid-July 1994. An estimated 500,000 to 1 million Rwandans were massacred. The genocide was planned and encouraged by the Hutu-backed elite and carried out by all levels of society. Communities were destroyed as people went on killing sprees, raping women and children and destroying property.

There has been a significant amount of international attention on Rwanda to try and ensure that peace and reconciliation becomes established in the country, as well as to assess what lessons can be learned for wider African conflicts. Karbo and Mutisi (2008) analysed the impact of a local court system known as the Gacaca courts that are intended to promote conflict resolution and what they term 'psychosocial healing'. They argue that post-conflict reconstruction in Africa is too focused on 'hardware components', such as infrastructure development, to the neglect of psychological (what they term 'software') aspects of reconstruction.

After the war ended, Rwanda's formal courts faced a backlog of over 120,000 prisoners suspected of genocidal crimes and it was clear the Rwandan formal legal system and the international criminal tribunal were not going to be able to deal with all these cases. The introduction of a local court system was a mechanism to decongest the country's prisons, but it was also a tool to promote culturally relevant approaches to conflict resolution in localized settings.

Endogenous means 'to come from within' and can be compared with a conflict resolution approach that originates from external sources such as international bodies or from central government. Endogenous conflict resolution methods are unique, informal, communal, spiritual, context-specific, integrated into life experiences, and respect the cultural viewpoint of the people they serve.

For example, the Rwandan government created the Gacaca Law (2001), which is a community-based judicial approach to conflict resolution and gave local areas the mandate to deal with cases of genocide. Gacaca is a traditional mechanism of

The Rwandan genocide, also known as the 'genocide against the Tutsi', was a mass slaughter of the Tutsi people by the Hutu people in a 100-day period from 7 April to mid-July 1994. An estimated 500,000 to 1 million Rwandans were massacred.

conflict resolution among the Banyarwanda of Rwanda and has traditionally been used to resolve conflict at local levels through dialogue and community justice systems. Gacaca courts are culturally specific to Rwanda and were used in the past to settle land, property, marital, and other interpersonal disputes. The system is based on voluntary confessions and apologies by perpetrators and is conducted outside: people sit on the grass in the presence of other community members.

Local residents give testimony for and against the suspects, who are usually tried in the communities where they are accused of committing crimes. The Gacaca approach is bound up with the African concept of Ubuntu, which translates to 'humaneness, solidarity'. Ubuntu aims to create an environment where people are able to recognize their humanity is inextricably linked with the shared humanity of others.

Ubuntu also encourages people to see beyond the crimes of the perpetrators by seeking to integrate them back into a single community. The emphasis is on building community cohesion and breaking down ingroup/outgroup perceptions through the shared experiences of truth telling, healing, reconciliation, and public acknowledgement of grief and suffering.

However, there have been key problems with the Gacaca court system:

- The reliance on eyewitness testimony means witnesses can use the system for their own ends because there is very little fact checking of the accounts. The Rwandan government addressed this by the sentencing of one to three years' imprisonment for anyone who makes a false testimony or refuses to testify. However, establishing 'truth' is still problematic.

- The perception became established that the courts were ethnically biased because they seemed focused on crimes committed by the Hutus against the Tutsis. This has led to the Tutsis adopting a group identity of 'genocide survivors', which has perpetuated feelings of ethnocentrism toward the

Gacaca is a traditional mechanism of conflict resolution in Rwanda and has traditionally been used to resolve conflict at local levels through dialogue and community justice systems. Gacaca courts are based on voluntary confessions and apologies by perpetrators and are culturally specific to Rwanda.

What are the psychological challenges facing the Gacaca court system in Rwanda and how can they be addressed?

A Gacaca court in session. This is quite formalized with the presence of furniture. In some cases, participants sit on the grass in an informal gathering.

Hutus as 'genocide perpetrators'. While this may be understandable given the historical facts, it undermines conflict resolution as it perpetuates a cycle of blame and victimhood.

- Sexual offences were not addressed by the court system, which is a reflection of traditional African approaches toward the treatment of sex and women. This has led to women (who were the main victims of sex crimes) becoming a marginalized outgroup with legitimate grievances toward male perpetrators who went unpunished. This has led to claims that the courts have resurrected the traditional Rwandan **patriarchal** culture.

- The genocide dispersed the two main ethnic groups across the geographical landscape. This led to new group identities being established ('Hutu-Tutsi', 'Tutsi-Tutsi' and 'Hutu-Hutu'). The combination of landscape and ethnicity is known as an ethnoscape and it was noted that the new groups did not always perceive the localized court system as working in their favour because dispersed people take their cultural expectations with them into new geographical spaces and the court system relied on community healing through shared experiences, which was not always possible.

- The courts are temporary as there is a lack of permanent infrastructure in rural communities (such as police forces or court systems). Therefore, the psychological effects of psychosocial healing and community building can also be temporary if they are not regularly reinforced. Therefore, some international non-governmental organizations (NGOs) not affiliated to national governments have created micro-credit schemes designed for Hutu and Tutsi cooperation to maintain community cohesion.

- The social and open nature of the court system allowed some perpetrators to project a remorseful appearance and receive reduced sentences, which led to feelings of indignation as they were not seen as genuine.

Research micro-credit schemes designed for Hutus and Tutsis and discover what the money is spent on. Some are designed for women. Why is there an emphasis on female empowerment in Africa?

GRIMACING MOUSE MAKES AN ARGUMENT FOR THE BENEFITS OF INDIVIDUALITY IN THE FACE OF FORCED COLLECTIVISM...

36 Social responsibility

Topic focus

Discuss factors influencing social responsibility.

36.1 Bystanderism

Content focus

Discuss factors thought to influence bystanderism.

Bystanderism is when bystanders do not help and have decided not to engage in prosocial behaviour.

When someone needs help in public and other people are around but not directly involved, they are called bystanders. **Bystanderism** is when bystanders do not help and have decided not to engage in prosocial behaviour. The following are factors thought to influence bystanderism.

36.1.1 Diffusion of responsibility and pluralistic ignorance

Diffusion of responsibility assumes bystanders are influenced by the number of people around at the time of an event. It can be summed up as: a victim is more likely to receive help the fewer people there are to take action. The more observers there are, the smaller the possibility of them helping.

It can be assumed that people seek cues on how to act from other people. This is known as informational social influence and can lead to **pluralistic ignorance**. Pluralistic ignorance is the notion of a combined group ignorance: large numbers of people can claim to be ignorant of the true nature of an event. If there is only one observer, they will feel a lot of responsibility to act. The more observers there are, the more responsibility has been diffused and there is a greater chance of being believed if they claimed they did not know what was happening.

Darley and Latané (1968) aimed to measure whether the number of other people present affects a person's decision to help. They tested 72 participants who had agreed to go into a room to be part of a recorded conversation about problems at university. Each person was in the room alone and heard the same standardized recorded voices in the same order. The researchers told them that there was either one other participant or five other participants. All of the others were just recorded voices. After some time one person seems to have a seizure and asks for help. The researchers measured how long it took for the real participant to come out of their room and try to help.

The independent variable was the number of people the real participant thought were also present to hear the call for help, and the dependent variable was the presence of informational social influence operationalized by the amount of time taken to try to help.

The results showed within the first two minutes, 85 per cent of the 'alone' participants tried to help, compared to 31 per cent of those who thought four other people could help. Within six minutes, 100 per cent of the alone group had tried to help, compared with 62 per cent of the other group. Therefore, the number of other people bystanders think are also present is a very powerful influence on whether they help or not. They sought cues on how to act from the other voices they could hear. Therefore, a diffusion of responsibility is more likely to lead to bystanderism.

Key study: Piliavin et al. (1969)

Aim: To investigate the effect of several variables on helping behaviour.

Procedure: The researchers created an emergency situation on a New York subway train: four teams of student researchers, each one made up of a victim, model, and two observers, staged standard collapses in which the type of victim (drunk or ill), race of victim (black or white) and presence or absence of a model were varied.

Findings: The victim with a stick was helped 62 out of 65 times and the drunken victim was helped 19 out of 38 times. The helpers were 90 per cent male and 64 per cent of the time they were white. Furthermore, an apparently ill person is more likely to receive aid than one who appears to be drunk, the race of the victim has little effect on the race of the helper, except when the victim is drunk, the longer the emergency continues without help being offered, the more likely it is that someone will leave the area of the emergency, and the expected decrease in speed of responding as group size increased did not actually occur.

Conclusions: The researchers suggest that the causes of the discrepancies are social and cognitive. Males are more likely to help males for two main reasons: that in this time period, it was more socially expected for men to help, and the possible costs for a woman helping are higher because of possible risks.

Evaluation: Piliavin et al. deliberately set out to test the diffusion of responsibility hypothesis put forward by Darley and Latané. In the Darley and Latané experiment it was predicted and found that as the number of bystanders increased, the likelihood that any individual would help decreased and the delay in response would also increase. It should be noted that their study involved bystanders who could not see each other or the victim.
Piliavin et al. (1969) found no evidence in their data for diffusion of responsibility. They suggested the fact that observers in their study could see the victim would have given them clear information regarding the situation. Because the episode was so clear, it may have overwhelmed any tendency to diffuse responsibility. Therefore, the results cannot be used to dismiss the notion of diffusion of responsibility, but does show how results from isolating variables in a laboratory will not always be replicated in a more **ecologically valid** setting.

Diffusion of responsibility assumes bystanders are influenced by the number of people around at the time of an event.

TOK Can an experiment setting have as much value or ecological validity as research carried out in naturalistic conditions?

36.1.2 Perceived similarity

Social identity theory (see p. 88) can be used to explain the behaviour of bystanders. The notion of social identity refers to how we perceive ourselves according to our membership of social groups. Social categorization means we naturally divide the social environment into ingroups, to which an individual belongs (us), and outgroups, to which the individual does not belong (them). It results in a reduction of perceived differences within the ingroup (we are similar to one another); a reduction of perceived differences in the outgroup (they are all the same); increases perceived differences between the ingroup and the outgroup (we are different from them), known as the category accentuation effect. There is further theoretical support in the form of kin selection theory, which assumes that individuals help other individuals if they are perceived to be 'kin' or have ingroup or family status.

Levine et al. (2005) aimed to test whether Manchester United football fans were more likely to help a Manchester United fan than a fan of a different team on a match day. They waited for Manchester United fans to walk between two buildings at a university campus. A man ran past each participant, wearing either a Manchester United football shirt, a Liverpool football shirt, or a plain white shirt. The man then fell over and pretended to be hurt, and observers recorded how much help the participant gave.

They found little difference in the help offered to the man when he wore a Liverpool shirt or a plain white shirt, but the participants were much more likely to help him if he was wearing a Manchester United shirt.

Such explicit isolation of variables in this **naturalistic** setting does show the impact of perceived ingroup status on whether to help or not. Although, like the Darley and Latané (1968) study, the deliberate isolation of the variables, even though they were naturally occuring, does limit the generalizability to some extent.

When Levine et al. restaged the fall after asking participants to fill in questionnaires that triggered their football fan identity rather than just a 'Manchester United fan' identity, the amount of help for the other victims went up, thereby demonstrating how group identity can be manipulated, which then impacts thoughts, feelings, and behaviours.

Piliavin et al. (1969) can also be used to illustrate the effect of perceived similarity. They found some tendency for same-race helping to be more frequent as well as same-gender helping, as men were more likely to help overall. Same-gender helping could be explained by perceived risk on the part of the women bystanders rather than perceived similarity on the part of the males.

36.1.3 Culture and geographical location

Research testing cultural differences in bystanderism assumes that behaviour is affected by economic development and also by cultural notions, such as **simpatia**. Simpatia is an important notion in Hispanic and Latino cultures and refers to social harmony, or 'liking for the other', and a general desire to avoid conflict.

Levine et al. (2001) compared the rate of helping behaviour in different cities around the world. Twenty-three countries were chosen, and the researchers visited one major city from each. They recorded how often someone helped in the following conditions: a person pretending to be blind waiting to cross the road; a person walking along the street in a leg brace and dropping magazines; a person dropping a pen while walking along the street. Rio de Janeiro, which has a low level of economic development, was the city where people helped most often in the three situations. Overall, helping across cultures was inversely related to a country's economic productivity; countries with the cultural tradition of simpatia were on average more helpful than countries with no such tradition. Such findings can also be explained via an ingroup paradigm. Poor people may be more inclined to band together because people experience less anxiety and tension the more cohesive the group (Myers, 1962). It was also found that people cope better with stress when they belong to a cohesive group (Zaccaro et al., 1995).

Caution should be used when generalizing from the findings of Levine et al. All of the confederates in the study were male, which will have decreased the chances of being helped by females; there was an emphasis on urban environments and the results would almost certainly have been different in rural locations; many variables overlap in this natural setting, which makes pinpointing exact causes problematic. Furthermore, different cities have different subcultural norms because different parts of the city have different norms and expectations. It would be difficult to standardize all these variables and compare the different cities. For example, Rio has many poor areas that may have been more hostile than the areas tested, and the geographical nuances of different cities cannot be replicated across the world (e.g. in crime centres, or because of traffic or pavement flow).

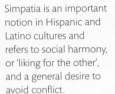

Simpatia is an important notion in Hispanic and Latino cultures and refers to social harmony, or 'liking for the other', and a general desire to avoid conflict.

Think about how you, as an IB student, can support or enforce the idea of simpatia in your student environment.

36.2 Prosocial behaviour

Content focus

Discuss factors that are thought to influence prosocial behaviour.

Prosocial behaviour is defined as behaviour that benefits another person or has positive social consequences (Staub, 1978). In the context of bystanderism, it is the behaviour of not standing by when someone needs help. This definition is often considered too vague, because although it discusses the outcome of the behaviour, it does not consider the motivation of the behaviour. For any useful study, the reasons behind prosocial behaviour should be considered.

Think about why you find pleasure in CAS activities.

Prosocial behaviour is defined as behaviour that benefits another person or has positive social consequences (Staub, 1978).

Altruism is often seen as a main motivator for prosocial behaviour. Batson (1991) defines altruism as 'a motivational state with the ultimate goal of increasing another's welfare'. However, some people argue that the ultimate goal of all human behaviour is personal pleasure; within this paradigm true altruism cannot exist. Personal pleasure is difficult to define and research, but it seems reasonable to assume that if a person engages in charity work in order to feel good or receive social rewards, **egoistic** motivation is behind the action.

There is a strong argument that prosocial behaviour may reduce or avoid negative feelings, as well as allowing people entry into an 'ingroup' of social do-gooders.

36.2.1 Sociocultural factors

Research testing cultural differences in bystanderism assumes that behaviour is affected by economic development and also by cultural notions (for example, the notion of simpatia, see p. 306). Therefore, prosocial behaviour can be said to be influenced by these factors.

Furthermore, prosocial behaviour usually occurs within a social situation with other people around. The notion of diffusion of responsibility assumes people are influenced by the number of people around at the time of an event and was discussed on page 304.

36.2.2 Cognitive and emotional factors

Social identity theory can be used to explain prosocial behaviour, as it assumes people naturally divide the social world into groups. Social identities are cognitive constructs where individuals perceive other individuals to be similar or dissimilar based on certain cues.

Latané and Darley (1970) propose five internal processes that must occur in order for a person to intervene. The person must:

- notice the situation

- appraise it as an emergency

- develop feelings of responsibility

- believe they have skills to succeed

- reach a conscious decision to help.

Therefore, the decision-making process involves cognitive factors (attention, appraising, perceiving, decision making) as well as an **affective** element, which Latané and Darley propose as the feeling of responsibility being a key motivating factor in the decision-making process.

This is supported by Batson's (1991) empathy-altruism model, which examines the emotional and motivational component of prosocial behaviour. It argues that a key component of deciding to act is feeling **empathy** toward an individual, which is known as **empathetic concern**. This is characterized by feelings of tenderness, compassion, and sympathy (Batson, 1991). Note that feelings are partly biological, and people may have different predispositions to feel empathy. Furthermore, empathy can be influenced by day-to-day biological factors such as diet, sleep, and other biological rhythms.

The empathy-altruism model has supporting research with humans. For example, Toi and Batson (1982) aimed to test whether levels of empathy and cost had an impact on how much people would help another person. They asked female psychology students to listen to a radio interview with a psychology student named Carol, who had apparently broken both her legs in a car accident. The researchers then gave participants the opportunity to help Carol with class notes.

- Independent variable A: Empathy level

  ○ Condition 1: Participants were asked to imagine how Carol is feeling (high empathy condition)

  ○ Condition 2: Participants were asked to be **objective** and not concerned with how Carol felt (low empathy condition)

- Independent variable B: High- or low-cost conditions

  ○ Condition 1: High cost. Carol would be in the class. It would be embarrassing to deny her the lecture notes.

  ○ Condition 2: Low cost. Carol would not be in the class. It would not be as embarrassing to deny her the lecture notes.

Results showed the groups who were told to focus on Carol's feelings were much more likely to offer to help her. In addition, the high empathy group were equally likely to help in either condition. The low empathy group was more likely to help Carol in the high-cost condition.

Researchers concluded the most important factors in people's decision to help is how much empathy they feel and the perceived cost to themselves for helping or not helping. The results can also be used to show how humans engage in a cost-benefit analysis before choosing to help others.

36.2.3 Biological factors

From a genetic perspective, evolutionary success is defined by the number of copies of itself a gene leaves behind in a population. In a gene-centred view of evolution the organism is merely a vehicle or a survival mechanism for the gene (Dawkins, 1976). Such a view helped shift the perspective of evolution from the individual and groups to that of the genes themselves.

Hamilton (1964) argued that members of any given population stand a good chance of sharing genes (for example, an individual's own child carries half of the individual's genes; the child from an individual's sibling will carry a quarter of those genes; and a cousin's child will also share a sixteenth). Therefore, a gene can increase its evolutionary success by indirectly promoting the reproduction and survival of other individuals who also carry that gene.

Inclusive fitness refers to the ability of an individual organism to pass on its genes to the next generation. The notion takes into account the direct descendants of the individual as well as the shared genes of close relatives. Therefore, it can be used to explain how a gene can increase its chances of evolutionary success by indirectly promoting the reproduction and survival of other individuals who share the same genes.

Inclusive fitness refers to the ability of an individual organism to pass on its genes to the next generation. The notion takes into account the direct descendants of the individual as well as the shared genes of close relatives.

To what extent can inclusive fitness be used to explain prosocial behaviour?

EE

Kin selection is an evolutionary theory that assumes prosocial behaviour exists because it has an adaptive function, meaning it has helped human beings survive and thrive over time.

To what extent does the use of animal models help or hinder knowledge creation in psychology?

TOK

This approach has been used to explain why individuals engage in behaviour that help their group but harm themselves. Inclusive fitness is the main assumption underpinning kin selection theory, which attempts to interpret altruistic social behaviour via genetic **relatedness** while taking into account the benefits and costs associated with altruistic acts.

Kin selection is an evolutionary theory that assumes prosocial behaviour exists because it has an adaptive function, meaning it has helped human beings survive and thrive over time. The theory suggests prosocial behaviour is instinctive rather than cognitive, and argues that organisms are motivated to help others who are genetically similar to increase the chances of the group surviving. For example, in an emergency situation people are more likely to help someone who is interpreted as being in their ingroup than someone in their outgroup.

Kin selection theory has been demonstrated cross-culturally and with animals in a cross-species approach. For example, vampire bats are more likely to share blood with close relatives (Wilkinson, 1984) and squirrels are more likely to warn relatives than non-relatives of predators (Sherman, 1985).

The theory also has empirical support from human participants. Madsen et al. (2007) aimed to test kin selection theory in a laboratory setting in two countries. The researchers asked student participants in the UK to do a painful physical exercise for as long as possible. They promised the students that one of their biological relatives would receive money according to how long the student could stay in this position. They then compared the length of time students were able to stay in the painful position and correlated this with how genetically close the relative was.

In South Africa, they used the same experiment with students of Zulu origin. The independent variable was the degree of biological relatedness and the dependent variable was the amount of time spent in a painful position.

The results showed that biological relatedness was correlated with the amount of time spent in a painful position. This result was the same in both countries. Madsen et al. argued that perceptions of kinship represent a baseline that individuals use when deciding how to behave toward others.

The study also shows the impact of culture on perception. Zulu males helped their cousins as much as their brothers. This is because in Zulu culture, cousins are perceived to be family and part of the social ingroup.

Therefore, while biological relatedness increases levels of prosocial behaviour, this is moderated by circumstantial cues, such as shared developmental environment, familiarity, and social bonding (Sherman et al., 1997). In this way, kinship refers to 'social kinship', not necessarily 'genetic kinship'.

These circumstantial cues do not necessarily reject an underlying genetic link, because it is possible animals have sophisticated ways of understanding who is more or less genetically related, as well as it being more likely that close social groups are genetically related.

Kin selection can be used to explain why individuals engage in acts that help the group but harm themselves. Group selection refers to the idea that natural selection sometimes acts on whole groups of organisms, favouring some groups over others.

This leads to the evolution of traits that are group-advantageous. This contrasts with the traditional 'individualist' view, which assumes Darwinian selection usually occurs at the individual level by favouring some individual organisms over others, which leads to the evolution of traits that benefit individuals (Okasha, 2006; 2015).

Empathy-altrusim and kin selection theory compared

There are key differences between the two main approaches to explaining prosocial behaviour.

Kin selection in its Darwinian form is an evolutionary theory, meaning it is focused on biological reasons for altruistic behaviour. For example, behaviour can be inherited through genes. This means that kin selection views altruism as an adaptive response that is natural in animals and humans. Therefore, kin selection assumes research with animals can inform our understanding of human behaviour.

Empathy-altruism comes from the cognitive level of analysis, meaning it is focused on internal psychological processes rather than social or biological ones. It is difficult to research cognitive processes with animal research. Animals cannot explain how they think and feel.

Kin selection assumes people put themselves in danger for other people and therefore, the approach usually focuses on extreme events that threaten the survival of the individual and group, whereas empathy-altruism studies focus more on day-to-day events.

In its purest form, kin selection theory fails to explain prosocial behaviour when helping non-related strangers. However, **nurture kinship** addresses this issue by incorporating an environmental explanation of the behaviour, and there are elements of SIT that can explain why people help others who are unrelated.

It should be noted that these two theories are not opposed to one another, but rather complement each other. For example, it can be seen as highly likely the cognitive processes outlined in the empathy-altruism model (empathy, perception, and motivation) are the result of evolutionary processes.

36.3 Promoting prosocial behaviour

Content focus

Evaluate strategies for promoting prosocial behaviour

Prosocial behaviour is defined as behaviour that benefits another person or has positive social consequences (Staub, 1978). Therefore, it is often promoted by institutions, such as schools, to create positive behavioural norms. There are various strategies to achieve these outcomes. The two strategies that will be evaluated in this section are:

* Kindness Curriculum (KC) in preschool children

* **emotion coaching**.

36.3.1 Sociocultural considerations

Parents are often the most immediate moderator on a child's prosocial development and therefore, any consideration of promoting prosocial behaviour needs to consider the cultural environment parents create in the home. For example, parents who are warm are likely to engage in pleasant and inherently rewarding interactions with their children, thus providing opportunities for parents to model or coach the regulation of positive emotions. It is thought a positive interaction style leads to a greater ability for the child to foster positive **peer** relationships.

Harsh or power-assertive discipline has consistently been found to be negatively related to prosocial behaviours (Romano et al., 2005), whereas other types of discipline where the emotions of others are emphasized have been found to promote sympathy and prosocial behaviours (Krevans and Gibbs, 1996). Therefore, parenting norms associated with warmth, secure attachment, and responsiveness to distress have been positively related to prosocial outcomes (Zhou et al., 2002).

36.3.2 Cognitive and emotional considerations

Compassion for others is thought to motivate an individual to engage in prosocial behaviour (McGinley, 2008). However, an individual has to regulate their own emotions, and research has shown that individuals who are prone to negative emotions are less likely to engage in prosocial behaviour. If an individual becomes overwhelmed with feelings of personal distress, they can then become focused on relieving their own negative feelings instead of engaging in prosocial behaviour (Eisenberg, 2005). For example, children who have higher levels of **temperamental fear** are more personally distressed in helping situations and are less likely to be labelled as a prosocial individual (Spinrad and Stifter, 2006, cited in McGinley, 2008).

Other aspects of vulnerable temperament, such as shyness, anger, frustration, and general negative emotionality have been similarly found to inhibit children and adolescents' prosocial behaviours (Eisenberg et al., 2004, cited in McGinley, 2008). These findings support the notion that children prone to negative emotions may experience high levels of personal distress, which lessens the likelihood of feeling sympathy and engaging in prosocial behaviours.

36.3.3 Biological considerations

Temperamental fearfulness is thought to strongly influence the ability of a child to internalize societal **standards** regarding prosocial behaviour. This personality trait occurs at such a young age it is assumed to be highly predetermined by biology. Children who are considered highly fearful are especially sensitive to minimal parental discipline that does not cause them to become too emotional. They may also internalize standards more readily than their less fearful counterparts. Children who lack such fear may alternatively adopt societal prosocial standards because they are motivated by a trusting and warm relationship with their caregiver (Kochanska, 1993).

36.3.4 Interactive approach

Studying prosocial behaviour by separating the sociocultural, cognitive, and biological factors is not always helpful. Kochanska (1993) proposed an interactive framework for studying internal **morality** and the internalization of societal standards of prosocial

---

Parents and children in Western societies tend to view thought violations relating to conscience as being separate to violations in prosocial behaviour.

Temperamental fearfulness is thought to strongly influence the ability of a child to internalize societal standards regarding prosocial behaviour. This personality trait occurs at such a young age it is assumed to be highly predetermined by biology.

To what extent can personality traits be measured?

behaviour. These standards, which define conscience, typically focus on a child's ability to refrain from behaviour that is prohibited by society. However, caution should be used when assuming children who refrain from violating societal norms are engaged in prosocial behaviour.

Prosocial behaviour is defined as behaviour that benefits another person or has positive social consequences (Staub, 1978). Technically, refraining from committing harm is a prosocial act, but it does meet the implicit assumption that prosocial behaviour must be an active assertive enterprise usually motivated by a willingness to help others. Kochanska (1993) herself noted that her theory centred around the idea of children prohibiting negative actions rather than engaging in prosocial behaviour. She presents the notion that conscience is better conceptualized as two constructs: moral emotions (e.g. guilt, empathy), and rule-compatible conduct (e.g. internalization of prohibitions and rules) (cited in McGinley, 2008), which are heavily influenced by biological predisposition in the form of temperament and the sociocultural surroundings that for young children is usually defined by the parenting style.

Furthermore, it is clear that anxiety and fearlessness interact with parenting and social norms. For example, anxious children may internalize moral standards from authoritative parents and also be aware of appropriate prosocial behaviour, but then be unable to act on this knowledge under socially challenging conditions (Hastings et al., 2007). Therefore, highly empathic individuals may be unable to cope with others' negative experiences because they also feel the distress of the 'other'. Consequently, the empathic individual becomes focused on their own personal distress instead of developing a sense of sympathy, which leads to prosocial responding. Therefore, any child prone to distress must somehow regulate these negative emotions before they can successfully become prosocial individuals (McGinley, 2008).

TOK How and by whom should notions of 'prosocial behaviour' be defined and implemented? To what extent should notions of multiculturalism and respect for diverse cultural norms be incorporated into moral discourses in the human sciences?

36.3.5 Strategies for promoting prosocial behaviour
Kindness Curriculum in preschool children

Flook et al. (2015) wanted to test the effectiveness of a 12-week **mindfulness**-based Kindness Curriculum delivered in a public school setting on executive function, **self-regulation**, and prosocial behaviour in a sample of 68 preschool children.

Mindfulness training enhances attention by bringing awareness to a particular attentional object, whether it is the breath, external stimuli, thoughts, or emotions. It entails noticing when the mind has wandered from its object of attention (monitoring) and returning attention back to the chosen object (shifting/cognitive flexibility) (Flook et al., 2015). In the context of the Kindness Curriculum, it is 'child facing' in the sense that the focus is on developing skills within the child to help them regulate their emotional worlds and act prosocially.

In Flook et al. (2015), seven classrooms were recruited from six different elementary schools within a public school district in a medium-sized Midwestern American city. Within these schools, 37.9 per cent of children are considered socioeconomically disadvantaged. A total of 99 children were invited to participate and parents of 68 indicated they wished to enrol their child in the study. The sample included a mixed ethnicity with a majority being Caucasian (58.8 per cent).

Participants were randomly assigned by classroom to either a mindfulness-based KC intervention or a wait-list **control** group where no KC was administered. Participants were assessed in individual testing sessions before and after the training period. **Informed consent** was obtained from parents of all child participants before evaluation, and the children were also asked individually whether they wanted to participate before the start of each evaluation session and their decisions were respected.

The intervention group received a 12-week mindfulness-based prosocial skills training course designed for preschool-age children. The foundation of the KC is mindfulness, which is aimed at cultivating attention and emotion regulation, with a shared emphasis on kindness practices (e.g. empathy, gratitude, sharing). The preschool KC incorporated children's literature, music, and movement to teach concepts related to kindness and compassion. The curriculum was taught by experienced mindfulness instructors in a **secular** manner. Student training in the KC consisted of two 20–30-minute lessons each week over a 12-week period, totalling approximately ten hours of training.

Among other measures, such as a sharing task scale, students were assessed by a teacher-rated social competence scale (TSC). The measure was comprised of two subscales: a prosocial behaviour subscale (seven items, showing empathy and compassion for others' feelings) and an emotion regulation subscale (five items, e.g. stopping and calming down when excited or upset). The factors were rated on a six-point Likert-type scale.

The results showed students who participated in the KC training showed larger gains in teacher-reported social competence as compared to the control group. In addition, the control group acted more selfishly (sharing fewer resources with others) over time as compared to the KC group. Comparison of the end-of-year school records showed higher marks/grades for children in the intervention as compared to control group on indicators of learning, social-emotional development, and health. Notably, these differences emerged for second semester report card grades assigned approximately three months after the end of the intervention.

These changes were observed after a relatively short intervention period with a very modest dose of the intervention, which supports the practicality and effectiveness of this approach. The training shows promise as an accessible and cost-effective strategy to promote well-being and prosocial behaviour by training non-cognitive skills. Flook et al. argues that taking a universal preventive approach may set children on a positive trajectory for ongoing development.

Emotion coaching

In a UK-based **pilot study**, Rose et al. (2015) wanted to test the effectiveness on children's behaviour if the adults who worked with them had been taught particular emotion-centric techniques. Adults who worked with the children were given a course in emotion coaching, which was designed to help them deal with children's emotional issues more effectively. It was assumed that the training of the adults would help children by enabling them to tune in more explicitly to their emotions and then engage in more consistently prosocial behaviour. The adults were shown how they could train children to manage their feelings and the behavioural consequences of those feelings.

While the project's training was adult focused, the results would manifest in the prosocial behaviour of the children. For example, the researchers sought to explore the adults' emotions and engage in discussion about their own beliefs and attitudes toward their own and others' emotions, as well as their perceptions of children's behaviour, the assumption being that an adult's underlying emotional functioning generates certain behaviours in children.

Emotion coaching is comprised of two key elements: empathy and guidance. These two elements express themselves whenever 'emotional moments' occur with children.

Emotional empathy involves recognizing, labelling, and validating a child's emotions, regardless of the behaviour. This is designed to promote self-awareness and understanding of emotions within the child. Acceptance by the adult of the child's internal emotional state creates feelings of security, which helps the child to engage with more reasonable solutions.

Guidance involves engagement with the child in problem-solving in order to support the child's ability to learn to self-regulate. The child and adult work together to find alternative courses of action to help manage emotions and prevent future transgressions.

Participants included senior and junior teaching staff, teaching assistants, school support staff, children's service staff including health and social care services, early years practitioners, youth workers and youth mentors, and some parents. The bulk of the data was, however, drawn from 11 schools and the majority (80 per cent) of participants were education staff (largely teachers). Moreover, the behavioural case study was focused on one school.

Participants were trained in emotion coaching techniques in workshops and then supported over the course of one full year where they were expected to implement emotion coaching into their everyday interactions with children.

The effectiveness of emotion coaching in professional practice was to be measured by a mixture of qualitative and quantitative data in three main areas:

- improved emotional philosophy and adult self-regulation on the part of the adults

- improved exchanges between adults and children

- improved self-regulation and prosocial behaviour on the part of the children.

These areas were measured qualitatively with data from focus groups and free text responses, with a particular focus on the structure of the participants' stories about emotion coaching usage. They were measured quantitatively through the use of questionnaires with Likert-type scales. For example, participants were asked to rate on a scale from one (strongly disagree) to five (strongly agree): 'When a child / young person is angry, I help him / her to identify / name the feeling'.

The improved self-regulation and prosocial behaviour on the part of the children was quantitatively measured by the amount of call outs in class and the amount of exclusions from school. There was also a case study approach to the research with six young people (four 13-year-old boys and two 15-year-old girls) who were considered by the staff to be 'at risk of exclusion'. The 'team around the child' (including the

Emotion coaching is comprised of two key elements: empathy and guidance. These two elements express themselves whenever 'emotional moments' occur with children.

parents) were trained in emotion coaching and then records were kept of internal exclusions.

The qualitative and quantitative data showed the emotion coaching enabled adults to communicate more effectively and consistently with children in stressful situations, to utilize fewer 'emotion dismissing' approaches, and help to de-escalate volatile situations. Furthermore, adults found difficult situations less stressful and exhausting, showing a positive impact on adult well-being. It promoted self-awareness on the part of the children with regards their emotions, positive self-regulation of their behaviour, and helped to generate nurturing relationships.

The quantitative data showed the emotion coaching had significantly reduced the amount of call outs in class and significantly reduced the amount of exclusions. In the case study children there was a total drop in numbers of internal exclusions – from 21 to 13 – and call outs – from 84 to 36 – which was considered by the deputy head of the school to show 'real improvement'.

Prepare a five-point action plan to improve pro-social behaviour based on the Rose et al. study.

Overall, the findings from Rose et al. (2015) revealed a reduction in disruptive behaviour and improved prosocial behaviour on the part of the children across the different settings.

Kindness Curriculum and emotion coaching compared

Mindfulness training enhances attention by bringing awareness to a particular attentional object, whether it is the breath, external stimuli, thoughts, or emotions, whereas emotion coaching focuses on improved emotional philosophy and self-regulation on the part of the adults. It focuses on improved exchanges between adults and children, improved self-regulation, and prosocial behaviour on the part of the children after being around adults who have been emotionally coached. There is a slight issue of semantics and cultural differences because it could be argued the emotion coaching presented here by Rose et al. (2015) is actually a form of kindness curriculum for adults.

In this instance, mindfulness training was 'child facing' in the sense that the focus is on developing skills within the child to help them regulate their emotional worlds and act prosocially, whereas emotion coaching was 'adult facing'. It was assumed that the emotion coaching of the adults would in turn help children by enabling them to tune in more explicitly to their emotions and then engage in more consistent prosocial behaviour.

In this instance, mindfulness training was assessed by a teacher-rated social competence scale (TSC), whereas emotion coaching and the factors were rated on a six-point Likert-type scale and measured by a mixture of qualitative and quantitative data.

37 Approaches to research: psychology of human relationships

Learning focus

Discuss approaches to research dealing with human relationships.

Research dealing with human relationships creates a number of special considerations for researchers. Studying human relationships poses challenges and it is tempting to oversimplify complex social and psychological issues from a research standpoint.

Key goals of social psychologists are to understand the complexities of human relationships, improve interpersonal relations, and promote social responsibility as well as reduce violence between groups. However, it should be noted that groups are not static, they are dynamic and represent social and personal constructions. An individual may perceive someone else as belonging to several groups, whereas the individual themselves may not consider themselves to be identifiable with those groups or may have completely different understandings of what those group labels mean.

Therefore, research into human relationships has to be **credible** and trustworthy if it is to be used as a foundation for public and academic discussion.

Studying human relationships poses challenges and it is tempting to oversimplify complex social and psychological issues from a research standpoint.

37.1 Participant expectations

One of the more important factors to consider in relationship-related research is that the participants are less like to respond **passively** to the research process; they are intimately engaged in it and its findings because the issues relate to their own personal relationships. Researchers need to be aware that relationship research is an active process that requires reflection and interrogation of the data, the participant, and the research context, but it may also lead to participant expectations (also called **reactivity**).

Participant expectations are an issue for all types of social science research but are particularly relevant in relationship-related research. Participants may try to guess the nature of the research or programme and influence the results. If the participant feels they have to behave in certain ways in order to please the researcher, this will affect the value of the data in a negative way.

For example, prejudice has affective as well as cognitive components, whereas discrimination is the behavioural extension of these. An individual can hold prejudicial views, but these do not always manifest themselves in behaviour. Therefore, prejudice and discrimination are very difficult for psychology researchers to study and measure because people are usually aware of how socially unattractive prejudice and discrimination can be and can be prone to the social desirability bias.

Taylor and Moriarty (1987) refer to this as the 'bending over backward' effect where participants try to appear as socially desirable as possible. Researchers have to consider very carefully how to avoid such biases. For example, Fiske et al. (2002) measured the extent to which outgroups are defined by mixed perceptions and feelings (see p. 296 for details). The choosing of the 'outgroups' by the researchers in this study made it more socially acceptable to express an opinion of them and the researchers were able to further reduce social desirability concerns by stating, 'We are not interested in your personal beliefs, but in how you think they are viewed by others'.

The instruction was intended to tap perceived cultural stereotypes, but it also runs the risk of producing data that does not accurately measure prejudice in society, but instead shows what participants assume represents prejudice in society. One way to minimize the effect of participant expectations and researcher bias is reflexivity throughout the research process.

37.2 The importance of reflexivity

> Reflexivity is a process that occurs throughout the research and is based on the assumption that it is important the researcher is aware of his or her own contribution to the construction of meaning in the research process and then makes the reader of their research aware.

Reflexivity is a process that occurs throughout the research and is based on the assumption that it is important the researcher is aware of his or her own contribution to the construction of meaning in the research process and then makes the reader of their research aware. Such an approach allows the social researcher to reflect on ways in which bias may occur, by acknowledging that his or her own background and beliefs can influence the way the research is conducted.

This line of thinking argues that social researchers should provide sufficient details about issues that may potentially bias the investigation – for example, revealing where they stand in terms of political ideology pertinent to explaining social phenomena (such as feminism or the effects of capitalism).

Fiske et al. (2002) state their own stereotype perceptions may not have been shared with the participants. For example, for 'sexy women' they were originally thinking 'brainless bimbo', but some of their own respondents may have been thinking 'villainous vamp'. This criticism by Fiske et al. is in itself a fairly narrow-minded prediction as many people would have other stereotypes in mind when presented with the phrase 'sexy woman' rather than the two listed here. It might be suggested that the reflexive process engaged in by Fiske et al. (2002) was not deep enough and even when they self-criticized they were still immersed in their own views of the world.

37.3 Choosing an appropriate methodology

Relationship issues are often intertwined. For example, the perception of others is a combination of past experience, biological influences, family expectations, and sociocultural contexts. Therefore, it is important researchers do not apply one method as a definitive approach to researching complex issues. It is likely that a combination of qualitative and quantitative mixed methods is appropriate, with **triangulation** of different data sources. Triangulation refers to the validation of data through cross-verification from two or more sources. The sources are usually theoretical and/or methodological.

37.3.1 Types of triangulation

- **Methodological triangulation:** different methods (e.g. interviews plus observations, questionnaires, and diary analysis)

- **Theoretical triangulation:** the search for evidence or approaches that could contradict their interpretation (e.g. a feminist lens; a behaviourist lens; a collectivist lens).

- **Researcher triangulation:** the use of other researchers who would bring different perspectives and experience that might challenge the findings of the report.

For example, Tyler and Blader (2001) aimed to measure the influence of identification on the degree to which people cooperate with groups. They asked participants to complete questionnaires anonymously, assessing on a scale of one to six. However, the issue of measurement poses problems for relationship researchers. Puts (2005) aimed to measure the effect of ovulation on attractiveness of male voices. The study assumed females' perception of 'attraction' changed as they move through their ovulation cycle. Puts obtained voice recordings of 30 men attempting to persuade a woman to go out on a romantic date. One hundred and forty-two heterosexual women then listened to the recordings and rated each man's attractiveness for a short-term sexual encounter and a long-term committed relationship. Puts found a clear link between the ovulation cycles and the perception of attractive characteristics in prospective mates.

Puts et al. (2012) also asked 500 men to rate the attractiveness of the women's faces as they moved through their menstrual cycle. They found men rate women as more attractive when they are at the most fertile phase of their ovulation cycle. They also tested female participants and asked 500 women to rate other women's attractiveness across their cycles and found the female participants also rated the subjects higher on both measures when the subjects were in their most fertile phase.

Relationship issues are often intertwined. For example, the perception of others is a combination of past experience, biological influences, family expectations, and sociocultural contexts. Therefore it is important researchers do not apply one method as a definitive approach to researching complex issues.

However, it can be noted that complex behaviour such as attraction and relationship formation cannot be explained by reducing the explanation to simple processes. It is realistic to assume it is a combination of many factors. For example, perception is dynamic and open to influence. It can be influenced by schemas from life experiences, biological events (e.g. ovulation; arousal), physical stimulants such as face shape/symmetry, self-esteem, or perceptions of similarity. Relationships are a complex issue and researchers may be tempted to measure the self-perception aspects of relationships, as they can be readily investigated using traditional methods such as questionnaires, surveys, and self-reports. However, while quantitative measurements may be attractive for eliciting large amounts of data from a relatively large sample size, they may miss the personal nuances inherent within personal relationships.

37.4 The issue of generalization

Generalization refers to the extent to which results are relevant outside the context of the study. Relationship researchers have to carefully consider the extent to which they want their findings to apply to people other than those who participate in a particular study. Given the importance of sociocultural elements in human relationships, to what extent is it feasible to generalize to other cultures and peoples?

Furthermore, personal relationships are a complex and deeply personal phenomenon that is difficult to access from a research standpoint. For example, many studies assume their participants are heterosexual. How should researchers go about finding out the sexuality of their participants, and to what extent can that be generalized to other populations?

According to Ritchie and Lewis (2003), it is useful to consider the following forms of generalization.

- **Representational generalization** means findings from research can be applied to populations outside the specific population of the study. Many researchers use psychology students as they are readily available for researchers who work in universities. If a researcher has used small samples that are not selected to be statistically representative, and other non-standardized methods may be used (such as interviews), it makes it difficult to generalize findings to other populations. Therefore, considerations of the uniqueness of certain populations have to be built into relationship-related research. For example, Fiske et al.'s (2002) participants were University of Massachusetts undergraduates, so they may have accorded some positive attributes to any given outgroup because of their potential liberal political orientation, 'North-East American subcultural norms', or because of an adherence to the college ethos of egalitarianism.

- **Theoretical generalization** means theoretical concepts derived from the study can be used to develop further theory. Human relationship issues deal with sensitive topics such as prejudice and discrimination. Fiske et al. (2002) dealt with this problem by choosing the stereotypes for the participants themselves, whereas Worchel et al. (1978) operationalized physical distinctiveness as differences in dress, so participants in two groups either dressed similarly (both groups wore white lab coats) or dressed dissimilarly (participants in one group wore white lab coats while subjects in a second group wore red lab coats). It was found that distinctive groups in a competitive relationship were least attracted to each other. They concluded that competition decreases ratings of attractiveness between groups who are seen as physically distinctive. However, the extent to which these findings can be generalized to racial distinctiveness and wider social theory is open to debate.

38 Ethical considerations: psychology of human relationships

Learning focus

Discuss ethical considerations in human relationship psychology.

Look back at section 23.1, page 175, which looked at Research Ethics Committees (RECs), what they are responsible for and the ethical considerations that they must think about before approving research.

38.1 Informed consent

As a starting point, participants should know that taking part in research is voluntary and the researcher must provide participants with sufficient information about the study. This is particularly important if the research is conducted by people who have some kind of relation to members of the sample (for example, relationship counsellor;

Relationship researchers have to carefully consider the extent to which they want their findings to apply to people other than those who participate in a particular study. Given the importance of sociocultural elements in human relationships, to what extent is it feasible to generalize to other cultures and peoples?

To what extent do ethical boundaries help or hinder knowledge creation in human relationship psychology?

Most respected academic institutions have some form of REC consisting of a multidisciplinary team of professional researchers and/or experienced academics with a balance of gender and cultural backgrounds.

a university professor), since participation could then be motivated by feelings of obligation. The researcher must provide participants with sufficient information about the study, such as who funded the study, who will conduct the study, how the data will be used, and what the research requires of the participants – for example, in terms of time and the topics the study will address. However, this does not mean the researcher has to give away the overall aim of the study.

It should also be made clear that consent can always be renegotiated. In cases where children aged under 16 years are involved, consent must be obtained from parents or legal guardians. For example, Flook et al. (2015) wanted to test the effectiveness of a 12-week mindfulness-based Kindness Curriculum (KC) delivered in a public school setting on executive function, self-regulation, and prosocial behaviour in a sample of 68 preschool children. Participants were randomly assigned by classroom to either a mindfulness-based KC intervention or a wait-list control group. Informed consent was obtained from parents of all child participants before evaluation and the children were also asked individually whether they wanted to participate before the start of each evaluation session and their decisions were respected.

In this kind of study, informed consent is relatively easy to obtain as the researchers were offering something the parents might want. In other instances, researchers may have to use **mild deception**. For example, Aronson and Linder (1965) aimed to test the effect of how a specific series of 'accidentally' overheard compliments would affect male attraction toward women. The participant 'accidentally' overheard the experimenter describe them in one of four ways: all positive; all negative; initially negative but becoming positive; or initially positive but becoming negative. Aronson and Linder (1965) concluded that males prefer a situation when they feel they have overcome an obstacle by changing from unattractive to attractive; winning over people is more rewarding and boosts self-esteem. However, Aronson and Linder had to deceive their participants as well as subject them to a humiliating ritual of overhearing negative comments about themselves. It is also doubtful whether the insight gained was genuinely 'new knowledge' and worth the risk of deliberately manipulating the participants' self-esteem.

TOK To what extent does psychology produce knowledge that has not been produced in the sciences, literature, or philosophy?

38.2 Protecting participants from (psychological or emotional) harm

Researchers should take preventive action in all research to avoid harming participants. This is particularly true in sensitive research topics, such as relationship problems or prejudice, discrimination, and violence. Due to the nature of certain methods (e.g. qualitative methods) such as in-depth interviews, participants may disclose very private information that they have never shared with anyone before. This can happen because the interview situation seems like a friendly encounter, where the participant may feel comfortable and safe with an individual who cares about them. However, the participant may regret such revelations and feel upset and so this situation should be avoided wherever possible.

Researchers into human relationships need to be particularly sensitive to people's feelings. For example, Kiesler and Baral (1970) aimed to test whether boosting the feelings of self-esteem in male participants would increase their chances of talking to an attractive woman. They issued a fake IQ test that was given to male participants. They were then given fake scores that were either high or low. The men were asked to wait in a room and an 'attractive' female entered. They found the men who had been given high IQ scores were quicker to talk to the woman. Kiesler and Baral (1970) concluded that self-esteem influences the chances of individuals interacting. However, deliberately manipulating people's self esteem in this way would raise serious questions from a modern REC committee. Full debriefs are needed to make sure that participants understand what they have experienced is part of a research study, although this does not mean they are protected from psychological harm while they are taking part.

TOK

To what extent should findings from studies that violate modern ethical rules be considered as valid in psychology?

Therefore, prior to the research and before they agree to participate, participants should have a clear understanding of the topics to be addressed. The researchers must approach sensitive issues through clear and direct questions, so that participants are not drawn into irrelevant and sensitive details by mistake. If participants show signs of discomfort, the researcher should be empathetic and consider stopping the research. If the research has dealt with emotional and sensitive issues, the researcher should try to return to less sensitive topics toward the end. It is not advised that the researcher should provide advice or counsel the participant, but he or she might provide useful information about where to find help if necessary. The researcher has to decide what they will do in these situations and present their intentions to the REC.

38.3 Anonymity and confidentiality

Anonymity and **confidentiality** are a key part of psychological research. Usually, the identity of participants should not be known outside the research team and not usually be identifiable to each other. Potential researchers have to show their RECs how they will guarantee their participants remain anonymous and how the data will be held securely. At no point should any reader of the eventual report be able to guess the identity of the participants.

Confidentiality means that research data will not be known to anyone outside the study. The researcher may have to change minor details in the report to avoid the possibility of participants being recognized. Confidentiality also relates to the way data is stored after the research. If interviews or observations have been recorded and archived, it can be difficult to guarantee total anonymity, so these should be destroyed when transcripts have been made. If the researcher finds it necessary to archive non-anonymized data, the participant should give written informed consent.

In addition, ethical issues in terms of anonymity may arise in case studies or in research designs with a small number of participants, because of the risk that they may be identified in research reports – it is difficult to lose people in a small qualitative crowd.

Activity

Find all of the new words or expressions from this chapter and write them into a document with their definitions and explanations next to them. Be creative and use diagrams or boxes to help make your personal glossary unique and effective.

Theory of knowledge

Theory of Knowledge (TOK) can ask an endless set of questions about knowledge, how it is created and communicated and how it is consumed by the knower.

The basic assumptions of TOK are:

- Knowledge is not fixed; it is dynamic and therefore open to influence from a variety of sources both inside the knower and out 'there' in the ether as a shared construction between humans.

- The processes that create knowledge (e.g. the assumptions or methods of the creator/s) influence knowledge itself and therefore influence what becomes known.

- The processes that communicate knowledge (e.g. the type of language used or the platform on which is it is communicated) also influence its 'appearance', and therefore influence what becomes known.

- The processes that act on the knower when knowledge is consumed (e.g. emotions, perceptions, culture, values) influence what becomes known.

TOK is invaluable for exploring some of the bigger questions relevant to the teaching, learning and practice of psychology. The questions explored in this chapter are:

- Can models and theories be used to understand and predict human behaviour?

- Does a researcher's choice of methodology affect the **reliability** or **credibility** of research?

- Is what we know about human behaviour limited by our ethical considerations?

- Are emotions universal?

- Are the methods of the natural sciences applicable in the human sciences?

- Are there human qualities or behaviours that will remain beyond the scope of science?

Can models and theories be used to understand and predict human behaviour?

Most researchers have an underlying aim to be published in a **peer-reviewed** journal. If they are working with predominantly **qualitative** data, they hope their findings will be seen as 'credible'; if they are working with **quantitative** data they hope their findings can be replicated by others and thus achieve reliability; and they hope their conclusions are seen as valid in the eyes of their peers.

Because those who propose models and theories are working with these pressures in mind, their models and theories are developed and tested as deliberate **constructs** of research methodology.

RODENT'S
THE THINKER

COGITO ERGO MUS

Models

A **model** is a representation of a complex process used to aid understanding via visualization and simplification. All models have inherent flaws because they omit some of the detail and nuance of the process or object that the model represents. For example, in the dominant models of memory, the focus is on stored and recalled information, with little attention to how information is dis-remembered or forgotten.

To be considered robust, models need to be supported with empirical evidence as well as giving predictions. However, there is often a trade-off of some kind where a model might sacrifice some complexity in order to accommodate the demands of evidence and prediction.

For example, there is little explanation for how emotion influences memory in the **multi-store model of memory** (MSM) from Atkinson and Shiffrin, (1968). Emotion undoubtedly plays a role in memory formation, storage, and retrieval, but because memory is a personal, abstract concept not easily observed and described empirically, it is difficult to model the relationship between emotion and memory in a way that can be generalized to large populations. Therefore, the processes that the MSM does focus on tend to be those that can be replicated, such as word recall, which then strengthens the model's observability and predictive **validity**.

Theories

Theories in the human sciences provide a framework to explain behaviour. As such, they are coherent, predictive explanations or interpretations of empirically determined facts. For example, **social learning theory** (SLT) assumes that humans learn behaviour, and even attitudes and values, through observation.

The theory is well-supported with quantitative and qualitative evidence. For example, the SLT theory has been used to explain how aggression can be acquired via the presence of models. One criticism of this theory is that it does not include key **causative** factors on behaviour, such as the biological influences of **testosterone**, brain structures, body shape or **neurotransmitters**.

In fact, few theories in the human sciences claim to offer an all-encompassing explanation for complex behaviour. Thus, as in the SLT example, the explanation may be strong on description, but limited in terms of explanation in any intentional or causative way.

A key question facing the human sciences, and psychology in particular, is: To what extent do theories and models actually add to our understanding of human behaviour? For example, does the SLT offer any genuinely new insights into the origins of human behaviour that could not be learnt from literature and films, or from authority figures such as parents, teachers, friends, or even a TV series?

While it is accepted within the discipline that a good theory provides a framework for understanding that can be shared and tested by other researchers, the question remains: How much genuinely new knowledge was generated by the process of theory construction?

In summary, it can be argued that because of their simplifications, models and theories can be used to understand and predict human behaviour as long as their limitations as research constructs are understood. Given these restraints, the **generalizations** or 'laws of large numbers' may not apply to individuals in terms of explanatory or predictive power.

TOK

To what extent do theories help or hinder knowledge creation in psychology?

Does a researcher's choice of methodology affect the reliability or credibility of research?

Human science research methods are usually classified into two broad categories: qualitative research and quantitative research.

Qualitative research

Qualitative researchers want to understand 'what it is like' to experience particular conditions, how people assign meaning to their experiences, and how they deal with them. People are usually studied in their own environment, preferably in naturally occurring settings, such as schools, homes, hospitals, and streets. The aim of this kind of research is to describe and explain events and experiences, but rarely will a definitive, single conclusion be reached. Qualitative research is more about gaining understandings (note the plural) and generating rich insights that represent participant experiences rather than reliable data sets that can be replicated by other researchers. However, the qualitative process can lead to suggestions about how to overcome the problems identified in qualitative studies.

Qualitative researchers are concerned with meaning and experience – that is, they are interested in how people make sense of the world. The emphasis is on producing credible interpretations that represent participant(s) experiences rather than reliable data sets that can be replicated by others.

Examples of qualitative methods are:

* **Case study:** a detailed analysis over time of an area of interest to produce context-dependent knowledge.

* **Naturalistic:** detailed observations of naturally occurring behaviour in a normal social setting.

* Interviews: unstructured, semi-structured and focus group-type approaches used to gain insights into people's thoughts, opinions and feelings.

Qualitative interviews may be followed by **surveys** (a quantitative method) to collect data from a representative sample so that the findings can be generalized to a larger population.

The deeply personal nature of capturing 'meaning and experience' means that there is less emphasis on reliability and more emphasis on credibility. Credibility is used in qualitative research to indicate whether or not the findings of the study are congruent with the participants' perceptions and experiences.

There is a reliance on the researchers' decisions, such as choosing participants, deciding on questions, designing interview settings, and interpreting data, all of which are linked to the researchers' personal circumstance. Because of these subjective elements, it is difficult for other researchers to replicate findings.

However, others can check whether the accounts and interpretations are credible by applying alternative methods of analysis in relation to the same subject matter. For instance, a form of peer review in qualitative research is the use of research diaries, to construct a 'data decision trail' to chart their decision-making for readers.

Quantitative research

Quantitative methods emphasize objective measurements that allow for mathematical analysis. As such, data can be tested and possibly replicated by others through peer review. Examples of quantitative methods are:

- **Experiments:** independent variables (IV) are manipulated to measure their effect on dependent variables (DV), which are controlled as far as possible.

- **Field experiments:** the experiment takes place in a real-life environment.

- **Quasi-experiments:** the participants are grouped by characteristics such as gender, **ethnicity**, or scores on a depression scale.

- **Natural experiments:** where researchers find naturally occurring variables and study them, such as observing how children play according to gender.

Credibility in quantitative research is measured using the notion of **validity**, which refers to 'correctness' or 'accuracy'. For instance: To what extent are researchers confident that an identifiable cause has had an identifiable effect? Validity is established through **cause-effect** experimental methods that are open to peer review.

Reliability in quantitative research is measured by using the notion of replicability. For instance: To what extent can other researchers produce the same results with the same methodology?

In summary, the aim of qualitative methods is more focused on producing credible accounts and interpretations of participants' experiences (although not always open to replication). The aim of quantitative methods is to produce reliable data sets that can be tested for validity by others.

TOK

Should reliability be as important as credibility in the human sciences?

Quantitative methods emphasize objective measurements and usually produce data that lends itself to statistical, mathematical, or numerical analysis. The emphasis is on producing reliable and valid interpretations that can be tested through peer review to achieve similar results and conclusions.

Is what we know about human behaviour limited by our ethical considerations?

Ethics refers to a moral framework that differentiates 'right' from 'wrong'. All human science research carries ethical responsibilities in respect of the **autonomy** and **dignity** of the persons involved in their studies. Within a research context this means that participants should understand what is involved in the research process, and that they have the right to withdraw if emotional trauma is experienced as part of the research.

The question, 'Is what we know about human behaviour limited by our ethical considerations?' assumes a universal ethical framework ('our ethical considerations') for human science research. This assumption is supported by Research Ethics Committees (RECs) found in most respected academic institutions. RECs are usually a multidisciplinary team of professional researchers and/or experienced academics with a balance of **gender** and **cultural** backgrounds.

A REC is normally responsible for (based on the BPS Ethical guidelines 2010):

- reviewing all research involving human participants conducted by individuals employed within or by that institution

- ensuring that the ethics review is independent, competent, and timely

- protecting the dignity, rights, and welfare of research participants

- considering the safety of the researcher(s)

- considering the legitimate interests of other stakeholders

- making informed judgements on the scientific merit of proposals

- making informed recommendations to the researcher if the proposal is found to be wanting in some respect.

If there were no ethical limits on psychological experiments and other kinds of studies, then researchers would be free to violate the basic human rights of participants in their pursuit of knowledge. Such violations of ethical principals have happened throughout history under political regimes that do not recognize the dignity of the individual. Well-known examples include those conducted under the Nazi human experimentation programme during the Second World War (United States Holocaust Museum).

Among others, the Nazis conducted research on the:

- effects of mustard gas on the human body

- effects of bone, muscle, and nerve transplantation on the human body

- effects of freezing on the human body

- effects of head injuries on the human body

- effects of immunizations on the human body.

It is theoretically possible that the results of these studies found their way into Allied hands and that the findings were useful to them. It is thought that pharmaceutical knowledge in particular was used by companies after the war to develop drugs.

Ethics refers to a moral framework that differentiates 'right' from 'wrong'. All human science research carries ethical responsibilities because researchers interact with their participants on a humane level, unlike the natural sciences where the objects of study do not have consciousness or feelings (so far as we know).

Are ethics a uniquely human construct? Do other species have ethics?

To what extent should ethical frameworks be universal within the human sciences? What would the implications be for such a view? What are the implications for differing and culturally-specific ethical frameworks?

327

Research the Abu Ghraib Prison and the Dozier School for Boys in Florida and use Zimbardo's and Milgram's research to answer, 'How could rational, educated people treat other human beings in this way?'

And then answer this question: 'Should knowledge gained through research judged to be unethical later be used in research?

Other examples of ethical importance include the obedience studies conducted by Stanley Milgram (1963) and Philip Zimbardo (1971). Milgram's interest in human obedience produced genuinely new knowledge at a time when it was assumed that people would not obey orders resulting in another's pain. However, his experiments showed that people will obey orders they know to be wrong if placed in a certain context.

Context-dependent behaviour was also investigated by Zimbardo in studies that showed that situational cues within a mock prison produced behaviour in violation of ethical norms. In both cases, Zimbardo and Milgram acknowledged the emotional trauma visited on their participants who took their roles too seriously. It is unlikely that these types of studies would get REC approval today in human science experimental settings.

Are emotions universal?

Any approach to feelings and emotions should consider **physiology**, **cognition**, and behavioural elements. Emotions perform a number of roles in human behaviour.

Emotions are difficult to define but usually are considered to have physiological, cognitive, and behavioural elements.

*   They attach meaning to basic physiological changes.

*   They play an informational role in the cognitive sense. For example, emotions contribute to cognition by flagging what needs attention while devaluing what is less important (DeSousa, 1987).

*   They can bring about change in the environment through facial or bodily expressions (James, 2009), such as smiling or grimacing.

Although 'emotion' is a broad term, Forgas (1992) and Fineman (1993) take the view that feelings are what humans experience, while emotions are the expression of those feelings. A working definition should be discussed and agreed upon before trying to understand their role in human behaviour. It is worth breaking the question down into the following elements.

To what extent are emotions universal?

Physiological changes

While there are slight bodily differences across the world, the human body has universal commonalities that make it 'human'. For example, the physical and chemical structures as well as the role of the **endocrine** system is the same in every human. The endocrine system is a collection of glands that secretes hormones directly into the circulatory system. It is therefore an information signalling system that operates via a process known as endocrine signalling. The **adrenal glands** are endocrine glands that secrete **adrenaline**, among other hormones. Adrenaline is known as the 'fight or flight' hormone because it readies the individual in situations of perceived danger and produces physiological arousal. Therefore, when the human body secretes adrenaline the individual will experience a heightened physiological arousal. However, secretion will not occur in the same way in the same situations for different individuals. For example, someone who is new to skydiving will have a different physiological reaction to an instructor who has been skydiving for many years.

Are underlying physiological changes universal?

Cognitive interpretations of physiological changes

While physiological arousal is a biological phenomenon, the stimulant that is context and person specific has to be interpreted. For example, Dutton and Aron (1974) aimed to test whether physiological arousal can influence attraction by comparing attraction levels in two different environments (see bridge experiment p. 279) Their research suggested attraction occurs when physiological arousal is interpreted as sexual excitement.

However, not everyone will interpret the physiological arousal in the same way. The individual nature of emotions causes further troubles for analysis. For example, attraction is a deeply personal experience influenced both by biological determinism in the form of sexual orientation, as well as cultural **norms**. The woman in the Dutton and Aron (1974) study was uncovered, unaccompanied, and approaching men themselves. Therefore, men from cultures who are not used to seeing women act in this way may also have had mixed responses and may not have interpreted those reactions as attraction.

Behavioural projections

Such projections of emotions are regulated by **sociocultural** norms. How humans express themselves in a social context is highly culturally specific, as well as being influenced by other factors such as gender expectations. For example, Kessler et al. (1994) reported that women in the USA are about two-thirds more likely than men to be depressed, with a similar trend in the UK. However, gender differences in depression rates may be the result of the two genders responding to sociocultural pressures in terms of how to act and feel, which would mean their underlying depression symptoms manifest themselves in gender-specific ways (Nazroo, 2001).

For example, men may have been **socialized** to express depression symptoms in the form of anger, being alone, or turning to drugs, or other forms of acting out, whereas women are more likely to talk about their feelings in social settings and peer groups.

These projected social behaviours mean they are more likely to be labelled as 'depressed' and seek help, which may account for the gender differences in **prevalence rates** of depression. Women may also feel more comfortable seeking help with personal problems from healthcare professionals as a result of sociocultural norms. Studies have shown that expected gender differences in depressive disorders were balanced out by higher male rates of alcohol abuse and drug dependency (e.g. Metzler et al., 1995), suggesting there is no underlying biological difference between men and women in experiencing feelings of depression, but there are differences in emotional expression due to sociocultural expectations for how different genders should act.

The physiological underpinnings of humans are generally universal. However, emotions are part of a complex feedback mechanism that includes the body, cognition, and sociocultural influences, as well as other physiological phenomena such as drugs or food that can all heavily impact emotion and emotional expression. Therefore, while there are general emotions that might be considered universal (e.g. sadness or happiness), the context of when, why, and how they manifest themselves is heavily influenced by specific factors.

Are the methods of the natural sciences applicable in the human sciences?

The natural sciences use a variety of methods to generate, interpret, and present data and analysis.

TOK Are cognitive interpretations of physiological changes universal?

TOK Are the behavioural projections universal?

The scientific method is a formal method used by scientists that consists of systematic observation, measurement, and experiment, and the formulation, testing, and modification of hypotheses.

Methods of the natural sciences

The scientific method

The **scientific method** is a formal method used by scientists that consists of systematic pursuit of knowledge involving the recognition and formulation of a problem, the collection of data through observation and experiment, and the formulation and testing of **hypotheses**. It encourages the reduction of complex phenomena to the level of self-contained and isolated **variables**, which can then be manipulated and measured.

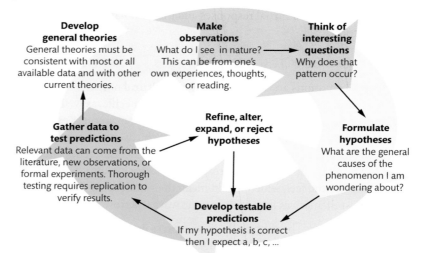

Develop general theories
General theories must be consistent with most or all available data and with other current theories.

Make observations
What do I see in nature? This can be from one's own experiences, thoughts, or reading.

Think of interesting questions
Why does that pattern occur?

Gather data to test predictions
Relevant data can come from the literature, new observations, or formal experiments. Thorough testing requires replication to verify results.

Refine, alter, expand, or reject hypotheses

Formulate hypotheses
What are the general causes of the phenomenon I am wondering about?

Develop testable predictions
If my hypothesis is correct then I expect a, b, c, ...

A diagram showing the cyclical process of the scientific method.

TOK Does the scientific method help or hinder knowledge creation in the human sciences?

The scientific method generates knowledge by providing a framework for developing and testing new ideas then allowing the results to be tested by others.

The use of peer review

The natural sciences are shared knowledge (the results of scientific studies are available to others working in the same field). Peer review is the process where other scholars evaluate a specific study and its conclusions in journals periodically published and read by experts in the field. For example: The *Journal of Neuroscience Methods* publishes papers that describe new methods specifically for neuroscience research conducted on invertebrates, vertebrates, or humans.

The use of theory

A theory is an explanation of some aspect of the natural world that has been acquired through the scientific method. Therefore, it has been repeatedly tested and confirmed through observation and experimentation, as well as peer review. Theories provide a framework for understanding and articulating knowledge and they allow new ideas to be developed (predicted) that support the basic assumptions of the original theory.

The scientific method has a clear set of methods to generate knowledge.

The use of models

Models are representations of complex processes. Characteristics of models are:

They are a simpler version of a complex system or object.

They focus on one feature of a system or object, descriptions of objects or processes.

They have explanatory power.

They generate predictions.

Models are representations of complex processes that are useful because they simplify complex phenomena, making it easier to study a concept or process or object.

The use of classification

Natural science seeks to find patterns and order in the natural world through classifications. Classification helps explain relationships in the natural world and helps improve prediction. For example, animal species are classified according to their body type and breeding habits.

Assumptions of the natural sciences

Scientific law: a phenomenon that will invariably occur whenever certain conditions exist. The formal statement about such a phenomenon is called a natural law – a generalized rule to describe a body of observations. For example, Newton's First Law states that an object will remain at rest or in uniform motion in a straight line unless acted upon by an external force.

Empiricism: refers to the emphasis placed on physical evidence (usually quantitative) to test hypotheses, support lawful relationships, and build theories. Evidence is usually collected by carrying out experiments and observation. It is a key part of the scientific method that all hypotheses and theories must be tested under scientific conditions rather than using pure reasoning, revelation, or imagination.

Induction: science can never test all possible examples. For example, the natural sciences cannot observe every polar bear to test if they are all white, even though all polar bears to date have been white. Therefore, it is not possible to say with absolute certainty that all polar bears are white. The natural sciences assume that conclusions that apply to a few samples will apply to all examples. This is the process of induction linked to the assumption mentioned above that nature has laws and principles that can be applied to other individuals not included in the sample.

Generalizability: the natural sciences make generalizations from a smaller sample that applies to a larger population. For example, because scientists cannot study all tree roots, they study a small sample to find similarities and differences that they can generalize to all tree roots.

Positivism: the belief that emphasizes knowledge creation by the use of empirical evidence and scientific methods (Jakobsen, 2013).

Falsifiability/disconfirmation: the ability to test scientific ideas and have the opportunity to demonstrate them to be false. Karl Popper argues that science theories can be clearly separated from non-science theories through falsification: if a theory cannot be tested and falsified by scientific means, then it is not scientific (Resnik, 2000).

Causation: the belief that one event leads to another and that events occur in predictable ways (Shepard and Greene, 2003).

To what extent are these methods and assumptions applicable in the human sciences?

Human scientists ask questions about human behaviour that can be tested under consistent conditions to form predictions and models/theories. The scientific method promotes the notion that variables should be isolated and studied via manipulation and measurement to test whether one variable will have a cause-effect relationship with another.

Peer review allows others to share the knowledge while evaluating the methodologies and conclusions.

Theories provide explanatory frameworks for understanding and articulating knowledge about human behaviour. They can be tested for their robustness to see how valid they are in explaining human phenomena.

Human behaviour can be classified to allow predictions and understandings to develop. It should always be remembered, humans are products of evolution and are classified on a very basic level as mammals, and therefore have many characteristics in common with other mammals.

Models can help describe and explain complex human processes and behaviours such as memory, perception, and relationship formation.

It can be assumed that humans will act in a certain way under certain conditions that allows for them to be studied and the results generalized to larger populations. Just as in science, problems can occur when the generalizations become too broad or are applied to populations that have different characteristics.

It is assumed that human behaviour can be measured and quantified using the methods of the natural sciences. For example, thought processes such as attitudes and behaviours (e.g. aggression) can be measured and observed.

Therefore, scientific methodologies and assumptions can be applied to the human sciences. The methodologies and assumptions will help and/or hinder knowledge creation depending on how they are used and applied. It is the role of the human scientist to be aware of the strengths and limitations of the various methodologies and assumptions to ensure their data and interpretations do not presume ultimate truth, while also considering how other methods may be an equally valid way for discovering the complexities of human nature.

Are there human qualities or behaviours that will remain beyond the scope of science?

Academic psychology deals with a broad range of areas, from the action of single hormones to large scale social group behavior. The diversity among the fields of psychology means that different methods are used to gather and analyze data dependent on a number of factors, such as the purpose of the research, the characteristics of the participants, and the researchers' beliefs about the nature of knowledge and how it can be acquired.

Despite the ability to apply the methods of the natural sciences to the human sciences, questions remain about the extent to which these methods should be applied and whether there are human qualities or behaviours that remain beyond the scope of psychology and science. Noam Chomsky suggested that the methods of psychology and the natural sciences are far from the only avenue that humans have available to them:

> 'There is, incidentally, no reason to suppose that all the problems we face are best approached in these terms. It is quite possible – overwhelmingly probable, one might guess – that we will always learn more about human life and personality from novels than from scientific psychology. The science forming capacity is only one facet of our mental endowment. We use it where we can but are not restricted to it, fortunately' (Chomsky, 2008: 249).

Chomsky's remarks suggest that while psychology has a role to play, it is far from the only approach to learning about human behaviour. Psychology has been heavily influenced by the natural sciences, which encourage the reduction of complex phenomena to the level of generally self-contained and isolated variables that can then be manipulated and measured.

For example, love is a deeply personal phenomenon but it can be explained using the methods and assumptions of science. It can be seen as an **adaptive** function that has evolved as a way to keep couples who have procreated together. Therefore, researchers assume the evolutionary consequences of love are so important that there must be some long-established biological mechanisms that regulate and promote it.

Through this lens, love can be reduced to a series of chemical reactions that increase the chances of the resulting offspring surviving and thriving. For example, Marazziti et al. (1999) measured the density of the platelet 5-HT transporter in 20 subjects who had recently fallen in love within the previous six months and were compared with 20 non-medicated **obsessive compulsive disorder** (OCD) patients and 20 **controls** (see p. 16 for details). They found subjects who were in the early romantic phase of a love relationship were no different from OCD patients in terms of the low density level of the platelet 5-HT, and both groups had significantly lower levels than in the controls. They concluded that **serotonin** could act as a biological mechanism to explain 'falling in love' and pair bonding behaviour.

However, the problem with the scientific approach to understanding 'love' is that it tells us very little about the personal experiences of people who are 'in love'. It does not address the sociocultural nature of love and how different people from different cultures may have different views and experiences of the phenomena. It fails to explain why some people can 'love' inanimate objects such as cars, or have close emotional bonds with pets. If love is reduced to the level of biochemical reactions, then we may learn about the physiological basis of love but learn little about the experience of it.

Chomsky's view suggests literature is an equally valid way to access and learn about human experiences. For example, the following poem by the Bengali poet Rabindranath Tagore tells us a great deal about the emotions and sentiment of love:

Unending Love (edited)

'I seem to have loved you in numberless forms, numberless times…
In life after life, in age after age, forever.
My spellbound heart has made and remade the necklace of songs,
That you take as a gift, wear round your neck in your many forms,
In life after life, in age after age, forever.'

Poems are products of the human capacity to imagine. Poems cause us to think and feel in ways that we might otherwise not. They cause us to ask questions about human nature, about the world around us, and about ourselves. They do this in a way that perhaps psychology and science are not able to do.

The existence of other approaches to understanding the human condition does not automatically make psychology and science less or more valid. It simply posits them as one of the many avenues that humans can come to know their world while trying to make sense of what it is to be human.

Internal assessment

Every IB Diploma Psychology student must submit one simple experimental study as part of the requirements for the course. This is marked by your teacher and moderated externally by an examiner. The mark for this piece of work makes up 20 per cent of your overall grade for your Diploma Psychology course. It is up to you to plan, carry out and then write up your experiment. The internal assessment (IA) is compulsory for both SL and HL students. The requirements for SL and HL students are the same.

The purpose of this section is to enable you to obtain the best marks possible.

The two most important things to remember are:

*   your experiment needs to be ethical

*   your experiment needs to be an actual experiment with only one **independent variable** (IV) that you have deliberately manipulated.

Making sure your study is ethical

For the experiment to be considered ethical, it must not cause any harm to anyone. This includes participants, researchers, bystanders, teachers/supervisors, moderators, and eventual readers. Harm can mean a number of different things such as: hurting, injuring, tormenting, teasing, torturing, traumatizing, impairing, wounding, mistreating, punishing, maltreating, misusing, abusing, molesting, damaging, or adversely affecting. It is important to understand that IB considers harm as psychological and emotional and not just in a physical sense. Your IA may well receive a mark of 0 if you do not take these ethical responsibilities seriously.

The following guidelines must be followed.

*   Any experimental study that creates anxiety, stress, pain or discomfort for participants is not permitted.

*   Experiments involving deception, conformity, obedience, or any other form of harm are not permitted.

*   Any experiment that offends the sensitivities of the particular school, community, culture, or country is not permitted.

*   Any experimental study that involves unjustified deception, involuntary participation or invasion of privacy, including the inappropriate use of information and communication technology (ICT), email and the internet, must be avoided. However, it should be noted:

    o   there may be rare occasions when such infringements cannot be avoided, in which case the approval of other experienced psychologists should be sought before proceeding

    o   **partial deception** may be allowed for some experiments where full knowledge of the experiment would fundamentally affect the outcome – such experiments are permissible provided they do no harm and participants are fully debriefed at the end. Participants retain their right to withdraw their data at this point and this should be stated clearly in the design section.

- Any experiment involving conformity and obedience studies is not permitted under any circumstances.

- Consent must be explicitly gained from participants through the use of a consent form. **Implied consent** is not acceptable. This process should be clearly documented.

- All participants must be informed of the aims and objectives of the experiment – however, partial deception is allowed (see above).

- All participants must be informed before commencing the experimental study that they have the right to withdraw at any time. Pressure must not be placed on any individual participant to continue with the investigation.

- Young children (under 12 years) must not be used as participants as they cannot give **informed consent**.

- Experimental studies involving older children (from 12 years up to 16 years) need the written consent of parent(s) or guardian(s). Students must ensure that parents are fully informed about the implications for children who take part in such research. Where an experimental study is conducted with children in a school, the written consent of the teachers concerned must also be obtained. This process must be documented, although names should be removed from the documentation to guarantee **anonymity**.

- Participants must be debriefed and given the right to withdraw their own personal data and responses.

- Anonymity for each participant must be guaranteed even after the experiment has finished.

- Participants must be shown the results of the research and if reasonable deception was involved, the participants must have the deception explained and justified to them.

- You must not conduct research with any participant who is not in a fit state of mind and cannot respond freely and independently.

- If any participant shows stress or pain at any stage of an experimental study, the investigation must finish immediately, and the participant must be allowed to withdraw.

- Animals must not be used for the experimental study.

- All data collected must be kept in a confidential and responsible manner and not disclosed to any other person outside of the experimental work group.

- Data must not be used for purposes other than that agreed to by the participants.

- Teachers should be informed immediately if you suspect other groups or individual students are breaching guidelines. If you witness something that you consider to be a breach of ethical guidelines then it is your duty to report it.

- Experimental studies that are conducted online are subject to the same guidelines. Any data collected online must be deleted once the research is complete. Such data must not be used for any purpose other than the conduct of the experimental study.

Making sure your study is an experiment

You should decide on your choice of topic. The following points will serve as a guide.

- The topic can be from any area of psychology.

- The theory or model on which your investigation is based is known as the **base-study**. It must be psychological in nature and must have appeared in a **peer-reviewed** publication.

- The link between the study or model used and your aims and objectives for your experiment must be made clear.

- The relevance of the experiment, that is, the reason for carrying out the experiment, must be made clear.

You are only allowed to use the experimental method in your IA. The experimental method looks for a relationship between two variables to support a **hypothesis** of **cause-and-effect**.

The two variables are:

- the independent variable (IV): the variable manipulated by the experimenters

- the **dependent variable** (DV): the variable that is measured

All other factors that could affect the DV should be controlled as far as possible. The study you are using as a base for your IA may guide you towards appropriate controls, but it may be adapted to suit the context in which you and your group are working.

Approaches to the independent variable

It is important that there is only one IV in the experiment. You should use your base-study to help guide how you manipulate the IV. You may wish to conduct a simple experiment, in which case the IV should only have two conditions. However, you should remember that your base-study may have several conditions for the IV. You may choose to replicate all the conditions or choose to simplify the experiment and select two conditions for your own experiment. Furthermore, details of how the IV is **operationalized** may also differ from the base-study.

For example, you may choose different words for a word list, or a different type of music for the study to suit your own circumstances, provided the link between the study and your own experiment remains clear.

Variables that are based on pre-existing characteristics of the participants are not suitable for the IA. These include, but are not limited to:

- **gender** (e.g. comparing the results of female and male participants)

- age (e.g. comparing the performance of 10-year-old participants and 18-year-old participants)

- native language (e.g. comparing native French speakers and native Mandarin speakers)

- **culture** (e.g. comparing the results of Afro-Caribbean participants and Swedish participants)

- education level (e.g. comparing the performance of students in grade 5 and grade 11)

- **socioeconomic** status (e.g. poor participants and rich participants)

- handedness (e.g. left-handed and right-handed participants).

If you use any of these as an IV, your experiment will not meet IB requirements and will not earn marks.

In addition, experiments involving the following elements are not acceptable and will not earn marks: **placebos**, ingestion or inhalation (e.g. food, drink, smoking, drugs), or deprivation (e.g. sleep, food).

Approaches to the dependent variable

The DV is the variable being measured. There are a number of approaches you can take.

You can replicate the operationalization of the DV used in the study on which you base your experiment.

You can adapt the operationalization of the DV to suit your own circumstances or resources. For example, you could alter the number of measurements taken, the type of measurements taken or use a different DV altogether. However, you must make the link between your base-study and your own experiment clear and be able to justify your alterations.

In addition, you may choose to alter the method of the base-study in a variety of different ways to better suit the context in which you are working.

For example, you may alter:

*   the type of participants (as the most feasible participants for a school experiment would be other students)

*   the number of participants involved (the base-study may have had access to participant numbers that are impossible to replicate in a school)

*   the design (the base-study may have used a **matched pairs** design that cannot be replicated in school as there are too few participants to choose from, making matching problematic).

The marking criteria are designed to allow for a degree of flexibility and full marks can be achieved if the variations outlined above are applied.

Group work

You are required to work as part of a group to plan and conduct the investigation. You cannot work alone. Your research method, subjects and materials, as well as the operationalization of the IVs and DVs, will be the result of the group working together. Once the data has been generated, the collaboration is complete and your group should disperse. Each member of the group must write up the report independently of other group members. The data should be analysed and conclusions drawn independently.

You should not discuss the results with other members of the group. Likewise, your evaluation should be carried out independently. While there will be some similarities (as you will be drawing on the same data as other members of the group), it is important that you remember the expectations for **academic honesty** and the consequences of academic malpractice.

Your group must consist of a minimum of two students and a maximum of four students. SL and HL students may work together. You may also choose to collaborate virtually with another student or students in other IB World Schools. Alternatively, you may work with another student studying a psychology course from another curriculum provider (such as A-levels or AP), or a student studying a related course such as an experimental science or social science course.

Assessing group work

Collaboration represents an authentic way of working in the field of research, but as it is difficult to assess a team member's contribution completely objectively, the reporting of the method is awarded fewer marks than the other sections. However, your evaluation of the method (including protocols, participants and materials) is where a clear understanding of the exploration will be rewarded, as this is carried out independently of the group. It is expected that you will point out the strengths as well as the limitations of the method as part of your evaluation – a good design will generate as much opportunity for comment as a less effective design, but it is anticipated that you will only gain the higher marks for the evaluation if you are fully engaged in the thinking behind the design of the investigation.

Make sure you fully understand the difference between collaboration and collusion before you begin.

Organization and presentation

The following details should be stated on the front page of the IA:

- title of the investigation

- IB candidate code (alphanumeric, e.g. XYZ123)

- IB candidate code for all the other group members

- date, month and year of submission

- number of words.

Your final report should be between 1800 and 2200 words in length and consist of the following components. You should use these as subheadings to subdivide your work:

- Introduction
- Exploration
- Analysis
- Evaluation
- References

The references are not assessed but must be included to meet the requirements of honest academic practice. Not attributing the ideas of others included in your work amounts to academic misconduct. If academic misconduct is discovered in any work you submit for IB assessment, you will not be awarded a grade for the subject.

It should be noted:

- you are not expected to define existing ideas or create new knowledge
- you are expected to research and represent existing definitions and the work of published academics.

Your reference section should reflect this.

The appendices do not count towards the word count but should be kept to a minimum. Appendices should include:

- raw data tables
- print-outs of calculations and/or results from statistics software or calculations made for analytical purposes
- consent form pro forma (unfilled)
- copy of standardized instructions and debriefing notes
- supplementary materials.

How to write an internal assessment

The following section is divided into the subheadings you should you use for your IA.

Introduction

In this section you have to:

- clearly state the aim of your investigation
- explain the relevance of the aim – why it is important
- explain the theory or model on which your investigation is based

- describe the link between the base-study or model and your investigation and explain why it is important

- clearly state the IVs and DVs

- clearly operationalize the **null** or **research hypotheses**.

Suggested word count: 600 words

The introduction should contain the academic background to the study. It should clearly show how your investigation is linked to the original base-study/theory. You must explain the base-study in depth. Explain the aim, method, results, and conclusion. The aim can be defined as the overall research goal (usually the research question). It does not need to be copied from the original study, you can use your own words. The method can be defined as what happened in the study. The results can be defined as exactly what was found in terms of their data. The conclusions can be defined as the broader meaning that comes from the results.

Example paragraph showing how to explain a base-study:

> *Loftus and Palmer (1974) aimed to show that eyewitnesses do not accurately 'replay' what they saw. Instead they reconstruct events based on their schemas or simplified mental representations. Loftus and Palmer aimed to show that participants' perceptions of a car's speed could be manipulated by leading questions. An independent measures laboratory experiment was conducted, with 45 undergraduate students being presented with seven film clips of traffic accidents. The experiment's IV was a key verb that took five conditions in the question: 'About how fast were the cars going when they smashed into each other?' 'Smashed' was substituted with 'collided', 'bumped', 'contacted' and 'hit'. The mean speed associated with 'smashed' was 40.8 mph while the mean for 'hit' was 31.8 mph. Loftus and Palmer (1974) concluded that eyewitness testimony can be manipulated by using different words in a leading question.*

The aim of the study is clearly stated.

The aims are statements of what the research tries to show. Do not use the word 'investigate' when stating the aim because the IA is an investigation. You should state the aim precisely, so use words such as measure, discover, explain and evaluate. You can also use the aim of the IA in the title. The aim should include the target population.

Example of an aim being clearly stated:

> *Aim: To measure the effect of leading verbs (IV) on speed perceptions (DV) on international high school students.*

The experimental and null hypotheses must be appropriately stated and fully operationalized. The prediction made in the experimental hypothesis is justified by your explanation of the original base-study/theory.

The hypothesis is a statement that predicts the experiment's outcome. An operationalized hypothesis clearly contains the IV and shows the effect on the DV. There should be an experimental hypothesis (H1) and a null hypothesis (H0). The null hypothesis predicts that the IV will have no effect on the DV. The experimental hypothesis predicts that there will be an effect. You should clearly state what this effect will be, and indicate how it will be observed. Based on the results of the experiment, one hypothesis will be rejected. The hypothesis should follow logically from previous research.

Examples of experimental and null hypotheses:

> H1: Participants exposed to the leading verb 'smash' when asked to estimate the speed of a car crash will have significantly higher speed estimations than participants who are exposed to the verb 'hit' when asked to estimate the speed of a car crash.
>
> H0: Participants exposed to the leading verb 'smash' when asked to estimate the speed of a car crash will have no significant difference in their speed estimation than participants who are exposed to the verb 'hit' when asked to estimate the speed of a car crash.

> H1: Participants exposed to a more emotionally intense verb (smash) will have significantly higher speed perceptions (measured in mph) than participants who were exposed to a less emotionally intense verb (hit) when asked to estimate the speed of a car on a video.
>
> H0: Participants exposed to a more emotionally intense verb (smash) will not have significantly higher speed perceptions (measured in mph) than participants who were exposed to a less emotionally intense verb (hit) when asked to estimate the speed of a car on a video.

Exploration

In this section you have to:

- state and explain the research design

- state and explain the **sampling technique**

- describe the sample and explain why they were chosen

- state the variables that you controlled (the **controlled** variables) and explain why they were controlled

- state and explain why you chose the materials you did.

State and explain the research design

Experimental designs are usually either:

- **repeated measures** (the same participants experience the IV's conditions); or

- **independent measures** (different participants experience the IV's conditions).

'Explain' means to give reasons for using a particular design and how it was used in your investigation.

For example:

> Repeated measures are used because they require fewer participants, and variables such as participants' intelligence can be controlled in each condition.

Independent measures avoid **demand characteristics**, such as participants guessing what the experiment is trying to find out and then not responding naturally.

Example paragraph:

> *Independent measures were used to control demand characteristics. Participants would probably guess the nature of the study if they were exposed to both verbs and so their responses would be unnatural. We gathered the participants in a room and asked them to draw pieces of paper from a hat labelled with letters A or B.*

State and explain the sampling technique

Sampling means choosing participants from the wider population and this section requires you to describe how and why you chose the participants.

There are three main types of sampling.

Purposive sampling: targets a particular group of people who would make good study participants because of their characteristics. 'Appropriate' characteristics would depend on the aim of the study.

Example:

> *We chose purposive sampling because the experiment required a good command of English. We deliberately approached good English speakers who we knew because having some participants with native English skills and others who have English as a second or third language would make the results less reliable.*

Opportunity sampling: where members of a target population are asked to take part just because they are available. In this situation, you ask possible participants that you see in the corridor or in lessons. This is sometimes called convenience sampling.

Example:

> *We chose an opportunity sampling method because it is quick and convenient and because we needed the full agreement of a teacher in advance to use their classes for our experiment. We approached a supportive teacher and agreed in advance to use their lesson time for our experiment. We used 22 participants because this was the class size.*

Random sampling: each member of a target population has the same chance of being sampled. In this situation, you write each name on a separate piece of paper and put the names into a container and then pull out the required number of participants. Do not use the phrase 'random selection' as it is not a suitable way to describe this process.

Example:

> *We chose a random sampling method to achieve an unbiased sample. We placed every name from our grade level onto a piece of paper and then put them in a hat and pulled out 20 names.*

Describe the sample and explain why they were chosen

The sample refers to the participants who will take part in the experiment. You need to describe the group in terms of:

- age range

- gender ratio

- nationality

- language proficiency

- whether they are psychology students or not.

These characteristics can be collected when giving out the consent forms. The potential participants could be asked to answer questions relating to their personal characteristics.

State how you allocated your participants to the groups

Example:

> *We put the participants' names in a hat and then pulled them out. In this way we randomly allocated them to each condition before the experiment began.*

State the relevant characteristics of the sample and explain why they are important

Example:

> *Fifteen out of our 20 participants were fluent in English or considered it their first language. However, five stated English was their second language. This is relevant because the investigation was conducted in English.*

State the controlled variables and explain why they were controlled

The controlled variables are not the variables you are interested in. However, they have to be held constant so the experimenter can focus on the IV and DV. You can list the controlled variables and, next to each, explain why you considered it a variable you needed to control and then state how you controlled it.

For example:

> *Pre-existing knowledge of IB DP Psychology: this is a variable that needs to be controlled because knowing the outcome or the background to the investigation may impact how a participant behaves and responds. We controlled for this variable by screening potential participants and asking them on the consent form if they had studied IB DP Psychology or had a sibling who had done so. Any potential participant who answered in the affirmative was not asked to participate.*

Age: this is a variable that needs to be controlled because the task in the investigation is cognitive in nature and cognitive development is linked to age. We controlled for this variable by only choosing students in Grades 11 and 12. We also asked for their age on the consent form and excluded anyone who was below the age of 16.

State and explain why you chose the materials you did

Materials refers to any object or apparatus you used to conduct your investigation. You can list them and provide an explanation next to each.

Example:

Clock: we used a clock to make sure the responses were timed and kept consistent between the two groups.

Pens: we provided pens to make sure they were kept constant between each group because the colour and type of pen may influence the participants' perception of the task they were asked to do.

Quiet room: we found a quiet room in the school because we needed to isolate the participants from intruding noise as this would distract them from the task they were asked to do.

Analysis

In this section you have to:

- state and explain the use of **descriptive** and **inferential statistics**

- present a clear and accurate graph that addresses the hypothesis

- interpret the statistical findings in a way that links them to the hypothesis.

Your analysis section should not include any raw data of any kind. Usually if you can see any individual participant scores then this can be considered raw data. All raw data should be available in an appendix. You can make reference to it in the Analysis section by labelling the place where you have put it (e.g. Appendices I) with Roman numerals.

The data collected should be appropriately displayed.

This means you use appropriate headings for each section of your results.

You need one graph with an appropriate title and one descriptive results table with an appropriate title.

Your analysis section should be further subdivided with the following titles: 'Descriptive statistics' and 'Inferential statistics'. Descriptive statistics describe a data set without drawing any inferences or conclusions about what is being described. Inferential statistics draw conclusions or inferences regarding to what extent the independent variable caused a change in the dependent variable.

The graph of results must be accurate, clear and directly relevant to the hypotheses of the study. Make sure that the graph has a title, a legend (a key), and a clear label for each axis. They should be simple representations of the results (descriptive), not the raw data.

The graph should show whether the experiment's DV is affected by the change in the IV. This could be as simple as showing a bar chart representing the mean of IV1 and the mean of IV2. It is often better to draw the graph by hand (with a pencil and ruler), scan it and paste it into the report because computer-generated graphs sometimes show too much or inappropriate information. Good graphs are clear and simple.

In order to make sure that the graph is clear you should:

- make it large

- give it a title, and include (N = ...) after the title to show the number of participants

- give it a border

- label the axes (include units)

- label the data either on the graph or with a key (legend)

- show the measure of central tendency and the measure of dispersion, if possible.

The data should be analysed in terms of descriptive statistics to highlight the **variability** and spread of the data.

Your results section must show whether the IV caused a change in the DV.

Your descriptive results should usually involve one measure of **central tendency** and one measure of **dispersion**. These should be applied to the data and their use explained. A common mistake is to calculate more than one measure of central tendency (mean, median, mode) and more than one measure of dispersion averages (range, standard deviation, variance, interquartile range). Use one of each.

A measure of central tendency shows the most likely, the most probable, the typical piece, or the average piece of data. Choose from the mean, median, or mode.

Use the mean to describe the typical, most likely, piece of data. If there are extreme outliers, (unusually high or low pieces of data) the mean will be distorted. As a result, it does not describe the typical data. If there are outliers, use the median.

If the data is not **continuous**, use the mode. If a group includes five girls and 15 boys, the most likely gender is male. It would not make sense to say that the typical gender is 0.75 male.

A measure of dispersion shows how varied the group of data is or how dispersed the data is from the normal or central data. The actual measure used depends on the data set you have collected.

Use the standard deviation if the data is continuous and the data set is **normally distributed** and use the interquartile range if the data is skewed.

Make sure that you include information on what the statistics are describing. For example, the mean speed is not 35.5, it is 35.5 miles per hour.

Examples:

> *The low value indicates that the data tends to be very close to the mean, suggesting there is a great deal of similarity in the data set.*
>
> *The high standard deviation indicates the data is spread out over a large range of values, suggesting there is less similarity in the data set.*

The median and interquartile range go together because they both ignore outliers. Mean and standard deviation go together because standard deviation measures the spread from the mean.

Results

You should put the results in a table showing the values. You should explain what you see in the table. For example:

> *The median estimate of speed for the question using 'smashed' was XX mph, while the median estimate of speed for the question using 'hit' was XX mph. The standard deviation of the data set associated with 'smashed' was XX mph. The standard deviation of the data set associated with 'hit' was XX mph.*

Inferential statistics are used to draw conclusions about the significance of the data generated in terms of supporting a hypothesis. Cause and effect should be treated with caution and conclusions should be tentative.

Social scientists need to know if the difference seen in the DV data sets is large enough to be the result of them manipulating the IV. If it is, they can be confident the manipulation of the IV caused the effect on the DV and their hypothesis has been supported. In statistical terms, they need to know whether the difference between the two conditions is significant enough. Therefore a statistical test needs to be applied to the data.

In summary, inferential statistics help answer the question: To what extent are we confident that the IV caused the DV to change, and that the DV did not change by chance?

You need to choose an appropriate inferential statistical test and explicitly justify why you have chosen it. There are two questions that need to be asked before a statistical test can be chosen:

Which design was used (repeated measures or independent measures)?

Is the data nominal, ordinal, or interval/ratio?

Nominal data

Nominal data is where the values/observations can be given a number. The numbers are simply labels. For example, in a data set, males could be coded as 0 and females as 1. The marital status of an individual could be coded as Y if married and N if single. Where people are required to estimate speed of cars they could be asked: 'Are they going fast or slow?'. Participants' responses could be coded 'f' for fast or 's' for slow.

Ordinal data

Ordinal data is where the values or observations can be put in order. For example, asking people to estimate the speed of cars on a scale of one to ten (ten being the fastest). In this way, the data can be ranked (placed in order). In ordinal data, the order is important (e.g. large to small; slow to fast) but the difference between the values is not because there is no standardized way of measuring the difference.

Interval data

Interval data is where the values/observations can be put in order and the difference (or interval) between the values is standardized and is the same. Miles per hour (mph) and temperature (Celsius) are examples of interval data. They are standardized measuring scales that are recognised throughout the world.

Choosing the correct inferential statistical test

	Choosing a statistical test	
	Independent measures design	**Repeated measures or matched pairs design**
Nominal data	Chi squared test	Sign test
Ordinal data	Mann–Whitney U Test	Wilcoxon signed-rank test
Interval or ratio data	Unrelated t-test	Related t-test

You then need to make sure the results of the inferential statistical test are accurately stated. Each statistical test produces different values. It is important that you include all of the values. For example, Wilcoxon signed-rank tests produce an N value, a critical value and an observed value.

An example showing how to justify and explain the use of an inferential statistical test:

> *I used a repeated measures design and my data was at least ordinal status. Therefore, the appropriate statistical test to use was the Wilcoxon signed-rank test. All calculations can be found in Appendix III.*
>
> *The observed value (T) was calculated to be 0 because none of the paired scores had a negative value when the differences were subtracted.*
>
> *The critical value was calculated to be 3 for a one tailed hypothesis at the 0.005 level of significance when N= 10 (Wilcoxon and Wilcox, 1964). N is the number of paired scores used.*
>
> *T must be equal or less than the critical value for the results to be considered significant. Therefore, my results can be considered to be highly significant.*

You then need to state whether the null hypothesis has been accepted or rejected appropriately according to the results of the statistical test and make your statement of statistical significance appropriate and clear. You must include a sentence where you accept or reject the null hypothesis based on the results of the test.

An example showing how to interpret the statistical findings in a way that links them to the hypothesis:

> *Statement of significance: The difference between condition A and condition B is significant at the 0.05 level of significance when N=10. I can reject my null hypothesis and accept my experimental hypothesis.*

You should never use the words 'proof' as your conclusions are only tentative. Your results will either help support the hypothesis or not.

Evaluation

In this section you have to:

- discuss your findings with reference to the background theory or model

- discuss strengths and limitations of the design, sample, and procedure, explain them and make them relevant to the investigation

- explain and justify modifications that are explicitly linked to the limitations of your investigation.

Your evaluation of the experiment should focus on:

- the limitations of the method – those factors that are likely to have had an influence on the outcome of the experiment but could not have been avoided (human error or accidents and omissions that could easily have been avoided with a little foresight and planning are not acceptable as limitations)

- suggestions for improving the method to generate more data or more effective data in order to arrive at a firmer conclusion. These may be based on the limitations identified or proposed on the basis of a fresh consideration of the experimental design.

You can divide your evaluation section into four subsections. You can use these subheadings:

- Discussion with reference to the background theory

- Strengths

- Limitations

- Suggested modifications

Discussion with reference to the background theory

You need to discuss your findings in the context of the base-study. You should include a statement about whether the results from your experiment support or refute the study. Repeat the descriptive results. Write the same sentence that you used below the graph. State how the results support or refute the experimental hypothesis. Repeat your statement of significance.

Strengths

Strengths of the design need to be clearly stated and explained. Even if your results are non-significant, it is likely that your descriptive results were generally as expected. You could divide your strengths into design, sample, and procedure, and say one strength for each.

Limitations

Limitations of the design need to be clearly stated and explained. You must give at least three problems with the design and procedure and say why they occurred and why you consider them to be limitations. You could divide your weaknesses into design, sample, and procedure, and state one weakness for each. Only include factors that are likely to have had an influence on the outcome of the experiment but could not have been avoided. For example, do not claim the small sample size affected your results unless you make it clear the sample size could not have been avoided and you are absolutely certain, and can support it with evidence, that a larger group would have changed the result. Furthermore, do not claim any limitation that could easily have been remedied with better planning on your part. You may wish to discuss variables that may have affected the result, but the nature of the experimental method made it difficult to include.

Suggested modifications

For each limitation, explicitly state how you would modify the study in the future to eliminate those weaknesses. Assume you have slightly more resources at your disposal. You may wish to focus on the design element and include more variables to improve **ecological validity**. You may wish to introduce qualitative data techniques to reduce the limiting effects of using an experiment to investigate complex human behaviour. You need to explain why this modification is useful or essential for future study. Therefore, after each modification you can state: 'This modification is essential because…'

A MINOR MODIFICATION … HOW FAST WAS THE BLUE CAT GOING WHEN IT SMASHED INTO THE RED CAT?

Higher level paper 3

Paper 3 assesses the approaches to research in psychology. The paper consists of a research scenario followed by three short-answer questions for a total of 24 marks.

Question 1

Question 1 will consist of all of the following questions, for a total of 9 marks. The questions will be assessed using an analytical mark scheme.

Questions	Marks
Identify the research method used and outline two characteristics of the method.	3
Describe the sampling method used in the study.	3
Suggest an alternative or additional research method giving one reason for your choice.	3

Question 2

Question 2 will consist of one of the following questions, for a total of 6 marks. The question will be assessed using an analytical mark scheme.

Questions	Marks
Describe the ethical considerations that were applied in the study and explain if further ethical considerations could be applied.	6
Describe the ethical considerations in reporting the results and explain additional ethical considerations that could be taken into account when applying the findings of the study.	6

Question 3

Question 3 will consist of one of the following questions, for a total of 9 marks. The question will be assessed using the rubric below.

Questions	Marks
Discuss the possibility of generalizing/transferring the findings of the study.	9
Discuss how a researcher could ensure that the results of the study are credible.	9
Discuss how the researcher in the study could avoid bias.	9

Rubric for question 3

Mark band	Level descriptor
0	The answer does not reach a standard described by the descriptors below.
1–3	The question is misunderstood and the central issue is not identified correctly, resulting in a mostly irrelevant argument. The response contains mostly inaccurate references to the approaches to research or these are irrelevant to the question. The reference to the stimulus material relies heavily on direct quotations from the text.
4–6	The question is understood but only partially answered resulting in an argument of limited scope. The response contains mostly accurate references to approaches to research which are linked explicitly to the question. The response makes appropriate but limited use of the stimulus material.
7–9	The question is understood and answered in a focused and effective manner with an accurate argument that addresses the requirements of the question. The response contains accurate references to approaches to research with regard to the question, describing their strengths and limitations. The response makes effective use of the stimulus material.

Research methods

You will be expected to:

* identify the research method used and outline two characteristics of the method

* suggest an alternative or additional research method giving one reason for your choice. Usually, this reason will stem from a shortcoming of the research method in the stimulus material and/or a strength of the alternative method you suggest.

The research methods identified by the IB are divided into **qualitative** and **quantitative** methods. In quantitative data, the aim is to produce **objective** knowledge where the emphasis is on the isolation and measurement of key **variables**. Qualitative researchers are concerned with meaning and experience – that is, they are interested in how people make sense of the world and how they experience events. The two methods can be used in conjunction with one another, such as interview data bolstered by survey data.

Qualitative methods

Case studies

A **case study** is a detailed analysis over time of a singular area of interest (a case) to produce in-depth, context-dependent knowledge. The area of interest is defined by the research and while it can be an in-depth study of one individual, it does not have to be. It is not a singular method but an approach to gathering data using a variety of research methods. Case studies often include a certain amount of **triangulation** and therefore it is believed that using different perspectives will result in rich data and a better all-round understanding of the situation. Conclusions based on multiple sources are considered to be more **credible**.

Main data collection methods in case studies include:

- focus groups

- **semi-structured interviews**

- observations

- diary accounts

- newspaper articles

- participant observation

- personal notes (e.g. letters, photographs, notes)

- official documents (e.g. case notes, clinical notes, appraisal reports)

- questionnaires.

Strengths of case studies

Case studies provide an opportunity to investigate phenomena that could not be studied otherwise because of the flexible nature of the approach.

They stimulate new research, because the case can highlight phenomena that need further investigation. For example, case studies of people with brain damage have encouraged research in memory processes and biological correlates of memory, using animal research to test theories. Case study research on intervention programmes for at-risk youths has resulted in more case studies to evaluate the effectiveness of interventions, in terms of how the users see them.

They can contradict established theories and help to develop new theories.

Limitations of case studies

It can be difficult to determine whether a series of related studies constitute a proper case study or if they are just a collection of studies dealing with the same question. Therefore, they are difficult to replicate as a whole research approach.

There is a potential risk for **researcher bias** in case studies. The researcher's own beliefs can influence the way the data is collected and analysed, but this could be controlled via **reflexivity** and other strategies to maintain credibility.

The reliance on memory when reconstructing the case history will be subject to distortion. Participants in case studies may also change their accounts in order to appear more socially acceptable to a researcher who they want to build a rapport with.

Naturalistic observations

Naturalistic observations are observations of naturally occurring behaviour in a natural setting. Several different recording techniques can be used, but field notes are an important part of the data. Observations may be participant or non-participant observations.

Strengths of naturalistic observations

Naturalistic observations have high **ecological validity** as the collection of data takes place in a natural environment and it is assumed that the participants behave in natural ways (in contrast to research in laboratories).

Naturalistic observations can be used to collect data in cases where it would be impossible or unethical to do so otherwise.

Limitations of naturalistic observations

There can be ethical considerations concerning the appropriateness of observing strangers without their knowledge. The researcher should also be careful not to violate the privacy of participants.

Naturalistic observations generate a lot of data and researchers have to make a decision about what, when, and how they will observe it. This can be addressed by recording behaviour, which raises ethical issues, and/or having more than one researcher, which raises inter-observer **reliability** issues.

Participant observations

In **participant observations**, the researcher becomes part of the group he or she observes. The aim of this research strategy is to gain a close and intimate familiarity with a given area of interest in a natural setting. The researcher enters the social world of other people, but they also affect the researcher in certain ways. It is important that the researcher is aware of this and that continuous reflections become part of the interpretation of the data. Critical thinking like this is always important, but particularly when the researcher chooses to study a group in which he or she has a personal or political engagement. In the analysis, the researcher includes this and any other relevant biographical data because this is an important perspective in the interpretation of the data. This is an example of reflexivity.

Strengths of participant observations

Participant observations provide very detailed and in-depth personal knowledge of a topic, which cannot be gained by other methods.

They are one of the best methods to avoid researcher bias because the researchers seek to understand how and why the social processes are the way they are, instead of imposing their own reality on the phenomenon. The researcher cites the research in the universe of the participants.

They provide a **holistic** interpretation of a topic, because the researcher takes into account as many aspects as possible of that particular group of people, in order to synthesize observations into a whole. The researcher uses material from the participants themselves to generate 'theory', and tries to explain one set of observations in terms of its relationship with others.

Limitations of participant observations

The researcher can become too immersed in the environment. Proper reflexivity needs to be maintained.

Participant observations can be time-consuming and demanding. The researcher needs to be physically present and try to live the life of the people he or she is studying.

There is a risk that researchers lose objectivity, but this always has to be managed with qualitative data. Researchers are supposed to see the world from the point of view of the participants, but this may present problems in terms of objectivity. In participant observation there is a delicate balance between involvement and detachment.

Every participant observer has to ask themselves: To what extent has their mere presence changed the behaviour of the group they are observing?

Deception is necessary (for **covert** methods), but this raises serious ethical issues. For example, friendships are formed on false pretences and peoples' feelings and lives are changed as a result of the research.

Non-participant observation

Non-participant observation means that the researcher is not part of the group being studied. It is a research technique by which the researcher observes participants, with or without their knowledge. The researcher does not take an active part in the situation as in participant observation. Some observational research takes place in psychological laboratories using one-way mirrors.

Strengths of non-participant observation

Non-participant observations can be seen as more objective because the researcher is not taking part in the behaviour being studied.

They can be seen as more ethical because the researcher cannot be said to actively influence the behaviour they are studying.

Limitations of non-participant observation

Participants often react to being observed. This is called **reactivity**, and it is assumed that reactivity will make the data less trustworthy/valid. This can be addressed by not informing people they are being studied, which raises clear ethical issues.

Overt and covert observation

Participant and non-participant observations can be **overt** or covert. The researcher decides in advance which technique is most appropriate for the research. In an overt observation, the participants know they are being observed whereas in a covert observation, the participants are not aware of being studied, so they have not agreed to it. Therefore, in a covert observation the researcher has to 'make up a story' to justify his or her presence in the setting in order to mask his or her real purpose for being there. Therefore, there are serious ethical issues involved in covert observations because not all (if any) of the participants will have been asked if they want to take part in a research study. Therefore, careful thought needs to be given to the ethical considerations usually by the **Research Ethics Committee** (REC). Furthermore, during covert observations it can be dangerous for the researcher if he or she is investigating a group of people who are known to be violent, such as street gangs. Any 'cover' that is established will need to be convincing and known to only a few people.

Interviews

Qualitative interviews include **unstructured**, semi-structured and focus group interviews. These are used to gain an insight into people's thoughts, opinions, and feelings from their own point of view. Qualitative interviews may be followed by surveys (a quantitative method) to collect data from a representative sample so that the findings can be **generalized** to a larger population. This could, for example, be a useful way to explore a psychological phenomenon in a case study.

Unstructured interviews

Unstructured interviews are interviews where the questions are not prearranged. They contain open questions and are informal, free flowing, and resemble a probing conversation.

Strengths of unstructured interviews

Unstructured interviews produce in-depth, rich, and nuanced data. A 'primal telling' in the participants' own language and expression.

They allow the researcher to be creative and adapt to the situation.

Limitations of unstructured interviews

Unstructured interviews offer limited scope to be replicated by other researchers or even the same researcher who wants to interview other participants because of their free-flowing nature.

They produce a large amount of data, much of which may not be relevant. It has to be sorted, transcribed, edited, and interpreted. This often means fewer participants in a particular research study because otherwise the data becomes overwhelming.

The researcher can more easily introduce their own biases and lead the interview in any direction they choose.

Semi-structured interviews

Semi-structured interviews involve the preparation of an interview guide that lists themes that should be explored during the interview. This guide serves as a checklist during the interview, but there is a great deal of flexibility in that the order of questions and the actual wording of questions are not determined in advance. Furthermore, the interview guide allows the interviewer to pursue questions on the list in more depth than others.

Strengths of semi-structured interviews

Semi-structured interviews still allow for a 'primal telling' of experiences in the interviewee's own language and expression while still following a semi-structured pattern. There is less potential bias by the researcher because there is some structure to the questions.

They have the flexibility of open-ended approaches, as well as the advantage of a structural approach. It enables the researcher to make interventions, asking participants to either clarify or expand on areas of interest.

They allow for analysis in a variety of ways because it is compatible with many methods of data analysis.

They allow for some consistency between different researchers.

Limitations of semi-structured interviews

Semi-structured interviews can limit how much the researcher pursues interesting data trails if they tie themselves too tightly to their schedule.

Researchers could impose their own expectations (**confirmation bias**) on the data through the use of specific questioning. Decision trails are necessary to improve credibility/trustworthiness.

Focus groups

A focus group normally consists of around six to ten people. Members of a focus group often have a common characteristic that is relevant for the topic of investigation, which is why **purposive sampling** is often used. The researcher has the role of facilitator, which means they are in charge of the group to make sure it stays on task by monitoring and prompting the group discussion.

Strengths of focus groups

Focus groups offer a quick and convenient way to collect large amounts of data from several individuals simultaneously.

They are particularly useful for exploring people's knowledge and experiences because it can be used to gain insight into what they think, how they think, and why they think that way.

They highlight cultural values or group **norms**.

Limitations of focus groups

Focus groups are not suitable for producing intimate data from the participants.

The presence of other participants may result in group dynamics such as **conformity** and **groupthink**, where individuals express views they do not hold as individuals in a group.

Quantitative methods

Experiments

Experiments are designed with one clear **independent variable** (IV) and a **dependent variable** (DV). All other factors that could affect the DV are controlled as far as possible. The IV may be graduated, resulting in a range of conditions on a scale. Alternatively there may be only two conditions for the IV: one is the **control**, the other the test condition. This is a simple experiment.

Strengths of experiments

Experiments can establish a **cause-effect relationship** between an IV and DV **(validity)**.

They can be easily replicated by other researchers (reliability).

Limitations of experiments

There is a lack of ecological validity in experiments as the environments and testing methods have to be so tightly controlled.

The isolation of variables sometimes means more nuanced factors are ignored or downplayed as the emphasis is placed on establishing cause-effect between variables rather than a grand narrative to explain complex events.

Field experiments

In **field experiments**, the researcher manipulates the IV but conducts the experiment in a real-life environment. As a result extraneous variables cannot be controlled.

Strengths of field experiments

There is a higher degree of ecological validity as the environments are more natural.

The participants do not have to know they are being studied so they do not react as much, if at all, to the presence of a researcher.

Limitations of field experiments

Field experiments lack complete replication as they take place in a natural environment.

There are problems with **informed consent** as not every participant will be aware they are taking part in a social science study.

Quasi-experiments

In **quasi-experiments**, participants are grouped based on a characteristic of interest, such as **gender**, **ethnicity**, or scores on a depression scale.

Strengths of quasi-experiments

Quasi-experiments allow one characteristic to be isolated and researched in a controlled way.

There is a higher degree of ecological validity as the environments are more natural.

Limitations of quasi-experiments

Care has to be taken to create a comparable control group, otherwise there is a problem with **internal validity** as the participants are grouped based on a characteristic of interest. This characteristic needs to be reflected in a the control group for meaningful comparison to take place.

The amount of confounding variables means **causality** between variables is difficult to establish.

Natural experiments

In natural experiments, researchers find naturally occurring variables and study them. The researcher does not manipulate the variables but simply records the possible effects of identified IVs on identified dependent variables.

Strengths of natural experiments

There is a higher degree of ecological validity in natural experiments as the environments are more natural.

Natural experiments allow variables to be isolated and researched in a semi-controlled way.

Limitations of natural experiments

The researcher does not manipulate the variables in a natural experiment, so it is not possible to establish a cause-effect relationship.

There are problems with informed consent as not every participant will be aware they are taking part in a social science study.

Correlations research

In **correlations research** there is a focus on two variables, but these are not termed independent and dependent variables as the **hypothesis** is not based on a potential cause and effect, instead they are referred to as **co-variables**. They have similar strengths and limitations to natural experiments.

Strengths of correlations research

There is a higher degree of ecological validity in correlations research as the environments are more natural.

Allows variables to be isolated and researched in a semi-controlled way.

Limitations of correlations research

The researcher does not manipulate the variables in correlations research, so it is not possible to establish a cause-effect relationship.

There are problems with informed consent as not every participant will be aware they are taking part in a social science study.

Surveys

Surveys can be quantitative or qualitative in nature. Quantitative surveys usually involve tightly focused questions that can be answered with a numbered answer response on a scale.

Strengths of surveys

A large amount of data can be collected from large populations in a relatively quick and easy way.

Patterns of behaviour can be seen before more in-depth research is carried out.

Limitations of surveys

The researcher does not manipulate the variables, so it is not possible to establish a cause-effect relationship.

The data is not very in-depth or rich.

Sampling methods

You will be expected to describe the sampling method used in the study.

Researchers cannot research an entire population. They first have to decide what group they are interested in (known as the **target population**) and then select a group of people from it. This is the sample. The method they use to extract the sample will influence the characteristics of the sample.

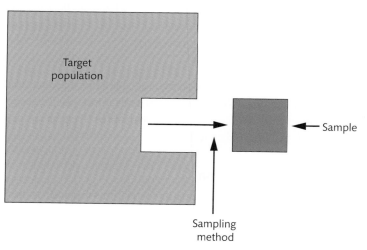

A diagram showing the relationship between the target population, sampling method, and sample.

The following are common methods:

Random sampling: the process where every member in the target population has an equal chance of being selected.

Convenience/opportunity sampling: the process of selecting people who are able to participate in the study at a given time. They may be known to the researcher or within a place the researcher has access to.

Volunteer sampling: when individuals choose to participate in the study.

Purposive sampling: participants are chosen because they possess characteristics relevant to the research study.

Snowball sampling: participants who are already in a study help the researcher to recruit more participants through their social network. This is particularly useful and gains access to subgroups or people who might not otherwise allow themselves to be interviewed.

Ethical considerations

You will be expected to:

- describe the ethical considerations that were applied in the study and explain whether further ethical considerations could be applied

- describe the ethical considerations in reporting the results and explain additional ethical considerations that could be taken into account when applying the findings of the study.

There are, overall, the same ethical issues involved in qualitative research as in quantitative research. These include informed consent, protection of participants from psychological or physical harm, respect for the participants' integrity and privacy, and the right to withdraw from the research. However, there are special ethical considerations to be made due to the very nature of qualitative research. The characteristics of qualitative or field research usually include long term and close personal contact with participants, which may have implications for what the participants disclose to the researcher.

Informed consent

Informed consent should always be obtained wherever possible unless it conflicts with the aims of the research. This is stressed in all guidelines on ethical conduct in research by reputable RECs. However, in some cases, where it would not otherwise be possible to study a phenomenon (e.g. use of violence in a street gang), ethics committees may offer dispensation from the rule because the goal of the research is to obtain knowledge that may eventually prevent violence.

However, generally, participants should know their participation is voluntary. This is particularly important if the research is conducted by people who have some kind of relation to members of the sample, since participation could then be motivated by feelings of obligation. The researcher must provide the participants with sufficient information about the study, such as who funded the study, who will conduct the study, how the data will be used, and what the research requires of the participants – for example, in terms of time and the topics the study will address. It should also be made clear that consent can always be renegotiated. In cases where children aged under 16 years are involved, consent must be obtained from parents or legal guardians.

Protecting participants from harm

Researchers should take preventive action in all research to avoid harming participants. This is particularly true in sensitive research topics, such as drug abuse, domestic violence, or alcoholism in the family. Due to the nature of qualitative methods, participants may disclose very private information that they have never shared with anyone before.

Prior to the interview, and before they agree to participate, participants should have a clear understanding of the topics to be addressed. Researchers must approach sensitive issues through clear and direct questions, so that participants are not drawn into irrelevant and sensitive details by mistake. If the participants show signs of discomfort, the researcher should be empathetic and consider stopping the interview.

Anonymity and confidentiality

Participants should be informed about the issues surrounding **anonymity** and **confidentiality**. The identity of the participants should not be known outside the research team, but in cases where sampling has involved a third party (e.g. managers, friends, teachers), this cannot be done, and in this case the participants should be informed.

Confidentiality means that research data will not be known to anyone outside the study. The researcher may have to change minor details in the report to avoid the possibility of participants being recognised. Confidentiality also relates to the way data is stored after the research. If interviews or observations have been recorded and archived, it can be difficult to guarantee total anonymity, so these should be destroyed when transcripts have been made. If the researcher finds it necessary to archive non-anonymized data, the participant should give written informed consent.

Use of quotes

Using extensive quotes can reveal the identity of the participant. If proper checks are not in place to ensure anonymity it can have lasting consequences for participants. It is difficult to lose participants in a small qualitative crowd because readers can guess the identity of the participants by the way they speak or what they are saying. Therefore, careful consideration needs to be given to the use of quotes.

Who to include

In case studies where covert observation is used, participants may not have consented to their involvement and will not know they have the right to withdraw from the research, because they do not know that they are being studied.

Generalizing findings

You will be expected to discuss the possibility of generalizing the findings of the study.

Generalization for quantitative research is based on **probability sampling** and the results are applicable to the whole target population. However, the IB also states that qualitative researchers should consider **transferability** where findings from a study can be transferred to settings and/or populations outside the study only if the findings of a particular study are corroborated by findings of similar studies (for example, in multiple case studies).

The following forms of generalization can be distinguished in qualitative research:

Representational generalization: findings from qualitative research studies can be applied to populations outside the population of the study. Qualitative research normally involves small samples that are not selected to be statistically representative, and non-standardized interview methods may be used. This makes it difficult to generalize findings. However, if evidence from other studies confirms the findings, it is argued that generalization is possible. For example, qualitative interviews may be followed by surveys (a quantitative method) to collect data from a representative sample so that the findings can be generalized to a larger population.

Inferential generalization: findings of the study can be applied to settings outside the setting of the study. This is also called transferability or external validity. If the study on homeless people is a pilot programme to test the effectiveness of a service to resettle homeless people, the question is whether the findings can be applied to other services that provide help to the homeless. Whether or not the findings can be transferred to another setting will depend on the depth of the description of the researched context and the phenomenon. This description may allow for inferences to be made, but it will rest as a hypothesis until it is supported or disproved by further evidence.

Theoretical generalization: theoretical concepts derived from the study can be used to develop further theory. The findings from a study might lead to inferences about possible effective policies to help homeless people. In that way, the findings from the study may contribute to wider social theory.

Achieving credibility

You will be expected to discuss how a researcher could ensure that the results of the study are credible.

It is usually difficult to replicate findings in qualitative research because qualitative data relies on researcher interpretation, subjective decisions (e.g. choosing participants, deciding on questions, deciding on interview settings, choosing segments of interviews, interpreting the data), which all have the influence of the researchers' personal decisions. Therefore, credibility is used in qualitative research to indicate whether or not the findings of the study are in line with the participants' perceptions and experiences.

The following techniques increase credibility in qualitative research:

- inclusion of samples from interviews

- claims supported with excerpts from the interview

- use of a 'decision trail'

- explanations for the decisions the researcher came to (to help the reader understand where, why, and how the researcher conducted the research in the way they did)

- use of **peer review** to check the interpretations

- other researchers who are interested in the same area can add further insight as well as question the original findings.

The use of reflexivity

Reflexivity is based on the assumption that it is important the researcher is aware of his or her own contribution to the construction of meaning in the research process. Reflexivity is a process that occurs throughout the research. It allows the researcher to reflect on ways in which bias may occur. Researchers should provide sufficient details about issues that may potentially bias the investigation. For example, revealing where they stand in terms of political ideology.

The use of triangulation

Triangulation is the validation of data through cross verification from two or more sources. The sources are usually theoretical and/or, methodological.

Methodological triangulation: different methods (e.g. interviews plus observations and questionnaires and diary analysis) are used to research the same phenomena.

Theoretical triangulation: the search for evidence or approaches that could contradict their interpretation is conducted through a different theoretical lens (e.g. a feminist lens; a behaviourist lens; a collectivist lens).

Researcher triangulation: the use of other researchers who would bring different perspectives and experience that might challenge the findings of the lead researcher.

Avoiding bias

You will be expected to discuss how the researcher in the study could avoid bias.

Bias refers to human factors that may affect the results of the study. The following are common biases.

Researcher bias

Researcher bias is when the researcher themselves influences the results of the study because of a personal view they hold. For example, they may want a certain treatment to work or they hold a political view on how a certain group is being treated by a government. This may manifest itself in terms of who and how they choose for the study, how they act towards participants, how they emphasize and de-emphasize certain themes in the data, and the conclusions they come to. The researcher should apply reflexivity to control this during the study and then provide information to the reader in the final report.

Participant bias, or demand characteristics

Participant bias is when participants act according to how they think the researcher may want them to act. For example, the social desirability effect refers to the idea that participants may give answers they presume are socially desirable but not necessarily what they truly believe. Researchers need to ask: What have I done to control this? How might the participants act under different conditions? How can I ask the same question in different ways to see if the participants are consistent?

Sampling bias

Sampling bias occurs when the sample is not representative of the target population. Researchers need to ask: If I changed the sample how would it affect the findings?

The assumption that bias can be completely avoided is problematic for philosophical and practical reasons. However, bias can be addressed by the researcher engaging in a reflexive process throughout the study and making that process available for peer review and for their readers.

Practice scenarios

The paper 3 exam will consist of stimulus material followed by short-answer questions.

The questions will be:

Question 1

Identify the research method used and outline two characteristics of the method. (3)

This question wants you to label the research method and then state two characteristics of this method.

AND

Describe the sampling method used in the study. (3)

This question wants you to state and describe the sampling method.

AND

Suggest an alternative or additional research method giving one reason for your choice. (3)

This question wants you to label an additional method that might be useful for the subject being studied and then state a reason why it would be appropriate.

Question 2

Describe the ethical considerations that were applied in the study and explain if further ethical considerations could be applied. (6)

Human science research usually has some explicit ethical issue. For example, it will investigate young people, sick people, and people in difficult situations such as homelessness. This question wants you to consider the ethical considerations in reporting and applying the results.

OR

Describe the ethical considerations in reporting the results and explain additional ethical considerations that could be taken into account when applying the findings of the study. (6)

This question wants you to consider the wider ethical considerations in applying the research. Human science research usually has some element of applicability to a social need. What would the applicability of the results look like (e.g. some form of

Use different coloured highlighter pens to mark off various sections that are relevant to the questions being asked. These are:

- The research method
- The sampling method
- Ethical aspects
- What did they do?
- To whom did they do it?
- How did they do it?
- What are the findings?

Write in the margins:

- What were the basic problems?
- How can the study be improved?

365

new therapy; educational campaign) and what would be the ethical considerations surrounding a potential application?

Question 3

Discuss how the researcher in the study could avoid bias. (9)

This question wants you to consider how the researcher could avoid bias should the research be carried out again. You will need to spot ways in which bias has already affected the methodology of the research. You will need to discuss the various ways bias can be avoided.

OR

Discuss how a researcher could ensure that the results of the study are credible. (9)

This question wants you to consider how the researcher could improve the credibility should the research be carried out again. You will need to spot ways in which credibility has already been challenged in the methodology of the research. You will need to discuss the various ways credibility can be improved.

OR

Discuss the possibility of generalizing/transferring the findings of the study. (9)

This question wants you to consider how the findings of the study can be generalized (quantitative studies) or transferred (qualitative studies). You will need to discuss the various forms of generalization and transferability.

Scenario 1

The aim of this case study was to investigate gender differences in online learning for students in higher education in a US university. A US Department of Education statistic suggests university enrolments in the US will be more than 20 million by 2020. As student enrolment increases, there will be pressure on classroom and lecture hall space and so it is expected that more universities will make use of computers to deliver education and communicate with students. Therefore, using computer-based communication (CBC) is one of the main ways these institutions are addressing rising student enrolment. For example, digital seminars can be delivered online where participants take part via cameras and microphones. A seminar is a small group focused learning environment where students can discuss issues led by the tutor.

A female researcher in the USA was interested in communication patterns of students using computer-based communication (CBC) while studying at university. The researcher herself was a tutor at the same university where she carried out her research. The research project used unstructured interviews to collect data from 60 participants (47 female; 13 male) who were chosen using convenience sampling. The sample consisted of adult professionals studying for bachelor and master's degrees. They were asked to sign informed consent forms and were fully debriefed after the interviews were completed. They were guaranteed anonymity and confidentiality. At the end of the interviews the researcher carried out a focus group with ten female participants who were chosen using convenience sampling. They were asked to discuss their experiences of being in a CBC environment. Participant quotes and stories from the focus group were used heavily in the results section of the report.

The overall results showed male and female preferred learning styles and communication patterns, and participation barriers were compared for differences in gender. Results showed there are gender differences between male and females in communication styles. For example, there was a tolerance of male domination in online communication patterns, which was seen as effectively silencing female students and making it more difficult for them to communicate on an equal footing with the males. Implications for practice were discussed. The main results that emerged were that training was needed for the male participants to help them understand how they could improve their communication styles to better accommodate the female participants.

Question 1

Identify the research method used and outline two characteristics of the method. (3)

Describe the sampling method used in the study. (3)

Suggest an alternative or additional research method giving one reason for your choice. (3)

Question 2

Describe the ethical considerations that were applied in the study and explain if further ethical considerations could be applied. (6)

Question 3

Discuss the possibility of generalizing/transferring the findings of the study. (9)

Answers

Question 1

Identify the research method used and outline two characteristics of the method. (3)

The research method is a case study that consists of a detailed analysis over time of a singular area of interest (a case) to produce in-depth, context-dependent knowledge. The case study consisted of unstructured interviews and focus groups to collect data. The case was a university that made use of computer based communications (CBC) to deliver education and communicate with students.

Describe the sampling method used in the study. (3)

The sampling method used in the study was convenience sampling, which is the process of selecting people who are able to participate in the study at a given time. They may be known to the researcher or within a place the researcher has access to, which means the researcher who worked at the university may well have taught some of the students or been aware of their concerns.

Suggest an alternative or additional research method giving one reason for your choice. (3)

The researcher could have also used covert naturalistic observations to observe the participants interacting in a CBC environment, such as a digital seminar. This would have produced results with high ecological validity, assuming the participants would behave in natural ways as they would not know they are being observed. In this way, she would not only rely on the participants to provide a description of the CBC, but also observe the communication dynamics within a CBC context herself.

Question 2

Describe the ethical considerations that were applied in the study and explain if further ethical considerations could be applied. (6)

The participants were asked to sign informed consent forms and were fully debriefed after the interviews were completed. They were guaranteed anonymity and confidentiality. At the end of the interviews the researcher carried out a focus group with ten female participants were they were asked to discuss their experiences of being in a CBC environment. However, because participant quotes and stories were used in the final report, this may mean their identities could be revealed as it is difficult to lose people in a small qualitative setting as the voices and stories may be recognizable. It should have been part of the consent process to make it clear to the participants that what they said may well be used as a quote in the published report to allow them the chance to reconsider if they want to take part in a focus group or not.

Question 3

Discuss the possibility of generalizing/transferring the findings of the study. (9)

The study offers very little scope for generalization outside of its setting. It is a case study of one particular university in the USA with a sample weighted heavily in favour of one gender (female), even though the primary focus of the case study is gender-related behaviour. There is some possibility of representational generalization to other universities who run a CBC program. However, it is not clear whether all the participants (both male and female) would agree with the main findings of the report. It is also not clear how or why the participants were chosen to take part in the focus group or if the focus group sample was deemed representative of the unstructured interview group sample. Given the researcher's gender, it may be she chose participants for the focus group that reflected her own experiences as a female within a CBC setting, which again limits the generalizability of the findings.

Scenario 2

The aim of this study was to investigate the effectiveness of drama therapy and art therapy on crime rates with young offenders who commit petty crime in the Netherlands and Germany. Petty crime is defined as low-level or less-serious crime such as stealing from shops or spraying graffiti on walls. Previous research had suggested such therapies were not good value for the tax payer and there was a possibility that future governments may reduce funding.

Two researchers (one male; one female), working in a university social science department, used surveys to collect data from 42 experienced art therapists working in five institutions in the Netherlands and Germany who were found using snowball sampling. They were asked to sign informed consent forms and were guaranteed anonymity and confidentiality. The survey asked questions about the effectiveness of drama therapy and art therapy on crime rates with young offenders, which were scaled from one through to five. For example, one question was: How effective do you think art therapy has been on helping young offenders you have worked with transition into a non-criminal lifestyle? There was a space at the end of the surveys for the participants to add further thoughts. The surveys were conducted on a digital internet platform. The results were published in a peer-reviewed journal and quotes from the participants were used to add support for the quantitative results.

The overall results showed drama and art therapy was seen as an effective way to help young offenders deal with their emotional problems; it reduced the chances of young offenders reoffending; it required more funding to make it more accessible for more young people. Some participants expressed concern that funding may be cut in the future and they worried about the effect on the young people they worked with.

Question 1

Identify the research method used and outline two characteristics of the method. (3)

Describe the sampling method used in the study. (3)

Suggest an alternative or additional research method giving one reason for your choice. (3)

Question 2

Describe the ethical considerations in reporting the results and explain additional ethical considerations that could be taken into account when applying the findings of the study. (6)

Question 3

Discuss how a researcher could ensure that the results of the study are credible. (9)

Answers

Question 1

Identify the research method used and outline two characteristics of the method. (3)

The research method is a quantitative survey to investigate the effectiveness of drama therapy and art therapy on crime rates with young offenders who commit petty crime in the Netherlands and Germany. Quantitative surveys usually involve tightly focused questions that can be answered by placing a number on a scale.

Describe the sampling method used in the study. (3)

The sampling method used in the study was snowball sampling, which means some initial therapists who are already in a study helped the researcher to recruit more participants through their social network. This is particularly useful for gaining access to subgroups or people who might not otherwise allow themselves to be interviewed. This may have meant the therapists decided that being involved in the study would bring benefits to themselves or the profession.

Suggest an alternative or additional research method giving one reason for your choice. (3)

An additional research method could be the use of unstructured interviews. These are interviews where the questions are not prearranged. They contain open questions and are informal, free flowing, and resemble a probing conversation. These will produce in-depth, rich and nuanced data and allow the researcher to go beyond the results of the survey. They allow the researcher to be creative and adapt to the situation, which meant they could have asked follow-up questions to any response the therapists gave.

Question 2

Describe the ethical considerations in reporting the results and explain additional ethical considerations that could be taken into account when applying the findings of the study. (6)

The participants were asked to sign informed consent forms and were guaranteed anonymity and confidentiality. However, the qualitative nature of one part of the survey may mean the therapists' identities could be revealed as their responses may be recognizable. It should have been clear in the consent process to make sure the participants knew that what they said may well be used as a quote in the published report to allow them the opportunity to consider how much information they may wish to reveal in the qualitative element of the survey. Moreover, the political nature of the debate (regarding funding for these types of therapies) should mean the authors take great care to make sure the identities of the participants are completely protected. Social science research can influence public opinion, which in turn influences government decisions and so greater care should have been taken to produce more in-depth and less one-sided results.

Question 3

Discuss how a researcher could ensure that the results of the study are credible. (9)

The results can be seen to lack credibility because they state the therapies are effective, but this was based on a sample of therapists. It would be expected for therapists to claim their work was effective. Therefore, the researchers could have used triangulation to help ensure that the results of the study were more credible. Triangulation is the validation of data through cross-verification from two or more sources. For example, they could have used methodological triangulation, which would have meant using different methods such as unstructured interviews and observations to produce more in-depth data. They also could have researched the young offenders themselves to discuss how effective they thought the therapy was. The researchers could also have observed the art therapists at work with the young offenders and then followed up with a focus group with the therapists and young offenders to discuss their experiences.

They could also have used theoretical triangulation, which would involve the search for evidence or approaches that could contradict their interpretation or the interpretation of their participants. For example, the provision of therapy for young offenders can be seen through a conservative political lens by questioning to what extent the tax payer should pay for therapy for young offenders who commit petty crime. Such a critical viewpoint might have stimulated the participants to provide more in-depth justification for their work. Finally, the researchers could have used researcher triangulation by using other researchers who would bring different perspectives and experience that might challenge the findings. For example, they could have invited researchers or participants who had a critical view of therapy for young offenders (such as serving police officers) to check or peer review their work and suggest improvements for future research.

Extended essay

An extended essay (EE) in psychology gives you the chance to broaden your interest in this diverse field. However, there are many pitfalls with an EE in psychology. Therefore, the following advice should be considered.

Only consider an EE in psychology if:

- you are studying psychology at HL or you want to study psychology at university
- you have a clear personal interest in the subject outside of school
- you have access to academic psychology journals.

On the other hand:

- do not do an EE in psychology if you are not a psychology student
- do not consider collecting data of any kind
- do not see an EE in psychology as an 'easy' or fallback subject
- do not choose an EE in psychology because you could not think of a suitable question in your other subjects.

You need to remember that a psychology EE is not an extension of the internal assessment (IA). You cannot confuse the two in any way, shape, or form, nor can you use the research you collect for one to help with the other.

Psychology is an academic subject with a body of work supporting it. 'Pop psychology' is an idea aimed at selling products to the mass market. Your essay needs to stay away from any topic that resembles 'pop psychology' and only work with sources that are considered within the realm of academic psychology.

Pop psychology can be defined as:

- a product or idea that is intended to have mass-market appeal
- a product or idea that is not supported by academic sources.

Academic psychology is supported by **peer-reviewed** research that is published in academic journals. The material has an academic tone and is aimed at fellow academics who are researching the same area.

Developing a research question

You must frame your research question as a question. A **hypothesis** or statement of intent is not acceptable. The reason for this is that a question helps you to retain focus throughout the essay.

A research question is a clear and focused question centred on a research topic. A strong research question helps you to focus the research, providing a path through the writing process.

A clear and well-focused research question, which has a specific aim, will allow you to work towards developing a reasoned argument within the scope of the task, rather than the kind of 'all about' essay that an unfocused research question can lead to.

Sometimes you will need to revise your research question; therefore, a research question should always be considered provisional until you have enough research data to make a reasoned argument.

Analysis and evaluation

You need to engage seriously with analysis and evaluation to earn marks in a psychology EE.

The following are relevant questions to keep in mind when discussing theories. You do not have to answer all of them, but they do represent effective critical thinking.

- What are the essential claims made by the theories?
- How do they relate to one another?
- How do they relate to the essential claims of other theories?
- What are the underlying assumptions of the theories?
- How do they relate to one another?
- How do they relate to the assumptions of other theories?
- What have other researchers published about the strengths and weaknesses of the theories?
- What kind of evidence supports the theories?
- Is there evidence of data or methodological triangulation to support the theories?
- Which theories are emerging as stronger or more valid in my particular research field?
- Why are they emerging as stronger or more valid?
- Why are weaker theories dismissed or considered weaker?

The following are relevant questions to keep in mind when discussing studies.

- What are the underlying assumptions of the studies?
- What are the underlying assumptions of the methodologies the studies used?
- Do other researchers have different assumptions about how the phenomena can be studied?
- What have other researchers published about the strengths and weaknesses of the studies?
- What kind of evidence supports the studies – is it quantitative or qualitative?
- Have other researchers used different methodologies and arrived at different conclusions? If so, research and state the differences and conclusions and state why they are different.
- Is there evidence of data or methodological triangulation to support the studies?
- Which studies are emerging as stronger or more valid in my particular research field?
- Why are they emerging as stronger or more valid?

- Why are weaker studies dismissed or considered weaker?

- Which studies contradict the major findings in the field?

- Why do they contradict the major findings?

- How can validity or credibility be defined in your field of study?

- Do all researchers agree? If not, why do they disagree?

- What was the context of the research and how may this have affected the results?

- Who were the participants?

- What was the time period or the cultural setting?

Advice on structure and paragraphing

Your essay should be subdivided into clear sections using subheadings. Each subheading should provide a clear focus for the section. These subheadings could be seen as mini-essay questions, so aim to answer them in the section that follows. You can also use mini-introductions under each subheading to tell the reader what each subsection focuses on. This should be three to five sentences long and be in italics to separate it from the main body of the text. You can start this mini-introduction with the words: 'In this section I will discuss…'

Paragraphs should be tightly focused around a particular point. You can follow the PEAL approach to achieve this.

Point – make a clear thesis statement in one or two sentences.
Evidence / Examples – support the thesis with a clear example described in two or three sentences.
Analyse / Evaluate – engage in some form of analysis or discussion. See the discussion questions above for guidance.
Link back to the question (or 'mini-conclusion') – conclude the paragraph by rewording your thesis statement to include the main points of your analysis.

The EE contains (in the following recommended order):

- Title page with the title and the research question

- Contents page

- Introduction

- Body (development/methods/results)

- Conclusion

- References and bibliography

- Appendices.

The title page must only include:

- the title of the essay, which should be a clear, focused summative statement of your research that gives the reader an indication of your research topic. It should not be phrased as a research question.

- the research question

- the subject for which the essay is registered

- word count.

An important note:

Please note that name of the student or the school should not appear on the title page or on any page headers. This is because the work is assessed anonymously.

Make sure you use the required presentation format:

- 12-point, readable font

- double spacing

- page numbering

- no candidate or school name on the title page or page headers.

The upper limit is 4000 words for all extended essays. Examiners will not read past this point.

Included in the word count:

- Introduction

- Main body

- Conclusion

- Quotations

- Footnotes and endnotes that are not references.

Not included in the word count:

- Contents page

- Maps, charts, diagrams, etc.

- Tables

- Citations/references

- Bibliography

- The reflection on planning and progress form.

Essays containing more than 4000 words are subject to penalties and examiners are not required to read material in excess of the word limit.

Citations and referencing

Citations

Citations allow ideas to be connected to their authors. They should appear in the text of an essay, either as an in-text citation or footnote/endnote. These must then be linked to the full references at the end of the essay. If you do not cite ideas then you are implicitly stating that those ideas belong to you. Therefore, all ideas need to be cited appropriately. How sources are cited varies with the particular referencing system you have chosen. Page numbers should almost certainly be given in the case of direct quotations. Whichever citation and referencing system you use, you need to be consistent.

Referencing

A reference provides all the information needed to find the source material. References enable the reader to consult the work and verify the data that has been presented. References can come from many different sources, including books, magazines, journals and websites.

When you choose your citation and referencing style, you need to have a full understanding of how it is to be used before embarking on the research task. You should record and keep your references as you move through your research process.

The IB's minimum requirements for references include:

- name of author

- date of publication

- title of source

- page numbers (print sources only)

- date of access (electronic sources only).

URLs

It will be assumed by EE examiners that many of the sources will be electronic in nature so make sure the URL and date of access are included.

Referencing online materials

References to online materials should include the the website address, the date it was accessed and, wherever possible, the author's name. If a source does not openly publish the author's name then you should be asking if it is a suitable source to use as most academics want to be associated with their work. All electronic sources must be date stamped so the examiner can see when you accessed them.

Appendix

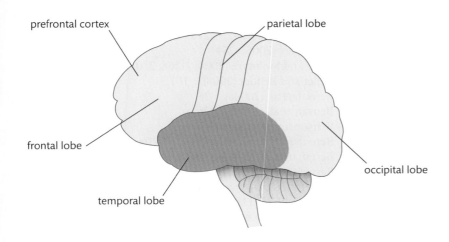

prefrontal cortex

parietal lobe

frontal lobe

occipital lobe

temporal lobe

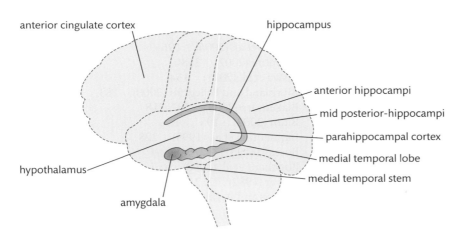

anterior cingulate cortex

hippocampus

anterior hippocampi

mid posterior-hippocampi

parahippocampal cortex

medial temporal lobe

medial temporal stem

hypothalamus

amygdala

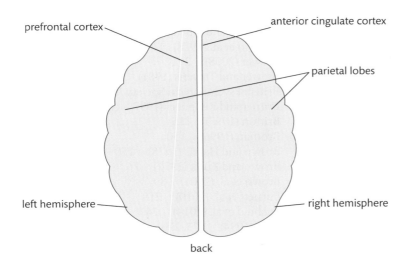

prefrontal cortex

anterior cingulate cortex

parietal lobes

left hemisphere

right hemisphere

back

Researchers' index

General index